Joseph Smith

Supplement to a Descriptive Catalogue of Friends' Books

Or Books Written by Members of the Society of Friends

Joseph Smith

Supplement to a Descriptive Catalogue of Friends' Books
Or Books Written by Members of the Society of Friends

ISBN/EAN: 9783337098780

Printed in Europe, USA, Canada, Australia, Japan

Cover: Foto ©ninafisch / pixelio.de

More available books at **www.hansebooks.com**

SUPPLEMENT

TO A

DESCRIPTIVE CATALOGUE

OF

FRIENDS' BOOKS,

OR BOOKS WRITTEN BY MEMBERS

OF

THE SOCIETY OF FRIENDS.

SUPPLEMENT

TO A

DESCRIPTIVE CATALOGUE

OF

FRIENDS' BOOKS,

OR

BOOKS WRITTEN BY MEMBERS OF THE SOCIETY OF
FRIENDS, COMMONLY CALLED QUAKERS,

FROM THEIR FIRST RISE TO THE PRESENT TIME;

INTERSPERSED WITH CRITICAL REMARKS,

AND

OCCASIONAL BIOGRAPHICAL NOTICES,

AND INCLUDING

ALL WRITINGS BY AUTHORS BEFORE JOINING AND BY THOSE
AFTER HAVING LEFT THE SOCIETY,

WHETHER ADVERSE OR NOT, AS FAR AS KNOWN.

BY JOSEPH SMITH.

LONDON:
EDWARD HICKS, JUN., 14, BISHOPSGATE STREET WITHOUT, E.C

1893.

Ashford, Kent :

H. D. & B. HEADLEY, INVICTA PRINTING WORKS.

1892.

ARRANGEMENT, &c.

---o---

First, the Authors' Surnames are carried on Alphabetically and the places of their Birth or Residence as far as known.

Then the Titles of the Books, and the number of editions printed, as near as can be ascertained, in chronological order, then the size and date and number of sheets,—and lastly, the time and place of the death of the deceased Authors, if known.

Some are set down twice for the more ready finding them, as some that have *two Authors* under both their names, and some not only under the Authors' names, but also under the title of *King and Parliament*, *Sufferings*, and *Testimonies* of, and concerning Friends deceased, because they fall properly under those heads.

And such as have no Authors' names may be found under "*Anonymous*, or *Nameless*, *Friends*, *Quakers*," &c., &c.

Periodical Publications may be found under that head.

At the end of those Pieces by Authors whose works have been collected, the page is given where they may be found; where that is omitted it must be understood that such Tract or Piece is not in their collected works.

EXPLANATION OF SIGNS USED IN THIS CATALOGUE.

* * to indicate those individuals who at some time were disunited from the Society, and not known to have returned.
* † „ those who condemned their error, and were restored into unity with their friends.
* ‡ „ those who were disunited, and returned, but believed to have again backslided.
* § „ those individuals about whom there is some uncertainty as to whether they left the Society or not.
* ‖ „ those Authors about whom there is some doubt as to whether they ever belonged to the Society, and those *Anonymous* Books with the same mark must be considered doubtful, i.e. whether written by Members or not.
* ¶ „ Books and Editions of Books printed before 1708, not named by John Whiting in his Catalogue. Those written by individuals before joining, and those by Authors after having left the Society, have no such mark, as it was not his intention to include such books.
* B „ that the article was printed on the *Broadside* of a sheet. If the date is known of a Book without any, it is enclosed in Crochets.

Many of the Books and Tracts enumerated in this Catalogue may be obtained on application to the Publisher.

SUPPLEMENT TO
"A Catalogue of Friends' Books"
By JOSEPH SMITH.

A.
Date, sheets.

A. A. S.—See ALICIA S. ASHWORTH.
A. E.—See EDWARD ASH.
A. J.
—— The Honest Country Quaker's PLEA for his Non-payment of TITHES, or any forced maintenance, in this Gospel Dispensation. By J. A.
Printed for J. Roberts, near the Oxford Arms, in Warwick Lane.
[In *Sion College Library*.] .   8vo. 1737. 1½

A. W., of *Saffron Walden*.
—— Memoir of.   .   .   .   .   8vo. [1835.]

ABBATT, Richard, son of Edward and Mary Abbatt, of *Preston*, in *Lancashire*. A Schoolmaster.
—— The Elements of Plane and Spherical Trigonometry; and its application to Astronomy, Dialling, and Trigonometrical Surveying. With plates. Designed for Mathematical Students. By RICHARD ABBATT.
London : John Richardson, Royal Exchange.
                                Small 8vo. 1832. 13
[*Brit. Mus.*, 717 C. 1.]
Reprinted.—2nd edition.
London : John Richardson, Royal Exchange.
                                Small 8vo. 1836. 13
NOTE.—There is added one page of *Errata* at the end.
Reprinted.—New edition, corrected, cloth, 2s.
London : Thomas Ostell & Co., 83, Leadenhall Street.   .   .   .   Small 8vo. 1841. 13

ABBATT, Richard, *continued*.

—— A Treatise on the Calculus of Variations. Illustrated by numerous Problems.
London. 8vo. 1836.
[*Brit. Mus.*, 5,291 B. 1.]
Reprinted.—2nd edition.

—— The Principles and Practice of Linear Perspective, divested of all difficulty.
London. 8vo. 1853.
[*Brit. Mus.*, 8,715 d.]

—— General Education. Learning made easy; or, teaching by reason and sight.
London. 8vo. 1854.
[*Brit. Mus.*, 8,308 c.]

—— Orthographic projection of the Globe on the plane of a given horizon.
London. 8vo. 1857.
[*Brit. Mus.*, 10,002 c.]

> He died the 15th of 9th mo., 1884, aged 84 years, at Marlbro' House, Burgess Hill, near Hurstpierpoint, in the county of Sussex, and was buried in Friends' Burial Ground, Stoke Newington.

ABBOTT, Benjamin, of *Hitchin*.

—— The Boys' Leisure Hours. A Monthly Miscellany, in Nos. from 184— to 184—.

> He died at Thornton Heath, near Croydon, the 6th of 12th mo., 1870, aged 77 years, and was buried in the Friends' Burial Ground, Croydon.

ABELL, Joshua, of *Dublin*.

—— The Dublin Literary Journal. See PERIODICAL PUBLICATIONS.

ABRAHAM, Daniel, George Fox and others. See GEORGE FOX.

—— Christian Epistle to John III., King of Poland.
4to. 1678.

ADAMS, Richard, of *Kilcott*, in *Devonshire*.

—— Some STRIKING and REMARKABLE PREDICTIONS, of the *Holy, Learned, and Excellent* Archbishop Usher, some time Lord Primate of Ireland, in the reign of King Charles the First. To which are added, 𝔄 𝔉𝔢𝔴 𝔍𝔫𝔱𝔢𝔯𝔢𝔰𝔱𝔦𝔫𝔤 𝔈𝔵𝔱𝔯𝔞𝔠𝔱𝔰, from other eminent religious authors, concerning *The* Nature *and* End of a Spiritual Life.

> *The Secret of the Lord is with them that fear Him, and He will shew them His Covenant.*
> PSALMS.

ADAMS Richard, *continued.*
Bristol : *Printed by R. Edwards, for Richard Adams, of Kitcott, Devonshire.*
8vo. 1797. 1½
NOTE.—The other eminent religious authors alluded to in the title, and from which the extracts are made are GEORGE FOX, WILLIAM PENN, and ROBERT BARCLAY, etc.

ADY, John, of *London.*
——Proposals for printing " The Harmony of the Divine Will," &c.
London : Printed by Henry Fry, Basinghall Street.
4to. 1807 ½

ALBRIGHT, William Henry, son of WILLIAM WHITLARK ALBRIGHT and ELIZABETH ALBRIGHT (*née* Smith) and nephew of Joseph Smith, the Bibliographer.
——" 𝕷𝖊𝖆𝖉 𝖒𝖊 𝖇𝖞 𝕿𝖍𝖞 𝕷𝖎𝖌𝖍𝖙." W. H. ALBRIGHT.
8vo. No date. ⅛

ALDIS, Chas., Surgeon. Account of him, with a *Portrait.*
See EUROPEAN MAGAZINE, 1817.

ALEXANDER, Alice.
——An Appeal to Christian Men on the Subject of Female Attire.
Dublin : John Gough, 6, Eustace Street. (*Printed by R. Chapman, Temple Lane, Dame Street, Dublin.*)
Price One Penny. Per hundred, 6s. 6d.
8vo. 1872. ½

ALEXANDER, Joseph Gundry, formerly of Leominster, now of London.
——LET NO MAN DESPISE THY YOUTH. 𝕿𝖍𝖔𝖚𝖌𝖍𝖙𝖘 𝖔𝖓 1 𝕿𝖎𝖒𝖔𝖙𝖍𝖞 iv. 12-16. Addressed to the YOUNGER MEMBERS OF THE SOCIETY OF FRIENDS, who are engaged in First Day School Teaching, and other branches of Home Mission Work. By Joseph G. Alexander.
London : F. B. Kitto, 5, Bishopsgate Street, Without.
[*John Bellows, Printer, Gloucester.*]
12mo. [1872.] 1¾

ALEXANDER, Richard Dykes, of *Ipswich.*
——OBSERVATIONS on the SUBJECT OF WAR, showing its inconsistency with Christianity. By Richard Dykes Alexander.
Second edition. *Burton, Printer, Ipswich.*
8vo. No date. ½

ALEXANDER, Richard Dykes, *continued*.
——The Ipswich Series of Temperance Tracts. Vol. I.
Nos. 1 to 66.
    Ipswich, printed. . 12mo. 1846.

ALEXANDER, Ann, his wife.
——FRUITS and FLOWERS : By the Author of " The Wheatsheaf."
    " The *proper* culture of the garden of thy mind will
      yield thee more than *summer* fruits and flowers."
    London : Printed for Darton and Harvey,
      Gracechurch Street.
                            18mo. 1833. 6
——THE SHRUBBERY. By the compiler of " FRUITS AND FLOWERS," and of " THE GARDEN," &c.
    " But truths on which depend our main concern,
      That 'tis our shame and misery not to learn,
      Shine by the side of every path we tread,
      With such a lustre, he that runs may read."
    [ANON.]   COWPER.
    London : Darton and Harvey, and all Booksellers.
                          18mo. 1835. $7\frac{1}{18}$
——To Friends of the Q.M. of Suffolk.   1843.
——Gleanings from Pious Authors. 𝔑 𝔑𝔢𝔴 𝔈𝔡𝔦𝔱𝔦𝔬𝔫.
    London : Simpkin, Marshall, and Co. ; Alfred
      W. Bennett, 5, Bishopsgate Without.
    Ipswich : J. M. Burton and Co.
              Foolscap 8vo. 436pp. 1858.

ALEXANDER, William, Bookseller, of *York*.
——True Liberty. [Anon.]
    York, printed. . . 4to. No date. ½

ALEXANDER, Ann, of *York*.
——A new set of Cards, calculated for general circulation ; selected by the Author of " Facts respecting Climbing Boys. On Card Playing, the Swearer's Prayer, &c. (Six different.) . . 16mo. No date.

ALEXANDER, William Henry, of *Ipswich*.
——The BOOK OF PRAISES : being the 𝔅𝔬𝔬𝔨 𝔬𝔣 𝔓𝔰𝔞𝔩𝔪𝔰, according to the authorised version, with 𝔑𝔬𝔱𝔢𝔰 𝔬𝔯𝔦𝔤𝔦𝔫𝔞𝔩 𝔞𝔫𝔡 𝔰𝔢𝔩𝔢𝔠𝔱𝔢𝔡. By WILLIAM HENRY ALEXANDER. Edited by his family.
    London : Jackson, Walford, and Hodder, 27,
      Paternoster Row, E.C. MDCCCLXVII.
    [*Unwin Brothers, Printers, Bucklersbury, E.C.*]
                        8vo. 1867. 30½

ALEXANDER, William Henry, *continued.*

—— Memorials of William H. Alexander and Sophia Alexander, of Ipswich.
London : F. B. Kitto, Bishopsgate Street Without.
Ipswich : Rees and Gripper.
         8vo. 1867. 10¾

 Wm. H. Alexander, died 14th of 1st mo., 1864, aged 64 ; and his widow Sophia the 25th of 11th mo., 1865, aged 59 years.

ALLEN, Alfred, of *Sydney, New South Wales.*

—— and others. A Letter from Friends in Sydney, to the Dear Friends in Melbourne, 1867.
         4to. 1867. ½

 Reprinted from the original and 2nd edition.
 Gloucester: John Bellows, Steam Press, Westgate-Street.
         12mo. 1868. ½

  Signed by
   James Mitchell,
   Joseph Dixon,
   Alfred Allen,
   William Tuting,
   Arthur Wood.

—— A Vindication of the Truth, and A TESTIMONY on behalf of the Ancient Principles of the People called Quakers, sincerely and affectionately commended to the Members of the Society of Friends in the *Colonies, the British Isles, and in other lands.*

 [This Vindication is given in answer to a Pamphlet dissenting from the doctrines contained in a Printed Epistle sent by some Members of the Society of Friends in Sydney to the Yearly Meeting of Friends in Melbourne.]

 Sydney : Gibbs, Shallard, & Co., 108, Pitt Street, Melbourne : Clarson, Massina & Co., 95, Little Collins Street. London : F. Bowyer Kitto, 5, Bishopsgate Without.
        8vo. [1868.] 3¾

  Signed by
   Alfred Allen,
   Joseph Dixon,
   James Mitchell,
   Arthur Wood.

ALLEN, Hannah, of *Stoke Newington,* formerly of *Ratcliff.*

—— A Compendium of History from THE CREATION to the COMMENCEMENT OF THE CHRISTIAN ERA.

ALLEN, Hannah, *continued.*
>Designed chiefly for the use of Schools and young persons. By H. ALLEN.
>>*London: Charles Bean, 1, James Terrace, Hoxton. (Richard Barrett, Printer, Mark Lane).* 8vo. 1862. 34¼
>>NOTE.—The copy from which I took the above title has written on the title page, " M. E. Darton, with love from H.A., 20 4 66 " ; also on the flyleaf in pencil, " T. G. Darton, Westleys & Co., Friar Street, Doctors' Commons " ; and has numerous "corrections and alterations" in ink, evidently with a view to a new edition.
>>She died the 12th of 4th month, 1867, aged 83 years, and was buried at Stoke Newington.

ALLEN, Hannah, wife of Stafford Allen, of *London,* and ELLEN CLARE MILLER, and others.—**An Appeal on behalf of Schools in Syria, Greece, &c.**
>4to. [1869.] ½

——A Beloved Mother. Life of Hannah S. Allen. By her daughter. London : Samuel Harris & Co., 5, Bishopsgate Without. 8vo. 1884. 12¼ (Portrait.)
>She died the 6th day of the 6th month, 1880, aged 67 years, and was buried at Stoke Newington.

ALLEN, John, of *Liskeard.*

——Brief Memoirs of George Fox, William Penn, and a Biographical Sketch of Elizabeth Fry.
>*London : Printed for the Tract Association of the Society of Friends.* . . 18mo. 1856-57.

ALLEN, Richard, of *Dublin.*

——Rambles in Egypt and Syria. (Peninsular and Oriental Hotel, Suez, 2nd of 4th mo. (April), 1869.) To the Editor of the General Advertiser.
>Paper No. 5. . . 4to. Broadside. 1869. ¼

——Rambles in Egypt and Palestine. Samaria, 26th of 5th mo. (May), 1869. To the Editor of the General Advertiser.
>Paper No. 9. . . Fol. Broadside. 1869. 1

——Rambles in Egypt and Palestine. Beyrout, 9th of 6th mo. (June), 1869. To the Editor of the General Advertiser
>Paper No. 10. . . Fol. Broadside. 1869. 1

——Rambles in Egypt and Palestine. Beyrout, 14th of 6th mo. (June), 1869.
>Paper No. 11. . . 4to. Broadside. 1869. ¼

ALLEN, Richard, *continued*.

—— Letters from Egypt, Syria, and Greece, by Richard Allen.
Reprinted from the General Advertiser.
Dublin : *Printed by Gunn and Cameron, 13, Fleet Street.* 8vo. 1869. 4¼

—— A Brief Sketch of the last days of Richard Allen.
Privately printed. . . 18mo. [1886.] ⅓

—— A Christian Philanthropist of Dublin. A Memoir of Richard Allen. By *Hannah Maria Wigham*.
8vo. 1886. 16¾
He died the 19th of 1st month, 1886, aged 83 years.

—— and others. At a Meeting held at Plough Court June 14, 1816, for the Formation of the Peace Society.
4to. 1816. ¼

—— A Circular on the " Scripture Lessons." . 4to. [1820.]

—— An Appeal to Friends on behalf of the Scripture Lesson Fund.
W. Phillips, Printer, George Yard, &c. 4to. [1820.] ½

—— and JOSIAH FORSTER.—Letter on the subject of the Bill for the general Education of the Poor. 4to. 1821. ¼

—— Defence of the British and Foreign School Society against the Remarks in the Sixty-seventh number of the " Edinburgh Review."
[Anon.] *London* : *Published by Hutchinson & Son.* 8vo. 1821. 3

ALLEN, William, of *Plough Court, London*, continued from p. 18 of Catalogue.

—— Prospectus of a New Work, entitled the PHILANTHROPIST, to be published in three months. *Price Half-a-Crown.*
Printed at J. Lancaster's Royal Free School Press, Borough Road, Southwark. . 8vo. [1810.] ⅛

—— Thoughts on the Importance of Religion.
London : *Printed and sold by W. Phillips, George Yard, Lombard Street.* . . 12mo. 1808. ⅔

—— Another Edition.
Gillingham : *Printed by E. Neave.* 8vo. 1808. ¾

The same. A new edition. Reprinted at Chichester by *W. Mason*. 8vo. 1809. 1⅛

—— Another edition. . B. 1

ALLEN, William, *continued.*
——Thoughts on the Importance of Religion.
☞ *Printed and sold by George Cooke, Dunstan's Hill, Tower Street; of whom may be had a variety of interesting Papers.*
                                                        Broadside. No date   1
——Another Edition.
    Stockport : Printed by J. Lomax, Underbank.
                                                        12mo. 1814.   ½
——**Pensees** Sur L'importance de la Religion.
    A. Montauban, Chez P. A. Fontanel, Imprimeur Du Roy.
    [Anon.]   .   .   .   12mo. 1817.   ½
——Story of the Spitalfields Genius. (*By Fayle*).
——Colonies at Home, &c. Second Edition.
    Lindfield : Printed by C. Green, &c.
                                                        8vo. No Date   1
    „   Third Edition.
    „   Fourth Edition.
    Lindfield : Printed by C. Green, &c.
                                                        8vo. 1827.   2
——Brief Remarks upon the Carnal and Spiritual State of Man. Translated into Welsh.
                                                        12mo. Bala, 1830.
——Vie et Voyages of William Allen. By R. N. Reyr.
                                                        16mo. Toulouse, 1853.
——BIOGRAPHIE de WILLIAM ALLEN, Membre de la Société des Amis, ou Quakers, Par G. De Félice, Auteur de *l'Histoire des Protestants de France*, etc.
    Paris : C. Meyrueis et Co., Lib., Rue des St. Pères, 43 et 45. Grassart, Libraire, Rue de la Paix, 2.
    Toulouse, Lagarde, Libraire, Rue Romiguières, 7.
                                                        12mo. 1869. 11½
——Engraving of his residence, " Plough Court, Lombard Street."
    Reprinted from " The Illustrated London News." [1872.]
ALLEN, William, son of Samuel Allen, of *Hitchin*, and nephew of the above Wm. Allen.
——Transactions of the 𝔉𝔯𝔢𝔢𝔡𝔪𝔢𝔫'𝔰 𝔄𝔦𝔡 𝔖𝔬𝔠𝔦𝔢𝔱𝔶, of London, from June 24th, 1864, to December 31st, 1865.
    G. Coventry, Printer, Tottenham, London.
                                                        8vo. [1866?] 1¼
——and Samuel Gurney.—Account (of do.) from January to March, 1866   .   .   .   8vo. [1866.] ⅛

ALLINSON, David, Compiler of Laws of *New Jersey*.
ALLINSON, William J., of *Philadelphia*.
——Memorials of the Life and Character of John Gummeré
By Wm. J. Allinson. 8vo. 6 leaves
——Poems. By William J. Allinson.
Philadelphia: Claxton, Remson and Hafelfinger.
1873.
ALLIS, Thomas.
——On the Sclerotic Ring of the Eyes of Birds and Reptiles.
8vo. 1855.
ALMANACKS.
See also Samuel Atkins, Philadelphia, 1685.
——The Protestant Dissenters Almanack for the year 1859.
8vo. 1859.
——Calendario Protestante de los Amigos Cristianos. Para el Ano de 1868. Editor responsable, Parra y Alvarez.
Mexico : Imprenta de Manuel Castro calle de las Escalerillas núm. 10,
[1868.] 64pp.

NOTE.—Containing a Spanish Translation of Nos. 2 and 7, Old Banner Tracts, by Juan G. Butler.

——The MORAL ALMANACK, for the year **1871**. The Calculations are for Pennsylvania, New Jersey, and the Northern and Western States, and are made to mean or CLOCK TIME.
Philadelphia : Published by the Tract Association of Friends, and to be had at their Depository, No. 304, Arch Street. Printed by William K. Bellows, S. W. corner of Fourth and Apple Tree Streets.
12mo. [1871.] 1½
ALSOP, Christiana, daughter of Ruhamah John and Elizabeth Alsop, of *Philadelphia*.
——A Short Testimony concerning her.
In Comly's Miscellany, vol. 4, p. 374.

She died the 24th of the 2nd month, 1832, aged about 34 years.

ALSOP, Robert, was born at *Maldon*, in *Essex*, 1803. Afterwards, in 1816-17, at Ackworth School. Chemist in Sloane Square, Chelsea, last of Stoke Newington.
——and JOSEPH COOPER—Extracts from Letter, &c., bearing upon the Immigration Slave Trade.
8vo. [1858.] 1⅛

ALSOP, Robert, *continued.*

——Letter on the welfare of young Friends, 3rd Month, 31st, 1864, on behalf of the Quarterly Meeting.
8vo. ⅛

——What is the Gospel ? In reply to a letter from a Friend.
(Second edition with postscript revised).
16mo. 1873.

NOTE.—Answered by Wm. Irwin, George Pitt, Joseph Armfield, and Chas. Elcock.

——A few remarks in reply to a tract by Joseph Armfield, entitled " The Spirituality of the Gospel re-asserted and defended."
16mo. 1874.

——Criminal Lunacy. Signed by Robert Alsop and others on behalf of the Howard Association.
8vo. 1869. ¼

——MEMOIRS of the LIFE AND GOSPEL LABOURS of STEPHEN GRELLET. Edited by Benjamin Seebohm.

" The fields in many parts I have visited are white unto harvest, so that sometimes I have wished that I might have the life of Methuselah, or that the sun might never go down, that I might do my share of that great work which is to be done in these Nations."—S. GRELLET, p. 133.

(Portrait of S. Grellet, and facsimile of his hand-writing.)

Third Edition abridged. By R. and C. R. Alsop.
London : Edward Marsh, 12, Bishopsgate Street Without, MDCCCLXX.
Printed by R. Barrett and Sons, Mark Lane, London.
8vo. 1870. 28

Translated into French by G. de Félice, of Montauban.

——A TRIBUTE TO the Memory of Robert Alsop.
(Edited by Christine R. Alsop.)
London : West, Newman, & Co., Printers, 54, Hatton Garden. [For private circulation.]
sq. 8vo. 1879. 13

ALSOP, Christine R., his wife.

——Mission Work in France, dated 74, Clissold Road, *Fifth Month,* 1876.
Printers: Warren Hall & J. J. Lovitt, 88, Camden Road, London, N.W.
12mo. [1876.] ⅓

ALSOP, Christine R., *continued.*

——FRAGMENTS relating to Christine R. Alsop, 𝔴𝔥𝔬 𝔡𝔦𝔢𝔡 at 𝔚𝔢𝔩𝔩𝔦𝔫𝔤𝔥𝔞𝔪 𝔥𝔬𝔲𝔰𝔢, 𝔫𝔢𝔞𝔯 𝔏𝔢𝔴𝔢𝔰, after a few days' illness, on the 19th of Sixth Month, 1879.
London : West, Newman, & Co., Printers, 54, Hatton Garden.
16mo. 1879. ½

——Memorials of Christine Alsop, Compiled by MARTHA BRAITHWAITE. (Portrait.)
8vo. 1881. 16

Robert Alsop died the 1st of 11mo., 1876, aged 72 years, and was interred at Stoke Newington, Christine his wife died as stated above in the year 1879.

ALSOP, Samuel, of *Philadelphia*, Mathematician.

——A Treatise on surveying in which the theory and practice are fully explained, preceded by a short treatise on Logarithms and also by a compendious system of plain trigonometry, the whole illustrated by numerous examples. By SAMUEL ALSOP, author of a treatise on Algebra.

Reprinted.—2nd edition.
Philadelphia. 8vo. 1858. 432pp.

AMINADAB.

——𝔄𝔪𝔦𝔫𝔞𝔡𝔞𝔟'𝔰 LETTER to the Author of a PAPER called The 𝔍𝔫𝔡𝔢𝔭𝔢𝔫𝔡𝔢𝔫𝔱 𝔚𝔥𝔦𝔤. Wherein is made appear that his taking upon himself the name of 𝔍𝔫𝔡𝔢𝔭𝔢𝔫𝔡𝔢𝔫𝔱 serves only to show who he does 𝔇𝔢𝔭𝔢𝔫𝔡 upon. Dedicated to the 𝔅   𝔩 𝔒𝔩𝔲𝔟. By a hearty lover of the CHURCH and MONARCHY.

Behold he is metamorphosed as it were, for his outward Man is turned inward, yea, and his inward Man is turned inside out.

London : Printed for T. Warner, at the Black Boy in Paternoster Row. Price Sixpence. 8vo. 1721. 2½

——AMINADAB, one of the People called QUAKERS. To the B———p of L———n, on his LETTER to the Clergy and Inhabitants of *London* and *Westminster*, concerning the late EARTHQUAKES.

London : Printed for Obadiah Prim. Price Threepence. 8vo. 1750. 1

ANDERDON, John, of *Bridgewater, Somersetshire.*

——His " Book Plate."

ANDREWS, Isaac, of *North America.*

——Account of the Early part of his Life, his religious exercises, and Call to the Ministry. In Comly's Miscellany, Vol. 4, page 1.
>He died about the 15th of the 12th month, 1775. See mention of him in Woolman's Journal, &c.

ANONYMOUS.

——TRUTH Seeks no CORNERS: or, Seven CASES of Conscience Humbly presented to the Army and Parliament. 4to. Printed in the year 1659. 1½
>Query, whether Friends? Not E. Hookes'

——A SERMON preached before the People called Quakers, in the Park of Southwark. By a Reverend and Dearly-beloved Sister, who came from *Scotland*, &c. Reprinted ; *Edinburgh, printed by John Reid, MDCLCCCVIII.* 8vo. 1688.
>NOTE.—The *First Edition* of this pamphlet, 1687, is entered in my catalogue with a note that it was a *mere fiction*, notwithstanding which, it was contributed by Matilda Sturge, to "The Friends' Quarterly Examiner," Vol. xvi. p. 91, as genuine from a copy of this 2nd Edition, in the possession of W. Rendle, of Forest Hill, S.E.

——‖ The Harmless Opinion of the REVOLUTION of Humane Souls; as a probable Hypothesis, and very serviceable to clear many Doubts, and answer many Objections of ATHEISTS against the Divine Providence, and the HOLY SCRIPTURES. Modestly defended in a Reply to a late Treatise, Signed by J.H., Printed at *Oxford*, and called by him, An Answer to some *Queries*, proposed by W.C., or a Refutation of *Helmont's* Pernicious Error, &c.

London : Printed for Sarah Howkins, *in Georgeyard, Lombard Street.* 8vo. 1694. 3

——‖ *Spira Respirans* : or, The WAY to the Kingdom of Heaven, by the Gates of Hell; in an Extraordinary Example. By a Person brought to the depths of Despair and Anguish, recovered by the mighty Grace and Power of God, and raised to Heights of Assurance and Joy. Wherein are some uncommon considerations concerning the manner of Salvation and Damnation, Life and Death, Happiness and Misery. With some Fundamental Arguments for the Immortality of the Soul.

ANONYMOUS, *continued.*

John 3, 8.—*The Wind bloweth where it listeth, and thou hearest the sound thereof, but canst not tell whence it cometh, and whither it goeth : so is every one that is born of the Spirit.*
London : Printed and Sold by T. Sowle, near the Meeting-house, in White Hart Court, in Gracious Street. 12mo. 1695.   3

——A WARNING PIECE (in verse).
London : Printed by J. Sowle, in White-Hart-Court, in Gracious Street.   Large B. 1709.   1

——Some QUERIES for the YEARLY MEETING to answer (about 1734 ?).
Folio. No printer's name, place, or date.   Suppose about JOHN HEWLET, who went to America.

——CONSIDERATIONS upon the present TEST LAW of PENNSYLVANIA : Addressed to the Legislature and Freemen of the State. [By BENJAMIN RUSH.]
Philadelphia : Printed by Hall and Sellers.
12mo. 1764.   1

——SERIOUS REFLECTIONS on the intended attempt to alter the COMMON LAW of *England*, in regard to the POSSESSIONS of the CLERGY (not Friends, I think).
Folio. 1772.   1

——REMARKS upon a BILL now depending in Parliament, entitled, *A Bill to prevent Suits, for Tythes, where none, nor any Composition for the same, have been paid within a certain Number of Years.*
Fol. No Printer's name, place, or date.   .   1

——" The Government being engaged in a War, proposes to borrow a Sum, &c."   The above was printed and dispersed, in a Handbill, by JOSEPH PHIPPS, to the remarks therein contained, the following are added by another hand, &c. (JOHN ROPER, supposed).
4to. [1781.]   ¼

——Address to Young Men.   Signed Senex.   Fol.   1783.

——The Polite Reasoner : in Letters addressed to a young Lady at a Boarding School in Hoddesdon, Hertfordshire.   By Mary Weightman, Hoddesdon.
London : Printed for W. Bent, Paternoster Row.
8vo. 1787,

ANONYMOUS, continued.

——The JUVENILE SPEAKER : or Dialogues, and Miscellaneous Pieces in Prose and Verse, for the instruction of Youth in the Art of Reading. By the Author of the POLITE REASONER.
London : Printed for W. Bent, Paternoster Row.
12mo. 1787. 5½

——A Short System of Polite Learning : being a concise introduction to the Arts and Sciences, and other branches of useful knowledge,

——The Friendly Monitor ; or Dialogues for Youth against the Fear of Ghosts, and other Irrational Apprehensions, with reflections on the Power of the imagination, and the folly of superstition. By the Author of the Polite Reasoner and Juvenile Speaker.
London : Printed for W. Bent, Paternoster Row.
12mo. 1791. 5½

——The Bee, a Selection of Poetry from the best AUTHORS. (Vignette, Bee Hive and Bees.)
A new edition.
London : Printed and sold by Darton and Harvey Gracechurch Street. . . 18mo. 1795.
Preface, &c., 9 pp., Text, 191 pp.
NOTE.—The title is engraved.

Reprinted.—A new edition.
London : Printed and sold by Darton and Harvey, Gracechurch Street. . . 12mo. 1797. 9

——The same.—A New Edition.
London, &c. (Imprint as above). Small 12mo. 1791.

——The same.—The Fifth Edition.
London : Printed by and for Darton and Harvey, Gracechurch Street. 1807.

——The Bee, a Selection of Poetry from approved authors.
London : Darton and Harvey, Gracechurch Street.
(J. May, Printer, Dover.) 12mo. No date. 9

——A GENTLE CAUTION. (against Talebearing, Backbiting, &c.)
G. Cooke, Printer, Dunstan's Hill, London.
Fol. N.D. ½

——Character of Buonaparte.
G. Cooke, Printer, Dunstan's Hill, Tower Street.
Fol. No date. ½

ANONYMOUS, *continued.*

—— An AFRICAN'S APPEAL to the BRITISH NATION. With, The AFRICAN'S COMPLAINT. *Sold by W. Darton and Co., No. 55, Gracechurch Street, London.* . . . Fol. N.D. ½

—— Strictures on the Conduct of the Quakers as a Society, No. 1. *Printed by James Montgomery, at the Iris Office.* 12mo. 1802.

—— To the Students at Oxford. [J.R.] 12mo. Oxford. 1809.

—— The following QUESTIONS were offered to the TEACHERS in the Nine—Partners' Boarding—School, to their Pupils, and the answers given in by them. The SCHOLARS had the liberty of recurring to BOOKS for aid, when they found themselves unable to give proper answers without such assistance. *Danville, Vt.: Published by Daniel Lowell. Isaac Hill, Printer.* 24mo. 1818. ½

—— The TRIUMPH OF FAITH over Unbelief : exemplified in the Conversion and Death of a Young Female, belonging to the Society of Friends, *who had formerly been entangled in the Snares of infidelity.* WRITTEN BY A PHYSICIAN.

" Faith lends its realizing light,
 The clouds disperse, the shadows fly ;
 The Invisible appears in sight,
 And God is seen by mortal eye."

London : Published and sold by J. Kershaw, 14, City Road, and 66, Paternoster Row. (Printed by T. Cordeaux, 14, City Road, London.)
(About 1818 ?) 12mo. No date. ½

—— ADDRESS to SERVANTS. [By CHARLES DUDLEY.] *Printed and sold by J. Low, 21, Gracechurch Street.* [*Circa.* 1819.] ¼

—— A LETTER to a Junior Member of the Society of Friends, occasioned by his Address to the YOUNG MEN AND WOMEN of the same Society.

"It is the not properly considering the extent of our capacity, the not clearly distinguishing the things to which our ideas are suited, from those to which they are inadequate, that has made many men fall into an irksome scepticism, and some into actual infidelity."
BISHOP WATSON,

ANONYMOUS, continued.

    Woodbridge : *Printed and sold by B. Smith; sold also by Cowell, Ipswich; Chaplin, Colchester; Marsden, Chelmsford ; Rackham, Bury ; Wilkin & Youngman, Norwich ; and Sloman, Yarmouth.* 12mo. 1820. 1

        Note.—This is an Answer to Chas. Elcock's Letter (see Catalogue, Vol. I., p. 559).

——The ENTERTAINING MEDLEY, being a Collection of 𝕿rue 𝕳istories and 𝕬necdotes, calculated for the Cottagers' Fireside. (Woodcuts.)

    Dublin : *Printed by Christopher Bentham, 19, Eustace Street.* . . 18mo. 1822. 5

——UN MOT contre la Mauraise Habitude de prendre le Nom de Dieu en Vain. (A word against the bad habit of taking God's name in vain.) LOUIS. MAJOLIER, *Nismes*, GAUDE, *Impr.—Libraire, Grand Rue.*

                                                              8vo. 1822. ½

——The History of TIM HIGGINS. The Cottage Visitor. *(Woodcuts.)*

    [By ABIGAIL ROBERTS, of *Mountrath* in *Ireland.*] *Dublin* : *Printed by C. Bentham, Eustace Street.* 18mo. 1823. 5

——EXTRACTS from LOCKE'S PARAPHRASE on *The Apostle Paul's Epistles*, on the Subject of the PUBLIC MINISTRY OF WOMEN.

    London: Printed for Gossling & Egley, No. 69, New Bond Street. [By T. BRETTELL, *Rupert Street, Haymarket, London.*

                                             Foolscap 8vo. 1826. 1

——A Collection of Prophecies, from the 𝕺ld 𝕿estament, which testify of our Lord and Saviour, Jesus Christ; with parallel Passages from the New Testament. Selected by a Mother for her only child.

——The FRIENDS' FAMILY. Intended for the Amusement and Instruction of CHILDREN.

    Philadelphia : *Published by T. E. Chapman, 74, North Fourth Street.* . 18mo. 1844. 92pp.

        CONTENTS.—Story of Thomas Ellwood and an account of James Parnell.

——The FOOL'S GOSPEL. [See BARTON DELL.]

    London : *Elliot Stock, 62, Paternoster Row.*

                                                       8vo. 1871. 11¼

ANONYMOUS, *continued.*
London : *Printed for Harvey & Gracechurch Street; and sold by W. Phillips, George-yard, Lombard Street; and J. & A. Arch, Cornhill.*
12mo. 1826. 4½

NOTE.—This is already entered in the Catalogue, but not the imprint.

——INSTRUCTION and ADVICE to GIRLS, intended to assist them in the performance of their several duties as SERVANTS. THIRD EDITION. [By Mary Hoare?]
London : *Printed and sold by William Phillips, George Yard, Lombard Street.*
18mo. 1826. 1⅓

——Chattering Disposition to be avoided.
James Whiting, Printer, Finsbury Place, London.
Folio. [*Circa* 1827.] ½

——Remarks on Drunkenness, with Cases and Advice to those persons who are in the Habit of Drinking Spirituous Liquors. By a Medical Man.
London : *Harvey & Darton, Gracechurch Street.*
8vo. 1830. 2½

——A Letter on Christian Doctrine. . . 1832.

——CONVERSATIONS as between PARENTS and CHILDREN. Designed for the instruction of Youth. (On the principles of Friends.)

" Train up a child in the way he should go, and when he is old he will not depart from it."—PROV. XXII., 6.

Second Edition.
Philadelphia : *William Brown, Printer.*
12mo. 1834. 5½

——Dialogue between Fox and Freeman . 1835.

——Letter on the Lord's Supper . . . 1836.

— —A few Hints to parents. (On the right training of chilren).
Darlington : *Printed by Coates and Farmer, High Row.*
12mo. 1836. ⅓

——Remarks on the Disuse of all Typical Rites, addressed to the Society of Friends. No. 132 of a series of Tracts. Gloucester, printed.
8vo. 1837. 1½
See M. II.

——Reflections on the Constitution and Duties of Man. 1811.

ANONYMOUS, *continued.*

——Dialogue on the CORN LAWS : Scene, The Steam-boat "Orwell."
    London : Effingham Wilson, 18, Bishopsgate Street, Within. . . . 8vo. 1841. 1½
    By Stephen Perry, Ipswich, now (1870) of Needham Market, Suffolk.

——A Dialogue on the Corn Laws between a Gentleman and a Farmer on board of the "Orwell Steamer."
    Printed by Stephen Piper. 8vo.
    NOTE.—This tract was afterwards adopted and largely circulated by the Anti-Corn Law League.

——The Law and the Gospel. . . . . 1843.

——Reflections on the Rise and Principles of the Society of Friends. . . . . . 1843.

——Letter respecting Joseph Marriage. . 4to. [1844]. ¼

——Observations on excluding females from participating in the Gospel Ministry. (America?) . 1844.

——An Affectionate Address to the Society of Friends in Great Britain and Ireland. By a Member. (A Reprint of 1831).
    Varty . . . . 1845.

——A Statistical Inquiry into the CONDITION OF THE PEOPLE OF COLOUR, of the City and Districts of Philadelphia.
    Philadelphia : Printed by Kite and Walton, No. 50, North Fourth Street. . 8vo. 1849. 3

——Observations on some of the Prize Essays.
    (*By W. Tanner, Bristol?*)

——A LETTER TO WILLIAM BENNETT, OF LONDON, Great Britain, upon the subject of the Religious Controversies among the Members of the Society of Friends in America. By Pacificus.
    (*No printer's name or place.*) . 12mo. 1854. ⅚

——A FRIENDLY LETTER to UNDER NURSES of the Sick, especially in Unions. By a Lady.
    London : A. W. Bennett, 5, Bishopsgate Without. 8vo. 1861. ¾

——A PILLAR OF REMEMBRANCE, &c. [See Eleanor Clifton.] . . . 16mo. London. 1861. 3/10

——The Children's History of the Society of Friends. Chiefly compiled from Sewell's History.

ANONYMOUS, *continued.*
>Reprinted.—2nd Edition.
Dublin : Hodges, Smith and Co., 104, Grafton Street. Publishers to the University.
London : Alfred W. Bennett, 5, Bishopsgate Street Without.
(By Josh. S. Sewell ?) . . Square, 16mo. 1864. 6
——Limits of Volitional Liberty. By a Modern Barclayan (non-religiously treated). 1865.
——The Preston Hymn Book.
>Fifth Edition . . . . 24mo. 1864.
——" Guide the House." An Address to Poor Mothers. **By a Mother.**
>Reprinted.—2nd Edition. *London : Alfred W. Bennett, 5, Bishopsgate Without, E.C.*
>12mo. 1866. $\frac{1}{2}$
——The CHRISTIAN MINISTRY, considered in relation to **The Priesthood of Believers,** and the free Exercise of Spiritual gifts.
>" Ye are a chosen generation ; a royal priesthood."—
>I. PET. II., 9.
>*London : Longmans, Green, Reader, and Dyer. (Printed by E. Couchman and Co., Throgmorton Street, London).* 8vo. 1867. 8
——Church Establishments, and the effect of their absence in America. (By the Meeting for Sufferings).
>*London : Edward Marsh, 12, Bishopsgate Street without.* 8vo. 1869. $\frac{3}{4}$
——Charleton *v.* Barclay. (Being an Answer to Robert Charleton's objections to Barclay's Apology).
>*Douglas, Printer, Dungannon.*
>Large 4to. November, 1868. $\frac{1}{2}$
>NOTE.—Extracted from " The Friend " (Philadelphia) of 6th Month, 6th, 1868.
——Birthright Church Membership in the Society of Friends.
>*Printed by R. Barrett and Sons, Mark Lane, London.* 8vo. [1869.] $\frac{1}{4}$
——Christ, the Giver of True Liberty, with, " What saith the Scripture ?" . . 8vo. No date. $\frac{1}{8}$
>NOTE.—Published by order of the Meeting for Sufferings, and translated also into Spanish for circulation in Spain.
——A Mystery. *Dialogue between Father and Son,* by " Uncle Ben." . . 8vo. [1869 ?] $\frac{1}{8}$

ANONYMOUS, *continued*.

——An Address to the Younger Females in the Society of Friends.
>London : F. Bowyer Kitto, 5, Bishopsgate Street Without. 32mo. 1869. ¼

——The Early Friends : their Message and the Secret of their Power.
>Philadelphia. . . . . 8vo. No date. 1

See H. W. Smith, wife of R. Pearsall Smith.
(By Sarah Grace Harvey, wife of Thomas Harvey of Leeds.)

——A Plea for the Oppressed : An address to the Christian Women of England.
>Leeds : Printed by Edward Baines & Sons.
>12mo. 1870. ⅓

——The Setting Sun. A Poem in seven books. (By JAMES HURNARD.)
>London : F. Bowyer Kitto, 5, Bishopsgate Street Without, E.C. . . . 8vo. 1870. 23

——LITTLE CAROLINE AND JASPER.

Died 2nd Month 28th, 1869, aged 2 years. | Died 4th Month 30th, 1869, aged 6 months.
>4to. [1869.] ¼

——The Society of Friends. A few familiar words. (? By Fardon, Maidstone.)
>12mo. 1d.

——LUMEN SICCUM : an Essay on the exercise of the intellect in matters of Religious belief. Addressed to Members of the Society of Friends. [By George Stewardson Brady, a surgeon, of Sunderland.]
>London : F. Bowyer Kitto. Manchester : Hale and Roworth. . . . 8vo. 1868. 1¾

The Imprint on the fly leaf is, "Sunderland : Printed by William Henry Hills. London : F. Bowyer Kitto, 5, Bishopsgate Street Without ; Joseph Smith, 2, Oxford Street, Whitechapel. Manchester : Hale and Roworth."

Answered by THOMAS DREWRY.

——The Sympathy of Our Lord. Reprinted from the Friends' Quarterly Examiner. By W. Westlake.
>Birmingham : White and Pike, Commercial Buildings. . . . 12mo. 1868. ½

——To the Owners and Drivers of Horses and other Animals. [By DANIEL MILLER.]
>Clowler, Printer, Croydon. . 8vo. [1858.] ¼

21

ANONYMOUS, *continued*.

——Thoughts on the Toleration of Important Differences of Opinion in the same Religious Community. Respectfully addressed to the Lancashire Committee by Trust-to-Truth.
London : *F. Bowyer Kitto, 5, Bishopsgate Without.*
Price Sixpence. 8vo. 1870. 1½

——A Few Remarks on *The Prayer-Book*, and some of the things now practised in the Church of England. By a Protestant. [Joshua Green, of Stanstead, Essex ?]
London : *F. Bowyer Kitto, 5, Bishopsgate Without.*
Price One Penny. . . . . . 12mo. 1870. ½

——Why should Charles Voysey be supported ? A LETTER TO A FRIEND, from a Member of the Society of Friends.
It may be well to inform the reader that neither the writer nor his correspondent are connected with Manchester Meeting.
London : *Provost & Co., Henrietta Street, Covent Garden.* . . . . . 12mo. 1871. ½
[By EDWARD T. BENNETT ?]

——Address to Religious Inquirers on the Subject of Silent Worship, or Waiting upon God.
J. Wright, Printer, 8, Market Hill, Sudbury.
8vo. No date. ½

——The MANCHESTER HERESY : its Theological Stand— Point and Rule of Belief critically considered. Ad Judicium.
Stratford-upon-Avon : *J. Morgan, Printer and Bookseller, High Street.* 8vo. 1871. ⅞

——The Happy Choice. [By MATILDA RICKMAN.]
Gloucester : *John Bellows, Steam Press.*
Small 8vo. [1872.] 1

——A Plan for Peace.
" I speak as unto wise men :
Judge ye what I say."
For
OF WISDOM IT IS TRULY SAID :
" Her ways are ways of pleasantness,
And all her paths are PEACE."
(No date.) Square 12mo. [1872.] ½

——BARCLAY and his Assailants. Reprinted, with additions, from the " British Friend." With a Supplementary Tract by the late Edward Alexander, of Limerick. [By William Bennett.]

ANONYMOUS, *continued*.
Glasgow : Robert Smeal.
London : F. B. Kitto, 5, Bishopsgate Street Without.
Manchester : W. Irwin, 24, Deansgate.
8vo. 1872. 3
NOTE.—For a reply to this pamphlet see THOS. DREWRY.

——Examination of Scripture evidence respecting the Lord's Supper. By a member of the Society of Friends.
Aberdeen: James Murry, 28, St. Nicholas Street.
1872.

——Quakerism : American and English.—The Ministry of Elias Hicks. By an American. Price sixpence.
London: F. B. Kitto, 5, Bishopsgate Street, Without. Joseph Smith, 6, Oxford Street, Whitechapel. Birmingham : James Guest, 52, Bull Street, and all Booksellers.
8vo. [1872]. ½
NOTE.—Signed "G" at the end, and dated Birmingham, July 1st, 1872.

——The REASON GIVEN by an early Constitution Friend for his SCRIPTURAL VIEW OF WORSHIP AND DISCIPLINE. (W. L. Bellows?)
London : Samuel Harris & Co., 5, Bishopsgate Street, Without, E.C. Gloucester : William L. Bellows.
Price One Shilling 8vo. 1873. 3¾
Any profits from the sale of this Edition will be given to the British and Foreign Bible Society.

——The Early Friends in Prayer.
Harrison Penney, Printer by Steam Power, Darlington. 8vo. No date. ⅛
NOTE.—Penn's description of George Fox—Edmundson's first interview with George Fox, Josh. Oxley's account of Edmund Peckover's departure for religious service in America.

——Work of the Future for the Society of Friends. [By WM. HY. RICHARDSON.]
London : W. Isbister and Co.
[*Hills, Printer, Sunderland.*] 8vo. 1874. 3⅛

——Quakerism : and its social change. [By a Member of the Society of Friends.] In "*The Daily News*, Thursday, April 5th, 1877."

——Remarks on the Quakers. (So called).
12mo. No. P.N.P. or Date. ⅙

——A Paper : "Dear Friend ; Let us remember." 8vo. ¼

——A Paper : "Are there earnest hearts." 8vo. ⅛

*ANTHONY, Susannah, of *North America*.

——Memoirs of Miss Susanna Anthony, who died at Newport, Rhode Island, June 23, 1791, consisting chiefly of Extracts from her writings, and criticisms on them. By S. Hopkins, *Clipstone*. 8vo. 1803.

APPLETON, Lewis, of *Birmingham*.

——REMINISCENCES OF A VISIT to the BATTLE FIELDS of Sedan, Gravelotte, Spicheren, and Wörth, and the BOMBARDED TOWNS of Thionville, Metz, Bitche, Strasburg, &c. With Illustrations. By Lewis Appleton.
London : Simpson, Marshall, & Co., Stationers' Hall Court. Gloucester : John Bellows.
8vo. 1872. 7¾

ARCHER, Elizabeth.

——An account of the penitent end of a Young Maid (Elizabeth Archer), daughter of Edward and Elizabeth Archer, of *Barbadoes*, of about 18 years. By her *Mother* ; p. 63 Tomkin's "Trumpet Sound."

ARMATAGE, George, M.R.C.V.S., now Secretary of the *Bedford Institute, Spitalfields, London.*

1——The Clinical Note Book, designed and arranged for the use of Students and Practitioners, with a view towards facilitating the taking and preserving the Records of cases in veterinary practice. Sanctioned and approved by the Principal of the Glasgow Veterinary College, for the use of the Clinical Students of that Institution. By George Armatage, M.R.C.V.S.
Glasgow : David Robertson. Edinburgh : MacLachlan and Stewart. Dublin : Hodges, Smith and Co. London : Longmans and Co.
Demy 8vo. 1866.

2——Education of the Veterinary Surgeon. Paper read at the Veterinary Congress, held in London 1867.
Published in *The Veterinarian*, June, 1867, and privately printed . . . . 10pp.

3——The Cattle Plague, and the best means to be adopted for preventing its importation to this country. A Lecture delivered at a meeting of the Devon and Cornwall Chamber of Agriculture, Thursday, the 12th of November, 1868, by Professor Armatage, of London.
Plymouth · Trythall, 5, Whimple Street.
Demy 8vo. 30pp.

ARMATAGE, George, *continued.*

4——The Horse : How to Feed Him, Avoid Disease, and Save Money. By George Armatage, M.R.C.V.S., Professor of Anatomy and Physiology in the Glasgow Veterinary College. Late Professor of Materia Medica in the Albert Veterinary College, &c., &c. (See No. 13.)
London : Frederick Warne & Co., 1868. 120 pp. foolscap 8vo.
Second edition . . . . 1870.

5——The Horse-owner's and Stableman's Companion : or, Hints on the Selection, Purchase, and General Management of the Horse, by George Armatage, M.R.C.V.S., Professor of Veterinary Medicine.
London : Frederick Warne & Co. 1869. 120 pp. foolscap 8vo.
Second edition . . . . 1870.
Third edition, revised . . . 1890.

6——Memoranda for Emergencies ; or the Veterinarian's Pocket Remembrancer ; being Concise Directions for the Treatment of Urgent or Rare Cases, embracing Semiology, Diagnosis, Prognosis, Surgery, Therapeutics, Toxicology, Detection of Poisons by their appropriate Tests, Hygiene, &c., &c. Demy 32mo., 168 pp. 1870.
London : John Churchill & Sons.
Second edition, revised . . . 1884.

7——Practical Horse Shoeing. Prize Essay to which the sum of £20 was awarded by the Scottish Society for the Prevention of Cruelty to Animals. Not published.

8——The Thermometer as an aid to Diagnosis in Veterinary Medicine, by George Armatage, M.R.C.V.S., formerly Lecturer in the Albert and Veterinary Colleges. 1869.
Leighton Buzzard : A. P. Muddiman. London : F. Warne & Co. Edinburgh : MacLachlan & Stewart.
64 pp. foolscap 8vo.
Second edition, revised and enlarged, 1890, foolscap 8vo, 64 pp.
London and New York : Frederick Warne & Co.

9——Every Man his own Cattle Doctor, by Francis Clater, entirely re-written to the present date by George Armatage, M.R.C.V.S., Late Professor of Anatomy, Physiology, &c, with Copious Notes, Additional Recipes, &c., and upwards of two hundred Practical Illustrations, showing forms of Disease and Treatment. . . . . 1870.

ARMATAGE, George, *continued.*
London : Frederick Warne & Co.
681 pp. demy 8vo.
Second edition . . . . 1873.
Third edition, 681 pp. . . . 1877.
Fourth edition, 681 pp. . . . 1879.

—— Every man his own Cattle Doctor, by George Armatage, Late Professor of Anatomy and Physiology, &c., with Copious Notes, Recipes, &c., and upwards of Three Hundred and Fifty Practical Illustrations, showing Forms of Disease and Treatment. Altered Title.
Fifth edition, 894 pp., entirely re-written . 1882.
Sixth edition, revised and enlarged, 920 pp. 1890.
London and New York : Frederick Warne & Co.

10 —— Every Man his own Horse Doctor, by George Armatage, M.R.C.V.S., Author of Every Man his own Cattle Doctor, &c., &c., with which is embodied Blaine's Veterinary Art, with Copious Notes, Recipes, Steel Plates, and Practical and Anatomical Illustrations . . . . . 1877.
London : Frederick Warne & Co. 830 pp. demy 8vo.
Second edition . . . . 1885.
Third edition . . . . 1887.
Fourth edition, Revised and Enlarged, pp. 1891.

11 —— Cattle : Their Varieties and Management in Health and Disease. By George Armatage, M.R.C.V.S., Author of "The Cattle Doctor," "The Horse Doctor," "Horse-owner's and Stableman's Companion," &c., &c. Revised and considerably enlarged. With Illustrations. 230 pp. foolscap 8vo. . . 1882.
London : Frederick Warne & Co.

12 —— The Sheep : Its Varieties and Management in Health and Disease. By George Armatage, M.R.C.V.S., Author of "The Horse Doctor," "The Cattle Doctor," "Horse-owner's and Stableman's Companion," &c., &c. Revised and considerably enlarged. With Illustrations. 212 pp. foolscap 8vo. . . 1882.
London : F. Warne & Co.

13 —— How to Feed the Horse, Avoid Disease, and Save Money. Altered Title. Third edition, Revised and Enlarged, (of No. 4.) 132 pp. foolscap 8vo. 1890.
London and New York ; Frederick Warne & Co.

—— The following Prize Essays were published in The Transactions of the Highland and Agricultural Society of Scotland :—

ARMATAGE, George, *continued*.

14——Report on Murrain, 1864. Premium, the Gold Medal.
15——Report on the Diseases of Farm Horses, 1867. Premium, £10.
16——Report on Pleuro-Pneumonia. No. 5, Fourth Series, 1870. Premium, £10.
17——Report on the Examination of Horses as to Soundness. No. 5, Fourth Series, 1870. Premium, £5.
18——Report on Veterinary Contracts. No 6, Fourth Series, 1871. Premium, £5.
19——Report on Different Modes of Horse Shoeing. Vol. iv., 1872. Premium, £5.
20——Report on Abortion and Premature Labour in Mares, Cows, and Ewes. Vol. iv., 1872. Premium, £10.
21——Report on The Operation of The Contagious Diseases (Animals) Act, 1869. Vol. v., 1873. Premium £10.
22——Report on Inoculation as a Means for the Prevention of Pleuro-Pneumonia. Vol. viii., 1876. Premium, £10.
23——Report on Septic, Anthrax, or Carbuncular Fevers, among Horses, Cattle, Sheep, and Pigs. Vol. viii., 1876. Premium, £15.
24——Report on Strangles. Vol. x., 1878. Premium, £10.
25——Report on Hoose or Husk in Calves and Lambs. Vol. x., 1878. Premium, £10.

    Numerous Papers read before the North of England, West of Scotland, and Central Veterinary Medical Associations, published with many others in the Veterinarian and Veterinary Review.

ARMFIELD, Joseph, of *London*.

——The Spirituality of the Gospel Re-asserted and Defended. By Joseph Armfield. In reply to a Printed Letter by Robert Alsop, entitled "WHAT IS THE GOSPEL?"

    London: S. Harris & Co., 5, Bishopsgate Street, without. Gloucester: John Bellows, Steam Press. . . . . . 16mo. [1873.] 1

ARSCOT, Alexander.—Continued from p. 132 of Catalogue, Vol. 1.

——Some considerations relating to the Present State of the Christian Religion, &c. (1st part.)

    Philadelphia: Printed by B. Franklin, at the New-Printing Office, near the Market.
                                  Small 8vo. 1731.

Reprinted; *London, printed; Reprinted by B. Franklin, at the New Printing Office, in Philadelphia.*
                                      1732. pp. 111.

ARSCOT, Alexander, *continued.*
——Some Consideration. Part II.
*London, Printed; reprinted by B. Franklin, at the
New Printing Office, in Philadelphia.*
1732. pp. 140.
——Part III.
*London: Printed 1734; Philadelphia: Reprinted
by Andrew Bradford, at the Sign of the
Bible.* . . . 1738. pp. vii. 175
ASH, Edward, of *Bristol.*
——A Contribution to the Interpretation of the New Testament, comprising:—I., An Introductory Essay; II.,
A Series of Illustrative Notes. By Edward Ash, M.D.
London: 1868.
Reprinted.—Second edition. . . 8vo. 1870. 26
*London: W. Macintosh, 24, Paternoster Row;
F. B. Kitto, 5, Bishopsgate Street Without.*
——" Ecce Homo ": Its Character and Teaching.
London. 1868.
——Memoir of Robert Charleton. See ROBERT CHARLETON. . . . . 8vo. [1873.]
——GEORGE FOX, his Character, Doctrine, and Work. AN
ESSAY. *By a Member of the Society of Friends.
London: Saml. Harris & Co., 5, Bishopsgate Street
Without. Bristol: Wm. Mack, Park Street.*
[Anonymous.] Price, 6d. 8vo. 1873. 2¾
——Supplementary Pages to Dean Alford's Revision of the
Authorised Version of the New Testament; with
Notes on New Testament Passages, the meaning of
which is more or less open to question.
London. . . . . 1874.
——A RETROSPECT of my Life. By Edward Ash, M.D.
[Edited by Fielden Thorp.]
Bristol: W. Mack, Steam Press, 38, Park Street.
8vo. 1874. 5¾
——Christian Holiness; What it is, and How to be Attained.
Reprinted. The second edition.
London. . . . . 1874.
    He died the 23rd of the 12th mo., 1873, aged 76 years, and
    was buried at Bristol.
ASHBY, Louisa—See LOUISA PEASE.
ASHWORTH, Alicia S., of *London.*
——Decision for Christ. *Lines sent by A.S.A., to her
precious Child, 3rd Month 18th, 1865; and now presented to her young friends,* In Loving Remembrance of ALICIA A. ASHWORTH, by her bereaved
Mother. 8vo. 11th Month, 1865. ⅛

ASHWORTH, Alicia S., *continued.*
—— A Hymn of Praise for sustaining Mercy. A.S.A.
8vo. No date. ⅛
—— ASYLUM for the Relief of Persons deprived of the Use of their Reason, Frankford, near Philadelphia. Annual Reports. See FRIENDS (America).

ATKINS, Samuel, of *Philadelphia.*
—— Kalendarium Pennsilvaniense, or America's Messenger. Being an Almanack for the Year of Grace, 1686, wherein is contained both the English and Foreign Account, the Motions of the Planets through the Signs, with the Luminaries, Conjunctions, Aspects, Eclipses: the rising, southing and setting of the Moon, with the time when she passeth by, or is with the most eminent fixed stars : Sun rising and setting, and the time of High-Water at the City of Philadelphia, &c., with Chronologies, and many other Notes, Rules, and Tables, very fitting for every man to know and have ; all which is accommodated to the Longitude of the Province of Pennsylvania, and Latitude of 40 Degr. north, with a Table of Houses for the same, which may indifferently serve New England, New York, East and West Jersey, Maryland, and most parts of Virginia. By Samuel Atkins, Student in the Mathematicks and Astrology.—"And the stars in their courses fought against Sesera," Judges 5c. 29v.
Printed and sold by William Bradford, Sold also by the Author and H. Murrey, in Philadelphia, and Philip Richards, in New York. 1685. . . . . 12mo. pp. (40).
Title from Hildeburn's "Pennsylvania Press," Vol. I.

ATKINS, Sarah, afterwards *Lucy Wilson.*
—— FRUITS OF ENTERPRISE, exhibited in the TRAVELS OF BELZONI in EGYPT AND NUBIA, to which is prefixed, A Short Account of the Traveller's Death ; by the Author of "Grove Cottage."
Eleventh Edition.
London : Grant and Griffiths, successors to Newbery and Harris, corner of St. Paul's Churchyard, MDCCCXLVIII.
Frontispiece, "Belzoni on his Travels."
18mo. 1848. 7½

ATLEE, Edwin A. (Dr.), Translator and Editor.

B.

B.J.—John Bellows ?
——"RITUALISM" OR "QUAKERISM?" Being remarks on
a Pamphlet by J.W.C., entitled, "Quakerism and the
Church." J.B.
*London : F. B. Kitto, Bishopsgate Street Without,
E.C.*
Price Threepence. 8vo. 1870. 2½

B.J.—From the Lune to the Neva, sixty years ago ; with
Ackworth and Quaker Life by the way.
Salford : Printed. . . . 8vo. 1879. 7⅛

B. (J.F.).—See JOSEPH FIRTH BOTTOMLEY.

BACKHOUSE, Edward, of *Sunderland*.
——Ritualism a Damage to Vital Christianity, and a Danger
to the Liberties of England. By one of the Religious
Society of Friends.
*Sunderland : Wm. Henry Hills, 188, High Street,
West.* . . . . . . 8vo. 1867 ⅓

——The RELIGIOUS SOCIETY OF FRIENDS : Doctrines and
Practices in which they agree with their fellow-
Christians, and others in which they differ. By
EDWARD BACKHOUSE.
*London : F. Bowyer Kitto. Sunderland : William
Henry Hills.* 8vo. 1870 1¼

——And CHAS. TYLOR.—EARLY CHURCH HISTORY to
the Death of Constantine. Compiled by the late
EDWARD BACKHOUSE. Edited and enlarged by
CHARLES TYLOR. (With a Biographical Preface by
Thomas Hodgkin,) and many illustrations.
*London : Hamilton, Adams & Co.
Philadelphia : J. B. Lippincott & Co.*
8vo. 1884.
NOTE.—At page V. is a Portrait of EDWARD BACKHOUSE.
Text, 553 pp. Preface, 20 pp.

——WITNESSES FOR CHRIST and Memorials of Church
Life, from the Fourth to the Thirteenth. A Sequel
to "Early Church History." By EDWARD BACK-
HOUSE and CHARLES TYLOR. In two Volumes.
London : Hamilton, Adams & Co. 8vo. 1887.
Vol. I., 418 pp. Vol. II., 578 pp.

——Martyr Scenes of the 16th and 17th centuries. Edited
by CHARLES TYLOR.
London 4to. 1888. 11
He died at HASTINGS, the 22nd of 5th month 1879, aged
71 years, and was buried at Bishop Wearmouth.

BACKHOUSE, James, of DARLINGTON,
A MAP *of the* MEETINGS, *belonging to the* QUARTER-
LY MEETINGS of LANCASTER, WESTMORELAND,
CUMBERLAND, NORTHUMBERLAND, DURHAM, &
YORK. *By James Backhouse.* 1773.
Engraved by Thos. Kitchin.
Published as the Act Directs 1st, 3rd Month, 1773, by the
Author at DARLINGTON. Price 1s. 6d., also sold by T.
Kitchin, No. 59, Holborn Hill, LONDON.
            Large Broadside.
  He died in 1804.

BACKHOUSE, Katherine, wife of Edward Backhouse, of
Sunderland.
——Mothers and Daughters. A Few words on 𝕿𝖍𝖊 𝕽𝖎𝖌𝖍𝖙
𝕿𝖗𝖆𝖎𝖓𝖎𝖓𝖌 𝖔𝖋 𝕲𝖎𝖗𝖑𝖘. By K. BACKHOUSE, Sunderland.
London : Morgan and Chase, 38, Ludgate Hill.
*Office of "*𝕿𝖍𝖊 𝕮𝖍𝖗𝖎𝖘𝖙𝖎𝖆𝖓*." And may be*
ordered of any Bookseller. Price One Penny.
            8vo. [1870]. 1

BACKHOUSE, James, of York,—*continued*, from "Cata-
logue of Friends' Books," vol. 1. page 152.
——and others.—A Declaration of the Views of the Trustees
of the Flounders' Institute, relative to the Educa-
tional Trust, reposed in them by the late Benjamin
Flounders, of Yarm.   8vo. 1848.
——Short Sketch of the last few weeks of his life.
            8vo. 1869. ¼
——MEMOIR of JAMES BACKHOUSE, by his Sister. [S.
BACKHOUSE.] (*With a Portrait and facsimile of*
his Autograph.)
York : William Sessions, Low Ousegate. London :
F. Bowyer Kitto, Bishopsgate Street, Without.
            8vo. 1870. 16
Reprinted,—2nd edition.
York. 8vo. 1877. 12½
  He died the 20th of 1st Month, 1869, in the 75th year of
his age.

BACKHOUSE, James, Jun.—*continued* from Catalogue of
Friends' Books, vol. 1, p. 156.
——A Lecture on French Protestantism in the 17th and
18th centuries.
York 8vo. 1884. 3¾
——A Handbook of European Birds, &c.
London : Gurney & Jackson. . 8vo. 1890.
            pp. vii., 334
  He died at *West Bank, York*, on the 31st of 8th Month,
1890, aged 65 years. For further particulars concerning
him, see *The Annual Monitor, for 1891.*

BACKHOUSE, William,—continued from "Catalogue," vol. 1, page 157.
——and JAMES JANSON.—A Guide to True Peace, etc.
Reprinted,—*London: William Darton & Son. W.P.*
Penny Printer, Frome . 32mo. No Date. 2½
Reprinted,—*London : Charles Gilpin, Bishopsgate*
Without 24mo. 1849. 2⅜
*BAGE, Robert, an ex-Friend,
Some publication of his.
BAKER, John Gilbert, late of *Thirsk*, in *Yorkshire*, now of *Kew*.
BAKER & NOWELL'S Supplement to the Yorkshire Flora.
It contains a Complete List of the Flowering Plants, Ferns, and Mosses of the County, with the localities of many of the rarer species.
W. Pamplin, 45, Frith Street, Soho. 8vo. 1854.
——North Yorkshire, Studies of its Botany, Geology, Climate and Physical Geography, with four Maps.
London : Longman. . 8vo. 1863. 352 pp.
BALDWIN, Thomas, of *Philadelphia*; Geographer, Author ; See also JOSEPH THOMAS, M.D.
——A Universal Pronouncing Gazeteer, containing Topographical, Statistical, and other information, of all the more important places in the known world, from the most recent and authentic sources ; with a map. By Thomas Baldwin ; assisted by several other gentlemen.
Philadelphia. . . . Post 8vo. 1845. 550pp.
——United States Gazateer ; giving a full and comprehensive review of the Present Condition, Industry, and Resources of the American Confederacy ; embracing also important Topographical, Statistical, and Historical Information, from recent and original sources ; together with the results of the Census of 1850, and Population and Statistics, in many cases to 1853. By Thomas Baldwin and J. Thomas, M.D., with a fine map.
Philadelphia. . . . . Royal 8vo. 1854.
*BALDWIN, William, M.D., a distinguished Botanist.
——Reliquie Baldwiniana, Selections from the correspondence of the late Wm. Baldwin, M.D., Surgeon in the U.S Navy, with occasional Notes, and a short biographical Memoir. Compiled by Wm. Darlington, M.D.
Philadelphia. 12mo. 1843. 346pp.

*BALL, Thomas Frederick. of *London*, continued from
Catalogue, *Vol. I.*, p. 163.
——Anecdotes of Aborigines; or, Illustrations of the
coloured races being " Men and Brethren." [Edited
by T. F. B.]
London. . . . . . 8vo. [1868.]
——The London Friends' Meetings, &c.
See WILLIAM BECK. 8vo. 1869. 25¼
——Extracts from Reviews of " Poems." . . 4to. 1866. ¼
——Queen Victoria : Scenes and Incidents of her Life and
Reign. By T. F. Ball.
London : S. W. Partridge & Co.
Second edition . . . . . 8vo. 1886.

BALL, William, of *Tottenham, near London*, and *Rydal,
Westmoreland*; continued from Catalogue, Vol. 1,
p. 163.
——The Tribute and Sequel. . . . 8vo. 1862.
——The Story of James Beattie, the Aberdeenshire School-
master, versified. 1866
——SALOME'S VERSE-BOOK.
TRANSCRIPT BOOK, I., p. 4. BY WILLIAM BALL.
" —— my little Follower ; Thou, sweet Loan of Parents
long to dwell on distant shore."
*Edinburgh : James Taylor, 31, Castle Street,
MDCCCLXVI.* . . . 8vo. 1866. 6
——" Calling upon God," in Old Testament ; instances of
Confession, Petition, and Praise.
Edinburgh : James Taylor, 31, Castle Street.
8vo. 1867
——The Root of Ritualism, and other contributions to the
Periodicals of the Society of Friends ; with added
papers chiefly relating to the Views and Practices of
that Society. By William Ball.
*London : F. Bowyer Kitto, 5, Bishopsgate With-
out, E.C. Edinburgh : J. Taylor, 31, Castle
Street.* 8vo. 1867. 15¼
——Cunningham and Kelly Refuted, and other contribu-
tions to the Periodicals of the Society of Friends, &c.
Second series.
Edinburgh : J. Taylor, 31, Castle Street.
8vo. 1869. 221 pp.
——THE YEARLY MEETING OF 1869, and other contribu-
tions to the PERIODICALS OF THE SOCIETY OF
FRIENDS ; with added Papers, chiefly relating to the
views and practices of that Society. By William
Ball. Third series.*

BALL, William, *continued*.
> *Edinburgh* : *J. Taylor, 31, Castle Street.* 8vo. 1870.
>> ° The First Series being entitled, "The Root of Ritualism," &c., and the Second Series, "Cunningham and Kelly Refuted," &c. In this as in those no attempt is made to alter their extempore character by any retouching.

——Verses composed since 1870 : some elegiac, others occasional, and miscellaneous.
> [Privately printed. *London.*] . 4o. 1875.

[Brit. Mus., 1652 h. 12.]

——THE ACKNOWLEDGMENTS of the 𝔥undred and 𝔖ixteenth 𝔓salm : arranged in portions (with short reflections) for each day in the month. By William Ball.
> [Not published.] . . . 16mo. 1877. 56 pp.
>> NOTE.—Half-title, but no other (?) but what is on the cover, and no printer's name or place. (Edinburgh, printed?)
>>> "PREFIX.
>>> To my Dear Friend,
>>> CHARLES FOX,
>>> of Trebah, near Falmouth,
>>> These Reflections,
>>> written at his suggestion on this Psalm,
>>> are very affectionately inscribed.
>>> W.B."
>> ALDERBRAE, *Winter of 1876-7.*

——NOTICES OF BOOKS AND OTHER PAPERS (Second Series) being chiefly reprints from the PERIODICALS OF THE SOCIETY OF FRIENDS; THIS VOLUME being also the Fifth Series of this Class.* By WILLIAM BALL.
> *Edinburgh: J. Taylor, 31, Castle Street.* 8vo. 1877. 10
>> ° The First being entitled, "The Root of Ritualism;" the Second, "Cunningham and Kelly refuted;" the Third, "The Yearly Meeting of 1869," &c.; and the Fourth, "Notices of Books," &c. In this, as in those (all privately printed), no attempt is made to alter their extempore character by any retouching.
>> NOTE.—Contains, "The Two Priscilla Gurneys—" Priscilla Hannah Gurney," and "Priscilla Gurney, Junior,"—also "My Cousin Anne Fry," etc., etc.

——On the Morning of an Execution. [ANON.]
> *Glasgow*: *W. G. Blackie & Co., Printers, Villafield.* . . . . . 16mo. [1877.] ¼
>> William Ball was also a contributor to *The Friend*, and *British Friend*.
>> He died the 30th of 7th Month, 1878, aged 78 years, and his remains were interred in Friends' Burial Ground at Winchmore Hill. For further particulars concerning him, see *The Annual Monitor* for 1879.

BALLANGER, James, of *America*.
——Journal and Essays . . . 1851.
‖ BARBER, Henry, M.D.
——SWARTHMOOR HALL AND ITS ASSOCIATIONS. By Henry Barber, M.D.
London : F. B. Kitto, 5, Bishopsgate Street. Ulverston : D. Atkinson, King Street.
8vo. [1871.] 3½
NOTE.—Contains a wood cut Frontispiece of "Swarthmoor Hall," "Fac-simile of Judge Fell's Signature," "Arms of Fell," and "Friends' Meeting House," and Pedigree of Fell of Swarthmoor.

BARBER, James Henry, of *Sheffield*.
——A NARRATIVE of the Proceedings at the CELEBRATION of THE CENTENARY of ACKWORTH SCHOOL. 26th and 27th of Sixth Month, 1879. Edited by James Henry Barber. Also ᚼ Sketch of the Life of Dr. Fothergill, by JAMES HACK TUKE : and ᚼ Short Sketch of the History of Ackworth School, by JOHN S. ROWNTREE ; with *a nearly verbatim report of the speeches delivered at the two meetings.*
Published by the Centenary Committee, Ackworth School.
London : Samuel Harris & Co., 5, Bishopsgate Without 8vo. 1879. 13½

‖ BARCLAY, Charles, of *Dorking*.
— —Letters from the Dorking Emigrants.
London : 8vo. 1833.
[*Brit. Mus.*, T. 1415—13.]

BARCLAY, David, of *Cheapside,—continued* from "Catalogue," Vol. 1, p. 167.
——An Account of David Barclay.
(From the Morning Chronicle of June 5th, 18 9.)
S. Hodgson, Printer, Newcastle. . 4to. [1809.] ¼
——Particulars of his house, and many family anecdotes, by M. C. Jones, of Gungrog, Welshpool.
12mo. 1864.
He died at *Bush Hill*, the 18th of 3rd month, 1769, aged 87 years, and was buried in Friends' Burial Ground, at Winchmore Hill, on the 23rd of the same month. Isaac Sharples attended his funeral.

BARCLAY, Ellen, Wife of Wm. Leatham Barclay, of *Reigate*.
— —MISSIONARY HELPERS' PRAYER UNION.
——" Brethren, pray for us."—I Thess. v., 25.
The Orphans' Printing Press, Leominster.
8vo. [1891.] ¼

BARCLAY, John.—*Continued* from "Catalogue," Vol. 1, p. 169.
——Select Anecdotes. . . 12mo. *New York.* 1833.
——Notice of Thomas Shillitoe's Journal. . 8vo. [1836.] ⅛
———A Selection from the Letters and Papers of.
    Reprinted in America. . . . 8vo. 1847.
———A Testimony to "The Word nigh in the Heart," &c.
    Reprinted,—*Dublin* : *John Gough, 6, Eustace Street.*
    12s. per 100. 12mo 1871. ⅛
——EXTRACTS FROM LETTERS of John Barclay to MARY B.
    To be had at Friends' Book Store, 304, Arch Street, Philadelphia.
    [*Wm. H. Pile, Printer, 422, Walnut Street.*]
    12mo. 1877. 2¼
    or 50 pages.

BARCLAY, Joseph Gurney, Banker, of *Lombard Street, London, and Knott's Green, Leyton, Essex.*
———Astronomical Observations taken during the years 1862 to 1864.
    London . . . . 8vo. 1865.
———ASTRONOMICAL OBSERVATIONS, taken during the years 1865-69, at the Private Observatory of Joseph Gurney Barclay, Esq., F.R.A.S., Leyton, Essex. Vol. II.
    London : *Williams & Norgate, 14, Henrietta Street.*
    4to. 1870. 18

BARCLAY, Robert, the Apologist, continued from Catalogue, Vol I., page 173.
———Catechism and Confession of Faith, &c. Reprinted, the Third Edition, corrected and very much amended. By R.B., a Servant of the Church of Christ.
    LICENSED and entered according to order.
    Small 8vo. No Date. 10⅜
———A Catechism and *Confession of Faith*, approved of and agreed unto, by the *General Assembly* of the *Patriarchs, Prophets*, and *Apostles*, CHRIST, himself *chief Speaker*, in and among them. Which containeth a true and faithful Account of the Principles and Doctrines, which are most surely believed by the Churches of Christ in *Great Britain* and *Ireland*, who are reproachfully called by the name of QUAKERS; yet are found in the one Faith with the Primitive Church and Saints, as is most clearly demonstrated by some plain Scripture Testimonies (without consequences, or commentaries), which are here collected and inserted by way of *Answer* to a few weighty,

BARCLAY, Robert, *continued.*
  yet easie and familiar *Questions*, fitted as well for the wisest and largest, as for the weakest and lowest Capacities. To which is added an expostulation with, and Appeal to, all other Professors.
              The Sixth Edition.
  By R.B., a Servant of the Church of Christ.
    Search the Scripture (or, ye search the Scriptures) *for in them ye think ye have Eternal Life, and they are they which testify of me. And ye will not come to me, that ye might have life.* John 5, 39, 40.
  Dublin : *Printed by* John Ray, *in Skinner Row,* and are to be sold by *John Softlaw, in Meath-street,* 1711.   .   .   .   .   Small 8vo.   11½
                                          (or 16mo.)   5¾
    NOTE.—At the end is a list of BOOKS *sold by* JOHN SOFTLAW in *Meath Street, Dublin.*
——A Catechism and confession of faith, &c.
           Reprinted in *America*, 1783 and 1864.
——Apology, &c., in *Latin*   .   .   .   .   .   1676.
    Translated into *English*, and first printed in *Holland*, 1678.
    See page 439 Whiting's Memoirs, 2nd edition.
——An Apology, &c.   .   .   .   .   .   .   1733.
                                                1783.
  Reprinted,—13th edition—Corrected by comparison with former editions.
    Manchester : *Printed and published by William Irwin, 24, Deansgate.*   .   .   8vo.   1869.   25
  Reprinted,—The 14th edition, Glasgow   .   8vo.   1886.
——An APOLOGY FOR THE *True Christian Divinity* as the same is held forth, and preached by the people called in scorn *QUAKERS* : BEING A full Explanation and Vindication of their *Principles* and *Doctrines,* by many Arguments, deduced from *Scripture* and *Right Reason,* and the Testimonies of FAMOUS AUTHORS, both ancient and modern : with a full Answer to the strongest Objections usually made against them. *Presented to the* KING. Written in *Latin* and *English* by *ROBERT BARCLAY.* And since Translated into *High Dutch, Low Dutch,* and *French,* for the information of strangers.
         THE SIXTH EDITION in *English.*
    NEWPORT, *Rhode Island* : *Printed by* JAMES FRANKLIN, 1729   .   .   .   .   8vo.   1729.   22
                         [22 leaves and 574 pages.
    NOTE. " Who have arrived."

BARCLAY, Robert, *continued.*
——Apology for the True Christian Divinity, &c.
 Published by the Meeting for Sufferings of Philadelphia Y.M.
 1848.
 " It was prepared with great care and after close examination of the earliest editions. It was stereotyped, and is thought here to be a standard edition."
——Apology (DUTCH).
——VERANTWOORDING Van de ware Christelyke GODGE-LEERTHEID, (Gelyk dezelve voorgedragen en gepredikt word van het volk, spotsgewyze *Quakers* genaamd. Behelzende een volkomen verklaring en verdediging hunner Beginselen en Leerstukken ; door vele bewysredenen, uit de Heilige Schrift, de ware Reden, en Getuigenissen van vermaarde, zo wel oude als nieuwe Schryvers, bekrachtigd. Mitsgaders een volkomen beantwoording der Krachtigste Tegenweerpingen, die hun doorgaans voor Komen. *Eerst in't Latyn geschreven door* ROBERT BARCLAY, *En in't Nederduitsch vertaald door* J. H. GLAZEMAKER.
Act. 24, 15.—Naar dien weg welken zy Secte noemen, diene ik den God der Vaderen, gelovende alles, dat in de Wet en in de Profeten geschreven is.
Tit. 2, 11.—De zaligmakende genade Gods is verschenen allen menschen en onderwyst ons, dat wy de godloosheid en de waereldsche begeerlykheden verzakende, matiglyk en rechtvaardiglyk, en godzaliglyk leven zouden in deze tegenwoordige waereld.
Verwachtende de zalige hope, en verschyninge der heerlykheid des groten Gods, ende onzes Zaligmakers Jesu Christi.
Die hem zelven voor ons gegeven heeft, op dat hy ons zonde verlossen van alle ongereeetigheid, en hem zelven een eigen volk zonde reinigen, yveverig in goede werken.
1 *Thess.* 5, 21.—Beproeft alle dingen : behoud het goede.
 TWEEDE DRUK.
 Van reele Druk-en Spelfonten gezuiverd en op verscheide plaatsen verbeterd.
  Te AMSTELDAM, by A. WALDORP, *Boekverkooper op het Rokkin,* 1757 . . . 4to. 1757. 64¼
   NOTE.—At the end on the last page is the following :—
   " OP T'VOORGAANDE WERK.
   Een Leeraar, die de zalving kend,
   Weet wat hy leert ; en wie hem vend.—W. EVERWYN."
——Views of Christian Doctrine held by the Religious Society of Friends, being passages taken from

BARCLAY, Robert, *continued.*
    Barclay's Apology.
        Philadelphia. 8vo. 1882. 18½
—— On Christian Worship: being the 11th Proposition of the 13th Edition of Barclay's Apology.
        Manchester: Printed. . . . 8vo. 1869.
—— The Life of Robert Barclay.—In Vol. VII. of "British Biography; or, An Accurate and Impartial Account of the Lives and Writings of Eminent Persons, in Great Britian and Ireland."
        Printed for R. Goadly; and sold by R. Baldwin, in Paternoster Row; and J. Towers, near Cripplegate, London. . . 8vo. 1772.
—— Extracts from Barclay's Proposition concerning the Scriptures.
        Clay, Printer, Stockport. 12mo. No date. ⅓

BARKLEY, Robert.
—— A Discourse on Prayer and Devotions, etc., 1704. See GEORGE KEITH.

BARCLAY, Robert, Jun. (his son), continued from Catalogue Vol. I., p. 189.
—— An ESSAY upon FAITH: shewing the Difference between that which is *true,* and that which is *false.*
        Aberdeen: Printed by James Chalmers.
        Small 12mo. 1740. 1

BARCLAY, Robert, of
—— His Book Plate.

BARCLAY (Allardice), Robert, of *Ury,* in *Kincardineshire* (commonly called Captain Barclay) was born in the 8th month, 1779. He was the son of Robert Barclay, M.P. for Kincardineshire in 3 Parliaments, and a Friend of Wm. Pitt's, the son of Robert Barclay, *Grandson* of the Apologist.
—— PEDESTRIANISM; or, An Account of The Performances of celebrated Pedestrians during the last and present century; with a full Narrative of Captain Barclay's Public and Private matches; and an Essay on Training.—By the Author of the History of Aberdeen, &c., &c., &c.
        Aberdeen: Printed by D. Chalmers & Co. *For A. Brown and F. Frost, Aberdeen; Constable and Co., and Greig, High Street, Edinburgh; Longman & Co., Paternoster Row; Forsyth, 114, Leadenhall Street; and Rice, 28, Berkeley Square, London.* 8vo. 1813.

BARCLAY (Allardice) Robert, *continued.*
> NOTE.—Prefixed is a Frontispiece, a whole length portrait of "Captain Barclay, in his walking dress,"—and at the end of the volume is a "Genealogy of the Family of Barclay, of Mathers and Ury, in the county of Mearns."

—— Letters from Captain Barclay and others.
[*Brit. Mus.* 10815. C.]
         Leith.   8vo. 1814.
> For further particulars see the Survey of Kincardineshire, by Robertson,—concerning his father Robert Barclay.

—— Agricultural Tour in the United States and Upper Canada, with miscellaneous notices.
  Edinburgh : Printed. . . .   8vo. 1842.

BARCLAY (Captain Robert)—*Who performed on New-market Heath the most remarkable feat ever recorded in the annals of Pedestrianism ; having walked one Thousand Miles in one Thousand successive hours at the rate of one Mile in each hour. This extraordinary performance commenced on Wednesday, May 31st, 1809, at 12 at Night, Captain Barclay walked half-a-mile out from the Horse and Jockey across the Norwich road up the Heath, and returned. He completed the distance on Wednesday, July 12th, at 37 minutes past 3 in the afternoon, in the presence of Ten Thousand spectators. N.B.—The Bet was for one Thousand Guineas aside, and it is supposed there was not less than one Hundred Thousand Guineas depending on the performance.*
> Engraved by Williams from a Drawing in the Possession of Captain Barclay. Published November 27th, 1809, by S. W. Fores, No. 50, Piccadilly.

A full-length coloured engraving   .   Folio.
  Portraits at Bury Hill.
David Barclay
Robert Barclay, of Bury Hill, son of the following
Alexander Barclay, } of Philadelphia
Ann Barclay,   }
Captain Barclay
Arthur Barclay
Wife of ditto, and others.

BARCLAYS OF URIE.
 Reliquiæ Barclaianæ. CORRESPONDENCE OF *Colonel David Barclay of Urie, and his Son, Robert, including* **Letters from** *Princess Elizabeth of the Rhine, the Earl of Perth, the Countess of Sutherland, William Penn, George Fox, and others ;* ALSO *the Act of the Scotch Parliament of 1685, settling Urie upon Robert*

BARCLAYS OF URIE, *continued.*
> *Barclay & his Descendants, and Robert Barclay's Vindication of his connexion with the Stuarts.*
>> HŒCOLIM MEMINISSE JUVABIT.
>>> LITHOGRAPHED BY WINTER & BAILEY, 24, CHANCERY LANE, LONDON.
>> [Edited by Joseph Bevan Braithwaite ?]
>>> large 4to. 1870. 169 pages.
>>> NOTE.—Contains Letters of George Whitehead to Robert Barclay, also Arthur Kett Barclay's account of his attending the funeral of Captain Barclay.
> [*British Museum*, 10921. K.]

BARCLAYS OF URY.—See F. A. BUDGE.

BARCLAY FAMILY.
> Births and Deaths of some of the BARCLAY FAMILY and their Burials in Winchmore Burial Ground :— David Barclay born 1729, died 1809 ; Robert Barclay, of Bury Hill, born 1751, died 1830 ; Robert Barclay, of Clapham, born 1759, died 1816 ; Ann Barclay (his wife) born 1763, died 1801. (Parents of John Barclay).

BARCLAY, Robert, of *Tottenham*, last of *Reigate, Surrey.* Continued from Catalogue, Vol. I., p. 190.

——On MEMBERSHIP in the SOCIETY OF FRIENDS, by Robert Barclay. Being some remarks on an article lately published in the "FRIENDS' QUARTERLY EXAMINER," on Birthright Membership, by John Stephenson Rowntree.
>> *London : Samuel Harris & Co., 5, Bishopsgate Street Without. Sessions, York. Scott, Carlisle. Penney, Darlington. Irwin, Manchester. White & Pike, Birmingham. Whereat, Bristol. Edmundson, Dublin.* . . 8vo. [1872.] 4¼

——The Inner Life of the Religious Societies of the Commonwealth : considered principally with reference to the influence of church organization on the spread of Christianity. By Robert Barclay.
>> With two Photographic Illustrations and Chronological Map ; also Reprints and Copies of MSS.
>>> Super Royal 8vo., 731 pp. . . 1876.
>> *London : Hodder & Stoughton, 27, Paternoster Row.*
>> Second edition.—MDCCCLXXVI.
>> Third edition.
>> *Barclay and Fry, Printers, 9, College Hill, London, E.C.*

BARCLAY, Robert, of *Tottenham, continued.*

> NOTE.—This Work gives information, drawn to a considerable extent from original sources, respecting the origin and internal development of the Societies called "Anabaptist," "Brownist," "Separatist," "Independent," "Presbyterian," "Familist," "Mennonite," "Schwenkfeldian," "The Friends," "The Seekers," "The Ranters," "Muggletonians," &c.
>
> A clear and connected account is given of the various external causes which led to the formation of these Societies, and the undercurrent of religious thought and feeling during the times of the Commonwealth; with many curious details of their customs, &c.
>
> It also deals generally with the subject of the influence of these Societies, on the spread of Christianity, and contains a complete series of the Statistics of Modern Religious Societies, drawn from reliable sources.

——SERMONS by ROBERT BARCLAY, Author of "The Inner Life of the Religious Societies of the Commonwealth," with a BRIEF MEMOIR edited by HIS WIDOW. (Portrait and fac-simile of his writing.)

> *London : Hodder & Stoughton, 27, Paternoster Row* 8vo. 1878. 25¾
>
> He died 11th of 11th Mo., 1876, aged 43 years, and was buried at Winchmore Hill.

BARKER, Abigail and others, of *America.*

——COMMENTS on MUTILATED EXTRACTS FROM THE WRITINGS OF JOSEPH JOHN GURNEY, contrasted with Selections from the Writings of Fox, Barclay, Penn, and others; by the late Abigail Barker, and other Friends in America.

> *London : Printed by John Hasler, 4, Crane Court, Fleet Street* . . . . . 8vo. 1845.
>
> NOTE.—This forms part of "CALUMNY REFUTED; or a GLANCE AT JOHN WILBUR'S BOOK," commencing at page 7 and ending at page 92.

BARKER, Rachel, of *America.*

——Sermon . . . . 1835.

BARKER, Jacob of *North America*, Banker, Journalist, &c.

——Incidents in the Life of JACOB BARKER, of New Orleans, Louisiana. With Historical Facts, his Financial Transactions with the Government, and his Course on Important Political Questions, from 1800 to 1855. With Portraits of JACOB BARKER and JOHN WELLS.

> *Washington* . . . . . 8vo. 1855.

*BARNARD, Sir John, a patriotic Citizen, and distinguished Alderman of *Dowgate Ward, London*, being appointed in 1727, was born at *Reading* in *Berkshire*, in 1685, of Quaker parents, being educated at Wandsworth School ; but in his 19th year he quitted the Society of Friends, and became a member of the Established Church, and was baptised at Fulham by Bishop Compton. In 1721, on account of his reputation and abilities, he was nominated to represent the City of London in Parliament, and notwithstanding the contest was as warm as ever had been known in the city, and he declined all personal solicitation, he was, by the exertion of his friends, returned in 1722. He continued to represent the city in the most independent manner for 40 years ; during which time he acquired considerable influence by his vigorous opposition to the measures of administration, then conducted by Sir Robert Walpole, and particularly by his opposition to the extension of the excise, which he induced the minister to abandon. In 1732, he was knighted on presenting a congratulatory address to Geo. II., and in 1738 he was invested with the high dignity of Chief Magistrate of the City of London, the duties of which he discharged with credit to himself and advantage to the public. In 1746 he was solicited by Geo. II., to accept the office of Chancellor of the Exchequer, which he refused. Mr. Pitt, afterwards Lord Chatham, used sometimes to call him the *great commoner ;* and Pope, obliquely sarcastic, exhibits him in contrast with worthless wealth and title, which would arrogate that respect which is only due to such men as Barnard :—

 Barnard in spirit, sense, and truth abounds ;
 Pray, then, what wants he? four score thousand pounds.
 He died at Clapham in 1764, leaving one son and two daughters.

—— A Defence of several Proposals for raising THREE MILLIONS for the SERVICE of the Government for the YEAR 1746 ; with a POSTSCRIPT, containing some NOTIONS relating to PUBLIC CREDIT. By SIR JOHN BARNARD, Knight.
 London : Printed for J. Osborn, at the Golden-Ball, in Paternoster Row.
        Price One Shilling.
[*Guildhall Library.*] . . . 8vo. 1746   5

—— Remarks on a LETTER to SIR JOHN BARNARD ; in

*BARNARD, Sir John, *continued*.

which the Proposals of that Worthy PATRIOT are vindicated, and a late *Important Transaction* set in a TRUE LIGHT. *By an Enemy to* JOBBS.

> London: *Printed for J. Hinton, at the King's Arms, in St. Paul's Churchyard.* 8vo. 1746.   2
> [*Guildhall Library.*]
>> NOTE.—The half-title is, "REMARKS on a LETTER to SIR JOHN BARNARD, &c. The SECOND EDITION.
>> Price Sixpence.

—— Letter to Sir John Barnard upon his Proposals.

—— Sir John Barnard's Letter to a Member of Parliament, occasioned by the Rejection of his Scheme . 1746.

—— Sir John Barnard's Defence, &c., and three Replies to the same.

—— Catalogue of John Barnard's Cabinet of Drawings, sold in February, 1787 . . . . . 4to.

—— An ESSAY on the many ADVANTAGES accruing to the COMMUNITY, from the superior NEATNESS, CONVENIENCES, DECORATIONS, *and* EMBELLISHMENTS *of* Great *and* Capital CITIES. Particularly applied to the CITY and SUBURBS of LONDON, the Renowned Capital of the *British* EMPIRE. Addressed to *Sir* JOHN BARNARD, *Knt.*, Senior *Alderman, and* Senior *Representative in Parliament of the said* CITY.

> London: *Printed for Henry Whitridge, at the Royal Exchange* . . . 8vo. 1754.   3½
> [*Guildhall Library*]. [Price One Shilling].

—— Memoirs of the late Sir John Barnard, Knt., and Alderman of the City of London.

> London: *Printed by R. and A. Taylor, Shoe Lane; sold by T. Boys, Ludgate Hill.* 16mo. 1820. 35 pp.
>
> He died on the 29th day of August, 1764, at *Clapham*, in *Surrey*, and was buried at *Mortlake*.
>
> Many years before his death his fellow-citizens expressed their sense of his virtues by erecting his Statue.
>
> Saturday, 23rd May, 1747, the Statue of Sir John Barnard, Knt., was erected at the Royal Exchange.—*Gents. Mag. for May, 1747.* This number also contains a group of 5 portraits, viz :—Head of George II ; Philip, Lord Hardwicke, Lord High Chancellor ; Philip, Earl of Chesterfield, Secretary of State ; George, Lord Anson, Vice Admiral ; and *Sir John Barnard.*

*BARNARD, Hannah, Wife of PETER BARNARD, of *Hudson*, in the *State of New York*, formerly Hannah Jenkins,—*continued* from " Catalogue," Vol. 1., p. 192.

BARNARD, Hannah, *continued.*

> Hannah Jenkins was born about the year 1754 of parents who were members of the religious Society denominated *Baptists* and was educated in communion with them. About the 18th year of her age she became convinced of the truth of the principles professed by Friends, and at her own request was admitted into membership with them.
>
> She was afterwards married to PETER BARNARD, of Hudson, in the State of *New York*, a member of that Society.
>
> For further particulars concerning her, see "A Narrative in the Proceedings of America,—in the Case of Hannah Barnard, 1804.—Introduction, p. ix.

—— The Short Cut, dated 1st Mo., 1801.

> A paper issued during the Hannah Barnard controversy imputing *Deism* to her, and insinuating that such opinions as hers, concerning war, have a tendency to lead to *Atheism.*

—— Another Paper by the same Author.

> NOTE.—Printed in Matthew's "The Recorder," Vol. 1, pp. 144, 145, and 156 to 188.

—— Dialogues on Domestic and Rural Economy, and the Fashionable Follies of the World. Interspersed with occasional observations on some popular opinions.— To which is added an Appendix on Burns, &c., with their Treatment. By Hannah Barnard.

> *Hudson : Printed for the Author.*   12mo.   1820.   3½

BARNARD, Mary, afterwards DICKENSON.

—— To the Memory of the late Samuel Fothergill, &c.

> Reprinted,— *York*, printed . . Broadside. [1815.] 1

*BARNES, Robert, of *Cockermouth.*

—— Poetical Works, with Memoir, 1823.

BARRETT, Richard Henry, Son of Richard Barrett, the Printer.

—— A Refutation of Mr. W. H. Gillespie's Argument, à *PRIORI* for the existence of A Great First Cause. By R.H.B.

> *London : Frederick Farrah, 282, Strand, W.C.*
>   Price Sixpence.   8vo.   1868.   1½

*BARRETT, Thomas Squire, A.A., F.A.S.L., of *Camberwell, Surrey* (Son of Richard Barrett, the Printer, and brother of the preceding).

—— Satire : its nature and effects. By G.F.G. Edited by T. S. Barrett.

> *London : Printed in the year 1865.*
>   12mo.   ½

*BARRETT, Thomas Squire, *continued*.

——An Examination of Mr. W. H. Gillespie's Argument, *à priori* for the existence of A Great First Cause. (By T.S.B.)
London: J. Burns, 15, Southampton Row, Holborn.
8vo. 1869. 3½

——Reprinted, entitled: EXAMINATION OF GILLESPIE: being an Analytical Criticism of THE ARGUMENT A PRIORI for the existence of a First Great Cause, as developed by Mr. W. H. Gillespie in his " Necessary Existence of God." By THOMAS SQUIRE BARRETT, Associate in Arts, of the University of Oxford ; Member of the Anthropological Institute of Great Britain and Ireland ; and Member of the London Dialectical Society.
> "The reasonings which would *demonstrate* his [God's] being, are called *a priori*. Those which give *probable evidence*, only, for his being, *a posteriori*."

Second edition.—*London : Provost & Co., 36, Henrietta Street, Covent Garden.*
8vo. 1871. 3¼

——A New View of CAUSATION by Thomas Squire Barrett.
London: Provost and Co., 36, Henrietta Street, Covent Garden . . . 12mo. 1871. 10

——Reprinted, entitled : "The PHILOSOPHY OF SCIENCE," a contribution thereto, on CAUSE AND EFFECT. By T. S. Barrett.
Second edition. *London : Provost and Co., 36, Henrietta Street, Covent Garden* 12mo. 1872. 10

——An Analytical Criticism of the Argument, *A Priori* for the Being and Attributes.
Out of Print.

——An Introduction to the Study of LOGIC AND METAPHYSICS. By Thomas Squire Barrett, F.R. Hist. S., F.L.A.S.,
> Member of the Anthropological Institute of Great Britain and Ireland ; Member of the London Dialectical Society ; Member of the Scientific Club ; and Associate (in Arts) of the University of Oxford.
>
> " The discovery of what is true, and the practice of that which is good, are the two objects of Philosophy."— *Voltaire*.

London : *Provost and Co., 36, Henrietta Street, Covent Garden* . . . 8vo. 1875. 3½

> ⁂ Besides the foregoing, T.S.B. has contributed numerous papers and letters on *Metaphysical, Theological, Mathematical, Scientific, Social*, and *Literary* subjects to various

BARRETT, Thomas Squire, *continued.*
Newspapers, Periodicals, and Reviews. The following is a list of those in which communications from T.S.B have appeared:—
British Friend,
British Controversialist,
Chemical News,
Correspondent,
Daily Telegraph,
Friend,
Friends' Quarterly Examiner,
Inquirer,
Liverpool Leader,
Medium and Daybreak,
National Reformer,
Religious Opinion,
Truth Seeker,
United Kingdom Mineral Water Review,
Weekly Record.

BARROW, Robert,—*continued* from "Catalogue," vol. 1., p. 194.
——Some verses on William Brownsword, Vicar of Kendal, written by Robert Barrow, whilst confined in Kendal Goale, for not paying the Priests' dues. In an old 4to. volume of Friends' Tracts, 1669-70.—(Once his property.)
Printed in the "Kendal Mercury," July 25th, 1863.

BARTLETT, Benjamin, formerly an eminent Apothecary at *Bradford, Yorkshire,* in which he succeeded his father, who had for his apprentice the after celebrated Dr. Fothergill.
——*Manduessedum Romanorum* : being the HISTORY and ANTIQUITIES of the Parish of MANCETER,[including the Hamlets of Hartshill, Oldbury, and Atherstone], and also of the adjacent parish of ANSLEY, in the County of WARWICK. By the late BENJAMIN BARTLETT, Esq., F.A.S. Enlarged and corrected under the inspection of several gentlemen resident upon the Spot.
With numerous illustrations.
London : Printed by and for J. Nichols, Printer to the Society of Antiquaries. MDCCXCI.
4to. 1791. 168 pp.
Vol. IX.—See "Miscellaneous Antiquities," (In continuation of the Bibliotheca Topographica). No. 1 containing Mr. Bartlett's "Manduessedum Romanorum."
——*The Episcopal Coins of* DURHAM, *and the Monastic Coins of* READING, *minted during the Reigns of Edward I., II., and III., appropriated to their respec-*

BARTLETT, Benjamin, *continued.*
 tire owners. By Benjamin Bartlet, F.A.S.
         4to. 1778. 2 leaves.
  (From the 5th Volume of ARCHÆLOGIA, p. 335. Published
   by the Society of Antiquaries in " Collectanea.")
 Reprinted.—A new edition with notes and illustrations
 by John Trotter Brockett.
  Newcastle : Printed by S. Hodgson, Union Street,
   for Emerson Charnley. . . 8vo. 1817.
——A Catalogue of the Valuable Collection of Coins, &c.,
 (Rare?) of Benjamin Bartlett, Esq., which will be
 sold by auction on April 25, 1787, and 5 following
 days. Part 1.
  °₀° A very curious and interesting Catalogue !
  B. Bartlett, whose mother was a Green of (J.J.G.'s) family,
  was also the author of other pieces, &c., on Numismatics,
  and, I presume, another Catalogue was printed.
——The HISTORY AND ANTIQUITIES of HINCKLEY, in the
 County of Leicester, the 2nd edition, to which is
 added the History of Witherly—And a large tract of
 the Manduessedum Romanorum, being the History
 and Antiquities of Manceter, by the late BENJAMIN
 BARTLETT. By John Nichols, F.S.A. Folio. 1813.
  He died at Hertford the 2nd of the 3rd Month, 1787, of
  a confirmed dropsy, in the 73rd year of his age, and
  was interred in the Quakers' Burying Ground at Harts-
  hill, in Warwickshire.
  See an obituary notice of him in the *Gentleman's Magazine,*
  1787, and published in Armistead's Miscellanies, Vol. iii.,
  1851.
  Mr. Bartlett lost his wife Jan. 1, 1785 ; and his only son
  Benjamin Newton Bartlett, who survived him but 7
  months, came to a melancholy end, Oct. 20, 1787.
  (J.J.G. has a copy of Catalogue and Mancetta book.)
BARTON, Bernard, of *Woodbridge,—continued* from
 " Catalogue, vol. I., p. 196."
——Poems.
  2nd *(American.)*   1825.
——The Adieu ! a Farewell taken of Christian Friendship,
 consisting of entirely original pieces, in prose and
 verse. Edited by S. S. S., author of " Gideon," " The
 Lady at the Farmhouse," etc., etc. [The " Introduc-
 tory Sonnet," and the concluding poem, by BERNARD
 BARTON.]
  2nd edition. *Colchester : Enfield ; & Filer and*
   Totham. And Simpkin & Marshall; Longman
   & Co. ; Hamilton, Adams, & Co. ; Hatchard

BARTON, Bernard, *continued.*
    & Son ; Harvey & Darton ; H. Washbourne : Darton & Son, London. . . 16mo. 1833.
—— Mornings in the Library. By Ann Knight. With 𝕴𝖓𝖙𝖗𝖔𝖉𝖚𝖈𝖙𝖎𝖔𝖓 𝖆𝖓𝖉 𝕻𝖔𝖊𝖒𝖘, by BERNARD BARTON.
    London : Darton & Clark, Holborn Hill. C. & J. Adlard, Printers, Bartholomew Close.
                                  18mo. No date.
—— Bealing Bells. An Account of the Mysterious ringing of Bells, at Great Bealings, Suffolk, in 1834 ; and in other parts of England : with relations of farther unaccountable occurrences, in various places : By Major Edward Moor, F.R.S., &c. [The Introductory and Valedictory Verses, by BERNARD BARTON.]
    Woodbridge : Printed and Sold by John Loder, for the Benefit of the New Church.
                                  12mo. 1841.
—— Stanzas to the Members of the British and Foreign Bible Society.

BARTON, John, brother of BERNARD BARTON,—*continued* from " Catalogue, vol. 1., p. 200."
—— AN ENQUIRY into the EXPEDIENCY of the EXISTING RESTRICTIONS on the 𝕴𝖒𝖕𝖔𝖗𝖙𝖆𝖙𝖎𝖔𝖓 𝖔𝖋 𝕱𝖔𝖗𝖊𝖎𝖌𝖓 𝕮𝖔𝖗𝖓 : with observations on the present social and political prospects of GREAT BRITAIN. By John Barton.
    London : James Ridgway, Piccadilly.
                                  8vo. 1833.
        NOTE.—The preface is dated, " Stoughton, March 30th, 1833."

BARTON, Walter, of *Sydney, New South Wales.*
—— The " Quakers " and the Baptists. (Signed by Walter Barton on behalf of a Meeting).
                        8vo., 4th month 6th, 1869
        NOTE.—Issued on the occasion of the Baptism of Walter Robson, by B. G. Wilson, of *Brisbane, Australia.*

‖BASSET, Sarah Jarmy, of *Philadelphia*, was the daughter of George Francis Bassett, a silversmith of *Yorkshire*, and Sarah Jarmy of *Ipswich*, who emigrated to America in 1794, and who both fell victims to the yellow fever which broke out in Philadelphia in 1798.
—— MEMOIR of SARAH J. BASSETT. Compiled from authentic papers furnished by her Friends, and published at their request.

BASSET, Sarah Jarmy, *continued.*
> *Philadelphia: J. Harmstead, No. 40, N. Fourth*
> *Street* . . . 16mo. 1848. 1½
>> She died the 28th day of the 1st mo., 1819.

BASSETT, Hannah, of *Lynn, Massachusetts.*
——Memoir of Hannah Bassett, with extracts from her Diary.
> *Lynn: W. W. Kellogg, Printer, No. 8, Exchange*
> *Street.* . . . 12mo. 1860. 3

BASSETT, Wm., *Lynn, Massachusetts.*
——Society of Friends in the United States, &c.
> [Anon.]. . . 8vo. Darlington. 1840. 1⅜
>> See FRIENDS. In Catalogue, vol. I, p. 781.

BATES, Elisha, continued from Catalogue of Friends' Books, vol. I, p. 204.
——The Evangelical Union. Edited by Elisha Bates, vol. I, No. 7, Dec. 1st, to No. 12, Feb. 16th, 1846.
> 8vo. 1845-6.
>> NOTE.—I have only seen these numbers.

BATT, Jasper, continued from Catalogue, vol. 1, p. 211.
——The Testimony of Jasper Batt for George Russell.
>> See ROBERT FORD and G. RUSSELL in *Catalogue, vol. I,*
>> p. 621.
> 4to. [1680.]

BATTEY, Thomas C., *of North America.*
——The LIFE AND ADVENTURES of a QUAKER among the INDIANS. By Thomas C. Battey. ILLUSTRATED.
> *Boston: Lee and Shepard.*
> *York: William Sessions, 15, Low Ousegate.*
> *London: S. Harris & Co., 5, Bishopsgate Street,*
> *Without.*
>> " We have pleasure in drawing attention to this book."—*The Friend.*
>> " Intensely interesting, as well as instructive."—*British Friend.*

BEACON CONTROVERSY.
——A Few Queries and Remarks offered to the consideration of Dr. Wardlaw and the Writer of the Review in the Evangelical Magazine of his "Letters to the Society of Friends," &c. [ANON.]
> In *Manuscript.* . . . 4to. 1836. ½

BEALING, Benjamin, Recording Clerk of the Society. Continued from Catalogue, vol. I, p. 227.
>> He died at *Wellingborough*, the 26th of 3rd mo., 1739.

BECK, Mary Elizabeth, of *Brighton.*
———Heavenly Relationships.

BECK, Mary Elizabeth, *continued.*
—— RITES; OR THE LORD'S SUPPER and Baptism, under the new dispensation. By Mary E. Beck.
   Third Edition.—*London : Friends' Tract Association, 14, Bishopsgate Street Without, E.C.*
   16mo. 1890. ¾
—— Through Egypt to Palestine.
   Reprinted, with additions, entitled "East and West."
   8vo. 1875. 14¼
—— Turning Points and their results, in the lives of eminent Christians.
   8vo. 1888.
—— The PROMISED GIFT of the HOLY SPIRIT, by M. E. Beck.
   London : Friends' Tract Association, 5, Bishopsgate Street Without.
   18mo. No date. ½
—— COLLATERAL TESTIMONIES to "QUAKER PRINCIPLES." By M. E. Beck.
   Third Edition. Revised and Enlarged.
   Edward Hicks, Jun., 14, Bishopsgate Without, E.C.
   8vo. No date. 692pp.

BECK, Joseph, of *Stoke Newington.*
—— A letter "To the Editor of *The Times*," dated, "31, Cornhill, Sept. 14th, 1874," being a few remarks about brakes and lights upon Railways.
   He died the 18th of 4th Mo., 1891, aged 61 years.

BECK, William, of *Stoke Newington* (his brother).
—— Historical Account of Friends in Germany. *Presented Third Month, 1868, to the Meeting for Sufferings in London.* Compiled from Minutes of the Yearly Meeting—the Meeting for Sufferings, and its Continental Committee, and letters of its correspondents. Also Extracts from the Journal of Friends MS. History, by F. Schmidt, and other sources.
   8vo. 1868. 1⅜
—— Circular and Table of Contents of the Origin, History, and Circumstances of the London Meetings, which it is proposed to publish (as follows.)
   4to. [1869.]
—— The LONDON FRIENDS' MEETINGS: showing the rise of THE SOCIETY OF FRIENDS IN LONDON; its Progress, and the Development of its discipline; with accounts of the various 𝕸eeting 𝕳ouses and 𝕭urial 𝕲rounds, their History and general associations. 𝕮ompiled from original 𝕽ecords and other sources, by WILLIAM BECK and T. FREDERICK BALL.

BECK, William, *continued.*
> London. *F. Bowyer Kitto, 5, Bishopsgate Street, Without.*
> 8vo. 1869. 25½

——Lithographed circular-letter to the Clerks of Monthly Meetings, soliciting subscriptions for the above work for the Meeting-house Libraries.
> *London: 33, Finsbury Circus.*
> 14th of 6th Month, 1869. ½

——SUN WORSHIPPERS.—A Letter of *Wm. Beck's* in "The Times" Newspaper, Tuesday, June 25th, 1872.

——SIX LECTURES on GEORGE FOX AND HIS TIMES. By WILLIAM BECK. Delivered at the Friends' Meeting-House, Stoke Newington, and re-printed from "The Friends' Quarterly Examiner," with some additions.
> *London: Saml. Harris & Co., 5, Bishopsgate Without.* 8vo. 1877. 9

——BIOGRAPHICAL CATALOGUE being an account of THE LIVES OF FRIENDS and others whose 𝔓𝔬𝔯𝔱𝔯𝔞𝔦𝔱𝔰 are in the LONDON FRIENDS' Institute. Also Descriptive Notices of those of the 𝔉𝔯𝔦𝔢𝔫𝔡𝔰' 𝔖𝔠𝔥𝔬𝔬𝔩𝔰 𝔞𝔫𝔡 𝔍𝔫𝔰𝔱𝔦𝔱𝔲𝔱𝔦𝔬𝔫𝔰, of which the GALLERY CONTAINS ILLUSTRATIONS, &c., &c., &c.
> Signed by W. BECK. . . . . 8vo. 1888.
> HENRY G. CHALKLEY. Preface, 6 pages.
> WM. F. WELLS. . Text, 878 do.
> *London: Friends' Institute, 13, Bishopsgate Street Without. (Printed by West, Newman & Co., 54, Hatton Garden, E.C.)*

BELL, Daniel.
——The 𝔇𝔢𝔰𝔠𝔢𝔫𝔡𝔞𝔫𝔱𝔰 of Daniel Bell and Katherine Barclay, married in 1750.
> *On a large sheet, size, 51in. by 40in. width.*

BELL, Edward, of *Mullicarton,* near *Lisburn,* in *Ireland.*
——SOME ACCOUNT of the RISE AND PROGRESS of Brookfield Meeting, in the County of Antrim, Ireland. (*For private circulation amongst Friends.*) Price One Shilling.
> May be had on application to the Author, EDWARD BELL, near Lisburn, Ireland.
> *Manchester: Arthur Henshall, 2, Cannon Street.*
> 8vo. 1880. 1¼
>> NOTE.—At the end is added, a Letter from John Barclay to Peter Bedford, taken from the British Friend, of 3rd Mo., 1850.

BELL, Jacob, son of JOHN BELL, of *London*.
—— List of the Founders of the Pharmaceutical Society of
 Great Britain. . . . . 1841. 8vo. 22pp.
—— Pharmaceutical Journal and Transactions. Volume I.
 1841-2. Edited by Jacob Bell, F.L.S., M.R.I.
  *London : John Churchill, Princes Street, Soho ;
  Maclachlan & Stewart, Edinburgh ; & Fannin
  & Co., Dublin.*
           viii. pp., 670 pp. 8vo. 1842.
—— Volume II. 1842-3.
  Same imprint.   viii. pp., 788 pp. 8vo. 1843.
—— Volume III. 1843-4.
  Same imprint.   viii. pp., 604 pp. 8vo. 1844.
—— Volume IV. 1844-5.
  Same Imprint.   viii. pp., 588 pp. 8vo. 1845.
—— Volume V. 1845-6.
  Same imprint.   vii. pp., 584 pp. 8vo. 1846.
   NOTE.—In this volume is a portrait of " William Allen,
   F.R.S., First President of the *Pharmaceutical Society
   of Great Britain*. Painted by H. P. Briggs, R.A.
   Engraved by H. C. Shenton."
—— Volume VI. 1846-7.
  Same imprint.   viii. pp., 616 pp. 8vo. 1847.
—— Volume VII. 1847-8.
  Same imprint.   v. pp., 607 pp. 8vo. 1848.
—— Volume VIII. 1848-9.
  Same imprint.   v. pp., 608 pp. 8vo. 1849.
   NOTE.—In this volume is a portrait of "John Bell.
   H. P. Briggs, R.A., 1833. H. B. Hall, 1849."
—— Volume IX. 1849-50.
  Same imprint.   viii. pp., 612 pp. 8vo. 1850.
—— Volume X. 1850-1.
  Same imprint.   viii. pp., 640 pp. 8vo. 1851.
—— Volume XI. 1851-52.
  Same imprint.
   Title and contents, viii. pp ; text, 600 pp. 8vo. 1852.
—— Objects, Charter, and Bye-Laws of the Pharmaceutical
 Society of 𝕲𝖗𝖊𝖆𝖙 𝕭𝖗𝖎𝖙𝖆𝖎𝖓. Incorporated February
 18th, 1843.
  *London : Printed by C. Whiting, Beaufort House,
  Strand.*   8vo. 1841. 1¾
  Reprinted (same imprint). . . 8vo. 1851. 1½
   He died the 12th of 6th Mo., 1859, aged 49 years.
BELL, William (see Catalogue, Vol. I., p. 235), Editor of
 The Irish Friend, of *Belfast, Ireland*, lastly of
 Richmond, Indiana, North America, where he died
 5th of 3rd month, 1871, aged nearly 74 years.
   See *The Friend* for 4th mo., 1871.

BELLERS, John, continued from Catalogue, Vol. I., p. 235.
—— Watch unto Prayer, &c.
  Reprinted in America in the year 1802 (only 200
   printed). . . . . . Small 8vo.   1

BELLOWS, William L., continued from Catalogue, vol. I.,
 p. 239.
—— The Unchangeable Testimony of Faithful Friends,
 against Tithe and Tithe-Rent-Charge. (Written
 Fourth Month 17th, 1867). . 8vo. [1867.]   ¼
—— Barclay Vindicated. A Review of Robert Charleton's
 "Thoughts on Barclay's Apology." By William L.
 Bellows.
  Manchester : *William Irwin, 24, Deansgate.*
             8vo. 1868.   2½
—— The Friends' Foundation Principle, Is it True, or, is it
 False ? An Enquiry occasioned by reading a Tract,
 entitled, "The Oppugners of Barclay, are they right,
 or, are they wrong ?" By William L. Bellows.
  Gloucester : *John Bellows, Printer, Westgate.*
             8vo. 1869.   1
—— An Exposure, &c.
 Reprinted.—2nd, 1865.
—— The Reason given by an Early Constitution Friend for
 his Scriptural View of Worship and Discipline.
            12mo. 1873.   2½
  He died the 2nd of 12th Mo., 1877, aged 75 years, and was
  buried at Gloucester.

BELLOWS, John (his Son), of *Gloucester*, continued from
 Catalogue, vol. I, p. 240.
—— A Winter Journey from Gloucester to Norway.
  Gloucester : *John Bellows, Steam Press, Westgate
   Street.* . . . 16mo. 1867.   4
—— Capital Punishment. Signed Civis.
          12mo. No date.   ¼
——— Le Vrai Dictionnaire de Poche, 𝕬 𝕱𝖗𝖊𝖓𝖈𝖍 𝖆𝖓𝖉 𝕰𝖓𝖌𝖑𝖎𝖘𝖍
 𝕯𝖎𝖈𝖙𝖎𝖔𝖓𝖆𝖗𝖞, for the pocket, by JOHN BELLOWS.
  London : *Trübner & Co.* *Paris* : *E. Leroux.*
  Gloucester : *John Bellows.* . 12mo. 1876.
    Second Edition.
  Containing the French-English and English-French divi-
  sions on the same page ; conjugating all the verbs ;
  distinguishing the genders by different types ; giving
  numerous aids to pronunciation ; indicating the *liaison*
  or *non-liaison* of terminal consonants ; and translating
  units of weight, measure, and value, by a series of tables,
  differing entirely from any hitherto published.
  The new edition, which is but six ounces in weight, has
  been to a large extent re-modelled, and contains many

BELLOWS, John, *continued.*

  thousands of additional words and renderings. Miniature maps of France, the British Isles, Paris, and London, are added to the Geographical Section.

  It is, to say the least, as complete a Dictionary of the French and English languages as has ever been published.—*Times.*

  The Vocabulary abounds in translations of every day expressions which cannot be always literally rendered, and of new words and phrases not found anywhere else. [Here follow examples.] ° ° And so we might go on without intermission, *filling a whole Scotsman* with words and idiomatic phrases not to be found in any other Dictionary. It is *better than any book of this kind ever published in Great Britain,* and *superior to any Pocket Dictionary edited and printed in any country in Europe.*—*Scotsman.*

  By trying to remedy some of the faults in other books of the kind, and *by letting originality replace servile copying,* [the Author] has made a very *serviceable Dictionary.*—*Atlantic Monthly.*

  The plan is *really excellent.—Daily Telegraph.*

  Not only *as a Pocket Dictionary, without a rival,* but one which would be remarkable among Dictionaries of any size for the novelties introduced in both matter and arrangement.—*Spectator.*

  A triumph of brain-work and the printer's skill.—*Civil Service Gazette.*

  A compilation of verbal facts perfectly astounding.—*Liverpool Mercury.*

  A *marvellous specimen of typography,* and is at once *the smallest and most comprehensive* of Pocket Dictionaries.—*Graphic.*

  It deserves the highest praise.—*Birmingham Daily Post.*

  De tous les prétendus dictionnaires de poche le plus compact et le plus portatif, en même temps que le meilleur et le plus complet.—*Revue Anglo-Française.*

——The Track of the War around Metz. Second edition. By John Bellows, Gloucester. With map and illustrations.

  London: Trübner & Co; Gloucester, John Bellows.

——On some Archaeological Remains in Gloucester, relating to the BURNING OF BISHOP HOOPER, read at the Annual Meeting of the Cotteswold Club, at Gloucester, 1878, by John Bellows.

  Second edition.   1880.

       8vo. 34 pp., and Title (one leaf).

Frontispiece of the Stake to which Bishop Hooper was chained.

BELLOWS, John, *continued*.
—— Barclay's Apology—Prospectus of a New Edition.
              8vo. 1882. ¼
—— Education, Emigration, and Colonisation.—*Gloucester*: November 28th, 1887. By John Bellows.
> NOTE.—This is printed in and forms part of a book, entitled " PROSPERITY OR PAUPERISM "? Edited by The EARL OF MEATH (Lord Brabazon). Pages 318—328.

BELSON, Frederick, of *New York*?
—— Considerations in the Interests of the Colored People, being, " An Address to those Christians who sympathise with the Poor and Bereaved Colored People," and the " Orphans' Home."
              8vo. [1868.] ½

BENEZET, Anthony, lastly of *Philadelphia*, continued from Catalogue, Vol. I., p. 240.
—— A COLLECTION OF RELIGIOUS TRACTS.
> In Proportion as we die to the Love of material Objects and earthly Affections, we advance in a Spiritual Growth : we break our Bands asunder, and rise into the Liberty of the Sons of God. The proneness of the human Mind to confine itself to the Objects of Sense, joined to the inordinate Love of them ; strengthened by Example and Custom, do so familiarize material Nature to the thoughts of the learned and unlearned, that by Degrees, they become, as it were, chained down to it ; hence so great a Number fall under the Predicament of the Apostle, Jude, verse 19., " *Sensual, not having the Spirit.*"—Pref. to Swedeng. (Swedenborg).

> *Philadelphia* : *Printed by Joseph Crukshank, in Third-Street, opposite the Work-house.*
> MDCCLXXIII.   12mo.? 1773.
> Not mentioned by Hildeburn.
> This vol. contains :—
> " Plain Path to Christian Perfection," *1772.*
> " David Brainard and others."
> " Sermons by Stephen Crisp," *1773.*

—— Letter—CCCCXII.
> (From Anthony Benezet, to the Rev. J. Wesley.)
> *Philadelphia* : *the 23rd of fifth Month (May) 1774.*
> *In " The Arminian Magazine," Vol. X., p. 44, 1787.*

—— The Plain Path to Christian Perfection.
> Reprinted.—*Philadelphia* : *Printed by Joseph Rakestraw.* 18mo. 1831. 2¾

—— Life of Anthony Benezet.
> *Philadelphia* : *Sherman & Co., Printers.*
>   8vo. 1867. 2

BENNETT, Alfred W., of *London*.
——Circular soliciting subscriptions for the Bust of John Bright, M.P. (See also John Bright.) 4to. N.D. ¼
——Alpine Plants, painted from Nature. By Joseph Seboth. Edited by Alfred W. Bennett. Four vols., with 400 coloured illustrations.
> London : *W. Swan, Sonnenschein & Co.,*
> Small 4to. (not dated.)

——The Tourist's Guide to the Flora of the Alps, by W.K. Dalla Torre. Translated and edited by Alfred W. Bennett. Bound in mor. with flap.
> London: *Swan, Sonnenschein & Co.* 16mo. 1886. 392pp.

——and G. MURRAY.
——A Handbook of Cryptogamic Botany. viii. and 473pp., 378 illustrations.
> London : *Longmans, Green & Co.* 8vo. 1889.

——An Introduction to the Study of Flowerless Plants. 88pp. 35 illustrations.
> London : *Gurney and Jackson.* 12mo. 1891.

*BENNETT, Edward T. (his brother).
——THE CRUSADE. A Popular and High-Class Journal :— Devoted to the Promotion of the Great Temperance Reform.
>> Associated for Progress, we bind ourselves that others may be set free.—MAZZINI.
> No. 25. (Vol. III., No. 1), January 1, 1876.
> 4to. One Penny.
> Edited by E.T.B., The Holmes, Betchworth, near Reigate.

BENNETT, William, of *London*, continued from Catalogue, Vol. I., p. 247.
——Joint Stock Companies and other Associations, &c.
> Second edition. . . . . 12mo. 1861.
> **Third Edition** (with a postscript).
> *London : Effingham Wilson, 11, Royal Exchange.*
> One Shilling. 8vo. 1869. 2

——and ELIZABETH BENNETT.—Pages from the Life of the Apostle Paul, and analysis of his Epistles. With preliminary sketch of the History of the Jews. With Map, and Photograph of Athens. By F. Frith.
> 16mo. 1873. 12⅛
>> William Bennett died the 7th of 2nd Mo., 1873, aged 69 years. Buried at Stoke Newington.
>> Elizabeth Bennett died the 9th of 1st Mo., 1891, aged 92 years. Buried at Stoke Newington.

BENNITT, William, continued from Catalogue, Vol. I., p. 248.
——A Loving SALUTATION AND WARNING TO SEAMEN, and all others whom it doth concern. [A REPRINT of 1675.]
Johnston & Barrett, Printers, 13, Mark Lane, London.
8vo. No Date. ⅛

BETTLE, Jane, of *Philadelphia*, continued from Catalogue, Vol. I., page 258.
——Extracts from the Memorandum of Jane Bettle.
Philadelphia. Printed. 12mo. 1843. 5

BEVAN, Samuel, continued from Catalogue, Vol. I., p. 262.
He died "On the 18th inst., at 40, Sackville Street, W., Samuel Bevan, late of The Grange, Ramsgate, and Porteous House, Paddington, formerly of Pangbourne, Berks, youngest son of the late Paul Bevan, of Tottenham, aged 60."—*The Times, Saturday, September 23rd, 1876.*

BEVANS, James, of
——Short Statement of Facts in Vindication of himself.
London : Couchman. 12mo. 1832.

* BEWLEY, Henry, of *Dublin*, continued from Catalogue, Vol. I., p. 266.
——Brief observations on Scriptural subjects, submitted to the consideration of those engaged in Evangelistic Work.
London : Printed. 8vo. [1875.] 6¼
——Comments. By J. J. G.

BICKLEY, A. C., of *London*. A Lover of Friends, though not a member.
——GEORGE FOX and the Early Quakers. By A. C. BICKLEY.
"No grander thing was ever done than when George Fox, stitching himself a suit of leather, went forth determined to find truth for himself, and to do battle for it against all superstition, bigotry and intolerance."
CARLYLE, "*Sartor Resartus.*"
"There is no character in Christian History since the days of its Divine Founder more free from spot or stain than that of George Fox."
London : Hodder & Stoughton, 27, Paternoster Row.
8vo. 1884.
NOTE.—With a frontispiece fac-simile letter of Geo. Fox's to Robert Barclay.
Preface, xx pp.
Text, 426 pp.

BIDDLE, Owen, of *Philadelphia*, Architect.

——An Oration, delivered the 2nd of March, 1781, at the request of the American Philosophical Society for promoting Useful Knowledge, before the said Society, and a large and respectable Assembly of Citizens and Foreigners, by Owen Biddle, one of the secretaries to the said Society.
> *Philadelphia : Published by Order of the Society, and Printed by Francis Bailey, in Market Street, MDCCLXXXI.*
>
> 4to. 1781. 36pp.

BIGG, William, lastly of *Luton*, continued from Catalogue, Vol. I., p. 268.
> He died the 2nd of 3rd mo., 1878, aged 64 years. See *Annual Monitor* for 1879.

BIGG, Louisa (his daughter), of *Luton, Beds.*

——URBAN GRANDIER, and other Poems. By LOUIS BRAND (a fictitious name).
> *London : Chapman & Hall, 193, Piccadilly.*
>
> 8vo. 1872. 5¼

——Pansies and Asphodel.
> 8vo. 1878. 11¼

BINGHAM, Jane M. Widow of WM. BINGHAM, of *Chesterfield, Derbyshire.*

——A Tribute to the Memory of WILLIAM BINGHAM, of Chesterfield, Derbyshire, who departed this life on the 30th of 3rd month, 1877.
> N.B.—First written in Fourth Month, 1877 ; and now, in 1889, printed to prevent the spread of mistakes.
>
> 16mo. 1889. 4 pp.

BINNS, Jonathan, of *Ackworth, Yorkshire.*

——A Spelling Book for the use of Ackworth School.
> *London : Printed and Sold by James Phillips, George Yard, Lombard Street.*
>
> 12mo. 1790. 6

Reprinted, see under Schools, in the Catalogue of Friends' Books, Vol. I., p. 790.

BINNS, Jonathan, of *Lancaster* (his Son).

——The MISERIES AND BEAUTIES of IRELAND. By JONATHAN BINNS, Assistant Agricultural Commissioner on the late Irish Poor Inquiry. In two volumes. VOL. I.
> *London : Longman, Orme, Brown, & Co.* 8vo. 1837.
> Title, Dedication (to the Queen), Advertisement, and Contents, 12 pp. ; Text, 418 pp.
> Volume II. A map and six plates.
>> He died 10th of 3rd Month, 1871, aged 85 years, and was buried at Lancaster.

*BIRCH, Thomas, continued from Catalogue, Vol. I., p. 272.
—— The Life of the Honourable ROBERT BOYLE. By Thomas Birch, M.A. and F.R.S.
 London : Printed for A. MILLAR, *over-against Catharine Street, in the Strand.* MDCCXLIV.
            8vo. 1744.
 Title, Dedication, &c., 3 pp. ; Text, 458 pp. ; Index, 16 pp.
  NOTE.—Contains much about the Society for Propagating the Gospel in New England, and letters from John Eliot, and the Governor (John Endecott), and others ; also an account of Henry Stubbe, his writings and death.
—— AN HISTORICAL VIEW OF THE NEGOTIATIONS between the COURTS of *England, France,* and *Brussels,* from the year 1592 to 1617. Extracted chiefly from the MS. State-Papers of Sir *Thomas Edmondes,* Knt., Embassador in *France* and at *Brussels,* and Treasurer of the Household to the Kings *James I. and Charles I.,* and of *Anthony Bacon,* Esq., brother to the Lord Chancellor *Bacon ;* to which is added A Relation of the STATE of *France,* with the CHARACTERS of *Henry IV.* and the principal persons of that Court, drawn up by Sir *George Carew,* upon his return from his Embassy there in 1609, and addressed to King *James I.* Never before printed. By Thomas Birch, M.A., F.R.S., and Rector of the United Parishes of *St. Margaret-Pattens* and *St. Gabriel, Fenchurch.*
 London : Printed for A. MILLAR, *opposite to Katharine Street, in the Strand.* MDCCXLIX.
 Introduction, 26 pp. ; Text, 528 pp.   8vo. 1749.
—— The Life of Henry, Prince of Wales, eldest son of King James I.   8vo. 1760.
  °Dr. Birch, who died of a fall from his horse between London and Hampstead, January 9th, 1766, at sixty-one, was a pioneer of literature. Dr. Johnson was repeatedly obliged to him for literary information, and bestowed on him a great epigram, but is said to have satirically observed, " Tom Birch is as brisk as a bee in conversation, but no sooner does he take a pen in his hand than it becomes a torpedo to him, and benumbs all his faculties." His General Dictionary, including a new translation of M. Bayle, was interspersed with several thousand new lives, and completed in ten volumes (folio).

‖ BIRKBECK, A. M.—*10, Gloucester Place, Hyde Park, London.* Daughter of Dr. Birkbeck ?
—— Rural and Historical Gleanings from EASTERN EUROPE. By Miss A. M. Birkbeck.
 " PRO PATRIA ET LIBERTATE." *Rakóczi.*

BIRKBECK, A. M., *continued.*
> London: Published for the Author by Darton &
> Co., 58, Holborn Hill.
> *(Translation reserved.)* . . . 12mo. 1854. 19

*BIRKBECK, George.—Continued from Catalogue, Vol. I., p.273.

—— Mathematics practically applied to the Useful and Fine Arts. By Baron Charles Dupin, Member of the Institute; of the Academy of Sciences, &c., &c. Adapted to the state of the Arts in England. By George Birkbeck, Esq., M.D., President of the London Mechanics' Institution, &c., &c.

> This work is in the course of being published in Numbers, price One Shilling each, on the 15th and last days of each month. Two Numbers, to be had at the end of the Month, will constitute a Part, price Two Shillings. Each Number contains thirty-two pages of letter-press, and two large folding plates, engraved in the best manner by TURRELL. The work will be completed in Ten Numbers, or Five Parts, and will form a very handsome octavo volume.
>
> The original work forms three volumes; and if this, containing the first course of Lectures, be favourably received by the public, it will be immediately followed by the second and third volumes. Volume the second will contain a complete series of Lectures descriptive of the principal MACHINES EMPLOYED IN THE ARTS; and the third will contain a full account of the different motive powers, such as THE STRENGTH OF MEN and ANIMALS, THE FORCE OF WIND, STEAM, AND WATER. The whole will form the only complete Course of Mathematics applied to the Arts yet given to the public. Each volume, treating a distinct branch of the subject, will form a perfect work, and will be sold separately.
>
> ADDRESS.
>
> It has been long and justly regretted, that a treatise, exhibiting clearly and comprehensively the connexion of Science with the Arts, has never been placed in the hands of the public. Of such a work, however, an admirable specimen has at length been furnished by the celebrated Baron Dupin; and as its execution is in every respect commensurate with the importance of the subject, it must prove, I am persuaded, a valuable acquisition to the British student.
>
> It may not be improper here to state, that, for several years, this learned and scientific inquirer has been engaged in travelling through the most cultivated and enlightened parts of Europe, and especially of Great Britain; surveying with the greatest assiduity, attention, and intelligence, the actual condition of the arts, manu-

BIRKBECK, George, *continued.*

factures, and commerce ; and everywhere exploring, by means of a most powerful mind, the nature and operation of the various processes and machines by which they are conducted, from the most simple to the most complicated. Amongst the objects by which, during his last excursion through this empire, he seems to have been most powerfully impressed, were the establishments recently formed for the scientific education of the working classes ; and the effect of that impression was the immediate introduction of a similar measure, with the concurrence of the Government of France, amongst the artisans and masters of manufactories in Paris, by means of courses of popular and truly practical lectures, delivered in the *Conservatoire des Arts et Metiers.* Having farther succeeded in establishing more than thirty schools of a similar kind in the provinces, Baron Dupin proceeded to publish, for their use and that of the working classes at large, the Lectures on Geometry, the first of the courses which he had thus delivered. Speaking of this publication, in a letter which I had the pleasure of receiving from him with a copy of it, he says, " I wish earnestly that this course of Lectures may deserve your esteem and approbation. It is the fruit of very extensive research, and has cost me a great deal of labour. The last eight Lectures will, I hope, present to the public, matter clearly exposed, which, until this moment, has never been rendered accessible to them."

The very perspicuous and instructive manner in which the truths of Geometry are unfolded, and the continually attractive application of these truths to the proceedings of the workshop, an application never before to an equal extent even attempted—must place this treatise in the hands of every inquiring workman, and, on account of the amusing character of its contents, in the hands of the least scientific or practical. It is likewise so completely adapted to the purposes of Mechanics' Institutions, that I trust it will soon become not only the text-book for the elementary schools, but be introduced as the basis of Courses of Lectures, to be regularly delivered by suitable professors upon this fundamental branch of mathematical science. When to this pursuit has been added a similar appropriation of the principles of mechanics, the materials for which have already been provided by our distinguished author, we may confidently anticipate all the beneficial results promised by him in one of his animating addresses to the Workmen of France. " If you study," says he, " the application of Geometry and Mechanics to your arts and your implements, you will find in this exercise methods of working with more regularity, precision, intelligence, facility, and rapidity. You will execute your work at once more perfectly and more expeditiously : and you

BIRKBECK, George, *continued.*

will acquire the power of reasoning accurately, respecting your performances and your inventions."

GEORGE BIRKBECK.

Published by Charles Tait, 63, Fleet Street, London; and Sold by William Tait, 78, Prince's Street, Edinburgh; W. Curry & Co., Sackville Street, Dublin; Robertson and Atkinson, Trongate, Glasgow; and by all the Booksellers of the United Kingdom.

—— MATHEMATICS PRACTICALLY APPLIED TO THE USEFUL AND FINE ARTS. BY BARON CHARLES DUPIN, Member of the Institute of the Academy of Sciences, &c., &c. Adapted to the State of the Arts in England.

BY GEORGE BIRKBECK, ESQ., M.D., President of the London Mechanics' Institution, &c., &c. GEOMETRY OF THE ARTS.

London : *Printed for Charles Tait, 63, Fleet Street, and William Tait, 78, Prince's Street, Edinburgh.* 8vo. 1827. 20

—— Ditto 8vo. 1827. 20
New Title Page only?

—— George Birkbeck, the Pioneer of Popular Education. A Memoir and Review. By John George Godard. (*Portrait.*) . . . . 8vo. 1884.

He died the 1st of 12th Month, 1841, aged about 65 years, and his remains were laid in the Catacombs in the cemetery at *Kensal Green*; they were afterwards removed to the " Family Mausoleum" in that cemetery.

BIRKBECK, Morris, of *Guildford, Surrey,* continued from Catalogue, Vol. 1. p. 272.

—— A Catalogue of Adverse Books (in MS.).

4to. 1806.

—— A Catalogue of Miscellaneous Books (in MS.).

—— Cursory Remarks on some passages entitled " Facts," contained in an Address—"To the Friends of the Monthly Meeting at Birmingham." Printed and dispersed by Samuel Galton, Junior, 1795.

(in MS.) 4to.

*BIRKBECK, Morris, continued from Catalogue, Vol. I., p. 275.

—— LETTERS FROM ILLINOIS. BY Morris Birkbeck, Author of " Notes on a Tour through France," and of " Notes on a Journey in America," &c. Illustrated by A MAP OF THE UNITED STATES, shewing

BIRKBECK, Morris, *continued*.

    Mr. Birkbeck's journey from Norfolk to Illinois, and a map of English Prairie and the adjacent country, BY JOHN MELISH. " Vox clamantis è deserto."
Philadelphia: Published by M. Carey and Son, 126, Chestnut Street.
12mo. 1818. 6½

BLANSHARD, Mary (supposed).

·———Lines found written in the fly-leaf of an old controversial Pamphlet, dated 1663, and signed, "Mary Blanshard, her booke."
8vo. No date. ¼

BLAKEY, William, of *Middletown*, in *Bucks* County, *North America*.

———Journal of William Blakey, containing some account of his Religious Exercises, Observations and Travels.
In Comly's Miscellany, Vol. IV., p. 76.
    He died the 20th of the 6th Month, 1822, in the 84th year of his age.

‖ BLAKES, James, Jun.

———Reports of Sermons, *Saml. Fothergill and others*.

BOCKETT, Sarah, of *Staines*, in *Middlesex*.

———Original Letter, Account of William Morgan, a Quaker; in a Letter from Sarah Bockett to a Friend (dated *Staines, May 11, 1747.*
In *Gent's Magazine*, 1797 ? p. 137.
    She died, 26th of 1st Mo., 1761, aged 70 years, and was buried at Bunhill Fields.

BONIFEILD, Abraham.

    He died the 9th of the 11th month, 1701, buried on the 11th of the same.
    Sarah Bonifeild, his wife, was buried on the 7th of 3rd month, 1695. (No age given in the Register) Reading and Warboro Monthly Meeting.

BOORNE, James, of *Reading*.

———PUBLIC FASTS. From Rules of Discipline and Phipps' Dissertations.
Barcham, Printer, Reading.
4to. No date. ¼

———𝔒𝔭𝔢𝔫𝔦𝔫𝔤 𝔬𝔣 𝔱𝔥𝔢 𝔓𝔲𝔟𝔩𝔦𝔠 𝔑𝔢𝔠𝔯𝔢𝔞𝔱𝔦𝔬𝔫 𝔊𝔯𝔬𝔲𝔫𝔡𝔰 𝔞𝔫𝔡 𝔇𝔯𝔦𝔫𝔨𝔦𝔫𝔤 𝔉𝔬𝔲𝔫𝔱𝔞𝔦𝔫, *Reading, August 16th, 1861.*
SPEECH of the MAYOR OF READING (James Boorne, Esq.), upon the occasion, at the Forbury.
Reading : Printed by T. Barcham, Broad Street.
8vo. [1861.] ¾

―――Mary Boorne. In Memoriam. (Portrait of her, Vignette).
    Barcham and Beecroft, Printers, Reading.
                                            4to. [1876.] 1

BOTTOMLEY, Joseph Firth. See also J. F. B. FIRTH.
―――The VELOCIPEDE, its Past, its Present, and its Future. By J. F. B. How to Ride a Velocipede,...
    "Straddle a Saddle, then Paddle and Skedaddle."
With 25 Illustrations.
    London : Simpkin, Marshall, & Co.
                                  8vo. 1869. $6\tfrac{3}{4}$

BOUSTED, John, of *Cumberland.* See Catalogue, Vol. I., p. 304. Was born at Aglionby, near Carlisle, in the year 1659. He died in 1716, and was buried at Scotby. See Rd. Ferguson's Book.

BOULTON, ――― Coadjutor of James Watt. Ex-Friend?

BOUVIER, John, Judge, Law Writer, &c. of *America.*
―――Law Dictionary, adapted to the Constitution and Laws of the United States of America, and of the several States of the American Union ; with References to the Civil and other Systems of Foreign Law. By John Bouvier.
Reprinted, the 2nd Edition.
       ,,   the 3rd   ,,
       ,,   the 4th   ,,
       ,,   the 5th   ,,
       ,,   the 6th   ,,   revised, improved, and greatly enlarged.
    Philadelphia.
                        2 Vols. Royal 8vo. 1856.
―――Institutes of American Law. By John Bouvier. Four vols.
    Philadelphia.   8vo. 1854.

†BOWDEN, James, continued from Catalogue, Vol. 1., p. 304.
―――Some Account of the Charity founded by Michael Yoakley.
                    Large 4to. Croydon. 1869.
Lithographed (not published). Only 15 copies printed for the Trustees.

―――AN ESSAY on THE ANTI-SCRIPTURAL DOCTRINE of the RESURRECTION OF THE BODY. By James Bowden.
    "I am the resurrection and the life : he that believeth in me, though he were dead, yet shall he live : and whosoever liveth and believeth in me shall never die."―
                              John xi., 25-26.

BOWDEN, James, *continued*.
    London : *Published by Samuel Harris & Co.,
    Bishopsgate Street Without.*
    London : *Printed by Wertheimer, Lea, & Co.,
    Circus Place, Finsbury Circus.*
    Price One Shilling.   8vo. 1878.   3
        He died at Nailsworth, Gloucestershire, the 4th of 3rd Mo.,
        1887, aged 75 years, and was buried at Shortwood.

BOWDEN, Martha, of *London*.
——Circular, informing Friends of her having taken a large
    Manor House at Port Looe, Cornwall.   8vo.
        She died the 26th of 10th Mo., 1887, aged 77 years.

BOWEN, Simon Maw, of *Gainsborough*.
——A Statement of the Expenditure of the Parish of
    Gainsboro', and such other payments as are usually
    made out of the Poor's Rate.
    Printed by A. Stark, Market-Place, Gainsborough.
                                        12mo. [1816.] ½
        He died the 9th of 7th month, 1852, aged 80 years.

BOWLY, Samuel, of *Horsepools*, near *Stroud*, continued
    from Catalogue, Vol. I., p. 307.
——Reply to a Letter from Lewis Rugg to Joseph Sturge.
    Birmingham : John W. Showell.   1841.
        He died the 23rd of 3rd mo., 1884, aged 82 years. For further
        particulars concerning him see *The Annual Monitor* for
        1885.

BOWNAS, Samuel, continued from Catalogue, Vol. I., p. 309.
——Description of Qualifications of a Gospel Minister.
                                                                 1847.

BOYCE, Anne Ogden, of *The Cedars, Chertsey.*
——Records of a QUAKER FAMILY : 𝕿𝖍𝖊 𝕽𝖎𝖈𝖍𝖆𝖗𝖉𝖘𝖔𝖓𝖘 𝖔𝖋
    𝕮𝖑𝖊𝖛𝖊𝖑𝖆𝖓𝖉. With Portraits of Isabel Casson, Jona-
    than Priestman, and John Richardson Procter. By
    Anne Ogden Boyce.
    London : *Samuel Harris & Co., 5, Bishopsgate
    Without. Printed by West, Newman & Co.,
    Hatton Garden, E.C.*   4to. 1889.
        Preface and contents, xii. pp. ; text, 298 pp.
  Two editions as follows :
    One containing NINE PEDIGREE TABLES and an
    INDEX to the MARRIAGES recorded in them. Price,
    12 6.
    One without the above mentioned PEDIGREE TABLES
    and INDEX. Price, 7 6.

BRACHER, Philip H., of *Wincanton, Somersetshire.*
——The SOCIETY OF FRIENDS past and present state.

BRACHER, Philip H., *continued.*
    Considered and compared with the HISTORY of the CHILDREN OF ISRAEL, contained in the BOOK OF JEREMIAH, *chapters xlii. to li., inclusive,* by Philip H. Bracher, Wincanton.
        Newport: J. E. Southall, Printer, Dock Street.
                                      12mo. 1890. 1

*BRADFORD, William, was the son of WILLIAM and ANNE BRADFORD, of *Barwell, Leicestershire,* and was baptised May 30th, 1663, being born 20th May (3rd mo., 1663).
——Address, &c., on the Bi-centenary of the birth of William Bradford. By John William Wallace.
——Short BIOGRAPHICAL NOTICES of William Bradford, Reiner Jansen, Andrew Bradford, and Samuel Keimer, Early Printers in Pennsylvania. By Joseph Smith.
        London: Edward Hicks, Jun., 14, Bishopsgate Without, E.C. . . . 8vo. 1891. 1¼
            He died at New York, 23rd of 5th mo., 1752, aged 89 years.

*BRADLEY, Thomas, M.D., continued from Catalogue, Vol. I., p. 310.
——A New MEDICAL DICTIONARY, containing a concise Explanation of all the TERMS used in Medicine, Surgery, Pharmacy, Botany, Natural History, and Chymistry. Compiled by Joseph Fox, M.D., late Physician to the London Hospital. Revised and augmented by Thomas Bradley, M.D., Physician to the Westminster Hospital.
        London: Printed for Darton and Harvey, Gracechurch Street; Longman and Rees, Paternoster Row; and Murray and Highly, Fleet Street; by Darton and Harvey, Gracechurch Street.
                                    Small 8vo. 1803. 20½

BRADWAY, Edward, of *Alloways Creek, New Jersey.*
——Testimony concerning his wife, Elizabeth Bradway.
    —In *Comly's Miscellany, Vol. 4, p. 170.*

BRADY, Geo. Stewardson, of *Sunderland.* A Surgeon.
——Lumen Siccum.

BRADY, Henry E., of *Newcastle,* Botanist.

BRAITHWAITE, George H., of *Horsforth,* near *Leeds.*
——" A Reasonable Faith," by " Three Friends," refuted.
        Leek, printed . . . 8vo. 1885. 3¾

BRAITHWAITE, Josh Bevan,—*continued* from " Catalogue," Vol. I., p. 314.

BRAITHWAITE, Josh Bevan, *continued.*
——Thoughts on Books and Reading. (Anon.)
    London : Bull, Hunton, and Co., 19, Holles Street,
    Cavendish Square, York : William Simpson.
    (F. Shoberl, Printer to H.R.H. Prince Albert,
    51, Rupert Street.) . . 12mo. 1855. ½
  Reprinted.
——PAUL THE APOSTLE. A Poem. By Joseph Bevan
  Braithwaite.
    London : Seely and Co., Essex Street, Strand.
                                  8vo. 1885. 11
——and WILLIAM ROBINSON and THOMAS PUMPHERY.—A
  Loving Salutation from the deputation appointed by
  London Yearly Meeting in 1884, to all Friends in
  Canada.   .   .   .   8vo. 1885. 1
——Bi-Centenary of the Death of GEORGE FOX [Then
  follows his *Portrait*]. Born 1624. Died 1691. A
  Paper by Joseph Bevan Braithwaite.
    " We are nothing : Christ is all."—GEORGE FOX.
  Three pence.
    Published by the Friends' Book and Tract Depôt,
    14, Bishopsgate Without, London. 8vo. [1891.] 3½
BRAITHWAITE, Martha, his wife,—*continued* from
  "Catalogue," Vol. I., p. 314.
——The Fireside Hymn Book ; containing Selected and
  Original Hymns ; compiled by MARTHA BRAITH-
  WAITE. THIRD THOUSAND.
    London : Hamilton, Adams, & Co., 33, Paternoster
    Row . . . Square 16mo. 1875.
BRAND, Louis, a fictitious name.—See LOUISA BIGG.
BREWIN, Wm., of *Cirencester.*
——and Thomas Harvey.——Jamaica in 1866. A Narrative
  of a Tour through the Island.   8vo. 1867. 8½
BREWSTER, Martha, continued from Catalogue, p. 317.
——A Friendly Address. Third Commandment.
    Lomax, Stockport
BRIGHT, Jacob, of *Alderly Edge, Manchester,* is the son of
  the late JACOB BRIGHT, of Greenbank, near Roch-
  dale, and was born at Greenbank, 1821 ; married 1855.
  Ursula, daughter of the late Joseph Mellor, of Liverpool, is brother to the late John Bright, M.P. for Birmingham. Educated at Friends' School, York.
——SPEECH of JACOB BRIGHT, ESQ., M.P., on the ELEC-
  TORAL DISABILITIES OF WOMEN, delivered in Edinburgh, January 17th, 1870.
    Printed *by Spottiswoode & Co., New Street Square,*
    London. . . 8vo. 1870. ¾

BRIGHT, John, continued from Catalogue, vol. 1, p. 318.
—— Author's Popular Edition. SPEECHES ON QUESTIONS OF PUBLIC POLICY by the Right Honourable JOHN BRIGHT, M.P. Edited by James E. Thorold Rogers.
" Be Just and Fear not."
London : Macmillan and Co.
[All rights reserved].
            8vo. 1869. 37½

—— Speeches on the public affairs of the last twenty years by the Right Hon. John Bright, M.P., President of the Board of Trade. The Text carefully collated from the best reports taken at the time with a short introduction.
London : John Camden Hotten, Piccadilly.
          Sq. 8vo. 1869. 360pp.

—— The Life and Speeches of. By George Barnett Smith. Popular edition, 2 vols. in 1.
   London, Printed.   . . .   8vo. 1882. 24¾

—— John Bright, Statesman and Orator, a popular sketch of his life and work, by B. Rhodes. 8vo. 1884.

—— Testimonial of John Bright, Esq., M.P., to James Hargreaves, a well-known character amongst the Society of Friends.
Kenyon & Abbatt, Printers, Bolton. 8vo. No date. ⅛

—— A Word to Serious People.
(A Temperance Tract).

—— John Bright. A non-political sketch of a Good Man's Life. By the Rev. Charles Bullock, B.D.
            8vo. [1889.]

—— JOHN BRIGHT, **The Man of the People**. By JESSE PAGE. Author of " Samuel Crowther, the Slave Boy who became Bishop of the Niger," " Bishop Patterson, The Martyr of Melanesia," &c., &c.
London : S. W. Partridge & Co., 9, Paternoster Row.   8vo. [1889.] 10
NOTE.—Has many illustrations, one "A View of ACKWORTH SCHOOL."
He died the 27th of 3rd Mo., 1889, aged 77 years.

BROOK, Mary, continued from Catalogue, Vol. 1., p. 321.
—— On Silent Waiting.
Philadelphia : Reprinted by Joseph Crukshank, in Market Street, between Second and Third Streets.   8vo. 1780. 32pp.
        German, 8vo. 1786.

BROOK, Uriah, continued from Catalogue, Vol. 1., p. 323.
—— A Short Account of.
Reprinted.—*Gloucester* : John Bellows, Steam Press, Westgate Street.   12mo. 1868. ½

BROWN, Alfred W., *of Evesham*.
—— Evesham Friends in the Olden Times : A History of "Evesham Monthly Meeting of the Society of Friends."
London. 8vo. 1885. 14¾
<small>His death occurred on the 23rd of 3rd Mo., 1891, aged 31 years.</small>

BROWN, Edward, of *North America*. Poet.
—— Echoes of Nature. (Poems).
Philadelphia. 12mo. 1845.

BROWN'S (Francis) *Wife*, of *Brighton*.
—— Little Tommy. [ANON.]
Reprinted. 12mo. *Brighton*, 1856.

BROWN, Isaac, continued from Catalogue, Vol. I., p. 326, now of *Kendal* (1875).
—— The Interpretation of Scripture, in its relation to Jewish Modes of Thought.
By Isaac Brown. *Reprinted from "The Friends' Quarterly Examiner."*
London: F. B. Kitto, 5, Bishopsgate Without.
8vo. 1869. 2¾

—— The LORD'S SUPPER : A Scriptural Argument in relation to its True Character and Permanent Obligation. By Isaac Brown.
Second Edition.
York: William Sessions, 15, Low Ousegate.
London : F. Bowyer Kitto, 5, Bishopsgate St. Without.
Price Twopence. 8vo. 1872. 1⅝
London : The Friends' Tract Association
16mo. 1873.

BROWN, William Henry, son of ISAAC BROWN.
—— On Babylonian, &c.

BROWN, Josiah, of *London*, after of *Norwich*.
—— How Readest Thou ? Christian Truth as held by the Society of Friends.
Reprinted the 2nd edition. 12mo. 1873. 1⅗
<small>He died the 22nd of 9th Mo., 1877, aged 69 years, and was buried at Norwich.</small>

BROWN, Potto, of
—— Potto Brown : The Village Philanthropist.
St. Ives : Printed. 1878. 14¾
<small>He died in the year 1871.</small>

BROWN, William, Junr., of *Preston*, near *North Shields*, continued from Catalogue, Vol. I., p. 328.
<small>(?) He died 23rd of 2nd Mo., 1871, aged 56 years. See "The Friend" for 4th Mo., 1871.</small>

BROWNE, Samuel, of *Leicester*.
—— An Account and Testimony of 𝖘𝖆𝖒𝖚𝖊𝖑 𝕭𝖗𝖔𝖜𝖓𝖊, concerning his dear MOTHER, Sarah Browne, Widow.
      12mo. (A Reprint of 1693.)

BRYCE, James, of *Manchester*.
—— Ought Christian men to engage in War ? No date. 4pp.
—— How to avoid War and live in Peace.   " "
—— Who slew all these ?   " "
—— The Sword and the Gospel.   " "
—— Justice and the Conqueror's Sword.   " "
—— Patriotism.   " "
  He died the 11th of the 2nd Mo., 1869, aged 63 years.

BUCKLEY, Joseph, of *Manchester*.
—— and others.—To Friends of Manchester Meeting.
           Folio. 1866. 1
—— Memoirs of Joseph Buckley. Edited by his daughter. (Portrait).
  Glasgow : Robert Smeal, Crosshill, Printer.
         8vo. 1874. 4⅛
  He died the 27th of 9th month, 1868, aged 61 years.

BUDD, Thomas, of *Somersetshire* after of *Pennsylvania*.
—— *Good Order Established* in Pennsylvania and New Jersey in America.
  Reprinted in America.

BUDGE, Frances Anne, of *Stoke Newington*.
—— 𝕬𝖓𝖓𝖆𝖑𝖘 𝖔𝖋 𝖙𝖍𝖊 𝕰𝖆𝖗𝖑𝖞 𝕱𝖗𝖎𝖊𝖓𝖉𝖘. A Series of Biographical Sketches. By Frances Anne Budge.
 [Reprinted from "The Friends' Quarterly Examiner."]
  With Preface by Edward Backhouse.
  " We are nothing, Christ is all."
         GEORGE FOX.
 London : Samuel Harris & Co., 5, Bishopsgate Without.   8vo. 1877. 29⅜

  CONTENTS.—William Caton - - - - page 1
   John Audland and his Friends - - - 28
   Edward Burrough - - - - - 53
   Elizabeth Stirredge - - - - - 72
   William Dewsbury and his Words of Counsel
    and Consolation - - - - 92
   John Crook - - - - - - 104
   Stephen Crisp and his Sermons - - - 119
   John Banks - - - - - - 136
   Humphry Smith and his Works - - - 157
   Mary Fisher - - - - - - 185
   The Martyrs of Boston and their Friends - - 208
   Passages in the Life of John Gratton - - 238
   James Dickenson and his Friends - - - 251
   William Edmundson - - - - 285

BUDGE, Frances Anne, *continued.*
 Contents—*continued.*   Page.
  William Ellis and his Friends - - - - 316
  Richard Claridge - - - - - 347
  Thomas Story - - - - - - 372
  Gilbert Latey and his Friends - - - - 401
  George Whitehead - - - - - 428
——The Barclays of Ury, including a Sketch of Samuel Watson and Roger Hebden.   8vo. 1881.
——Annals of the Early Friends.
 2nd edition.
        Thick 8vo. 1886. 31
——New series. Richard Davies and other Biographical Sketches.   8vo.
——A Missionary Life : Stephen Grellett.
 London, Printed. . . . 8vo. 1886. 8
   Annals (in *packets*).
——THOMAS ELLWOOD and other worthies of the olden times. By FRANCES ANNE BUDGE.
 London : James Nisbet & Co., 21, Berners Street.
        8vo. 1891. 165pp.

BUDGE, Jane, of (her Sister) *Stoke Newington.*
——Poems. By Jane Budge. Author of "Our Country's Story," "Great Events in England's History," &c.
        16mo. 1877. 4¾
——Glimpses of GEORGE FOX and his Friends. By JANE BUDGE.
 London : S. W. Partridge & Co., 9, Paternoster Row, E.C.—Leominster: The Orphans' Printing Press, 10 & 12, Broad Street. 8vo. [1888.] 20½
——William Penn (Life of)
 Leominster, printed. . . . 8vo. [1884.] 5

BURROWS, Joseph, was born at *Southminster.* He was a Wesleyan Methodist.
——A Brief Memorial of Joseph Burrows, who died at Maldon, *Sixteenth of 2nd Month, 1864,* aged 32 years. (Edited by a Friend ?)
 Sudbury : J. Wright, Market Hill. 18mo. ? 1864.

*BUGG, Francis, *continued* from Catalogue, Vol. I., p. 332.
——The Last Will of George Fox.
 7th Edition. . . . . . B. 1703. 1
——A Third Bomb thrown into the Quakers' Camp or, a Farther Manifestation of a Spirit of Persecution in the Quakers, &c.
 London, printed.   . Fol. 1706. ½

BUGG, Francis, *continued.*

——Some further consideration on the Quakers' Bill now depending,—for their Solemn Affirmation, &c.
Fol. May 23. 1715.   ½

BURY, Richard, of *London,—continued* from "Catalogue," Vol. I., p. 369.

——See JOHN MULLINER.—A TESTIMONY against Perriwigs, and Perriwig, &c. " Reprinted in obedience to the LORD, by *Richard Bury*, 1708."   4to.   1708.   3

BUXTON, Anna, afterwards Forster. See ANNA FORSTER.

*BUXTON, Thomas Fowell,—*continued* from " Catalogue," Vol. I., p. 372.

——THE REMEDY, by Thomas Fowell Buxton, Esq.
"Thou sellest thy people for nought, and dost not increase thy wealth by their price."—*44th Psalm, 12th verse.*
London : Printed by W Clowes & Sons, Stamford Street.
This Edition is not to be published.
Title page, ii. ; Text, 152, 8vo. (No date.) 9⅜
NOTE.—On the Paper Cover is written, " *Private and Confidential.*

——Severity of Punishment. Speech—May 23rd. 1821.
London : Printed by T. C. Hansard, Peterborough Court, Fleet Street, and sold by John and Arthur Arch, Cornhill.   .   8vo.   1821.   4¾

BUTCHER, Robert, Steward to the Duke of Bedford.

——Letter to Sophia Hume. In Comly's Miscellany, Vol. IV., p. 235.
Worth reprinting.
Query, whether a Friend ? and query should be " Boucher," the editor of three books of Jacob Behmen's (published by a gentleman retired from business).

BYRD, Ann, daughter of Joseph and Elizabeth Byrd, of *New York.*

———A Brief Memorial of the Monthly Meeting of New York concerning her, with some extracts from her memorandums.
In Comly's Miscellany, Vol. IV., p. 227.

——Narrative, Pious Meditations, and Religious Exercises of Ann Byrd.
Reprinted, second edition.
Byberry : Published by John Comly.
.   16mo.   1844.   4⅜

C.

*C. (J.W.) *i.e.* JOHN WILLIAM CUDWORTH, of *Leeds*.

——QUAKERISM and THE CHURCH : being my Reasons for leaving the Society of Friends and joining the Church. J.W.C.
    London : *F. B. Kitto, 5, Bishopsgate Street Without, E.C.* . . . 8vo. 1870. 6
    (*Edward Baines and Sons, Printers, Leeds*).
    NOTE.—Answered by J.B. in his Pamphlet, entitled, "Ritualism" or "Quakerism?" 8vo. 1870.

CADBURY, James, of *Banbury* in *Oxfordshire*. A Minister.

——To the Frequenters of Country Markets and Fairs. (On Alcoholic drinks).
    8vo. *Banbury*, 30th of 10th Month. . 1866. ¼

——WHITE MEAT. *To the Editor of the Banbury Guardian*. (On the dwarfish character of the agricultural population).
    Folio. *Banbury*, 6th of 8th Month. . 1867. ½

——" England Expects every Man to do his Duty."
    LORD NELSON.
    (A Paper on a "Permissive Prohibitory Liquor Bill.")
    John Potts, General Machine Printer, 51, Parson's Street, Banbury.
    Large Broadside. *Banbury*, 15th of 2nd Month. 1875. 1
    He died the 17th of 2nd Month, 1888, aged 85 years.

CADWALLADER, Priscilla, of *Philadelphia*.

——Memoir of Priscilla Cadwallader.
    Philadelphia. . . 18mo. 141 pp.

——Sermon . . . . . 1830.

*CALLAWAY, Henry, D.D., Oxon., L.R.C.P., first Bishop of St. John's, South Africa, was born 17th of 1st month, 1817. He was educated at the Grammar School at *Crediton, Devonshire*. Soon after leaving school, being brought in contact with some members of the Society of Friends, he began to read Quaker literature, and then became a member of the Society.

After which he entered the medical profession, commencing his Studies at *Bridgewater*. He subsequently pursued them at *St. Bartholomew's Hospital, London*, and commenced practice in London.

He gradually became convinced that he ought to re-join the Church of England, and ultimately became a Bishop.

*CALLAWAY, Henry, continued.
   For further particulars concerning him, see The Friend for 5th month, 1890, page 118 ; and for his works whilst a Friend, written from 1841 to 1851, see The Catalogue of Friends' Books, Vol 1, p. 375-6.
—— The Last Word of Modern Thought.
   Natal : Printed. . . . 8vo. 1866.
—— Nursery Tales of the Zulus, in Zulu and English.
   Natal. . . . . 1868.
—— A Volume of Sermons.
   He died at Ottery St. Mary, Devon, the 26th of 3rd Month, 1890, in his 74th year.

CALLOWHILL, Thomas, of Bristol, was the Father of HANNAH, the second wife of WILLIAM PENN.
—— Fac-Simile of his Autograph.
   (See Coleman's Catalogue of Original Deeds, &c., of William Penn, 1870.)

CAMBRIDGE, John, of No. 19, Walnut-Tree Walk, Lambeth, Surrey.
—— To the MINISTERS, and THOSE who love and fear the LORD, in the FRIENDS' Society. My Dear Friends, &c.—6th of 6th Month, 1783. . Folio. [1783].

CAMM, Anne.   } See Catalogue, Vol. I., p. 376-7.
CAMM, Thomas. }
—— A MEMOIR of the LIFE OF ANNE CAMM, and A Brief account of THOMAS CAMM ; Ministers of the Gospel, in the Society of Friends.
   York : Printed and Sold by John Lewis Linney, 15, Low Ousgate.
   [Price, 1s. per dozen.] . . 12mo. 1841.
   Anne Camm died the 30th of the 9th Month, 1705, in her 79th year.
   Thomas Camm died the 13th of the 1st Month, 1707-8, in the 67th year of his age.

CAPPER, Elizabeth N.
—— Voices of the Twilight and other poems, &c.
   London : S. Harris & Co. . 8vo. 1882.

CAPPER, Jasper, M.D.
—— The Turkish or Hot-Air Bath, with direction for its use.
   Hastings. . . . 16mo. 1865.

CAPPER, Mary, continued from Catalogue, Vol. I., p. 380.
—— Memoir of Mary Capper (abridged).
   Darlington. . . . . 1860.
—— A Memoir of MARY CAPPER, late of Birmingham, England.

CAPPER, Mary, *continued.*
Philadelphia : *For Sale at Friends' Book Store,*
304, Arch Street. . 8vo. 1882. 468 pp.

CAPPER, Samuel, continued from Catalogue, Vol. I., p. 380.
——Reply to the Bishop of Gloucester's Letter to his Clergy.
Hill, Printer, Bristol. . 1851. 4 pp.

——Sheam *v.* Capper ?

CAPPER, Samuel James.—Born 7th of 6th Mo., 1840. Son of Jasper Capper, of Liverpool, and grandson of Samuel Capper, of Bristol. His mother, Jane Fryer Gilpin, was eldest sister of Charles Gilpin, and niece of Joseph Sturge—now of the National Liberal Club, London.
> In 1870, contributed a long series of letters to the "*Times*" from every part of France during the Franco-German War, re-published by Bentley.
> In 1880, contributed to the "*Times*" series of letters, which formed basis of large illustrated work.
> He is also a frequent contributor to the "*Christian World;*" author of article in *Contemporary* on Siena.

——Sketches of and from Jean Paul Richter. . 1858.

——WANDERINGS IN WAR TIME : being notes of two Journeys taken in France and Germany, in the Autumn of 1870, and the Spring of 1871. By SAMUEL JAMES CAPPER.
London : *Richard Bentley and Son, New Burlington Street,* 𝔓𝔲𝔟𝔩𝔦𝔰𝔥𝔢𝔯𝔰 𝔦𝔫 𝔒𝔯𝔡𝔦𝔫𝔞𝔯𝔶 𝔱𝔬 𝔥𝔢𝔯 𝔐𝔞𝔧𝔢𝔰𝔱𝔶. . . . 8vo. 1871. 2/

——Contents of the above. . . 4to. 1871. ½

——The Shores and Cities of the Boden See. Rambles in 1879 and 1880, with Maps ... and ... Etchings. H. Smidth-Pecht.
T. De la Rue & Co.: London, 1881.
8vo. [1880.] pp. xxvi. 452.

——𝔓𝔞𝔵 𝔦𝔫 𝔗𝔢𝔯𝔯𝔞.—NOTES of the POPULAR PEACE CONGRESS, held at Rome, in the Palace of the Fine Arts, *Sunday, Nov.* 29th, 1891.
Rome : *Printed by the Società Laziale Piazza del Popolo, 8-14.* . . . 4to. 1891. 15pp.

CARLILE, Ann, was the daughter of DANIEL and ELIZABETH CARLILE, of *Plumstead,* in *Bucks County, Pennsylvania.*

——Account of her. In Comly's Miscellany, Vol. IV., p. 61.

CARPENTER, Samuel, of *Pennsylvania*.

———Biographical Memoir of Samuel Carpenter, *with facsimile of his autograph*.
>See Bowden's " History of Friends in America," Vol. II. Pennsylvania and New Jersey, page 270.
>He died in the year 1713.

CARVER, Richard, Ship Master of *London*, dyed at Corke, 8th Month 19th, 1670, aged —
>Munster Q. M. Registers.

*CASSIN, John, of *Philadelphia*.
>" An excellent Ornithologist, was a West-town Scholar. He is the Author of many papers in the Smithsonian publications, in the Journal of the Academy of Natural Sciences and of the Birds of California."

———Illustrations of the Birds of California, Texas, Oregon, British and Russian America; intended to contain Descriptions and Figures of all North American Birds not given by former American Authors; and a general Synopsis of North American Ornithology. By John Cassin. 50 Coloured Plates.
>*Philadelphia* :
>Royal 8vo. 1856. 294 pp.

CATALOGUES.

———A Catalogue of Books belonging to Colchester Monthly Meeting.
>*London* : *Printed by Phillips & Fardon, George Yard, Lombard Street.* . 16mo. 1805. ½

———A List of Books belonging to Tottenham Monthly Meeting of Friends.
>*London* : *Printed by W. Phillips, George Yard, Lombard Street.* . . 12mo. 1818. ½

———Catalogue of the Books belonging to the Library of the Four Monthly Meetings of Friends of PHILADELPHIA ; with the Rules for the government of the Library.
>*Philadelphia* : *Printed by Joseph Rakestraw.*
>12mo. 1831. 7

———Catalogue of Books belonging to the LIBRARY of LEWES AND CHICHESTER Monthly Meeting, with its Rules and Regulations.
>*Brighton* : *Printed by Arthur Wallis, 5, Bartholomews.* . . . 12mo. 1850. ½

———Catalogue of Books for Sale at FRIENDS' BOOK STORE, No. 304, Arch Street, Philadelphia.
>*Thomas W. Stuckey, Printer, No. 403, North Sixth Street.* . . 12mo. 1869. ½

CATALOGUES, *continued.*
—-Catalogue of the LIBRARIES of EARLHAM COLLEGE.
> *Richmond, Ind.: Telegram Steam Book and Job Press.* 8vo. 1870. 5½

—-List of Books in the BANBURY FRIENDS' LIBRARY.
> 8vo. 1870. ¼

—-A List of Books belonging to Tottenham Monthly Meeting of Friends.
> *Printed by G. H. Farrington, 17 & 19, Great Knight Rider Street, Doctors' Commons, London, E.C.* . . . Large B. [.] 1

—-CATALOGUES OF BOOKS in THE LIBRARIES belonging to the Preparative Meeting of the SOCIETY OF FRIENDS in DARLINGTON.
> **Darlington**: *Harrison Penney, Printer, &c., Prebend Row.* . . . 8vo. 1885. 5

—-BEVAN-NAISH LIBRARY. **Catalogue.**
PART I.—BOOKS.
> *Birmingham: White & Pike, Limited, Moor Street Printing Works.* . . 12mo. 1891. 1½

CHALK, Thomas, of *Kingston-upon-Thames, Surrey*, was born at Brighton, 1786, and sent when 9 years old to Ackworth School. Continued from Catalogue, Vol. I., p. 398.

—-Life and Writings of John Whitehead.
> [Edited by THOMAS CHALK.] Foolscap 8vo. 1852. 18¾
>> He died the 2nd of 2nd Month, 1869, aged 82 years.
>> A Minister. For further particulars concerning him, see *The Annual Monitor for 1870.*

CHALKLEY, Thomas, born in *Southwark, London*, afterwards of *Philadelphia*, lastly of *Frankfort, Pennsylvania*, died in *Tortola*, 1741.

—-A Small Broom to sweep away the falshoods which Daniel Leeds has Thrown into the way of Thos. Chalkley.
>> NOTE.—This is an appendix to "Some brief Observations Made on Daniel Leeds his Book, Entituled 'The Second Part of the Mystery of Fox-Craft.'" By Caleb Pusey.
> *Printed at Philadelphia by Joseph Reyners.*
>> Small 4to. 1706. 4
>> In the Library of the *Meeting for Sufferings, Philadelphia.*
>> Since my Catalogue was printed in 1867, I have discovered through CHAS. R. HILDEBURN'S "Issues of the Pennsylvania Press," that the above was issued as an appendix to Caleb Pusey's book as above, and I now find that it was DANIEL LEEDS to which the note in my book referred to in one of his almanacks. See Vol. I., p. 399.

CHALKLEY, Thomas, *continued.*
—— Forcing A Maintenance Not Warrantable from the Holy Scripture, for a Minister of the Gospel. Being An Answer to some false and Erronius pages, writ by Joseph Metcalfe tending to stir up Persecution. By Thomas Chalkley.
 Printed at Philadelphia [*by Andrew Bradford.*]
          16mo. 1714.
—— A Letter to a Friend in Ireland, containing a Relation of some sorrowful Instances of the sad Effects of Intemperance as a Warning to Young People. By Thomas Chalkley.
 Third Edition.
 Philadelphia : Samuel Keimer.   1723.
—— A Collection of the Works of Thomas Chalkley. In Two Volumes. The Second Edition.
 Philadelphia : Printed and Sold by James Chattin, in Church Alley. Small 8vo. 1754. 3 6
—— MEMOIRES de THOMAS CHALKLEY, extraits principalement D'UN JOURNAL DE SA VIE et DE SES VOYAGES.
 Paris, Typographie de Firmin, Didot Freres, rue Jacob, 56. . . 12mo. 1840. 3½

CHAMPION, Richard, of *Bristol.* Connected with Cookworthy in the Porcelain manufactory.
  Portraits of Richard Champion and his Wife. From Jewitt's "Ceramic Art in Great Britain," in Gray's Catalogue of the late L. Jewitt's books.

CHARLETON, Robert, of *Bristol.* Continued from Catalogue, Vol. I., p. 405.
—— Thoughts on Barclay's Apology addressed to the Society of Friends, and especially to the Members of the Meeting for Sufferings. By Robert Charleton.
 Bristol: Printed by Ackland & Son, Dolphin Street. . . . 8vo. 1868. 1
  Answered by William Irwin, William Lean, and William L. Bellows, also by T.G. (see "An Antidote, &c."), and by an Anonymous Writer (see, under date 1868, Charleton *v.* Barclay).
—— Brief Thoughts on the ATONEMENT. By Robert Charleton.
 Bristol : Ackland & Son, Printers and Stationers, Union Street. . . 8vo. 1869. 1
  This is a reprint, with some slight amendments, of an article which appeared in the *Friends' Quarterly Examiner,* with a brief Preface. For private circulation only.

               1

CHARLETON, Robert, *continued.*
—— Brief Thoughts on THE ATONEMENT, By Robert
Charleton.
 London : *Friends' Tract Association, Bishopsgate
 Without, E.C.*
 Price, One Halfpenny. . . 8vo. 1879.   ¾
—— Strictures on a Pamphlet, &c., by the Rev. Jacob Stanley,
in a Letter addressed to the Wesleyan Methodists of
the Bristol North Circuit. By Robert Charleton.
Second Thousand, 2d.
—— Observations on Mr. Stanley's Second Tract. By Robert
Charleton.
—— MEMOIR of the late Robert Charleton (by E. ASH and
J. S. FRY) ; also, 𝕭𝖗𝖎𝖊𝖋 𝕿𝖍𝖔𝖚𝖌𝖍𝖙𝖘 𝖔𝖓 𝖙𝖍𝖊 𝕬𝖙𝖔𝖓𝖊𝖒𝖊𝖓𝖙 ;
and a Lecture on the Protestant Reformation in
England.
 *London : Samuel Harris & Co., Publishers, 5,
 Bishopsgate Street Without, E.C.*
 One Shilling. . . . 8vo. [1873.]   3½
—— MEMOIR of ROBERT CHARLETON. 𝕮𝖔𝖒𝖕𝖎𝖑𝖊𝖉
𝖈𝖍𝖎𝖊𝖋𝖑𝖞 𝖋𝖗𝖔𝖒 𝖍𝖎𝖘 𝕷𝖊𝖙𝖙𝖊𝖗𝖘. Edited by his Sister-in-
Law, ANNA F. FOX. (With a *Portrait and fac-
simile of his Autograph*).
 *London: Samuel Harris & Co., 5, Bishopsgate
 Street Without.*
 [*R. Barrett & Son, Printers, 13, Mark Lane,
 London.*] . . . 8vo. 1873.   19¼
 Reprinted—The 2nd Edition, with considerable ad-
  ditions (same imprint). . 8vo. 1876.
 <small>He died on the 5th of 12th Month, 1872, aged 63 years, and
 his remains were interred in the Friends' Burial Ground,
 Bristol.</small>

*CHASE, Pliny Earle, M.A., of Harvard College, *Cambridge,
U.S.A.*, was born at *Worcester, Massachusetts*, the
18th of 8th Month, 1820.
    PUBLICATIONS.
 Elements of Arithmetic. Parts First and Second.
  Philadelphia, 1844.
 The Common-School Arithmetic, designed for learners
  of every class, and particularly for those who are
  desirous of acquiring a thorough Knowledge of
  Practical Mathematics. Worcester (Mass.)
        12mo. 1848.   12
  I. The Primary School Arithmetic. 18mo.   4½
  II. The Grammar School Arithmetic. 12mo.   11
  III. Arithmetic Practically Applied. 12mo.   16

*CHASE, Pliny Earle, *continued*.

By Horace Mann, LL.D., the First Secretary of the Massachusetts Board of Education, and Pliny E. Chase, A.M., Author of " The Common-School Arithmetic. Philadelphia, 1850.

The Philosophy of George Fox. An Address delivered before the Alumni Association of Friends' Yearly Meeting School, at their Sixth Annual Meeting, at Newport, 1864.

And the following papers in the publications of the American Philosophical Society.

1—Sanscrit and English Analogues, Proceedings, v. 7, p. 177-291. 1860.
2—Chinese and Indo-European Roots and Analogues, Proceedings, v. 8, p. 5-48. 1861.
3—Intellectual Symbolism, Transactions, v. 12, p. 463-594. 1862.
4—Description of a Chinese Seal, Pro., v. 9, p. 139-141. 1863.
5—Chinese and Hebrew Analogues, Pro., v. 9, p. 145. 1863.
6—Probable Asiatic Origin of the Alphabet, Proceedings, v. 9, p. 172-182. 1863.
7—Chinese and Aryan Affinity, Pro., v. 9, p. 231-232. 1863.
8—Catalogue of Trade Tokens, during the Rebellion, Proceedings, v. 9, p. 242-258. 1863.
9—Comparative Etymology of the Yoruba Language, Transactions, v. 13, p. 35-68. 1863.
10—Probability of Accidental Linguistic Resemblances, Transactions, v. 13, p. 25-33. 1863.
11—On the Barometer, as an indication of the earth's rotation and the sun's distance, Proceedings, v. 9, p. 283-288. 1863.
12—Barometric Indications of a Resisting Aether, Proceedings, v. 9, p. 291-294. 1864.
13—Barometric Fluctuations and Temperature, Proceedings, v. 9, p. 345-349. 1864.
14—Gravity and Mechanical Polarity, Proceedings, v. 9, p. 355-360. 1864.
15—Connection of Terrestrial Magnetism with Atmospheric Currents, Proceedings, v. 9, p. 367-371. 1864.
16—Aerial Tides, Proceedings, v. 9, p. 395-399.° 1864.
17—Principal Causes of Barometric Fluctuations, Proceedings, v. 9, p. 405-411. 1864.
18—Comparative Fitness of Languages for Musical Expression, Proceedings, v. 9, p. 419-420. 1864.
19—On some primitive names of Deity, Proceedings, v. 9, p. 420-424. 1864.
20—On Terrestrial Magnetism as " a mode of motion," Proceedings, v. 9, p. 427-440. 1864.
21—Numerical Relations of Gravity and Magnetism,† Proceedings, v. 9, p. 487-495. 1864.
22—Numerical Relations of Gravity and Magnetism, Transactions, v. 13, p. 117-136. 1864.
23—Radical Significance of Numerals, Pro., v. 10, p. 18-23. 1865.
24—Copto-Egyptian Vocabulary, Pro., v. 10. p. 69-94. 1865.

*CHASE, Pliny Earle, *continued*.
- 25—Influence of Gravity on Magnetic Declination, Proceedings, v. 10, p. 97-104. 1865.
- 26—Gravity and Magnetic Inclination, Proceedings, v. 10, p. 111-118. 1865.
- 27—Experiments upon the Mechanical Polarization of Magnetic Needles, under the influence of fluid currents, or " lines of force," Proceedings, v. 10, p. 151-166. 1865.
- 28—Observations on Skylight Polarization, Proceedings, v. 10, p. 196-197. 1866.
- 29—On the comparative visibility of Arago's, Babinet's, and Brewster's Neutral Points, Pro., v. 10, p. 223-226. 1866.
- 30—Relations of Temperature to Gravity and Density, Proceedings, v. 10, p. 261-269. 1866.

Aggregate of above papers in publications of A.P.S. Society.
340 pages, octavo, 21¼ sheets.
195 pages, quarto, 12¼ sheets.

The 11th Article was copied by the Abbi Moigno, in his scientific annual. This and many of the other articles have been copied by Silliman's American Journal of Science, London, Dublin, and Edinburgh Philosophical Magazine, &c.

° Published also in Proceedings of the Royal Society, June 16, 1864.

† Magellanic Premium (a gold medal) awarded.

(Although a birthright member of the Society of Friends, my connection with the Society terminated some years ago. —P. E. C.)

CHASE, Thomas, M.A., of Harvard College, *Cambridge*, and now Professor at Haverford College, *Pennsylvania*, was born the 16th of the 6th Month, 1827, at *Worcester, Massachusetts*.

——Cicero on Immortality: The Tusculan Disputations, Book First; the Dream of Scipio; and Extracts from the Dialogues on Old Age and Friendship. With English Notes (and an Introduction).
Cambridge (Mass.) . . 16mo. 1851. 14
——The same, Third Edition 1856, revised; and since reprinted in eight editions.
——(The Scholar's Ideal). An Address before the Euethean Association, at Haverford College. 16mo. 1856. 1½
——Goethe and Schiller. An Address before the Haverford Loganian Society. . . 16mo. 1859. 2½
——The Connection between Æsthetic Culture and Religion. An Address delivered at Newport before the Alumni Association of the Friends' School, at Providence.
8vo. 1860. 1¼
——Hellas, her Monuments and Scenery. 16mo. 1863. 14¼

CHASE, Thomas, *continued*.

——An Address on the Character and Example of President Lincoln, delivered before the Athenæum and Everett Societies of Haverford College. . 16mo. 1865. 2¼

——The Homeric Question (An Article in the North American Review for October, 1850.) . 8vo. 21pp.

——The Life and Poetry of Wordsworth. (An Article in the North American Review for October, 1851.)
8vo. 22pp.

——The Early Days of Hellas. (An Article in the North American Review for October, 1858.) . 8vo. 27pp.
The same, reprinted in pamphlet form. . 1858.

——The Churches of Christendom responsible for the Continuance of War. By T. Chase, M.A.
American Peace Association.
See "Friend." 10th Month, '69.

CHASE, William Henry, of *Union Springs, Cayuga Co., New York.*

——DAY BY DAY : a Compilation from the writings of ANCIENT AND MODERN FRIENDS. By William Henry Chase. . . . . . 1869.
Third Edition.
Auburn : Dennis Bros. & Thorne, Publishers.
8vo. 1870. 27⅛
NOTE.—At the end of this edition are "Testimonials," in favour of the book.
Reprinted--The Fourth Edition (same imprint).
8vo. 1871. 27
NOTE.—Contains a nice portrait of Joseph Talleot, also a frontispiece, a group, viz., George Fox, Elizabeth Fry, Stephen Grellet, Hannah C. Backhouse, Richard Reynolds, George Howland, and Joseph J. Gurney.

CHEW, Samuel, of *Pennsylvania.*

——The Speech of Samuel Chew, Esq., Chief Justice of the Government of New-Castle, Kent and Sussex, upon Delaware : Delivered from the Bench to the Grand-Jury of the County of New-Castle, Nov. 21, 1741 ; and now published at their Request.
Philadelphia : Printed and Sold by B. Franklin, M.,DCC.,XLI. . Small 4to. 1741. 16pp.
Reprinted—The Second Edition.
Philadelphia : Printed and Sold by B. Franklin.
Small 4to. 1741. 16pp.

——The Speech of Samuel Chew, Esq., Chief Justice of the Government of New-Castle, Kent and Sussex, upon Delaware : Delivered from the Bench to the Grand-

CHEW, Samuel, *continued.*
    Jury of the County of New-Castle, Aug. 20, 1742 ; and now published at their Request.
        Philadelphia : Printed and Sold by B. Franklin, M., DCC., XLII. . 8vo. 1742. 16pp.
—— The Speech of Samuel Chew, Esq., Chief Judge of the Counties of New-Castle, Kent and Sussex, on Delaware : On the Lawfulness of Defence against an armed Enemy. Delivered from the Bench to the Grand Jury of the County of New-Castle, Nov. 21, 1741. First published at the request of said Grand Jury; and now re-published by desire of several Gentlemen.
        Philadelphia : Printed and Sold by R. Aitken, Front Street, M., DCC., LXXV. 8vo. 1775. 8pp.

CHILD, L. Maria. (Not a Member).
—— Life of Benjamin Lay.—American Anti-Slavery Society.

CHILTON, Thomas, of *Reading, Berkshire.*
—— The WAY of deliverance from BONDAGE. Set forth in love to the simple, who have erred for lack of knowledge. The Redemption of the holy *Seed,* is through Judgement on that which hath hindered its growth *Isa.* i., 27, and purification is by the fire of *Zion,* and and the furnace of *Jerusalem,* the which comes to be known by owning and submitting unto the power of the burning *Light* in its operation of Judgement against the transgressor, which breaks the peace of the wicked that he hath in his wickedness, and hereby through submission unto the sword of the Spirit of Judgement is learned to answer the requirings thereof, by which man comes to be purged, and made a vessel unto honour, meet for the Master's use.
    " *Oh! prepare to meet the Lord in the way of his Judgements, for all his wayes are Judgement.*"—Deut. 32, 4.
    By one that desires the enlargement of the righteous *Seed,* which is imprisoned in the unconverted.—THOMAS CHILTON.
        London, Printed for Thomas Simmons, at the Bull and Mouth, near Aldersgate, 1659.
                          Small 8vo. 1659. ½

‖CHORLEY, Henry Fothergill, of *London.*
—— HENRY FOTHERGILL CHORLEY : 𝕬𝖚𝖙𝖔𝖇𝖎𝖔𝖌𝖗𝖆𝖕𝖍𝖞, 𝕸𝖊𝖒𝖔𝖎𝖗 𝖆𝖓𝖉 𝕷𝖊𝖙𝖙𝖊𝖗𝖘. Compiled by Henry G. Hewlett. In Two Volumes. (*With a Portrait*).
        London : Richard Bentley & Son, 𝕻𝖚𝖇𝖑𝖎𝖘𝖍𝖊𝖗𝖘 𝖎𝖓 𝕺𝖗𝖉𝖎𝖓𝖆𝖗𝖞 𝖙𝖔 𝕳𝖊𝖗 𝕸𝖆𝖏𝖊𝖘𝖙𝖞.

‖CHORLEY, Henry Fothergill, *continued*.
> *(Printed by Clowes & Son, Stamford Street and Charing Cross).*
> Collation—Preface and Contents XII.
> > Vol. I. 344 pages.
> > Vol. II. Title Page and Contents, VIII.
> > > Text 340 pages.
> > > > He was born the 15th December, 1808, and died 16th February, 1872, aged 63 years and 2 months, and was interred in Brompton Cemetery.

‖CHORLEY, John Rutter.
——Catalogue of the Select Library of the late John Rutter Chorley, Esq.
> *Sold by Puttick & Simpson, Nov. 27th, 28th, 1867.*

CHRISTY, William Miller.

CHRISTY, Robert Miller, of *Saffron Walden*.
——The FLYING SERPENT, or Strange News out of ESSEX, being a True Relation of a Monstrous Serpent which hath divers times been seen at a Parish called *Henham-on-the-Mount*, within four miles of *Saffron Walden, &c.*
> LONDON : *Printed and Sold by Peter Lillicrup, in Clerkenwell Close.* . . . [1669.]
> SAFFRON WALDEN : *Reproduced in fac-simile by W. Masland, with Introduction, by Robert Miller Christy.*
> Price Sixpence. 4to. 1885. 1½

CHURCHMAN, John, Author of " MAGNETIC ATLAS," was the Son of *George Churchman*, and the *Grandson* of the *Preacher*.

CLARK, Dougan, M.D., of *America*.
——CHRIST OUR SANCTIFICATION. By Dougan Clark, M.D.
> *New Vienna, Ohio : Friends' Publishing House Press* . . . 16mo. 1876. 20pp. or ⅝

——Instructions to Christian Converts. By Dougan Clark, M.D.
> *Leominster : Orphans' Printing Press, 10 and 12, Broad Street.* . . . 120pp.

CLARK, Joseph, of *Doncaster*.
——LIFE of JOSEPH CLARK, with SELECTIONS from his CORRESPONDENCE. Edited by his Son, Henry Ecroyd Clark.
> > " How happy for us that there is a city that hath foundations, whose builder and maker is God ! Yes, sooner or

CLARK, Joseph, *continued.*
later, our dependence on earth must be broken. How blessed to know this conviction to abide in the mind and blend harmoniously with the conscientious performance of every day duties, which, however trivial in themselves, are of vast importance as essential parts of that discipline which aids in a preparation for a brighter scene."
—*Extract from a letter from Joseph Clark.*

For Private Circulation only.
Leeds: Printed by Edward Baines and Sons.
         8vo. 1870. 21¼

NOTE.—Contains a photographic portrait of Joseph Clark. —a view of Upper Haugh, the Residence of Joseph Clark. —CHART (A) showing Joseph Clark's Descent from the families of Clark and Ecroyd.—CHART (B) showing Ann Clark's Descent from the families of Firth and Woodhead.

CLARK, Henry Ecroyd, of 5, *Grosvenor Place, Leeds.*
See above.

‖ CLARK, Robert, of
——A SHORT DESCRIPTION of the ISLAND of ST. JOHN, in the GULPH of ST. LAWRENCE, NORTH AMERICA.
We whose Names are hereunto subscribed, do, for the satisfaction of those who may be inclined to purchase Land of ROBERT CLARK, *unanimously recommend the Plan, &c.—June 25th, 1779.*
  WILLIAM COOKWORTHY, Plymouth;
  JOHN TOWNSEND, Fenchurch St., London;
  (and others).
        Folio. [1779.] 1

CLAUS, John, of *Amsterdam,* in *Holland.*
——VERTOOGH DER WAARHEYT Die na de Godzaligheyt is, Uyt de Heylige Schriften; Door J.C. *In zyn Ouderdom van 86 Jaaren,* Zynen, Nageslachte, Geloofsgenóten, en andere Goede Bekenden, Ter zyner Gedachtenisse, en Opscherpinge van Liefde en goede Werken. Overgelevert *op den 11. April Ao.* 1727. Zynde de Vyftigste Verjaardagh van zyn staande Houwelyk, met zyn Ge-eerde Echtgenoot A.M.H. t'Amsterdam, By JACOB CLAUS.
      Small 8vo. Ao. 1727. 12

CLEMENT, John, of *Haddonfield, New Jersey.* (Not a Member.)
——𝔊𝔢𝔫𝔢𝔞𝔩𝔬𝔤𝔶 of the THREE DAUGHTERS of SAMUEL and ROSANNA COLLINS, late of Waterford Township, in Gloucester County, and State of New Jersey. (In the Paternal and Maternal line.) Collected and Arranged from Deeds, Wills, Memoranda, &c., by JOHN CLEMENT, Haddonfield, New Jersey.

CLEMENT, John, *continued.*
> *Philadelphia : The Leisenring Steam Printing House, Jayne's Building, Nos. 237 and 239, Dock Street.* . . . 8vo. 1871. 1

CLIBBORN (Colonel), Salvationist.
——Bought up !
> *Glasgow* : *R. L. Allan, 143, Sauchiehall Street.*
> *London* : *Alfred Holness, 14, Paternoster Row.*
> 24mo. No date. 16pp.

CLIFTON, Elinor, of
——A PILLAR OF REMEMBRANCE, according to the Example of Jacob. Gen. xxxv., 14, "And Jacob set up a Pillar in the place where He [God] talked with him." 102 PORTIONS OF SCRIPTURE which have at various periods been brought very near the heart of the writer. And it is earnestly desired that they may as nearly reach the heart of the reader, affording an instruction and comfort which the Divine Author of the text *alone* could give. [Anon.]
> *London : A. W. Bennett, 5, Bishopsgate Street Without.* . . . 16mo. 1861. 3½

CLIFFTON, Henry, of *Kingwood, New Jersey*, was born in *Philadelphia*, in 1753.
——Testimony concerning him.—In Comly's Miscellany, vol. IV., p. 73.

COALE, Benjamin, continued from Catalogue, Vol. I., p. 436.
——*A few Things proposed, as* EXPEDIENTS, *for a true Reconciliation among the people of God, called* QUAKERS.—𝔅enjamin 𝔄oal. With a Postscript by 𝔒harles 𝔅arris.
> 4to. [1693.] ¼

COALE, Joseph, of *Reading.*
——*To all the Bishops in Ireland, These.*
> See CONSTANT WILMER'S " Some Religious Affaires, &c." . . . . 4to. No Date. ¼

COATES, Benjamin H., M.D. Poet, Medical Writer.
——Epistle to Joseph John Gurney on the Society of Friends : a Poem.
> *Philadelphia*, 2nd mo., 1841. . 18mo. 23pp.
> Only 50 copies printed.

——A Narrative of an Embassy to the Western Indians, from the Original Manuscript of Hendrick Anpaumut, with Prefatory Remarks by Dr. B. H. Coates. *Communicated to the Society, April 19th, 1826.*
> In Vol. 2 of " The Memoirs of the Pennsylvania Historical Society," page 61.

*COATES, Reynell, M.D.
——A System of Physiology for Schools.

COFFIN, Elijah, of North America.
——Brief Remarks on the Marriage State.
——Scripture Exercises on Genesis.
——Ditto   Ditto on Matthew, Mark, Luke and John, &c.
——Tract on Amusements.
——Fuller's Catechism, published by E. Coffin.
——The Life of Elijah Coffin, with a reminiscence, by his Son, Charles F. Coffin, edited by his daughter, Mary C. Johnson. Printed for the family only (with steel portrait).
   E. Morgan & Sons (Cincinnati).   8vo. 1863. 307pp.

COFFIN, Charles F. (his Son).
   See above.

COFFIN, Levi, of *Cincinnati, Ohio.* Son of LEVI and PRUDENCE COFFIN (*née* Williams).
——REMINISCENCES of LEVI COFFIN, *The Reputed President of the Underground Railroad;* being a Brief History of the Labors of a lifetime in behalf of the Slave, with the stories of numerous fugitives who gained their freedom through his instrumentality, and many other incidents. With 2 Portraits and fac-simile autographs, of Levi Coffin and his wife, Catherine Coffin.
   London : Sampson Low, Marston, Searle, & Rivington, Crown Buildings, 188, Fleet Street. Western Tract Society, Cincinnati, Ohio.
                                 8vo. 1876. 45 sheets.

COGGESHALL, Elizabeth, daughter of Giles and Elizabeth Hosier, and Wife of Caleb Coggeshall, was born at Newport, Rhode Island, on the 14th of 3rd Month, 1770.
——MEMORIAL of the MONTHLY MEETING OF NEW YORK, concerning ELIZABETH COGGESHALL.
   New York : James Egbert, Printer, 374, Pearl Street. (Successor to M. Day's Press).
                                 8vo. 1852. 1⅜
   She died the 20th of 6th Month, 1851, aged 81 years.

COLLINS, Mary Forster, of *Philadelphia.*
——SOME OF THE TITLES OF THE SAVIOUR, as found in the HOLY SCRIPTURES. Selected by Mary Forster Collins.

COLLINS, Mary Forster, *continued*.
    Philadelphia : Joseph Rakestraw, Printer.
                                    16mo. 1854. ¼

COLLINSON, Peter, continued from Catalogue, Vol. I., p. 443.
    A List of *Peter Collinson's* Communications, Published in the *Philosophical Transactions* :—
— —Some Observations on the Hardness of Shells, and on the Food of the Sole-Fish. Read *May* 15th, 1744. Vol. 43, p. 37-9.
— —An Account of some very curious Wasps Nests, made of Clay, in *Pennsylvania*. *April* 25th, 1745. Vol. 43, p. 363-6.
——A Note concerning the Infection of the Distemper among the cows. Vol. 44, p. 7.
——Some observations on the *Cancer major*. *February* 10th, 1745-6. Vol. 44, p. 70-4.
— —Some Observations on the Balluga-Stone. *March* 12th, 1746-7. Vol. 44, p. 451-4.
——An Observation of an uncommon Gleam of Light proceeding from the Sun. *March* 19th, 1746-7. Vol. 44, p. 456-7.
——Some Observations on a sort of *Lisella*, or Ephemeron. *January* 31st, 1744-5. Vol. 44, p. 329-33.
——Some further Observations on the *Cancer Major*, communicated in a letter to Mr. *Klein*, secretary of *Dantzick*. *January* 1st, 1750. Vol. 47, p. 40-2.
— —A letter to the Honourable *J. T. Klein*, Secretary to the city of *Dantzick*, concerning the migration of Swallows. *March* 9th, 1758. Vol. 51, p. 459-64.
——Some Observations on the *Cycada* of *North America*. *February* 23rd, 1764. Vol. 54, p. 65-8.
——An Account of some very large Fossil Teeth, found in *North America*. *November* 26, 1767. Vol. 57, p. 464-7.
——Sequel to the foregoing Account of the large Fossil Teeth. Vol. 57, p. 468-9.

COMLY, John,—*continued* from Catalogue, Vol. 1, p. 445.
——English Grammar made easy to the Teacher and Pupil principally compiled for the use of West-Town Boarding-school by John Comly.
       Philadelphia.   .   .   . 18mo. 1803. 214pp.
          NOTE.—This book is a slightly altered edition of Murray, and has gone through 20 or more editions.

COMPTON, Theodore, of *Winscombe, Somersetshire*.
——Winscombe Sketches : of country life and scenery amongst the Mendip Hills. By Theodore Compton.

COMPTON. Theodore, *continued*.
> London: F. B. Kitto, 5, Bishopsgate Without;
> Axbridge: Richardson; Banwell, Purrett;
> Cheddar: Bryne; and Robbins & Scotney,
> Weston-Super-Mare. . . 8vo. 1867. 5½

—— THE LIFE AND CORRESPONDENCE of the REVEREND JOHN CLOWES, M.A. Rector for sixty-two years of St. John's Church, Manchester, and formerly Fellow of Trinity College, Cambridge.
> "Holy, apostolic—the most saint-like of all human beings I have known through life."—*De Quincey*.

Edited from materials collected by the late George Harrison, Esq., with the addition of other documents and information by THEODORE COMPTON.
> London: Longmans, Green & Co. [*Printed by Spottiswoode and Co., New-street Square, and Parliament Street.*]
> All rights reserved. . . 8vo. 1874. 16¾

COMSTOCK, Andrew, M.D., of *Philadelphia*.
—— A System of Elocution, with special reference to gesture, to the treatment of Stammering and defective articulation, comprising numerous diagrams and engraved figures illustrative of the subject. By Andrew Comstock, M.D.
> Philadelphia:
> 12mo. 1843. 364pp.

CONGDON, James B., of *Massachusetts, New England, N. America*.
—— Quaker Quiddities; or, Friends in Council.

CONRAD, Timothy A. Geologist, Author, of *Philadelphia*.
—— New Fresh-water Shells of the United States, with coloured illustrations and a monograph of the genus Auculotus of Say: also a synopsis of the American Naiades. T. A. Conrad, Member of the Academy of Natural Sciences of Philadelphia.
> Philadelphia:
> 12mo. 1834. 76pp.

—— Monograph of the Family Unionidæ; or Naides of Lamarck (fresh water bivalve shells), of North America: illustrated by Figures Drawn on Stone, from Nature, and finely Coloured. By T. A. Conrad, Curator of the Academy of Natural Sciences of Philadelphia; each Part containing 5 Coloured Illustrations. (6s.)

—— American Marine Conchology.
> Philadelphia:
> 1 Vol. 8vo., unfinished (3 Nos.)

CONRAD, Timothy A., *continued.*
—— Fossils of the Tertiary Formation of the United States.
Philadelphia :
8vo., unfinished.

—— The New Diogenes : a cynical poem.
> "Is happiness our aim ?
> Why contentment in a tub is safer
> Than piling glory on ambition's crest,
> Till it overtops Olympus."

Philadelphia :
12mo. 1800. 100pp.

COOK, Obed, of *Southwark*. Continued from Catalogue, Vol., p. 447.
> Obed Cook was a Schoolmaster, son of Alexander and Abigail Cook, of Glasgow. He married 25th of 9th Month, 1760, Elizabeth Archer, and after her death, Sophia Norris (2nd of 1st Month, 1787). He died at Gainsford Street, Horslydown, Southwark, the 23rd of 1st Month, 1795, aged 70 years.

COOKE, James, of *Pentonville, London*. Continued from Catalogue, Vol. I., p. 447.

—— CHRISTIAN COUNSEL, IN TWO PARTS. Part First, TO MANKIND IN GENERAL; Part Second, *Addressed more particularly to those with whom he is in Religious Profession*; in order to promote A CLOSER WALKING WITH GOD, by Believers in Christ of every denomination. By JAMES COOKE.
> "As the branch cannot bear fruit, of itself except it abide in the Vine ; no more can ye, except ye abide in Me."— John c. xv., v. 4.
> "Every man's works shall be made manifest : for the day shall declare it, because it shall be revealed by fire ; and the fire shall try every man's work of what sort it is."— I Corinthians c. iii., v. 13.

London : *Printed by G. Pigott, 60, Old Street. May be had of all Booksellers, and of the Publisher, No. 54, Chapel Street, Pentonville.*

PRICE, 3d. 8vo. 1813. 1

COOKWORTHY, William. Continued from Catalogue, Vol. I., p. 448.

—— A SECOND APPENDIX to the MEMOIR OF WILLIAM COOKWORTHY, by his Grandson.
> *Published by W. & F. G. Cash, 1854.*
> Printed for Theodore Compton.
> (*Birmingham* : *White & Pike, Moor Street Printing Works.*) . . . 8vo. 1872. ¾

COOKWORTHY, William, continued.
> NOTE.—The above is chiefly "Extracts from the Journal of Sarah Fox (née Champion) respecting William Cookworthy."
> The Life of Josiah Wedgewood, by L. Jewitt, F.S.A., Contains some account of Cookworthy's discovery.
> See also Art Journal, September, 1863.
> See also article, "Clay."—*Penny Cyclopædia*.

——The Divine Instinct.
> An edition 1751. Exon. Printed, Preface states, by a Tradesman.

*COOPER, Frederick, of *Manchester*.
——To my Friends and Fellow-Members of Manchester Meeting. . . . Folio. [1868]. 1
——The Crisis in Manchester Meeting. 𝔚𝔦𝔱𝔥 𝔞 𝔑𝔢𝔳𝔦𝔢𝔴 of the Pamphlets of David Duncan and Joseph B. Forster. By Frederick Cooper.
> *For Private Circulation in the Society of Friends.*
> 𝔑𝔬𝔱 𝔓𝔲𝔟𝔩𝔦𝔰𝔥𝔢𝔡.
> *Manchester*: *Printed by William Irwin, 24, Deansgate*. . . . 8vo. 1869. 4¾

COOPER, Joseph, of *Essex Hall, Walthamstow*.
——THE SLAVE-TRADE IN AFRICA in 1872. Principally carried on for the supply of Turkey, Egypt, Persia, and Zanzibar. By ELIENNE-FELIX BERLIOUX. From the French, with a Preface by Joseph Cooper.
> London : 27, *New Broad Street*. . 8vo. 1872.
——The LOST CONTINENT; or, 𝔖𝔩𝔞𝔳𝔢𝔯𝔶 𝔞𝔫𝔡 𝔱𝔥𝔢 𝔖𝔩𝔞𝔳𝔢-𝔗𝔯𝔞𝔡𝔢 in Africa, 1875. *With observations on the Asiatic Slave-trade, carried on under the name of the labour traffic, and some other subjects.* By JOSEPH COOPER. (Map).
> London : *Longmans, Green & Co.* 8vo. 1875. 8½

COPE, Edward D., Naturalist, Professor.

COPE, Gilbert,
——Record of the Cope family, 1861.
——Genealogy of the Dutton family, 1871.

COPE, Thomas P., President of the Mercantile Library Company, of *Philadelphia*, was a native of *Lancaster County, Pennsylvania*. He was descended from OLIVER COPE, one of the first purchasers from WILLIAM PENN.
——Biographical Sketch of THOMAS P. COPE, ESQ. [with a fine Portrait, engraved by Jno. Sartain after the original Portrait painted by J. Neagle in 1848.]

COPE, Thomas P., *continued*.
   *In The Merchants' Magazine, by Freeman Hunt,
   Editor and Proprietor.*—Vol. 20, p. 355.
                              8vo.   *New York*, 1849.
CORBETT, Maria, of
——and I. T. A.—Rhythms and Rhymes

CORDER, Susanna, continued from Catalogue, Vol I, p. 453.
——Life of Elizabeth Fry. By Susanna Corder.
   Philadelphia:
                              8vo.   1853.
COSINS, Nathaniel, of *No. 8, Brunswick Place, Southampton*.
——NON-PAYMENT OF CHURCH RATES. To the Members of the Church of England in Southampton, &c. (A Paper to clear himself from the serious charge of Injustice, in refusing to pay the Rates, &c.) 5th month 2nd, 1831.
   T. King, Printer, Southampton.   Folio. [1831.]   ½

CRACKANTHORP, John, was a Schoolmaster of *Warwick*, afterwards of *Birmingham*. See Catalogue, Vol. I., p. 459.

CRANE, Richard, continued from Catalogue, Vol 1., p. 460.
——Something spoken in Vindication, &c.
   Translated into High Dutch or German, with an Addition by Geo. Fox.
                              Broadside. No date.   1

‖CRAWFORD, Charles, of *Philadelphia*.
——AN ESSAY on the Propagation of the Gospel; in which there are numerous Facts and Arguments *Adduced to prove that many of the* INDIANS IN AMERICA *are descended from the* TEN TRIBES.
   "But when he saw the multitudes he was moved with compassion on them, because they fainted, and were scattered abroad, as Sheep having no Shepherd. Then saith he unto his disciples, the harvest truly is plenteous, but the labourers are few: Pray ye, therefore, the Lord of the Harvest, that He will send forth labourers into His harvest."—Matthew ix., 36, 37, 38.
   "Go ye into all the world, and preach the gospel to every creature."—Mark xvi., 15.
   The Second Edition. *By* CHARLES CRAWFORD, *Esq.*
   𝔓𝔥𝔦𝔩𝔞𝔡𝔢𝔩𝔭𝔥𝔦𝔞 : *Printed and Sold by James Humphreys.* . . . 12mo. 1801.   6½

CRESSON, Caleb, of *North America*.
——Diary of

CRESSON, Elliott, of *Philadelphia*.
—— REPORTS of the BOARD OF MANAGERS of the Pennsylvania Colonisation Society, with an INTRODUCTION AND APPENDIX. [By Elliott Cresson.]
Philadelphia : Printed for the Society. London : John Miller, Henrietta Street, Covent Garden.
Price, 1s. 6d. . . . 8vo. 1831. 3 sheets.

*CRESSWELL (Mrs. Francis), of
—— A MEMOIR OF ELIZABETH FRY : by her Daughter, Mrs Francis Cresswell. Abridged from the larger memoir, with alterations and additions.
"I was sick, and ye visited me : I was in prison, and ye came unto me."—MATTHEW xxv. 36.
London : James Nisbet and Co., Berners Street.
8vo. 1869. 22

*CREWDSON, Isaac. continued from Catalogue, Vol. I., p. 462.
—— On the NATURE and DESIGN of Christianity. [Anon.]
Stockport: Printed by J. Lomax, Great Underbank.
16mo. 1819. ¾
—— Glad Tidings for Sinners.
No. 575 Religious Tract Society.
—— Proceedings of the Y.M., 1837.
— - Portrait of Isaac Crewdson.
He died suddenly at Bowness, Windermere, in 1854, aged 64 years.

*CREWDSON, Jane, Wife of T. D. Crewdson.
—— Aunt Jane's Verses for Children.
2nd Edition.
—— Scripture Lyrics.
—— The Singer of Eisenach.
—— Lays of the Reformation.
—— 100 Assorted Leaflets.
—— "A LITTLE WHILE," and other Poems. By Mrs. T. D. Crewdson.
Manchester : William Bremner & Co., 11, Market Street ; London : F. Pitman, 20, Paternoster Row. . . . 16mo. No date. 108pp.

CRISP, Jane Palmer, of *Lynn, Norfolk*.
—— THE PAST AND PRESENT OF THE SOCIETY OF FRIENDS, exhibited in letters to the Daily News, commencing with the insertion therein of "*Quakerism : Its Social Change*," on the 5th of 4th month, 1877. Issued by JANE PALMER CRISP.
NOTE.—The above is the title on the printed cover outside, the inside title is,—

CRISP, Jane Palmer, *continued*.
—— The PAST AND PRESENT of the 𝔖𝔬𝔠𝔦𝔢𝔱𝔶 𝔬𝔣 𝔉𝔯𝔦𝔢𝔫𝔡𝔰, briefly exhibited in letters addressed to the Editor of the "Daily News." With Preface, Notes, &c.
Manchester : William Irwin, Cathedral Chambers, Half Street. 8vo. 1877. 1¼

CRISP, Stephen,—*continued* from Catalogue, Vol. 1., p. 466.
—— De WEG tót het KONINGRYK der HEMELEN, Aangeweezen in *Zeventien* PREDIKACIEN, Uytgesprooken te LONDEN, Door STEVEN CRISP *van Colchester*, In zyn leeven getrouw Bedienaar des Evangeliums, onder die Christenen, welke gemeenlyk QUAKERS worden genaamd. *Uyt het Engelsch vertaald, door* Wm. Séwel.
t' Amsterdam, by de Wed : van STEVEN SWART, Boekverkoopster in de Beursstraat in den gekroonden Bybel, 1695. Small 8vo. 1695. 19½
NOTE.—At the end of the Preface in my copy is the autograph of Wm. Séwel.

—— EXTRACTS from SERMONS of STEPHEN CRISP. 𝔓𝔯𝔢𝔞𝔠𝔥𝔢𝔡 at Gracechurch Street and Devonshire House from 1688 to 1697. (With a preface by H. S. A.)
London : Printed by E. Newman, Devonshire Street, Bishopsgate . . . 8vo. 1874. 1

—— Stephen Crisp and his Collection of MSS. 1667—1892. Containing letters from William Penn, Robert Barclay, George Whitehead, William Dewsbury, George Fox, Jun., James Parnell, and others. The property of Colchester Monthly Meeting. Now first edited, with Notes, explanatory and biographical, by C. Fell Smith.
London : Edward Hicks, Jun., 14 Bishopsgate Without. . . . . . . 1892.

CROPPER, James, continued from Catalogue, Vol. 1. p. 492.
—— Recollections of the late James Cropper, addressed to his grandchildren by their very affectionate mother, A. C.
(Lithographed) . . . large 4to. No date. 1½
—— Some of the ideas respecting the currency.
(Unpublished.) *Liverpool* . . 8vo. No date. 4
A Portrait of James Cropper has been published.

CRUIKSHANK, Edward, of *Edinburgh*.
—— An Appeal to the Society of Friends regarding the Doctrine contained in certain of their Tracts. By Edward Cruikshank . . . . . 1871.
See a review in B. Friend, 8th mo., '71.

*CUDWORTH, John William, of *Leeds.*   See J. W C.

CUFFEE, Paul,—*continued* from Catalogue, Vol. 1., p. 500.
"Capt. Cuffee is of a very pleasing countenance, and his physiognomy truly interesting ; he is both tall and stout, speaks English well, dresses in the Quaker style, in a drab-coloured suit, and wears a large flapped white hat."—
From a Cutting from a Newspaper.

§CUMMING, Thomas, a Merchant of *London?*   Portrait of him in Hume and Smollett's History.

—— The Project for annexing Senegal to Great Britain was first conceived by him, and in which he assisted.
In Hume and Smollett's History (Valpy's edition), Vol. xii. p. 310 I find the following note :—" On this occasion Mr. Cumming may seem to have acted directly contrary to the tenets of his religious profession ; but he ever declared to the ministry, that he was fully persuaded his schemes might be accomplished without the effusion of human blood ; and that if he thought otherwise, he would by no means have concerned himself about them ; he also desired, let the consequence be what it might, his brethren should not be chargeable with what was his own single act : if it was the first military scheme of any Quaker, let it be remembered it was also the first successful expedition of this war ; and one of the first that ever was carried on, according to the pacific system of the Quakers, without the loss of a drop of blood on either side." (1758.)

CURPHEY, Esther, was a *Methodist,* and was born in Ramsey, in the Isle of Man, 4th of 8th Month, 1782. The following account was, I believe, edited by a Friend. [Thos. Thompson ?]

——Some Account of Esther Curphey, who died, aged 28, at Ramsey, in the Isle of Man, in the year 1811.
London : Printed and Sold by William Phillips, George Yard, Lombard Street.   .   12mo.   1817.   1

CURTIS, John, Dr. (Father of JOHN HARRISON CURTIS.) (Whether an Author ?)

CURTIS, William,—*continued* from Cataloge, Vol. 1, p. 502.

—— The BOTANICAL MAGAZINE ; or, Flower Garden Displayed : in which the most Ornamental FOREIGN PLANTS, cultivated in the Open Ground, the Greenhouse, and the Stove, will be accurately represented in their natural Colours. TO WHICH WILL BE ADDED, their Names, Class, Order, Generic and Specific Characters, according to the celebrated LINNŒUS : their Places of Growth, and Times of

CURTIS, William, *continued*.

Flowering: together with the most approved Methods of Culture. A WORK intended for the use of such LADIES, GENTLEMEN, and GARDENERS, as wish to become scientifically acquainted with the Plants they cultivate.

LONDON: *Printed for W. Curtis, at his Botanic Garden, Lambeth Marsh; and Sold by all Booksellers, Stationers, and News-carriers, in Town and Country.* . . 8vo. 1787. 5

—— The BOTANICAL MAGAZINE; or Flower Garden Displayed, &c. By WILLIAM CURTIS, Author of the FLORA LONDINENSIS. VOL. II.

LONDON: *Printed by Couchman and Fry, Throgmorton-street, for W. Curtis, at his Botanic Garden, Lambeth Marsh; and Sold by the principal Booksellers in Great Britain and Ireland.* . . . 8vo. 1788. 4¾

—— The BOTANICAL MAGAZINE, &c. By WILLIAM CURTIS, Author of the FLORA LONDINENSIS.
(Same imprint.) . . . 8vo. 1790. 4¾

NOTE.—In the three Volumes there are 108 plates, No. 1 to 108.

—— PRACTICAL DIRECTIONS for Laying Down or Improving MEADOW AND PASTURE LAND, with an enumeration of the BRITISH GRASSES, pointing out such Seeds as are of the most nutritious property, and best adapted for Dairy Pasture, Hay, Green food, or for feeding and fattening stock: with full instructions for sowing, and the best Seasons for performing it. By WILLIAM CURTIS, *Author of the Flora Londinensis, Botanical Magazine, Lectures on Botany, &c., &c.* "Fiat Experimentum." Seventh Edition, with considerable Additions, by JOHN LAWRENCE, including, Hints for the General Management of all Descriptions of Grass Land, *as in Draining, Manuring, Harrowing, Rolling, and Weeding;* Also the Mode of expeditiously converting Arable Land into Pasture, by Turfing or Transplanting it, as extensively and successfully practised, with the patronage of Mr. Coke, of Holkham, on his Farms in Norfolk, under the instructions of his Steward, Mr. Blakie. To which is subjoined, a short Account of The Causes of the Diseases in Corn, called by Farmers the Blight, the Mildew, and the Rust; by Sir JOSEPH

CURTIS, William, *continued*.
    BANKS, Bart, 𝔍𝔩𝔩𝔲𝔰𝔱𝔯𝔞𝔱𝔢𝔡 𝔟𝔶 𝔫𝔲𝔪𝔢𝔯𝔬𝔲𝔰 𝔠𝔬𝔩𝔬𝔲𝔯𝔢𝔡 𝔓𝔩𝔞𝔱𝔢𝔰 𝔬𝔣 𝔊𝔯𝔞𝔰𝔰𝔢𝔰.
      𝔏𝔬𝔫𝔡𝔬𝔫 : *Sherwood, Gilbert, and Piper*, Paternoster Row. . . . 8vo. 1834. 10⅝

——Botanical Magazine. On the 1st of April will be published, containing four coloured plates with descriptions, price 1s., No. 1 of a new and improved edition of Curtis's BOTANICAL MAGAZINE, or Flower Garden Displayed, with amended characters of the species : the whole arranged according to the natural orders by W. J. Hooker, LL.D., F.R.A., and L.S., &c., &c., &c., and Regius Professor of Botany in the University of Glasgow, to which is added the most approved method of culture by Samuel Curtis, F.L.S., of the Glazenwood Horticultural Grounds, Essex, and Proprietor of the Botanical Magazine.

    London : *Printed by Edward Couchman, Throgmorton Street, for the Proprietor, Samuel Curtis, and Sherwood, Gilbert, and Piper, Paternoster Row.*

                ADDRESS.

    Few works, perhaps, connected with Botany, treated especially as an elegant amusement, have enjoyed a more extensive or a more deserved share of reputation and popularity than the BOTANICAL MAGAZINE, commenced, and for many so ably conducted, by the late Mr. Curtis. It was the first work of the kind that had ever been attempted in any country : though it has now met with imitators in many parts of Europe, and even in North America. The great expense, however, of keeping up complete sets of the entire stock of Fifty-three Volumes, and the heavy cost attending the purchase of the whole work to individuals who have not taken it from the commencement, have induced the present proprietor and conductor of the Botanical Magazine, Mr. Samuel Curtis, to resolve upon meeting the wishes of many lovers of Horticulture and Botany, Gardeners, and such as have it not in their power to procure the original edition, and to publish an entirely NEW EDITION of the OLD SERIES, on a more economical, but scarcely less beautiful, and in some respects more useful form.

    This new edition will be printed in royal octavo, on fine paper, and the plates will be *half* coloured. The descriptive part will be confined to what is necessary for the determination of the species, and the whole will be published in *systematic* order, commencing with the *Clematis* and *Ranunculus Tribe*, and following the arrangement of the celebrated DE CANDOLLE, as given in his "*Prodromus.*" There will be given at the head of

CURTIS, William, *continued.*

the species, the *characters* of the CLASSES, ORDERS, and GENERA. Such remarks will be made upon their uses, and properties and cultivation, derivation of generic names, &c., &c., as the subject may require; and the whole will be written in English. Any figure that may be requisite for the illustration of such Orders as are not given in the Old Series, will be selected from the New; so that the work will be an epitome of all that has been made known to Science, both by figures and descriptions, through the medium of the Botanical Magazine, during a period of forty-five years.

A number, price 1s. (or with the Plates full coloured, price 2s.), will appear twice in every month, containing four Plates accompanied by four pages of closely-printed Letter Press, more or less as the subject may require. A volume of ninety-six Plates will thus appear every year.

The Letterpress will be conducted by Dr. HOOKER, Regius Professor of Botany in the University of Glasgow; with the exception of what regards the cultivation of the species, which will invariably be supplied by Mr. CURTIS.

The New Series of the BOTANICAL MAGAZINE will continue to be published regularly on the first day of every month. Seventy-five numbers of this very highly interesting and beautiful work are now before the Public, in which are displayed, most accurately coloured from nature, with full descriptions of their uses, and valuable information as to their products in economical and commercial points of view, the rare and curious DOUBLE COCOA NUT, the CLOVE, NUTMEG, BLACK PEPPER, SAGO, TAPIOCA, the BREAD FRUIT TREE, CUSTARD APPLE, BUTTER NUT, PAPAW TREE, the COLUMBO ROOT, POISON TANGHIN, the COCHINEAL PLANT and INSECTS, &c., &c., with many interesting Plants never before figured in any European work.

This work is elegantly printed in royal 8vo. Each Number, price 3s. 6d., contains eight highly finished coloured Plates, with accurate descriptions. Twelve Numbers form a handsome Volume, and may be had of the Proprietor at Glazenwood; or of Messrs. SHERWOOD, GILBERT, & PIPER, Paternoster Row, and Messrs. ARCH'S, Cornhill.

Lately published, price 15s. boards.

——GENERAL INDEXES to the FIRST FIFTY-THREE VOLUMES of the BOTANICAL MAGAZINE: consisting of

1st.—A GENERAL ALPHABETICAL ENGLISH INDEX, with the Volume and Number of the Plate prefixed to each Plant: to which the Latin name is added.

2nd.—A GENERAL ALPHABETICAL LATIN INDEX, with the same reference to Volume and Plate; to which the English Names are added.

CURTIS, William, *continued.*
>3rd.—A GENERAL SYSTEMATICAL LATIN INDEX, with the same reference to Volume and Plate; to which the English names are added.
>
>As an additional interest to this appendage of the work, a Portrait, with a Sketch of the Life and Writings of Mr. WILLIAM CURTIS, the original Author of it is added; and at the end of the Index, blank leaves are inserted, for the continuation of the Index in manuscript.

D.

D.—See THOMAS DREWRY, of *Fleetwood.*

D.J.—See ISAAC DICKINSON, of *Whitehaven.*

DANT, Joan, of *Spitalfields, London, continued* from Catalogue, Vol. 1, p. 511.
>She died the 29th of 9th Month, being buried on the 2nd of 10th Month, 1715, aged 84 years, and was buried at Bunhill Fields.

DARBY, Deborah, *continued* from Catalogue, Vol. 1, p. 512.
——Account of Deborah Darby, in *Gent's Magazine*, 1810?

DARKE, Samuel, of *Worcester.*
——Tribute to his memory, in the *Worcester Herald*, of July 26, 1856.
>Republished in Noake's "Worcester Sects," &c. 1861.
>
>He died the 20th of 7th Month, 1856, aged 86 years.

DARLINGTON, William, M.D., LL.D., &c., *Botanist*, of *Pennsylvania, North America.* See also William Baldwin.
——Flora Cestrica; an Herborizing Companion for the young Botanists of Chester County, State of Pennsylvania. By William Darlington, M.D., LL.D., &c.
Reprinted, 2nd edition.
Reprinted, 3rd edition. . . . . Crown 8vo.

DARTON, Ann, of *33, Bishopsgate Street, Within, London.*
——" On a Consignment of Shells."
>8vo. 26th of 3rd Month, 1852. $\frac{1}{8}$

DARTON, Thomas Gates, *continued* from Catalogue, Vol. 1, p. 513.
——A Letter addressed to the "Christian Advocate," relative to the Society of Friends. By O.T.R. [*i.e.,* Thomas Gates Darton.]
>Ipswich: *Published by S. H. Cowell; and sold in London, etc.* . . . 12mo. 1836. $\frac{1}{4}$

DARTON, Thomas Gates, *continued*.
— —Introductory remarks to the 5th edition of the Life of Alice Hayes.
  London : Darton & Harvey, Gracechurch Street.
            12mo. 1836. 2⅔
— —The Total Abstinence agitation in its relation to intemperance 8vo. 1877. 1
— —The same.—Part Second.—Being further considerations suggested by the criticisms of Samuel Bowly and others on Part the First. . . . 8vo. 1877. 1
  He died the 16th of 12th Month, 1887, aged 77 years.

DARTON, Margaret E., his wife, *continued* from Catalogue, Vol. 1, p. 513.
— —THE EARTH and ITS INHABITANTS, 2nd edition.
              8vo. 1853.
 New Edition, revised.
  London : George Routledge and Sons, The Broadway, Ludgate. New York : 416, Broome Street . . . . . 8vo. 1868.
  She died the 6th of 2nd Month, 1886, aged 71 years.

DAVIES, Richard, *continued* from Catalogue, Vol. I, p. 514.
— —Life of Richard Davies.
 Reprinted in "The Friends' Family Library," Vol. 4.

DAVIS, Thomas, of *Milverton*.
— —Letter to Phillips and Fardon, dated the 5th of 12th Month, 1805. Respecting omissions and errors in the Life of Thomas Melhuish. (In M.S.) 4to. 1805. ½

DAVIS, William, of *Bath, continued* from Catalogue, Vol. 1, p. 516.
— —Friendly Advice to Industrious and Frugal Persons, &c. 4th edition, enlarged, title altered.
  London, printed. 8vo. 1817. 2

DAWSON, C. C., of *North America*.
— —A Collection of Family Records. . . . 1874.

DELL, Barton, of *Bristol, continued* from "*Catalogue of Friends' Books, Vol. 1,*" page 519.
— —The FOOL'S GOSPEL.
  "And a way shall be there, and it shall be called the Way of Holiness. . . . . The way-faring men, though Fools, shall not err therein."—ISAIAH xxxv.
  London : Elliott Stock, 62, Paternoster Row.
 [ANON.]   8vo. 1871. 11¼
  He died the 24th of 2nd Month, 1886, aged 78 years.

DEWHURST, Thomas, of *Lancaster*.
—— THE HAPPY MAN: or the scattered Thoughts of a POOR PILGRIM, addressed principally to the young, and occasionally to the middle-aged and those more advanced in years, by one who can truly subscribe himself A HAPPY MAN.
 "A Book is the expression of the thoughts of the writer."
 —C. H. SPURGEON.
 Lancaster : Printed by E. and J. L. Milner, Guardian Office, Church St. . 8vo. [1865.] 8¾
 NOTE.—On the copy from which I took the above, is written on the title page. "An affectionate token of remembrance from the Author to his dear cousin, Charles Gilpin, Esq., M.P."
 He died the 27th of 6th Month, 1869, aged 79 years.

DEWSBURY, William, *continued* from Catalogue, Vol. 1, p. 523.
—— The Discovery of Man's Returne, &c.
 Reprinted,—8vo. *London*, printed in the year 1665. 3
—— To all Nations, Kindreds, &c.
 Translated into *French* . . Folio. 1663. ½
—— To all the Faithful in Christ. . . . 1663. 1
 Reprinted.—4to. Printed in the year 1664 . . 1

DICKINSON, Isaac, of *Whitehaven*, father of Drewry Dickinson.
—— QUAKERISM: its Decline and Cause. An Essay that No prize did win. By J. D.
 Printed at "The Times" Office, Whitehaven.
 8vo. 1860. ¼

*DICKINSON, John, Politician, President of *Pennsylvania*.
—— The Political Writings of John Dickinson, 2 vols.
 Wilmington, Delaware. . . 8vo. 1801.
—— Life and Portrait of John Dickinson, contained in the 3rd volume of the National Portrait Gallery.
 Philadelphia. . . . . 1836.
 He died in the year 1808, aged 75 years. For further particulars see Blake's "Biographical Dictionary, 8th edition, Revised, *Boston*, 1853."

DILLWYN, George, of *Burlington, New Jersey*.
—— A Practical Syntax, &c. See ANONYMOUS.
 12mo. 1795.
—— Occasional Reflections. LATIN. . 1818.
—— Elixir Instituorum. . . 1823.

DILLWYN, William, continued from Catalogue, Vol. 1, p. 533.
> From Eli K. Price's Centennial Meeting of the Descendants of Philip and Rachel Price:—"In 1773 William Dillwyn, then of New Jersey, was one of a deputation of Friends to present a numerously signed petition to the Legislature of that State for the manumission of slaves, and he was heard at the bar of the house. In 1774 he went to England, and made the acquaintance of Granville Sharp, and soon after settled in London, and became a co-laborer with him. He formed a committee of Friends for the suppression of Slavery, before the subject had been thought of by Clarkson. When Clarkson took it up as a University Thesis in 1784, he found all his needed materials in the writings of Benezet.
>
> It is among the pleasing recollections of my visit to England in 1821, that I shared the hospitality of the veteran philanthropist, WILLIAM DILLWYN, at his beautiful home at Walthamstow, and saw him in the evening of life, of most venerable and benign appearance, surrounded by beloved and loving daughters, with feelings of yet warm and glowing interest in his native country, and of love for mankind."
>
> He died at *Walthamstow*, the 28th of the 9th Month, 1824, aged 81 years, and was buried in the Friends' Burial Ground, adjoining the Meeting-house, Tottenham.

*DILLWYN, Lewis Weston, *continued* from Catalogue, Vol. 1, p. 532.

—— A Descriptive Catalogue of Recent Shells, arranged according to the Linnœan Method, with particular attention to the 𝔖𝔶𝔫𝔬𝔫𝔶𝔪𝔶. By Lewis Weston Dillwyn, F.R.S. and F.L.S., Honorary Member of the Geological Society of London; the Linnœan Society of Philadelphia, &c. In 2 Vols.
> London: *Printed for John and Arthur Arch, Cornhill.* . . . 8vo. 1817. 71.

DIMSDALE, Sarah, widow of Robert Dimsdale and daughter of Francis Collins, of Ratcliff, died at Haddonfield, New Jersey, in 1739, and was buried in Friends' Burial Ground there.

DIXON, George, of *North of England Agricultural School, Great Ayton, Yorkshire,* near *Northallerton.*

—— Homes for the Freedmen of the United States of America, 8th mo. 20, 1870. . 8vo. [1870.] ¼

DOCWRA, Anne, *continued* from Catalogue, Vol. 1, p. 539.
—— A True Discovery, &c., . . Folio B. 1683.

DODSHON, Frances. See HENSHAW.
——A Serious Call, &c.
   Reprinted—*Macclesfield*.
DOUBLEDAY, Henry, *continued* from Catalogue, Vol. 1,
   p. 541. His portrait (oil painting) as well as his collection of insects is now in the Bethnal Green Museum.
   He died the 29th of 6th Month, 1875, aged 66 years.
DOUGLAS, John Henry, of *North America*.
——An Address to Parents on the Importance of Sabbath Schools. By John Henry Douglas. Price one penny.
   Chelmsford: *Printed by George Piper, High Street*.
            16mo.   No date.
DOW, Neal, Author of the "Maine Liquor Law."

D'OYLY, Bray, son of John D'Oyly, was born before 1634, and in 1656 succeeded his father in the Manors of Brownes and St. Amonds thence residing in the family mansion at Adderbury.
   But Bray D'Oyly was ill qualified to represent a proud and ancient family, for, like his relative Nathaniel Weston, he became a convert to Quakerism; and further, as soon as ever his father was laid in the grave, severed not only himself but his estates of St. Amonds and Brownes from the rest of his family, and suffering a common recovery thereof by indenture of bargain and sale enrolled, dated April, 1657, conveyed a considerable portion to Barnabas Horsman, of Banbury, to such uses as suited his wishes.
   Bray D'Oyly was not merely a staunch Quaker, but one of the most persecuted amongst the early members of that sect. He engaged too in the lengthy doctrinal controversy in defence of his new faith with his neighbour, William Fiennes, Lord Saye and Sele: who though himself an extreme Puritan, and a notorious enemy to the Established Church, spared no endeavours to persecute the Quakers. Some of the pamphlets which passed between them are enumerated in Beesley's History of Banbury. Bray D'Oyly's property too being considerable, increased the persecution against him.
   In 1661 he was prosecuted in the Hundred Court for non-payment of tithes, and was certainly most arbitrarily and unjustly treated. In 1662 he was heavily fined for attending meetings, as also in 1670 and 1674.
   Meanwhile his estates being unfettered, Bray D'Oyly gave the Quakers their Meeting House at Adderbury with land attached, being the building in which they

D'OYLY, Bray, *continued*.

still assemble. He died 5 p.m. in the summer of 1696, and was buried 2nd July, 1696, at Adderbury. He left a Will bequeathing his brother Edmund an annuity (on condition that he would not be troublesome to Anne, the testator's relict), and also a Widow the said Anne, who possessed the said Will in 1701, sharing a pretty jointure settled on her by Bray D'Oyly, married secondly January, 1698, at South Newington. John Toovey, of Henley-on-Thames, doubtlessly a Quaker but of a respectable family in Bucks and Oxfordshire, which was entitled to bear for arms, "Per fesse on and gules a wivern," with wings elevated, countercharged. On Bray D'Oyly's decease his Quakeress nieces succeeded to Brown and St. Amonds, but the male representation of the family devolved on his brother.

NOTE.—The above account is extracted from the work, " A Biog. Hist., &c., of the House of D'Oyly," 1845.

See Besse's Sufferings, Vol. 1, 567, 568-72, 3.; Beesley's Banbury; Quaker's Registry. A Biographical, Historical, Genealogical, and Heraldic Account of the House of D'Oyly, by William D'Oyly Bayley.

London : *Printed by J. B. Nichols and Son, 25, Parliament Street.* . . . . 1845.

The Registry says, "Bray D'Oyly was buried at Adderbury the 2nd of 7th Month (September), 1696. His age is not given.

Deed of Adderbury Ground dated 15th April, 1677, for £20, from Bray D'Oyly, Esq., and Anne his wife, to Edward Vivers, of Banbury, woollen draper, and others.

The deed mentions John D'Oyly, Esq., deceased, as late father of the said Bray.

Names signed Doiley.

The house in which Bray Doyley lived is still standing at Adderbury, near the Friends' Meeting House. Some large yew trees overhanging the outer wall of the ground in front must have been standing when B.D. lived there.

From a Memorandum.

DREWRY, Thomas, of *Fleetwood, Lancashire*, continued from Catalogue, Vol. I., p. 543.

—— EIGHT DAYS IN SCOTLAND.

[*For the Fleetwood Chronicle.*] 3 Papers as from the Type and Column of that work.

Large broadside.

November 29 ⎫
December 6 ⎬ . . 3 single leaves, 1867. 3 sheets.
December 13 ⎭

Single leaves.

DREWRY, Thomas, *continued*.

———A Few Notes on an anonymous pamphlet entitled, "Lumen Siccum: an Essay on the Exercise of the intellect in matters of Religious Belief."
London: F. B. Kitto, 5, Bishopsgate Street.
          8vo. 1868. 1

———To all whom it may concern. (A Protest against London Y.M.)
 Broadside . . . . . . [1871.] 1
  NOTE.—First Printed and inserted in the *advertising* Columns of "The British Friend," 9th and 10th month, 1871.

———The Last Days of John Wilbur. [ANON.]
          8vo. [1871.] ⅛

——BIRTH-MEMBERSHIP, AND MEETINGS FOR DISCIPLINE in the SOCIETY OF FRIENDS.
 [Chiefly extracted from "THE BRITISH FRIEND" OF 2ND MONTH 1ST, 1872.]

——The Assailants of Barclay, and his Quasi Defended.
 [From "The British Friend" of 9th Month 2nd, 1872, with some alterations and additions.]
        Folio. 1872. 2 pages

——The Conference of Friends in London, and the Yearly Meeting's Epistle of 1836.
 From *The British Friend* of 2nd Month 2nd, 1874, with additions.
        Single leaf. 1874.

———The Present Crisis in the Society of Friends. Signed, D. (a Reply to an Article of Wm. Pollard, in the 8th Month. Oblong folio, single leaf. [1875.] 1

———Birthright Membership.
 Reprinted from "THE BRITISH FRIEND" *of 5th Month 1st, 1884.*
      Thomas Drewry,
     Fleetwood, 4th Mo. 19, 1884.
        Single leaf. 1884

——SOME REMARKS on H. S. NEWMAN'S PREFACE to the AUTOBIOGRAPHY OF GEORGE FOX.
 Reprinted from "THE BRITISH FRIEND" *of 11th Month, 1886, with some additions and alterations.*
        Folio. 1886.

———The American Epistles.
 Reprinted from "The British Friend."
      Thomas Drewry,
     Fleetwood, *3rd Mo. 18*, 1886.
       Single leaf. 1886.

———A Chapter in Recent English History.

DREWRY, Thomas, *continued*.
(Reprinted from "The British Friend," 12th Month, 1886.)
Signed, D.
Single leaf. 1886.
——Some Remarks on a Publication entitled, " QUAKER STRONGHOLDS."
T. Woods, Printer, North Albert Street, Fleetwood.
8vo. 8th month, 1891. ¼

DRINKER, Anna. Poet.

DRINKER, Edward, for an account of him, see Blake's Biog. Dic., 8th Ed., Boston, 1853.

DRINKER, John.
——A Farewell to Rachel Wilson, by John Drinker.—In Comly's Miscellany, Vol. 4.

DUCK, Nehemiah,
——and James Duck, } Surgeons, of *Bristol*.
——**Prospectus of the Plan** of conducting CLEVE-HOUSE RETREAT (near Bristol). 4to. [1815.] ½
Nehemiah Duck died the 14th of the 3rd Month, 1842, aged 60 years, and was buried at the Friars, Bristol, on the 22nd of the same month.

DUCKETT, Thomas, of North America.

DUNCAN, David, of *Manchester*, continued from Catalogue, Vol. 1, p. 547.
——National Life. By David Duncan. Being the substance of a Paper read at the Manchester Friends' Institute, on Fourth Month 22nd, 1870.
London : F. B. Kitto, 5, Bishopsgate Street, Without.
1870.
——**Can an Outward Revelation be Perfect.** Revelations upon the claim of Biblical Infallibility. By David Duncan. Second Editio.
London : F. Bowyer Kitto ; Manchester ; Hale & Roworth. . . . Crown 8vo. 1871. 2¼
——John Woolman. A Paper read at the Friends' Institute, Manchester. By David Duncan.
London : F. Bowyer Kitto ; Manchester, W. Hale.
Crown 8vo. 1871. 2¼
He died

‖DUNCAN, P. B.
——Motives of Wars, an Essay before the Bath Royal Literary Institution.
12mo. 1844.

DUNCON, Samuel, of *Ipswich*, in *Suffolk*.

——¶ Several PROPOSALS offered (by a Friend to Peace and Truth) to the Serious Consideration of the Keepers of the Liberties of the People of England, in Reference to a Settlement of Peace and Truth in this Nation. As also a TRUE NARRATIVE in short is chiefly to make known two or three Sums of Money concealed ; and Many of the Actings of the Proposer, SAMUEL DUNCON, late of *Ipswich* in *Suffolk*, are declared. From the year 1640 to the year 1652.
Printed at *London, by James Cottrel.*
                                             4to. 1659. 1

DUNDAS, William, continued from catalogue vol. 1, p. 547.
    He died at *Kingston-upon-Thames*, 23rd of 10th month, 1673, and was buried at *Kingston.*

DYER, MARY, continued from Catalogue, Vol. 1, p. 548.

——NARRATIVE of the MARTYRDOM AT BOSTON, of William Robinson, Marmaduke Stevenson, Mary Dyer, and William Leddra, in the year 1659. *With other particulars.* Price sixpence. [Edited by JOHN HARRISON ?].
Manchester, printed. . . . 12mo. 1841. 2

DYER, William, of *Chesham, in Buckinghamshire.*

——Christ's Famous Titles. And a Believer's Golden Chain. Handled in divers sermons by *William Dyer*, Preacher of the Gospel.
London : Printed for the Author small 8vo. 1661. 26.
Reprinted—(with a portrait) - *London* :
                                             8vo. 1663.

——A Cabinet of Jewels : or, a Glympse of Sion's Glory.
[*London ?*] . . . 8vo. 1663.

——Christ's Famous Titles, and A BELIEVERS' Golden Chain. Handled in divers Sermons. Together with his CABINET of *Jewels*, or a Glimpse of Sion's Glory. By WILLIAM DYER, Preacher of the Gospel.
    " *Unto me who am less than the least of all Saints, is this grace given, that I should Preach among the Gentiles the unsearchable Riches of Christ.*"—Ephes. 3, 8.
London, Printed for the Author, and now divulged for the good of private Families, especially his Friends in the County of Devon, 1666.
                                              12mo. 1666.

——Christ's Voice to LONDON and The Great Day of God's Wrath. Being the Substance of Two Sermons Preached (in the CITY) in the time of the sad VISITATION, Together with the Necessity of Watching and Praying.

DYER, William, *continued*.
 With a small Treatise of DEATH. By William Dyer,
a Servant of JESUS CHRIST.
  " *The Lord's voice cryeth to the City.*"—Mich. 6, 9.
  *London : Printed for E. Calvert, and are to be sold
at the Black-spread Eagle, near the West end
of Paul's* . . small 8vo. 1666. 10½

——Christ's voice to LONDON, &c.
       12mo. Printed in the year, 1670. 5¼
  NOTE.—In this edition is an " Epistle to the Reader,"
wherein William Dyer says, " Kind *Reader* as soon as my
Books came forth, several men made a prize of them, by
printing them over divers times without my knowledge,
with many gross mistakes and abuses, which was not a
little trouble to me, to see how the Author and the Buyer
were both abused. Therefore Courteous *Reader*, this may
give thee to understand that if thou hast occasion for
any of my books thou mayest have them at the *Black-
Spread Eagle*, at the West End of *Paul's*, truly printed."

——Dyer's Works, viz., Christ's Famous Titles ; or a Be-
liever's Golden Chain : II. A Cabinet of Jewels.
III. Christ's Voice to London, and the Great Day of
God's Wrath. 3 parts.
  London : Printed in the Year 1671 and 1674.
       12mo. ? 1664. 1670.
  NOTE.—Each part has a distinct Title, Register and
Pagination.

— —Christ's Famous Titles, and *A Believer's Golden Chain*.
Handled in divers Sermons. Together with A Cabinet
of Jewels, or a Glimpse of Sion's Glory. As also
Christ's Voice to LONDON. The Great Day of God's
Wrath. The *Necessity* of *Watching* and *Praying*,
with a small Treatise of Death. By *William Dyer*,
Preacher of the *Gospel*.
  *London : Printed for the use of Private Families,
especially his Friends in Devon* 12mo. 1676. 16

——Cyfoeth i'r Cymru neu Dryssor y Ffyddloniaid. Wedi
ei Egoryd mewn amryw o Bregethau. . . Ar ne
foeddyn agored, a'r uniawn fford iddi, mewn dwy
bregeth Gyda galwad i bechadwriaid gan Grist ei hun,
etc.
  Llundain . . . . . 12mo. 1706.

——Christ's Famous Titles, and a Believer's Golden Chain,
handled in divers Sermons, together with his Cabinet
of Jewels, or, a Glimpse of Sion's Glory.
  Glasgow. . . . . . 12mo. 1735.

——The works of the Reverend William Dyer.
  Glasgow. . . . . . 12mo. 1771.

DYER, William, *continued.*
— —CHRIST'S FAMOUS TITLES, and a Believer's Golden Chain, Handled in diverse SERMONS. Together with with his CABINET OF JEWELS; or, A GLIMPSE OF SION'S GLORY. By the Reverend WILLIAM DYER, Minister of the Gospel.
> EPH. iii. 8.—Unto me who am less than the least of all Saints, is this grace given, that I should preach among the Gentiles the unsearchable riches of Christ.

Falkirk: Printed by **Daniel Reid***, and sold at his Shop, near the South-Gate of the Church, in High Street, and by the Booksellers in Great Britain and Ireland.*
8vo. 1777. 14½

— —CHRIST'S VOICE TO LONDON; Being the Substance of a Sermon preached in the City, in the Time of the sad Visitation. Together with the Necessity of Watching and Praying. With a small Treatise on Death. Written by the late Reverend Mr. WILLIAM DYER, Minister of the Gospel at *Chesham* and *Cloudesbury,* in the County of *Bucks.*
> The Lord's Voice crieth unto the City, Micah, vi. 9.

Falkirk: *Printed and sold by* **Daniel Reid***, at his Shop at the West entry of the Church.*
8vo. 1777. 3¾

— —CHRIST'S FAMOUS TITLES, and a Believer's Golden Chain, together with his Cabinet of Jewels; or, A Glimpse of Sion's Glory. By the Rev. WILLIAM DYER, Late Preacher of the Gospel at Chesham and Chouldsbury, in the county of Bucks.
EDINBURGH; *Printed for J. Dickson and J. Fairbairn.* With . 12mo. 1798.

— —CHRIST'S VOICE TO LONDON; &c.
Edinburgh: Printed for the Booksellers.
12mo. 1798. } 12⅙

— —Sermon [on Cant. v. 16, being No. 3 of Christ's Famous Titles."]
See Collection.—A Collection of scarce and valuable sermons, etc. 12mo. 1814.

— —Ainmeanna cliuteach, chriosd: Stabhrnidh oir a Chreidnchich: agus an t'slighe chumhann, do neamh, maille ri tri sear monibh eile; agus smuainteanan mu'n bhes . . . . Amis air eadar—theanga—chadh O Bheurla gu Gaidhlig le. C. Maclanruinn.
Glaschu. . . . . . 8vo. 1817.

— —Christ's Famous Titles, and a Believer's Golden Chain. Also a cabinet of Jewels; or a Glimpse of Sion's

DYER, William, *continued.*
    Glory. Together with Christ's voice to London, etc.
        Berwick. . . . . 12mo. 1827.
——The Follower of the Lamb ; a Discourse with an introduction, by the Rev. T. Page.
        London : . . . 12mo. 1840.
——Christ's Famous Title and a Believer's Golden Chain. (No portrait).
    2nd large type edition.
        Edinburgh : . . . 12mo. 1855.
——Christ's Famous Titles ; Believer's Golden Chain, and the Straight Way to Heaven, &c., Ainmeannan Chuiteach Chrisosd, &c. [Translated from the English into Gaelic.]
        Edinburgh : . . . 12mo. 1860.
——The Famous Titles of Christ.
        Glasgow : . . . 12mo. 1863.

    " He turned Quaker in the latter part of his life, and lies interred in the burying ground in Southwark. Ob. April, 1696, Æt. 60." Granger's "Biographical History of England, 4th edition. Vol. 3, p. 337. 1804.

    " William Dyer occurs Minister here (Choulsbury) in 1663. Bishop Kennet mentions that he became a Quaker in the latter part of his life ; and dying in 1696, was buried amongst persons of that persuasion in Southwark. He appears to have been of a very pious but melancholy cast of mind, and was the Author of . . . . all written in nearly a similar style ; and are, perhaps, portions of, or compilations from his discourses in the pulpit, much resembling the style of the noted John Bunyan. He is said to have been ejected for nonconformity in 1662." George Lipscomb's History of the County of Buckingham. Vol. 3, p. 322. Folio, 1847.

    He died of a hectic fever the 9th of the 2nd month (April), 1696, aged 63 years, and was interred in Friends' Burial Ground in the Park, Southwark.
                      London Burial Registers.

DYMOND, Alfred H., *continued* from Catalogue, Vol. I, p. 548.
——WHO'S RIGHT ? A LETTER to the RIGHT HON. SIR GEORGE GREY, BART., Secretary of State for the Home Department, in reply to his Speech in the House of Commons, June 10th, 1856, in opposition to the Motion of W. EWART, ESQ., M.P., "For a Select Committee to inquire into the operation of the Laws imposing the Penalty of Death," By A. H. DYMOND, *Secretary to the Society for Promoting the Abolition of Capital Punishment.*

DYMOND, Alfred H., *continued.*
Printed for the Society for Promoting the Abolition of Capital Punishment, 5, BISHOPSGATE WITHOUT, LONDON.
Price 1d., or 10d. per dozen.
8vo. [1856.] 1½

DYMOND, Edith.
——Poor Match-Seller of Croydon.
[ANON.] 12mo.

DYMOND, Henry, *continued* from Catalogue, Vol. I, p. 548.
Contents of Dymond's "Instructive Narratives, 1825."

	PAGE.
William Penn's Treaty with the Indians	1
A Commendable Practice	9
Extract from Gough's History of Friends	10
Extract from John Griffith's Journal	12
The Capture of a vessel by the French	14
A narrow escape from Capture	16
Faithfulness in minor matters, of good effect	18
Sketch of the History of Friends, 1	20
Extract from John Churchman's Journal	23
Grave-stones	25
Conflict between affection and principle	27
Patience under Suffering	32
Specimen of the cruelty exercised towards our early Friends	34
Drinking healths	38
Confidence in Divine Protection	39
Remarkable Preservation	42
Sketch of the History of Friends, 2	43
Convincement of Benjamin Bangs	60
Anecdote of Peter the Great	67
William Penn's Domestic Regulations	70
Narrative from T. Ellwood's life	73
Thomas Ellwood's account of his Imprisonment	78
Days of the week	98
John Richardson and some Indians	100
Shoe-making in Prison (Samuel Bownas)	102
A conscientious scruple	105
Sketch of the History of Friends, 3	108
Providential Escape	133
Extract from T. Chalkley's Journal	136
Extract from John Richardson's life	138
Robert Barrow's Captivity among the Indians	140
Establishment of Meetings for Discipline	158

DYMOND, Jonathan, *continued* from Catalogue, Vol. I, p. 549.
——Essays on the principles of morality, &c.
[Edited by WILLIAM DYMOND.] 8vo. 1829. 61½
——Essays, 7th edition.—London . 1880.

DYMOND, Jonathan, *continued.*
——Essays, 8th edition,—London 1886. 35½
——THE PRINCIPLES OF MORALITY, and the Private and Political Rights and Obligations of Mankind. By JONATHAN DYMOND. Abridged, and provided with questions for the use of Schools and young persons generally. By Caroline M. Kirkland.
New York : C. S. Francis & Co., 252, Broadway.
18mo. 1842. 1

"In its present shape, skilfully abridged and condensed as it is by our intelligent countrywoman, Mrs. Kirkland, it is not only a work peculiarly adapted to the use of schools and young persons."—The *Oneida Whig.*

——The Church and the Clergy.
6th edition.
London : Printed by E. Couchman, 10, Throgmorton Street, and sold by the principal Booksellers in Town and Country. . 8vo. 1835. 3¼

DYMOND, Joseph John, of *Bradford.*
——Substance of an Address delivered at the Temperance Hall, Brisbane, Queensland, May 3rd., 1875.
8vo. [1875.] ¾

——THE MAINTENANCE OF MINISTERS. A Bible Lesson. By J. J. DYMOND.
[*Reprinted by permission from the* "FRIENDS' QUARTERLY EXAMINER."]
London : Barrett, Sons & Co., Printers, Beer Lane, E.C. . . . . 16mo. 1886. ½

DYMOND, Robert, of *Exeter.*
——Early Records of THE SOCIETY OF FRIENDS in DEVONSHIRE. By Robert Dymond, F.S.A.
R. Barrett & Sons, Printers, 13, Mark Lane, London.
16mo. 1873. 72 pages or 2¼ sheets.

E.

E (S.).
——REASONS against VOLUNTEER RIFLE CORPS.
W. G. Blackie & Co., Printers, Glasgow.
Large 4to. 1859. ¼

EARLE, Pliny, of *New York.* DR. POET.
——An Examination of the Practice of Bloodletting in Mental Disorders. By Pliny Earle, M.D.
New York : . . . 8vo. 1855. 126pp.
——Institutions for the Insane in Prussia, Austria, and Germany. By Pliny Earle, M.D.
New York : . . . 8vo. 1855. 246pp.

ECCLESTONE, Theodor, *continued* from Catalogue, Vol. 1, p. 554.
——The Testimony of Devonshire House Monthly Meeting concerning our worthy Friend, Theodor Ecclestone, deceased. (In MS.) . . 3/3mo. 1727.
<blockquote>Theodor Ecclestone was born in *London, 1650*, died at *Mortlake*, in *Surrey, 1726*, and was buried at *Wandsworth*.</blockquote>

EDDY, Thomas, *continued* from Catalogue, Vol. 1, p. 554.
——An ACCOUNT of the STATE PRISON or Peniteniary House, in the CITY OF NEW YORK. By [Thomas Eddy] one of the Inspectors of the Prison. (ANONYMOUS).
New York: Printed by Isaac Collins & Son.
8vo. 1801. 6⅛

EDGERTON, Walter, *continued* from Catalogue, Vol 1, p. 556.
——Modern Quakerism examined and contrasted with that of the 𝕬ncient 𝕿ype. By Walter Edgerton, of *Spiceland, Henry Co., Indiana, U.S.A.*
Second edition: Reprinted from First American Edition.
Manchester: William Irwin, Cathedral Chambers, Half Street . . . 8vo. 1876. 2
<blockquote>NOTE.—To this Edition there is added an " Appeal to the English Reader," by George Pitt, of Mitcham, which is printed on the back of the title page, subsequent copies issued with a " Prefatory Note," by Walter Edgerton, and another by W. Irwin : in these later copies, the word " Appeal," is changed to " Address," printed on the back of the title page of the cover.</blockquote>
——WALTER EDGERTON'S DISOWNMENT by *Spiceland Monthly Meeting, within Indiana Yearly Meeting.* —STATEMENT OF THE CASE BY WALTER EDGERTON. . . . . 8vo. [1877.] ¼

EDWARDS, W. F. (Not a Friend).
——See DR. THOMAS HODGKIN.

EILERS, Jonas, *born at Timmel, in East Friesland.*
——Some Particulars of the LIFE and DEATH of JONAS EILERS.
<blockquote>" The child shall die an hundred years old ; but the sinner being an hundred years old shall be accursed."—Isa. lxv. 20.
BRADFORD, YORKSHIRE : Printed for the FRIENDS' TRACT ASSOCIATION ; Depository at their Meeting House Cottage, where persons may be supplied with Tracts on reasonable terms. (Edit. 5,000).</blockquote>
Henry Wardman, Printer, Bradford. 8vo. 1836. ½

ELCOCK, Charles, of *London, Gloucester, Belfast, &c.*, continued from Catalogue, Vol. 1., p. 559.

——The CONFESSION OF NON-BELIEF, issued by Ohio Select Yearly Meeting, EXAMINED. By CHARLES ELCOCK.
 London : *S. Harris & Co., 5, Bishopsgate Street, Without.*
 Dublin : Hodges, Figgis & Co., Grafton Street.
          Demy 8vo. $3\frac{1}{8}$

——IS THAT THE GOSPEL ? Being a reply to Robert Alsop's Controversial Tract, entitled "WHAT IS THE GOSPEL ?" Wherein his mis-translations of Greek and Latin, and his Garbled Extracts from Barclay's Apology, are exposed. By CHARLES ELCOCK.
 Our Testimony is not against the usefulness of the Holy Scriptures as an outward means, but against there being such an absolute necessity for them, as if without them, no knowledge of God, nor fellowship with Him, could be had.
 Manchester: *William Irwin, 35, Fennell Street.*
 NOTE.—The Preface is dated from "Manchester: 71, Market Street, 11th Month 1st, 1873."
        8vo.   1873.   3

——A GIFT OF SINGING.
 (*Reprinted from* "THE BRITISH FRIEND.")
    Signed Cardium.
         12mo.   No date. $\frac{1}{6}$

——To Friends in Ireland and to all to whom this may come. (10, Dunluce Street, Belfast, *Second of Fourth Month*, 1882.) . . . 24mo. [1882.] 4 pages.

ELLIS, Benjamin, M.D., Professor.
——The Medical Formular, being a Collection of Prescriptions derived from the writings and practice of many of the most eminent Physicians in America and Europe, Benjamin Ellis, Lecturer on Pharmacy.
 Philadelphia :
           8vo.   1826.

ELLIS, John, of *Leicester*.
——(An Account of) the late John Ellis. (*From the Leicester Journal, October 31, 1862.*)
  Crossley and Clarke, Printers, Leicester.
          8vo.   1862. $\frac{1}{2}$

*ELLIS, Sarah (Stickney).—Continued from Catalogue, Vol. 2, p. 626.
——PICTURES OF PRIVATE LIFE. 𝔉irst 𝔖eries. BY MRS. ELLIS, Author of "The Mothers of England," etc., etc. Seventh Edition.

ELLIS, Sarah, *continued.*
    London : *William Tegg and Co., 85, Queen-Street,*
      Cheapside. . . . . Small 8vo. 1850. 23
——(The Same.) 𝔖econd 𝔖eries.
    (Same imprint). . . . Small 8vo. 1850. 26½
——The Same. 𝔗hird 𝔖eries.
    (Same imprint). . . . Small 8vo. 1850. 23⅛
      NOTE.—Each Volume has a Frontispiece.
    She died at *Hoddesdon,* the 16th of 6th mo., 1872.

ELLWOOD, Thomas.—Continued from Catalogue, Vol. 1,
    p. 562.
——Sacred History.
    From the First American compared with the last
    London Edition. Complete in 2 Vols.
      Mountpleasant, Ohio : Republished by Enoch &
      Emily M. Harris. . . Large 8vo. 1854.
    First American Edition. . . . . 1804.
——Davideis.
    4th Edition [so called]. 1775.
    4th, 1st American. . 1838.
        1808.

ELLYTHORP, Sebastian, continued from Catalogue, Vol. 1,
    p. 571.
——A TESTIMONY WHEREIN is showed Weighty Reasons
Why the National Ministers, their Way and Practice,
is conscientiously disowned, and their Maintenance
by *Tythes* or other Hire denyed. Also, a Testimony,
from a certain Experience to the People called
Presbyterians, and all that are zealous in their way.
Also, a Testimony to them called *Anabaptists,* with
some Reflections upon a Book (propagated among
them) called, *The Child's Instructor,* wherein the
Author hath vented many Detractions and Slanders
against the *Light within,* and the People that bear
Testimony of it. Which, herein are plainly answered,
and the true Light and Way of Life, in which the
Antient *Christians* walked, and of which they testi-
fied, and which is now the same, is faithfully
vindicated.
*By a Sufferer in Bonds for the Testimony of Truth
against Deceit, and the Anti-christian Oppression of
Tythes, and other forced Maintenance for the
Ministry, Imposition of Oaths, &c.*
          𝔖ebastian 𝔈llythorp.
    *London, Printed and Sold by T. Sowle, at the
    Crooked Billet, in Holywell-Lane, in Shoreditch.*
                4to. 1692.

EMERY, Mary Ann, of *Bath*.
——Simple Truths : written under the influence of God's Love. [ANON.]
>London : *Charles Gilpin*.
>>18mo. [No date, 1851 ?] 103 pages.

EMERSON, William, of ?
——Questions for *John Bewick*, called Minister of *Stanhope*.
>NOTE.—These Questions are inserted in Bewick's Book ; Printed, 1660.

*EMMOT, George, of *Durham*.
This Pamphlet was entered in my Catalogue, Vol. 1, p. 576, but it seems I gave only the heading as on p. 1. I now give the correct title, which is as follows, viz. :—
——A NORTHERN BLAST or the SPIRITUAL QUAKER CONVERTED : Being Soul-saving Advice to the giddy people of *England*, who are running headlong to Destruction. Wherein are shewed the manner of their Meetings in the County of *Yorkshire* and *Durham* their Quakings, Shreekings, and ridiculous Actions ; also their fond and false restings of the Scriptures. With a full Examination, and Conviction of their Tenets. By G. EMMOT, of *Durham*, Gent., formerly a Brother amongst them, but now (by the help of God) Converted, and Established in the truth.
>London. Printed for *R. Lambert, and are to be sold at the signe of the Angel in Cornhill*, 1655.

——and title, for the same Book to promote its sale in *York*.
>London. Printed for *R. Lambert, Bookseller, at the Ministers' Gate in York*. . 4to. 1655.

At the end a single leaf was added, consisting of Scripture quotations, beginning with " *Acts 20, 30.—Also of our ourselves shall men arise, &c.*," ending :—
>" *Reader*, I entreat thee conscionably to study these Scriptures, and compare the doctrines of all Hereticall Enemies of the Ministry with them."

ESTAUGH, Elizabeth, was the daughter of JOHN HADDON, a Friend, who lived in the Parish of *St. George, Southwark*, and by trade a Blacksmith, or an Anchorsmith. ELIZABETH HADDON was born in 1682, and married JOHN ESTAUGH, of *Kelvedon, Essex*. She died March 30th, 1762, in the 80th year of her age.
——Account of Elizabeth Estaugh in the "West Jersey Press." June 17th, 1868.

EVANS, Charles, of *Philadelphia*, continued from Catalogue, Vol. I., p. 577 ; see also " The Friend," 7 mo., 1876.

EVANS, Charles, *continued*.

——AN EXAMEN of parts relating to the SOCIETY OF FRIENDS, in a recent work by Robert Barclay entitled "The Inner Life of the Religious Societies of the Commonwealth." By CHARLES EVANS, M.D.
Philadelphia : *Sold by Jacob Smedley, 304, Arch Street.* 8vo. 1878.   6½

EVANS, Edward, a Member of the Society of Friends, and Secretary of the Neath and South Wales Temperance Association, son of WILLIAM and MARY BINNS EVANS, and was born on the 27th of 7th month, 1833 ; nephew of JONATHAN REES, of *Neath*. His father was a grocer in *Birmingham*.

——Neath Total Abstinence Society. Report of the Proceedings of a PUBLIC MEETING, held in the Town Hall, Neath, on May 14th, 1859, In Memory of the late EDWARD EVANS.
"Them that honour Me I will honour, and they that despise Me shall be lightly esteemed."—I. Samuel, ii., 30.
Neath : *Whittington, Printer and Binder, Post Office.* . . . Small 8vo. 1859.   2

EVANS, William, continued from Catalogue, Vol. I., p. 580.
——Journal of the Life and Religious Services of WILLIAM EVANS, a Minister of the Gospel in the Society of Friends.
Philadelphia : For sale at Friends' Book Store, No. 304, Arch Street. . . 8vo. 1870. 44¾
[Edited by CHARLES EVANS, his brother.]
He died the 12th of the 5th month, 1867, in the 81st year of his age.

EVANS, Thomas, of *Philadelphia*, son of Jonathan and Hannah Evans, was born in Philadelphia in 1798. Continued from Catalogue, Vol. I., p. 579.
——A DEFENCE of the Christian Doctrines of the SOCIETY OF FRIENDS, &c. [ANON.]
Philadelphia. . . . 8vo. 1825. 21¾
See HICKSITE CONTROVERSY, Vol. I., p. 942, of Catalogue.

——Exposition of the Faith, &c.
1867.

——(Sketch of) Friends or Quakers. In a work entitled "An Original History of the Religious Denominations at present existing in the United States, &c." Compiled and arranged by I. Daniel Rupp.
Philadelphia : *Published by J. Y. Humphreys.*
Harrisbury : *Clyde & Williams.*   8vo. 1844.

EVANS, Thomas, *continued.*
—— MEMORIAL of THOMAS EVANS, a Deceased Minister, Member of the Yearly Meeting of Friends, held in Philadelphia, 1870.
> Friends' Book Store, No. 304, Arch Street.
> [*W. H. Pile, Printer, 422, Walnut Street.*]
> 12mo. [1870.] 1⅙
> He died the 24th of 5th month, 1868, aged 70 years.

EVENS, Samuel, of *Penketh.*
—— A few considerations on the DEFINITION OF FAITH, as professed by 𝔗𝔥𝔢 𝔖𝔬𝔠𝔦𝔢𝔱𝔶 𝔬𝔣 𝔉𝔯𝔦𝔢𝔫𝔡𝔰, to whom they are respectfully submitted. By Samuel Evens.
> *Manchester*: *William Irwin, Cathedral Chambers, behind the Cathedral, Half Street.* 8vo. 1874. ½
> Price, 1/2 per dozen, post free; or 6/6 per hundred.
> He died the 3rd of 1st mo., 1878, aged 85 years.

*EVERETT, John Richard, of *Islington*, a Schoolmaster, last of *Nottingham.* He left the Society and joined the Wesleyans. Continued from Catalogue, Vol. I., p. 581.
> He died 1871, see a memorial card. Theanna (his daughter), of Kingston, once lived with John Harris.

F.

F., S.
—— A Letter addressed to "My dear children," and beginning, "Religion is the one thing needful, &c."
> *J. F. Dove, Printer, St. John's Square.*
> 4to. [1825.] ½
> On my copy is written, "1825, 6/10. From the Author to Richard Phillips."

FABER, Albertus Otto. The following particulars respecting Albertus Otto Faber are given from the "Calendar of State Papers," mentioned in the "Catalogue," Vol. 1, p. 583, which I thought would be interesting to many Friends and others, during his imprisonment in Oxford Castle, viz :—
> April 11, 1667, Oxford.—[Alb. Otto] Faber to Williamson. Thanks for favours to his wife; entreats influence for delivery from his present purgatory and misery. [*French.*]
> April 23, 1667, Oxford.—Dr. A. O. F, to Williamson. Will give the reasons why at the Oxford Assizes he was not released, as were the others detained on the same business;

FABER, Albertus Otto, *continued*.

they were kept 20 weeks in prison, to be tried for the firing of Banbury; but at the trial, Judge Twysden enquired if he had not been before Council, and given recognizance to depart the land: said he had not, on which the judge said the matter should be referred to Lord Arlington, and sent him back to gaol. The judge spoke of him to Lord Lovelace, as a fortune-teller and mountebank, of whom the land should be rid. Hen. Stokes and others of Banbury tried to get the other three released, and the writer only detained, on pretence of orders from high quarters; the gaoler also, to increase his livelihood, complains of ill-conduct in his prisoners. The Calendar orders his detention, without bail, as a dangerous person, to abide the course of law. Begs favour for his deliverance; would think it folly to stay in the country contrary to the King's wishes. The society of debauched persons amongst whom he lives doubles the pain of his imprisonment. [*French*, 2 *pages*.]

April 30, 1667, Oxford. 109. Albertus Otto Faber to the King.—Since His Majesty sent for him to England, presented his discourses "De Magnetismo Vasorum maris" to him; being prevented by winter from returning to his Country, fell in with the people called Quakers, and mingled with them to penetrate into their profession, when three years ago he was taken prisoner at one of their meetings. Has always been supposed a Quaker since, although the Court of the Bishop of London has certified his attendance at the French Church. Assures His Majesty of the continuance of his devotion. Has never entertained a thought to his prejudice nor that of his government. Entreats the protection promised to him as a stranger at his first interview, and restoration to liberty. [*French*, 2 *pages*.]

78. Warham Jemmet, Jun., to Williamson.—The Flanders mails were detained by bad weather. One went thence this morning, having on board Albertus Otto Faber, who had His Majesty's pass for his transportation. *Annexing* 78. *1. Memorandum by Theophilus Wimple, master of a packet boat*, that he has *received from John Sumner*, messenger, *the person of Albertus Otto Faber, to convey him to Flanders. With note that he was put on board the boat on the 22nd instant. August 21, 1667.*

33. Albertus Otto Faber to [Lord Arlington].—Is a Stranger, and has no friend but his wife, also a stranger, and being left behind by the judge in arrest, begs his lordship to pardon this mode of presenting his requests to the King and himself, and to favour them. [French.] *Encloses.*

33. 1.—*Petition of Albertus Otto Faber* to Lord Arlington, to dismiss him in a *gracious way, being a stranger in doleful condition; after long detention, a pass was ordered for his departure, but the plague, and then the fire which*

FABER, Albertus Otto, *continued.*
>*destroyed his house, prevented; has behaved guiltlessly since, but having given in a petition for his departure, went meanwhile to Banbury to settle his affairs, was apprehended, sent to the common gaol, and on the assizes was referred to his lordship. Oxford Castle, March 29, 1667.*
>33. II.—*Petition of Albertus Otto Faber to the King, to receive him into favour, according to his proclamation in behalf of foreigners that live peaceably, and graciously to accept his sufferings, having been under restraint on mere suspicion, and nothing laid to his charge. Oxford Castle, March 29, 1667.*
>Whitehall, August, 2, 1667.—Order in Council,—on petition of Albertus Otto Faber, for release from his three years' imprisonment in Oxford Castle, as nothing has been proved against him—renewing the order of May 7 for his removal, and ordering that he be delivered to John Sumner, messenger, and brought before Lord Arlington. Page 355.

FARDON, William, of *Witney, Oxon.*
—— Outlines of a PLAN OF EDUCATION proposed by William Fardon, *Witney, Oxon.*
>Folio. 30th of 10th Month, 1798. ½

FARQUHAR, W. H., of *North America.*
—— Annals of Sandy Spring, 1884.

FARRAND, Banks, continued from Catalogue, Vol. 1, p. 593.
>He died at Stafford, of consumption, 29th of 4th Month, 1870, aged 46 years.

FARRINGTON, Geo. H., of *Watling Street and Winchmore Hill, near London.*
—— The Friends' Almanac.

FENWICK, John, late of *Binfield,* in the *County of Berks, England,* continued from Catalogue, Vol. 1, p. 602.
>Will—Probate at New Salem, 16th day of April, 1684. Recorded 5th day of May, 1684.
>>Samuel Hedge, Recorder.
>
>"And I declare this to be my last Will and Testament, and set my hand and Seal at Fenwick Grove upon my sick bed this the 7th day of August, 1683. John Fenwick.
>"Witnesses, Thomas Yorke, A. Carey, Thomas Webley."
>Priscilla Fenwick, daughter of John Fenwick, of *Binfield, Berkshire,* married at T. Curtis' House in Reading, 11th Mo. 16, 1671, to Edward Champneys, of *London.*

Berkshire and Oxfordshire Records.
>"Salem Deeds, B.," page 69. William Penn, John Smith, Samuel Hedge, and Richard Tindall, Executors of John Fenwick, deceased, &c.

* ?FERRIS, Benjamin, of *North America.*

—— A History of the Original Settlements on the Delaware from its discovery by Hudson to the Colonization, under William Penn, to which is added an account of the ecclesiastical affairs of the Swedish Settlers, and a History of Wilmington from its first settlement to the present time, illustrated by drawings by Benjamin Ferris.
Wilmington :
          8vo. 1846. 312 pages.

FERRIS, Caroline Murray, wife of Lindley Murray Ferris, and eldest daughter of Robert I. and Elizabeth Colden Murray. Her residence was at Coldenham, Orange County, in the State of New York.

—— A Christian's Testimony at Death : or, Memoirs of the Last Hours of Caroline Murray Ferris. [Edited by MARY MURRAY ?].
New York : John F. Trow, Printer, 49, Ann Street. . . . . . 12mo. 1853. ¾

NOTE.—With the above is printed (the pagination running on), " A Short Account of the Last Sickness and Death of Gertrude Colden Hussey " (her Sister).
 Caroline Murray Ferris died the 30th of 10th Month, 1852, aged 39 years.
 Gertrude G. Hussey died the 14th of 9th Month, ? 1848. ?

FIELD, John, was the son of John and Anne Field, and was born the 22nd of 3rd Month (May), 1652. His father was a Wire Drawer and flatter of Gold and Silver, and lived in Vine Street, alias *Grub Street, where his son John was born in the Parish of Giles Cripplegate, and was by Company a Blacksmith and Citizen of London. He gave his Son a good education, he learned both *Latin* and *Greek.* He appears to have been convinced when about 17 years of age.
 From " *Some Account of the Life and Sufferings of John Field* " (*in M.S. Devonshire House Archives*).
   * Now called Milton Street.
Continued from Catalogue, Vol. 1, p. 603.

—— Friendly Advice in the Spirit of Love unto Believing PARENTS, and their tender OFF-SPRING, in relation to their Christian Education. *The Third Edition.* With Additional Caution and Counsel unto Young Men and Maidens. By J.F.

FIELD, John, *continued*.
> " *And ye Fathers, provoke not your Children to wrath, but bring them up in the Nurture and Admonition of the Lord.*"
> —Eph. 6. 4.
> " *Children obey your Parents in the Lord, for this is right.*"
> —Eph. 6. 1.
>> *London : Printed for T. Northcott, in George-yard, near Lombard Street.* . Small 12 mo. 1695.   3
>>> NOTE.—To this book is a " Postscript," part by the Author, but chiefly by RICHARD SCORYER, dated, " *Wandsworth*, the *15th*, *7th* Month, 88."

FIRTH, Joseph Firth Bottomley, LL.B., son of JOSEPH BOTTOMLEY, was born near Huddersfield in the year 1842.

—— Municipal London ; or, London Government as it is, and London under a Municipal Council. By Joseph F. B. Firth, LL.B.
>> *London : Longmans & Co.* .   . 8vo. 1876.
>>> See a long Review of this book in " *The Weekly Dispatch, February 20, 1876.*"

—— CHELSEA SCHOOL BOARD ELECTION, 1876.—ADDRESS of JOSEPH F. B. FIRTH, ESQ., delivered during the Election. To which is added a copy of the Canon Cromwell Correspondence, and some Press Notices. Reprinted by order of the Executive.
>> *London : Printed for the Author by Yates & Alexander, Chancery Buildings, Chancery Lane, W.C. Price Twopence* . . 8vo. 1876. 3⅛
>>> He died suddenly on the 3rd of 9th mo., 1889, at *Chamounix*, in *Switzerland*, and was buried in the little English churchyard there.
>>> For an Account of him and his Portrait, see the " Pictorial News," Vol. XXV, No. 629, September 14th, 1889.

FISHER, Abraham, of *Holmwood* near *Dorking*, formerly of Ireland but now of Croydon, last of

—— Some Correspondence, &c., relating to a work, in private circulation, called, " Extracts from my Note-book." [By JOSIAH FORSTER.] For Members of the Society of Friends.
>> *John Bellows, Printer, Steam Press, Gloucester.*
>> 12mo. [1866.]   ½

FISHER, Mary, *continued* from Catalogue, Vol. 1, p. 612.

—— Mary Fisher ; or, the Quaker Maiden and the Grand Turk ; with other poems.
>> *Philadelphia.* .   . . 18mo. 1845. 36pp.

FISHER, Myers, a Lawyer at *Philadelphia*, and a Quaker, died March 12, 1819, aged 71. He was a man of science and an eloquent orator. He published an answer to Paine's "Age of Reason."
  Blake's Biographical Dictionary, 8th Edition, Boston, 1853.

FISHER, Samuel and Miers, of *Philadelphia*.
——Letter (printed) to Morris Birkbeck, date *Philadelphia, 11th Month, 18th,* 1793. (On the fever in Philadelphia.)
  Folio. [1793.] ½

*FISHER, Thomas, of *Philadelphia*.
——The Dial of the Seasons or a Portraiture of Nature, by Thomas Fisher.
  "The Sun with one eye seeth all the world."—*Shakespeare.*
  Philadelphia. . . . . 8vo. 1845. 217pp.
——The Songs of the Sea Shells,—A Collection of Poems.

FISHER, William Logan, of *Wakefield, Philadelphia County*.
——Pauperism and Crime, by William Logan Fisher.
  "The right use of riches is more commendable than that of arms. And not to desire them at all, more glorious than to use them well."—*Life of Coriolanus.*
  Philadelphia. Published by the Author.
  12mo. 1831. 119pp.
——THE HISTORY of the INSTITUTION OF THE SABBATH DAY, ITS USES AND ABUSES; with NOTICES OF THE PURITANS, THE QUAKERS, the national and other Sabbath Conventions, and of the Union between Church and State. By William Logan Fisher.
  Philadelphia: John Penington, 169, Chestnut-street.
  12mo. 1845. 8
Reprinted, 2nd Edition, revised and enlarged.
  Philadelphia. . . . 12mo 1859. 248pp.
——Observations on Mental Phenomena, Pauperism, and Crime.
  Philadelphia . . . . . 1851.
——Review of the Doctrine and Discipline of the Society of Friends.
  Philadelphia. . . . . . 1854.

*FOGGIT, Ann, imprisoned in *York Castle*, for the murder of her husband, Abraham Foggit.
——Her confession and clearance of the People called Quakers.
  Broadside. *York Castle, the 30th of December,* 1715. 1

FOLGER, Peter, was the *grandfather*, on the maternal side, of Dr. Benjamin Franklin; his mother was Abiah Folger, daughter of Peter Folger, one of the first colonists of *New England*. Peter Folger was invited to remove with his family to Nantucket, to officiate as miller, weaver, and interpreter of the Indian language; his son Eleazer was to act as shoemaker; and, as a proper encouragement to these several occupations, a grant of one-half of a share of land, with all the accommodations thereunto belonging, was made to the father. He accepted the invitation, and, in 1663, removed thither."
Macy's "*History of Nantucket*," *1835, p. 25.*

—— A Looking-glass for the Times, or the former spirit of New England revived in this generation. By Peter Folger. . . . . 1675.
See an extract from the above in verse, in Macy's " History of Nantucket," p. 287.

FOLGER, Peleg, of *Nantucket*, "was a Member and Elder of the Society of Friends. In early life he exhibited traits of character, which gave him a great superiority over others of his age. His literary acquirements were the result of his own unaided industry, for his school education was very limited, his youth being principally employed in the farming business. At about the age of 21 he began the business of a seaman, which he followed many years, both in whaling and cod fishing. In addition to keeping the run of the vessel, like an experienced navigator, he frequently introduced in his journals pieces of poetry and compositions in prose, and occasionally sentences in Latin, besides arithmetical and algebraical problems. His general deportment was serious and contemplative. It was rare that he indulged in levity, but he was free and sociable in conversation on useful subjects, whether moral or religious. He was considered as a monitor in all his conduct through life; beloved by all good people, he commanded the respect and obedience of those who looked to him for support and protection, among whom were several fatherless children. His knowledge of Mathematics and of the Natural Sciences generally, was considered by judges to be far superior to many who had had the advantages of a classical education. His character as a Christian, from his youth to the time of his decease, was almost without blemish. For several days previous to his departure he appeared to have a satisfac-

FOLGER, Peter, *continued.*
    tory presentiment of his approaching end, and that the sting of death was entirely removed. He had much to say by way of advice to his friends and neighbours, who visited him in his last moments. He died in the year 1789, aged 55 years."
    Macy's "History of Nantucket," p. 294.
——" Dominum Collandamus." [Let us praise the Lord.] Inserted in Macy's "History of Nantucket," &c., p. 295.

FORD, John, of York.
——At a conference of Friends on the subject of Education, held at Ackworth, the 27th of 7th mo., 1836, the following minute was adopted.—Signed, John Ford, Secretary, pro tem. . . . . 4to. [1836.]   ¼
——MEMOIR of WILLIAM TANNER, compiled chiefly from autobiographical memoranda. Edited by John Ford.
    London : F. Bowyer Kitto, Bishopsgate Street Without. York : William Sessions, Low Ousegate. 8vo. 1868. 17
    See WILLIAM TANNER.
——MEMORIALS of JOHN FORD. Edited by SILVANUS THOMPSON.
    London : Samuel Harris & Co., 5, Bishopsgate Street Without. York : William Sessions, 15, Low Ousegate. 8vo. 1877. 16¼

FORSTER, Joseph Binyon, of *Spring Bank, Altrincham,* near *Manchester.*
——On Liberty. An address to the Members of the Society of Friends. By their Fellow-Member, Joseph B. Forster. *Read at the Manchester Friends' Institute, on the Twelfth of Fourth Month,* 1867.
    London : F. Bowyer Kitto.
    Sunderland : W. H. Hills. . Crown 8vo. 1867. 2
      NOTE.—On the half-title page, the imprint is, "Sunderland : Printed by Wm. Henry Hills. London : F. Bowyer Kitto, 5, Bishopsgate Street Without ; Joseph Smith, 2, Oxford Street, Whitechapel.
      Manchester : Hale and Roworth.
——The Society of Friends and Freedom of Thought in 1871. By Joseph B. Forster. (On the disownment of David Duncan).
    London : F. Bowyer Kitto.
    Manchester : W. Hale. . Crown 8vo. 1871. 2
——The Manchester Friend, Published on the 15th of each month, commencing —— and ending 187—.

FORSTER, Josiah, of *Tottenham*, continued from Catalogue, Vol. 1., p. 623.
—— An Address to those who have been brought to a knowledge of the Truth as it is in Jesus. By Josiah Forster.
London: *Printed by Edward Newman, Devonshire Street, Bishopsgate.* . 12mo. 1865. ½
—— Some thoughts on Education in the love of an Elder Brother. J.F. . . . Folio. 1867. 1
—— and GEORGE S. GIBSON.—Madagascar Educational Fund. . . . Large 4to. [1869.] ½
—— Extracts from the Letters of Hannah Maria Whitwell, who died in 1866, at the age of 87.
[Edited by J. Forster.] Printed for private circulation only.
[*London: R. Barrett and Sons, Printers, Mark Lane.*] 8vo. 1869. 2
—— Letters to the Younger Members of the Religious Society of Friends; to which are added some further Reflections. (3rd Month, 1869).
[*London: R. Barrett and Sons, Printers, Mark Lane.*] . . . 8vo. [1869.] 2¼
—— Letters to FRIENDS in Great Britain, Ireland and America. (See B. Friend, 10th mo., 1869).
(Printed, but not published).
London: *Printed by Richard Barrett & Sons. Mark Lane.* . . . 8vo. 1869. 5⅞
—— MISCELLANEOUS ESSAYS; very generally with reference to THE CHRISTIAN PRINCIPLES OF THE RELIGIOUS SOCIETY OF FRIENDS. Printed for private circulation only.
London: Richard Barrett & Sons, Printers, Mark Lane. 8vo. 1870. 12

Contents.

	PAGE
I.—Suggestions on Education. Offered in love to Parents among Friends.	1
II.—Some Detached Thoughts on the Duties of a Teacher in a Boarding School.	14
III.—An Address to Friends in America.	21
IV.—Reflections on the Preaching of the Gospel. . .	35
V.—A Chronicle of some of the Historical Events of Past Years, most of them occurring in the course of the present Century, more or less in connection with our Religious Society in this land.	53
VI.—Meditations on Faith; on the Wisdom and Power of God; and on the Character of Holy Scripture . .	73

FORSTER, Josiah, *continued.*

    VII.—An Address to those who have been brought to a knowledge of the Truth as it is in Jesus. . . . PAGE 86

    VIII.—Letters to the Younger Members of the Religious Society of Friends; to which are added some further Reflections. 96

    IX.—To my Fellow-members of the Committee of the British and Foreign Bible Society. 144

    X.—A Retrospect of Past Days, at the age of eighty-two . 151

    XI.—Reflections after Reading the Sixty-seventh Report of the British and Foreign Bible Society. . . . 161

    XII.—Brief Notices of Two Proceedings at Rome. . . 164

    XIII.—Brief Summary of Meditations on the Practical Character of the Gospel. 171

    XIV.—A Few Observations on the Great Truths of the Christian Religion. 177

——" Memorial adopted by the Committee on occasion of the Decease of Josiah Forster, Esq." In the " Monthly Reporter of the British and Foreign Bible Society," August 1, 1870. No. 15, Vol. 9.

    London: Bible Society's House, Blackfriars, E.C.
                                                           8vo.   1870.

    He died the 27th of the 6th month, 1870, aged nearly 88 years, and was interred on the 2nd of 7th month, in Friends' Burial Ground at *Winchmore Hill*.

FORSTER, Thomas, of *London.*

——*A Guide to the Blind* Pointed to, or, a true 𝔗𝔢𝔰𝔱𝔦𝔪𝔬𝔫𝔶 to the LIGHT WITHIN. Wherein some men are reproved, others counselled and encouraged, but all (who are ignorant of their *true Guide*) directed to the *path of life*. With a Friendly CALL to all *Notionists* and high *Professors of Religion*, in what *Form* soever, to come speedily down from their *Pinnacles*, lest they *fall* into *temptation*. Also some *Queries* to the persecuting Ministers of the *Church of* ENGLAND. *Written for the Truth's sake by* T.F.

    " *The darkness is past, and the true light now shineth.*".— 1 John 2. 8. " *See therefore that ye walk circumspectly, not as fools, but as wise.*"—Eph. 5. 15.

    London: Printed for the Author, and are to be sold by G. Calvert, at the Black-spread-Eagle, near the west end of Pauls, & N. Brooks, at the Angel, in Cornhil, 1659.   Small 8vo.   1659.   6

    NOTE.—This is the full title of that entered in the Catalogue, Vol. 1., p. 624; there are also other editions.

FORSTER, Thomas.—" He was descended from the ancient family of Forster, formerly of *Bamborough Castle*, in *Northumberland*, so frequently alluded to in the History of England, and a relation of General Forster, who headed the Army in favour of the Stuarts in 1715." See *Forster's* "*Original Letters of Locke, &c,*" *Preface, p. 119.* He married DOROTHY FURLY, daughter of BENJOHAN FURLY, the son of BENJAMIN FURLY, of *Rotterdam.*

FORSTER, Edward, of *Walthamstow, Essex*, was the son of the above Thomas and Dorothy Forster. He married SUSANNA FURNEY, descended from an ancient and respectable family in *Gloucestershire*, by whom he had issue three sons; THOMAS FURLY FORSTER, BENJAMIN MEGGOT FORSTER, and EDWARD FORSTER.

FORSTER, Thomas Furly, of *Clapton*, near *London*, son of the above EDWARD FORSTER. He died in the 10th month, 1825, and was the author of the following.

——*Flora Tonbrigensis* ; or, a Catalogue of Plants growing wild in the neighbourhood of Tonbridge Wells, arranged according to the Linnæan System, from Sir J. E. Smith's *Flora Britannica*. With three plates of rare plants. By T. F. Forster, F.L.S., &c.
 London : *Printed by Richard and Arthur Taylor, Shoe Lane, and sold by J. and Arch, Cornhill; and J. Sprange, Library, Tonbridge Wells.*
          8vo. 1816. 14.

  He was also the Author jointly with his brothers, Benjamin Meggot and Edward Forster, of the Botanical Notices in Gough's Edition of Camden's Britannia, and of several publications on the subject of Botany.

FORSTER, Edward (his Brother) ⎫
FORSTER, Benjamin Meggot (his brother) ⎬ See above.

*FORSTER, Thomas, of *Boreham*, near *Chelmsford, Essex*, son of the above THOMAS FURLY FORSTER.

——ORIGINAL LETTERS of LOCKE ; ALGERNON SIDNEY : and ANTHONY, LORD SHAFTESBURY, Author of the " Characteristics." With an Analytical Sketch of THE WRITINGS AND OPINIONS OF LOCKE and other Metaphysicians, by T. FORSTER, M.B., F.LS., M.A.S., Corr. Memb. of the Acad. of N. Science at Philadelphia, &c.
 LONDON : *J. B. Nichols and Son, Parliament Street* 12mo. 1830. 33½
 Reprinted, with alterations,

FORSTER, Thomas, *continued.*
——Original Letters of John Locke, Alg. Sidney, and Lord Shaftesbury, with an Analytical Sketch of the Writings and Opinions of Locke and other Metaphysicians, by T. Forster, M.B., F.L.S., M.A.S., Corr. Memb. of the Acad. of N. Science at Philadelphia, &c.—The Second Edition.
 London : *Privately printed.* . . . 8vo. 1847. 18¼
 NOTE.—Most of these letters are addressed to Benjamin Furly and Arent Furly.
——Pocket Encyclopædia of Natural Phœnomena. By Thomas Forster, M.B., F.L.S., M.A.S. . . 12mo.
——Synoptical Catalogue of British Birds.
——Observations on the Genus Hirundo.
——Perennial Calendar. . . . 8vo.
——Researches on Atmospheric Phœnomena.
 He died at *Brussels*, in 1830 (a Roman Catholic).

FORSTER, William, *continued* from Catalogue, Vol. 1, p. 624.
——And others.—Extract from the Report of a Committee of Hardshaw East Monthly Meeting held at Manchester, the 8th of 12th Month, 1836, appointed to visit those who had sent in the resignation of their membership, and which report was received, read, and approved at an adjournment of the said meeting, held the 15th of 12th Month, 1836.
     (Lithograph) Folio. [1836.] 1
 The other signatures are :—Edward Pease, Thomas Robson, Peter Clare, George Richardson, Thomas Binyon, Richard Atkinson, Barnard Dickenson, and Isaac Robson.
——A Christian Exhortation to Sailors, &c.
 Reprinted,— *Newcastle* : *Printed by Edward Walker, Pilgrim Street* . . 12mo. 1821. ½
——Circular to accompany Yearly Meeting Address.
 Philadelphia : *Rakestraw* . . . . 1850.
——"A Brief Biographical Memoir of the late W. Forster."—In "The Anti-Slavery Reporter," Vol. 2. No. 5.—New series, May 1st, 1854.

FORSTER, William Edward, M.P. for Bradford, Yorkshire (continued from Catalogue, Vol. 1, p. 625), son of William and Anna Forster, was born at *Bradpole*, in *Dorsetshire*, in the year 1818; 1850 he married Jane Martha, eldest daughter of the late "Rev." Thomas Arnold, D.D., Head Master of Rugby School. He is a worsted manufacturer at *Bradford*. A

FORSTER, William Edward, *continued.*
    Magistrate, and Deputy-Lieut. for the *West Riding* of *York*, and Captain 23rd West Riding Volunteers. Was under-Secretary for the Colonies from 11th Month, 1865, till 7th Month, 1866, and is now [1870] Vice-President of the Committee of Council on Education ; and since Secretary for Ireland.
    Residence, *Burley*, near *Leeds*, *Yorkshire*, *80, Eccleston Square, S.W.*, and *Reform Club, Pall Mall, S.W.*

—— Biographical notice of "The Right Hon. William Edward Forster, M.P.," with a Portrait, and fac-simile of his autograph in "*The Leisure Hour*" for March, 1875, p. 153.

—— SPEECH of the Right Honourable WILLIAM E. FORSTER, M.P., on moving the Second Reading of the ENDOWED SCHOOLS BILL. In the House of Commons, Monday, March 15th, 1869. Extracted from "Hansard's Parliamentary Debates," Vol. CXCIV., p. 1356.
    London : *Cornelius Buck, 23, Paternoster Row*, E.C. 8vo. 1869.   1

—— Life of the Rt. Hon. W. E. Forster. By T. Wemyss Reid. 2 Vols. . . . 8vo. 1888.
    He was an occasional contributor to the pages of "The Westminster and Edinburgh Reviews." See the following, viz. :—
    "Quakers and Quakerism."—In "The Westminster Review," April, 1852.
    "British Philanthropy and Jamaica Distress."—"Westminster Review."
    American Slavery and Emancipation by the Free States.—"Westminster Review."
    Strikes and Lock-outs.—Ditto ? Written in 1854.
    The Autocracy of the Czars.—In "The Edinburgh Review," 1855.
    Kafir Wars and Cape Policy.—In "The Edinburgh Review."
    See also "*Cabinet Portraits*" for further particulars concerning him.
    He died the 5th of 4th month, 1886, in the 68th year of his age, and his interment took place at Burley-in-Wharfdale.

FOSTER, Charles Wilmer, B.A., of *St. John's College, Oxford* ; of Grosvenor Terrace, York. (Not a Member).

—— and JOSEPH JOSHUA GREEN—HISTORY of the WILMER FAMILY. . . . . 4to. 1888.
    See JOSEPH J. GREEN.

FOSTER, Thomas, of *Bromley, Middlesex,* from Catalogue, Vol. 1, p. 626.
> NOTE.—Concerning him. "This was Mr. Thomas Foster, for more than 50 years a respected member of the Society of Friends, in which he was born and educated. He was led early in life, by reading William Penn's Works, to embrace Unitarianism. Through the medium of Mr. William Rathbone, also a member of the Society of Friends, he became a subscriber to the London Unitarian Book Society. In the autumn of 1810, he printed in the *Monthly Repository* some remarks on the Yearly Meeting Epistle, which were afterwards distributed amongst the Friends. This circumstance led to proceedings being taken against him by the Society, and eventually he was disowned. He defended himself in "A Narrative of the Proceedings of the Society called Quakers, within the Quarterly Meeting of London and Middlesex, against Thomas Foster, for openly professing their Primitive Doctrines concerning the Unity of God, 1813." He was a man possessed with a simple and earnest love of truth, with a sound head and a truly warm heart. Mr. Aspland had the greatest esteem for him. He continued till 1818 to reside at Bromley Hall, where his friends were ever welcome, and where the most agreeable society, both in and out of the circle of the Friends, was constantly found. He then removed to Evesham, where he resided about 10 years. He died at Rushwick, near Worcester, July 9, 1834, in the 75th year of his age."
>
> *Memoir of the Life, Works and Correspondence of the Rev. Robert Aspland, of Hackney. By R. Brook Aspland, M.A.*
> 8vo. 1850.

FOTHERGILL, John, M.D., continued from Catalogue, Vol. 1, p. 629.

—— RULES for the PRESERVATION of HEALTH: containing All that has been recommended by the most eminent Physicians. With the easiest Prescriptions for most Disorders incident to Mankind, through the Four different Periods of Human Life. Being the Result of many Years' Practice. By JOHN FOTHERGILL. Dedicated to the College of PHYSICIANS.
> *London: Printed for John Pridden, at the Feathers, in Fleet Street, and sold by C. Etherington, York. MDCCLXII.* 12mo. 1762. 6
>> Dr. Fothergill's liberality, see Gawin Knight, to whom he gave *1,000 guineas.*—*Watkin's Biographical Dictionary,* p. 699.

—— LONDON, March 24, 1769.—" Lest the following Letters should have escaped the Notice of those to whom they are addressed, the MAGISTRATES and Representatives of this great City, &c. (On the dangerous

FOTHERGILL, John, *continued.*

Nuisances of Sugar Houses in the heart of the City.) N.L. [ANON.]
No Printer's name, place, or date.
Folio. [1769.] 1

—— A SKETCH of the late EPIDEMICK DISEASE, as it appeared in LONDON. Signed, *John Fothergill,* and dated London, 6th Dec., 1775.
No Printer's place or date. . . 4to. ½

—— " Biographical Anecdotes of the late John Fothergill, M.D., &c." In *The London Medical Journal,* Vol. IV. By *Dr. Simmons.* Anno 1784.
8vo. 27pp.

In the 4th Vol. of *The Histoire de la Société Royale de Médicine,* Anno 1780, 1781, Dr. *Vicq d' Azyr* has published *Eloge de M. Fothergill,* in 34 Quarto pages, wherein he politely acknowledges, " *Je dois à M. Lettsom la plus grande partie des renseignemens que j'ai reçus sur la vie de* M. FOTHERGILL.—See Appendix to Lettsom's Life of Fothergill, 4th edition.

—— A CATALOGUE of the CURIOUS and VALUABLE COLLECTION of Hot-House and Green-House Plants, Together with several Parcels of Seeds, Lately brought from the South-Seas, East-Indies, &c. ALSO, The FRAMES and GLASS of TWO HOT HOUSES: Late the Property of J. FOTHERGILL, M.D., deceased. Which will be sold by Auction, On MONDAY, the 20th Day, of August, 1781. (And the two following DAYS,) on the PREMISES, At UPTON, near STRATFORD, in ESSEX ; By Messrs. SAMPSON, and SPURRIER. The Sale to begin each Day at Eleven o'Clock. This Collection contains a variety of scarce Exotics, not to be found in any other Botanical Garden in Europe, and the whole has been collected at a vast Expense, from almost every Part of the Globe.

To be viewed One Week previous to the Sale. Catalogues may be had (without which no Person will be admitted) at 2s. 6d. each, to be returned to Purchasers, of Mr. Sampson, in Throgmorton-Street ; of Mr. Spurrier, in Copthall-Court ; and also at the Time of viewing may be had at the Garden. Sampson & Spurrier.
[*Guildhall Library.*]
8vo. [1781.] 52 pages (including title).

—— Anecdote of his [John Fothergill's] Eccentricity when a Student at Edinburgh. Inserted in Zimmerman, " On Solitude," 3rd edition, Vol. 2, 1802, p. 152.

FOTHERGILL, Samuel, continued from Catalogue, Vol. 1, p. 635.
—— Ten Discourses by Samuel Fothergill, from 1767 to 1770 inclusive.
Philadelphia. . . . . . . 1808.
—— Eleven DISCOURSES, delivered extempore, at Several Meeting-houses of the People called Quakers. By Samuel Fothergill. Mostly taken down in characters by a Member of the Church of England.
Wilmington: Printed for and published by Coale & Rumford. 12mo. 1817. 11
—— Letter to Samuel Fothergill by An Attender of Friends' Religious Meetings. (On babbling after the break-up of a meeting). [Anon]. . . 4to. No date. ¼

FOWLER, Robert, continued from Catalogue, Vol. 1, p. 643.
—— MEMOIR of ROBERT FOWLER, with **Extracts from his Letters**, and Fragments of an Address to the Youth of the Society of Friends.
London: Darton & Harvey, Gracechurch Street; J. & A. Arch, Cornhill; Edmund Fry, Bishopsgate Street; and Josiah Fletcher, Norwich.
12mo. 1835. 6⅝

*FOWLER, Robert Nicholas, of *London*.
Sir Robert Fowler was the son of Thomas Fowler, of London, banker, and was born at Tottenham on the 12th of the 9th Month, 1828. Educated at Grove House school, Tottenham, and at University College, London; he graduated B.A. (Lond.) in 1848, being second in mathematics and fifth in classics, and obtained his M.A. degree in 1850. Sir Robert's career may be said to have been of a two-fold character—civic and Parliamentary. His mayoralty (1883-4) is memorable from the fact that the Court of Aldermen deliberately passed over the alderman next on the rota selected by the Livery. Amongst the many important functions in which Lord Mayor Fowler took part were the openings of the Inner Circle Railway and the International Health Exhibition. Five months only had passed after his retirement, when by the sudden death of his successor —Lord Mayor Nottage—the civic chair became vacant. At the unanimous wish of the Livery Sir Robert resumed the duties and responsibilities of the office for the remainder of the year. For this her Majesty bestowed upon Sir Robert a baronetcy.
Lloyds Newspaper.

FOWLER, Robert Nicholas, *continued*.
—— To Tottenham Monthly Meeting, 1858.
—— A Visit to Japan, China, and India. By Robert Nicholas Fowler, M.A., F.R.G.S., F.S.A., Fellow of University College, London.
> London : *Sampson Low, Marston, Searle, and Rivington, Crown Buildings, 188, Fleet Street.* [All Rights Reserved.] 8vo. 1877.
>> He died suddenly the 21st of 5th Month, 1891, in his 63rd year, and his remains were removed to *Corsham, Wiltshire*, for interment in the family vault.

FOWLER, William, LL.B., and M.P. for Cambridge, of *London*, son of John Fowler, of *Chapel Ness*, near *Melksham, Wilts*, was born at *Melksham*, 1828 ; married 1865, Rachel Maria, daughter of Robert Howard, of *Tottenham*, and *Ashmore Manor, Dorset* (she died 1868). Educated at University College, London. Was called to the Bar at the Inner Temple January, 1852, and practised till January, 1856, when he became a partner in the firm of A. G. W. Alexander & Co. (now Alexander, Cunliffes, & Co.), Lombard Street, London.
—— The Crisis of 1866 ; a Financial Essay.
—— Morley and Tyndall on Miracles ; an Essay.

FOX, Albert, of *Kingsbridge*, in *Devonshire*, where he was born the 1st of 9th month, 1836. He afterwards removed to *London*, and from thence to *Liverpool*.
—— Albert Fox, 𝔱𝔥𝔢 𝔇𝔢𝔳𝔬𝔲𝔱 𝔐𝔢𝔯𝔠𝔥𝔞𝔫𝔱, A Memoir. By the Rev. John Jones, Congregational Minister, Liverpool. (With a Photographic Portrait.)
> *Liverpool: Edward Howell, Church Street. London : Hamilton, Adams & Co. F. B. Kitto, 5, Bishopsgate Without. Manchester : John Heywood.* 8vo. 1867. 12½
—— Memoir in *The Annual Monitor, for 1868*.
>> He died at Linares in Spain, the 27th of 1st Month, 1867, aged 30 years.

FOX, Caroline, of *Penjerrick, Cornwall*.
—— 𝔐𝔢𝔪𝔬𝔯𝔦𝔢𝔰 𝔬𝔣 𝔒𝔩𝔡 𝔉𝔯𝔦𝔢𝔫𝔡𝔰, being Extracts from the Journals and Letters of CAROLINE FOX. 𝔉𝔯𝔬𝔪 1835 𝔱𝔬 1871. Edited by HORACE N. PYM, to which are added Fourteen Original Letters from J. S. Mill. Never before published. (Portrait).

FOX, Caroline, *continued.*
>Third edition, 2 Vols.
>London : *Smith, Elder & Co., 15, Waterloo Place.*
>>8vo. 1882
>>Vol. 1, xxxi. 333 pages.
>>Vol. 2, xii. 353 pages.

FOX, Charles, of *Trebah,* near *Falmouth.*
——Game of Patience.

FOX, Charlotte S., Wife of Samuel Fox, late of *Tottenham,* now of *Falmouth.*
——Recollections of our Old Home.
>[Printed for private circulation.] . 8vo. [1868.] 2

FOX, George, continued from Catalogue, Vol. 1, p. 644.
——*The* Ancient Simplicity, *as it was* Once *Witnessed unto by* GEORGE FOX.
>>*This Letter was written to a Friend, the 24th of the 7th Month, 1661, and now stands a Witness against that Spirit of Enmity and Bitterness which broke forth against* JOHN PERROT.
>>>4to. ¼

——Narrative of his proceedings at Gracechurch Street Meeting. (From the Harleian MSS.) in Malcolm's London, Vol. 1.

——¶ Instructions for RIGHT SPELLING, and PLAIN DIRECTIONS for *Reading* and *Writing* TRUE ENGLISH. With several delightful things, very Useful and Necessary, both for Young and Old, to Read and Learn. By *G. Fox.*
>London, *Printed for Benjamin Clark, in George yard, in Lombard-street.* 12mo. 1683. 5½

——A Journal, &c., of George Fox. The Fifth Edition, corrected. In Two Volumes.
>*Philadelphia* : *Printed for B. & T. Kite, No. 20, North Third Street. Fry & Kammerer, Printers.*
>>8vo. 1808. 6¼

——The Eighth Edition. Two Volumes.
>>8vo. 1892.

——The Doctrines and Ministry of GEORGE FOX.
>*Philadelphia* : *Friends' Book Store, No. 304, Arch Street.* . . . 16mo. 1874. 1
>>NOTE.—This pamphlet consists of Extracts from his writings, by an anonymous Friend.

——SELECTIONS from THE EPISTLES of GEORGE FOX. By SAMUEL TUKE. Abridged.

FOX, George, *continued.*
>*Philadelphia : Published by the Association of Friends for the Diffusion of Religious and Useful Knowledge, No. 109, North Tenth Street.*
>
>12mo. 1858. 144pp.

——The Founder of the Quakers (George Fox.) In "*The Extractor,*" *p. 137.* . . . . 8vo. [1828?]

——George Fox preaching in a Tavern, with an engraving of the same from the Picture in South Kensington Museum. In "*The Family Friend, December, 1888,*" *page 188.*

——George Fox and his Times. By William Beck. See WILLIAM BECK.

——Life of George Fox. By A. C. Bickley. See A. C. BICKLEY.

——Portrait of "GEORGE FOX, Founder of the Society of Friends.
Sawyer, Junr., Sc.
>*Published by T. Rodd, 2, Great Newport Street.*"
>
>8vo. No date.

——PASSAGES FROM THE LIFE AND WRITINGS of GEORGE FOX, taken from his Journal. With the desire on the part of the editor to give a fair representation of his character and religious views, and to lead the reader to seek a fuller acquaintance with them.
>*Philadelphia: For sale at Friends' Book-Store, 304, Arch Street.* - - 8vo. 1881. 14½

——Autobiography of George Fox. By Henry Stanley Newman.—See HENRY STANLEY NEWMAN.

——GEORGE FOX : His Life, Travels, Sufferings, and Death, wherein is plainly discovered the real origin of the PEOPLE CALLED QUAKERS, and what a Quaker ought to be, as, also, the UNBELIEF, UNGODLINESS, AND FOLLY of all those who profess to believe in God, and yet do not fear to sin against him, or do not strive with all their might to make sinners tremble before him. BY GEO. R[AILTON.]
>*London : Salvation Army Headquarters, 101, Queen Victoria Street, E.C.*
>
>S. W. Partridge & Co., 9, Paternoster Row, E.C.
>Price One Penny ; 6,6 per 100 ; by Post 1/- extra.
>
>8vo. 1881. 2
>
>>NOTE.—The Title on the cover is, "GEORGE FOX : and his Salvation Army 200 years ago." And there are 4 wood cuts, viz., "Geo. Fox speaking in Ulverstone

FOX, George, *continued*.
    Church," " George Fox being Struck, and singing in the Lord's Power," " George Fox being stoned, beat, and dragged along the street besmeared with blood and dirt," and " Moving about to visit others when brought down to the very verge of the Grave himself."

FOX, George, the younger, continued from Catalogue, Vol. 1, p. 697.
——Begins,—" Oh People ! my Bowels yearn, my Bowels yearn towards you, whose desires in any measure are after the Lord, &c." (Published with a little addition by John Pennyman.) . . . 4to. [1670]. ¼
    See JOHN PENNYMAN.

FOX, Joseph John, of *Stoke Newington*, continued from Catalogue, Vol. 1, p. 704.
——The Province of the Statistician.
    Joseph John Fox contributed the following, viz. :—
Life of a Cloud.—" Leisure Hour."
The Coburg Family.—" Leisure Hour."
Historical Notices of Stoke Newington.—" The Sphinx."
The Sterrynore Lighthouse.—" James' Magazine."
——AUTUMN LEAVES : a Contribution to the Conference of 1873. By J. J. FOX.
    " Rebus angustus animosus atque Fortis appare."
    To be had of the Author, Lordship Road, Stoke Newington ; and of Samuel Harris & Co., 5, Bishopsgate Without, London. . 8vo. 1873. 2¼
Price One Shilling.

FOX, Charles Allen, of *Cardiff, Wales*, formerly of *Stoke Newington, London* ; son of JOSEPH JOHN FOX.
——To the Professors of every Name. Given in the motion of Life through CHARLES FOX. (On the observances of the day called Christmas.)
    8vo. *Stoke Newington Com., 12th Month.* 1880. ⅛
——The Christian's Duty upon Politics. (Signed, Charles Fox.)
    J. Davies, Cardiff, Printer. . . 8vo. 1886. ¼

FOX, Sarah Prideaux, of *Kingsbridge, Devonshire*.
——Estuary. 8vo. 1864. 11

FOX, Robert Were, F.R.S., of *Falmouth*, Mineralogist.
    His works being of a scientific character and numerous, a list of them may be found in The Catalogue of the Works of R. W. Fox, F.R.S., by T. H. Collins, 1878, and Boase and Courtney's " Bibliotheca Cornubiensis," &c.

FOX, Robert Were, *continued*.
>He died at his house, *Penjerrick*, near *Falmouth*, the 25th of 7th month, 1877, in the 88th year of his age, and was buried in the Friends' Burial-ground at *Budock*.

FRANKLIN, Matthew, of *New York*.
——Letter from Matthew Franklin to Charity Rotch.— New York, 2nd Month 21st 1805.
>In Comly's Miscellany, Vol. 4, p. 57.

FRASER, Allen, of *Western, Oneida County, New York*.
——THOUGHTS on the Schism and Waning of the Church of Friends; in A SERIES OF LETTERS, to Thomas Townsend, Ebenezer Hill and Frederic Mills, *Committee, &c.* BY ALLEN FRASER.
>*Western:* [*Oneida County, New York.*]
>8vo. 1845.   2

——Appendix (to ditto) - 12mo. 1845. Single leaf.
>NOTE.—This author speaks of Elisha Bates, as an ambitious and aspiring member, and that he had two selfish objects in writing "THE DOCTRINES OF FRIENDS," viz.:—
>I.—"To render the Church more popular in the Orthodox World."
>II.—"To make himself the visible head of it by writing its Creed."

FREEMAN, Henry, continued from Catalogue, Vol. 1, p. 708.
——An Address to the Society of Arminian Bible Christians, *in the* London Circuit (written at "Brighton, Sussex, 22nd day of 6th Month, 1824.")
>*Tew, Printer, 34, Queen Street, Cheapside, London.*
>12mo. [1824]. $\frac{1}{6}$

FREEMAN, Sarah Ann, of *Harborne*, near *Birmingham*.
——𝔍𝔫 𝔄𝔣𝔣𝔢𝔠𝔱𝔦𝔬𝔫𝔞𝔱𝔢 𝔑𝔢𝔪𝔢𝔪𝔟𝔯𝔞𝔫𝔠𝔢 of SARAH ANN FREEMAN, wife of Henry Freeman, *of Harborne, near Birmingham*, and eldest daughter of John and Hannah B. Bottomley, *Birmingham*, 𝔚𝔥𝔬 𝔡𝔦𝔢𝔡 𝔱𝔥𝔢 13𝔱𝔥 𝔬𝔣 9𝔱𝔥 𝔐𝔬𝔫𝔱𝔥, 1868, Aged 30 years.
>"Blessed are the pure in heart, for they shall see God."— MATTHEW v. 8.
>*Birmingham:* White & Pike, Printers, Commercial Buildings. . . 24mo. [1868?] $\frac{1}{2}$

FRETWELL, Ralph.
——Epistle to the Behmenites.
>Query, whether printed?

FRIENDS,—Books, Pamphlets, Papers, Minutes, etc., issued by or relating to the several Yearly, Quarterly, Monthly, and other Meetings, etc., arranged in the following order, viz. :—
    London Yearly Meeting.
    Meeting for Sufferings.
    Quarterly Meetings.
    Monthly Meetings.
    Dublin Yearly Meeting.
    Philadelphia Yearly Meeting, and other meetings.
    New York Y.M.
    Baltimore Y.M. (both branches) and other associations.
    Friends in Sydney.
    Miscellaneous Books and Papers.
    Schools, etc., etc.
    Women's Epistles.

YEARLY MEETING (London).

——Epistles from 1867 to 1892, inclusive.

———YEARLY MEETING, London, 1764. Meetings for Worship to be held this week.
    These Lists are to be had of *John Fudge*, Door-keeper of Gracechurch Street Meeting House.   4to. [1764].   ¼
    NOTE.—The Meetings in this list, are
        1. Devonshire House.
        2. Gracechurch Street.
        3. Peel.
        4. Ratcliff.
        5. Wapping.
        6. Horsley-down.
        7. Park.
        8. Deptford (discontinued this year on 4th day).
        9. Savoy.
        10. Westminster.

——The Yearly Meeting Epistle for 1867 (printed in a pamphlet form).
    E. Newman, Printer.   .   .   12mo. [1867].   ⅓

——Extracts from the Minutes and Proceedings of the Y.M. held in London, 1867 to 1892, etc.   8vo.

——Minute of the Y.M. on Ecclesiastical Establishments.
        8vo. 1869.   ¼

——Y.M. 1869, and Meetings for Sufferings, 4th of 6th mo, 1869. Lithographed Minute.—Copy, C. Hoyland.
        Folio. [1869].

FRIENDS, Yearly Meeting (London), *continued.*

——ADDRESS from the Committee appointed by the Yearly Meeting of 1870, to visit the Quarterly Meeting of Lancashire and Cheshire. Presented to Hardshaw East Monthly Meeting, *held at Manchester, 1st Month 12th, 1871.*

𝕷𝖔𝖓𝖉𝖔𝖓: *Edward Newman, Printer, 9, Devonshire Street, Bishopsgate.* 8vo. [1871]. ⅝

NOTE.—Names of the Committee.

Robert Alsop,	G. S. Gibson,
William Ball,	Thomas Harvey,
J. B. Braithwaite,	Joseph Huntley,
Isaac Brown,	Henry Pease,
Joseph Davis,	Arthur Pease,
John Dodshon,	J. G. Richardson,
Chas. Fox,	James Hack Tuke,
Joseph Storrs Fry,	William White.

——A Declaration of some Fundamental Principles of Christian Truth. Issued by the Committee appointed by the Yearly Meeting of the Religious Society of Friends to visit Lancashire and Cheshire Quarterly Meeting.

𝕷𝖔𝖓𝖉𝖔𝖓: *E. Newman, Printer, Devonshire Street, Bishopsgate.* . . . . 8vo. 1872. ½

——The Epistle from the Yearly Meeting, held in London, by adjournments from the 21st of the 5th Month to the 31st of the same inclusive, 1873.

𝕷𝖔𝖓𝖉𝖔𝖓: *Edward Newman, Printer, 9, Devonshire Street, Bishopsgate.* 16mo. 1873. ½

——Minute of the Yearly Meeting of Ministers and Elders, held 5th Month 30th, 1874. G. S. Gibson, *Clerk.*
4to. 1874. ¼

Meeting for Sufferings.

——Minute on Caffre War, 1851.

——The Church in its Relation to the State. 𝕬𝖓 𝕬𝖉𝖉𝖗𝖊𝖘𝖘 from the Religious Society of Friends to their Fellow-Countrymen.

London: Edward Marsh, 12, Bishopsgate Street Without. 8vo. 1868. 2

——Church Establishments, and the effect of their absence in America.

London: Edward Marsh, 12, Bishopsgate Street Without. . . . . . 8vo. 1869. ¾

FRIENDS, Meeting for Sufferings, *continued.*

———A Plea for entire Liberty of Conscience; addressed to Spain and her Rulers in this day of her happily recovered Civil Freedom.
London: *R. Barrett & Sons, Printers,* 13, *Mark Lane.*
Translated into Spanish. . . 8vo. [1869.] ¼

Printed also in the minutes of the Yearly Meeting, see appendix B.

———Christ the Giver of True Liberty. With "What saith the Scripture?" A leaflet for Spain.
Translated into Spanish. . . 8vo. [1869.] ⅛

Printed also in the minutes of the Yearly Meeting, see appendix B.

———Minute of the Meeting for Sufferings, held 2nd of 8th Month, 1872 (on Hannah Hall's visit to this country).
Signed Joseph Crosfield, *Clerk.* . 8vo. [1872.] ⅛

———Draft of Marriage Regulations. *As proposed to stand in lieu of present ones in "Doctrine, Practice, and Discipline."*
Signed, Charles Hoyland, 3rd Month, 1872.
. 8vo. [1872.] 1⅛

Quarterly Meetings.

Bedfordshire Q. M.

———List of Members of the Society of Friends belonging to the Bedfordshire Quarterly Meeting, which comprises the Monthly Meetings of Hertford and Hitchin, Luton and Leighton Buzzard, and Northampton and Wellingborough, showing their Postal Address.
London: *R. Barrett & Sons, Printers, Mark Lane.*
18mo. 1870. 2

———The REPORT OF THE COMMITTEE OF MEN AND WOMEN FRIENDS appointed by 𝕭𝖊𝖉𝖋𝖔𝖗𝖉𝖘𝖍𝖎𝖗𝖊 𝕼𝖚𝖆𝖗𝖙𝖊𝖗𝖑𝖞 𝕸𝖊𝖊𝖙𝖎𝖓𝖌 to visit the Monthly and Particular Meetings within its borders.
Printed by direction of the Quarterly Meeting, for the use of its Members.
London: *R. Barrett & Sons, Printers,* 13, *Mark Lane.* . . . . Small 8vo. [1873.] 1

NOTE.—This Report is signed "Richard Littleboy, *Clerk,*" and dated "*Hitchin,* 1st Month 15th, 1873." The names on the Committee are John Blunsom, Henry Brown, Jun., Joseph Glaisyer, Theodore Harris, Joseph Green Hopkins, Eli Johnson, Richard Littleboy, Alfred Ransom, Francis Ellington Wright, Mary Feltham, Elizabeth Hopkins, Margaret Sims May, Lucy Ransom, Caroline Read, Rebecca Thursfield.

FRIENDS, Quarterly Meetings, *continued.*
Berks and Oxon Q. M.
——A List of the Members of the SOCIETY OF FRIENDS, and **Attenders of their Meetings** in BERKS AND OXON Quarterly Meeting ; comprising the Monthly Meetings of Banbury, Reading, and Witney.
Reading : Barcham & Beecroft, Broad Street.
18mo. 1870. 32 leaves, one side blank.

London and Middlesex Q.M.
——A TABLE of First-day and other Meetings, within about forty miles of LONDON ; also of all the Meetings for Worship and Discipline in and about the said City. 1783. . . . . . . Large broadside. 1

——A LIST of the Meetings for Worship on First and week days, and of the Two-weeks, Monthly, Six-weeks, and Quarterly Meetings in LONDON ; also, the Committee of Friends' School and Workhouse, and when held, for the year 1785. . . . Oblong folio. ½

——List of Members of the **Quarterly Meeting** of London and Middlesex, comprising :—
  1. Devonshire House Monthly Meeting.
  2. Kingston Monthly Meeting.
  3. Ratcliff and Barking Monthly Meeting.
  4. Southwark Monthly Meeting.
  5. Tottenham Monthly Meeting.
  6. Westminster and Longford Monthly Meeting.
London : E. Newman, Printer, Devonshire Street, Bishopsgate. 18mo. 1868. 3

——**List of Members**, &c.   18mo. 1870.
——Ditto.   . . 18mo. 1871.
——Ditto. . . . . . 18mo. 1872 to 1892.
——Annual Reports of Friends' Institute, London, 1867 to 1892.

Bristol, Somerset, and Dorset Q.M.
——*List of Members* and Times of Holding Meetings in the Quarterly Meeting of Bristol, Somerset, and Dorset.
Bristol : Henry Hill, Printer, Small Street.
16mo. 1867. 70pp.

——Particulars of the Charitable Trusts, Meeting Houses, Burial Grounds, and Trust Properties of **Bristol and Somerset Quarterly Meeting of Friends**, and of its subordinate Meetings : with Reports and Ab-

FRIENDS, Quarterly Meetings, *continued.*
stracted Minutes of the Commission appointed by the Quarterly Meeting to enquire into the origin and application thereof.
Bristol: Henry Hill, Steam Printer and Stationer, 2, Baldwin Street.
Large paper folio. 1870. 54 leaves.

——Bristol, Somerset, and Dorset Quarterly Meeting's Commission on Charitable Trusts.—*Extract from Final Report of the Commission, held at the Friars, Bristol, 16th 1st mo.,* 1871. . . . . Folio. ½

Durham Quarterly Meeting.

——Report of Mission Meetings, Schools, Bible Classes, and other Christian Work carried on by Friends in Durham Quarterly Meeting.
Darlington : Printed by Harrison Penney, Prebend Row. . . . . 8vo. 1872. ¾

Essex Q.M.

——Times for holding the Meetings for Worship and Discipline in Essex. (About 1785 ?) . Large Broadside. 1

Warwick, Leicester, and Stafford Q.M.

——List of Members and Attenders of the Meetings of Friends, comprising the Quarterly Meeting of Warwick, Leicester, and Stafford. . . 18mo. 1869. 1 1/16

——Ditto. 18mo. 1870. 1½

Western Quarterly Meeting.

——List of Members of the Society of Friends belonging to the Western Quarterly Meeting showing their Postal Address. 18mo. 1869. 36 leaves, one side blank.

York Q.M., &c.

——A Table for the Year 1790, shewing the times and places of holding York Quarterly and Monthly Meetings.
4to. 1790. ¼

Monthly Meetings.
Banbury.

——List of Members and Attenders of Banbury Monthly Meeting, 1870.
Frederick Watts, Printer, High Street, Witney.
8vo. [1870]. ½

——List of Books in the Banbury Friends' Library, 1870.
Cheney, Printer, Banbury. . . 8vo. [1870]. ¼

FRIENDS, Monthly Meetings, *continued*.
   Darlington.
—— List of Members and Attenders belonging to Darlington Monthly Meeting, 5th Month, 1870.
   Darlington : Harrison Penney, Prebend Row,
   16mo. 1870. 1½
—— REPORT on CHRISTIAN WORK in Darlington Monthly Meeting.
   Darlington : Harrison Penney, Printer by Steam Power, Priestgate. . . . 12mo. 1871. ½
   NOTE.—The Report of the Committee is signed by Wm. Coor Parker. The Minute of the Monthly Meeting by Wm. Taylor, Clerk.
—— LIST of the MEMBERS AND ATTENDERS in the MONTHLY MEETINGS of DARLINGTON, GUISBOROUGH, and Richmond, to which are added LISTS OF STANDING COMMITTEES, and other information. 3mo. 1877.
   Darlington : Harrison Penney, Steam Printer, Prebend Row. . . . 16mo. 1877. 3
   NOTE.—Compiled by Jonathan Backhouse Hodgkin, with a "Map of Darlington, Richmond, and Guisbro' Monthly Meetings."

   Devonshire House.
—— List of Members of Devonshire House 𝔐onthly 𝔐eeting. With the Boundaries of the Monthly Meeting.
   London : E. Newman, Printer, Devonshire Street, Bishopsgate. 18mo. 1867. 1
—— A Catalogue of Books belonging to 𝔇evonshire 𝔥ouse 𝔓reparative 𝔐eeting, illustrative of the Christian Faith and Practice of the Religious Society of Friends.
   London : Printed by E. Newman, 9, Devonshire Street, Bishopsgate. . . 12mo. 1869. 1¾

   Kingston.
—— List of Member of Members of Kingston Monthly Meetings of Friend, 1867.
   S. Clouter, Printer, Croydon. . 8vo. 1867. 1
—— REGISTER BOOK for MARRIAGE CERTIFICATES, belonging to CROYDEN MEETING.
   London : Printed and Sold by S. Clark, in Bread Street, MDCCLX.
   (A Title Page only). . Royal folio. 1760.

FRIENDS, Monthly Meetings, *continued*.

Luton and Leighton.

——The Report of the Committee of Men and Women Friends appointed by Luton and Leighton Monthly Meeting to visit the Particular Meetings within its Borders.

For Private Circulation only.

London : R. Barrett & Sons, Printers, Mark Lane.
16mo. [1871?]   ¾

NOTE.—Signed by Daniel Norris, Henry Brown, William Chantler, Joseph Glaisyer, Richard Littleboy, Henry Brown, Jun., Theodore Harris, Joseph G. Hopkins, W. H. Cranstone, Sarah Hall Norris, Lucy How, Mary R. Littleboy, Elizabeth D. Hopkins.

Ratcliff and Barking.

——Minute of the last Y.M. on Poverty, 12th Month, 1889.
4to. 1890.   ½

Dublin Yearly Meeting.

——*Yearly Meeting of Friends in Ireland*, 1845.—Minute on the departure from Christian simplicity in apparel, language, and deportment, and on buying and selling shares in public undertakings.   .   . 4to. [1845.]   ¼

——A Summary of the History, Doctrine, and Discipline, etc. Printed by direction of the Dublin Y. M., the 2nd in Dublin.

——Supplement to " Rules of Discipline," &c.
8vo. 1848.   2⅛

——ADVICES and MINUTES issued and adopted by the YEARLY MEETING of the RELIGIOUS SOCIETY OF FRIENDS IN IRELAND, in relation to CHRISTIAN DOCTRINE, PRACTICE, and DISCIPLINE. Third Edition.

Dublin: Depository of the Society of Friends, 6, Eustace Street.   .   .   . 8vo. 1864.   20¾

Philadelphia Yearly Meeting.

——An Address of the Yearly Meeting of Friends, held in Philadelphia, to its own members, and to the members of other Yearly Meetings.

Published by direction of the Yearly Meeting.
8vo. 1868.   2½

NOTE.—This Address is "Signed on behalf and by direction of the Yearly Meeting. By Joseph Scattergood, Clerk."

FRIENDS, Yearly Meeting (Philadelphia), *continued.*
Reprinted in "The British Friend."

——An Epistle from the Yearly Meeting of Friends, held in Philadelphia, by adjournments, from the 18th of the 4th Month to the 21st of the same, inclusive, 1870. To its members.
Published by Direction of the Yearly Meeting.
Signed by Joseph Scattergood, Clerk   8vo. [1870.]   ¾
Reprinted in England.

> NOTE.—This Epistle was prepared under a religious concern for the preservation of our members from the influence of erroneous opinions and practices.

Printed Minutes and other papers.

——Extracts from the Minutes of our YEARLY MEETING, held in Philadelphia, by adjournments, from the 17th of the Fourth Month to the 20th of the same, inclusive, 1871.
Philadelphia : W. H. Pile, No. 422, Walnut Street. 12mo. 1871.   1¼
> NOTE.—List of Correspondents (at the end).

——JUDICIAL OATHS, and their effect. 16th day of 4th Month, 1883.
> NOTE.—This essay was prepared by the M. for S. and adopted by the Y. M., and signed by Joseph Walton, Clerk.

Friends' Book Store, No. 304, Arch Street, Philadelphia. . . . . . 8vo. 1883.   ½

——AN ADDRESS to its own MEMBERS, and to the Members of our Society elsewhere, issued by the Yearly Meeting of Friends of Philadelphia, Fourth Month 18th, 1883.
Friends' Book Store, No. 304, Arch Street, Philadelphia. 8vo. 1883.   2¼

Philadelphia Meeting for Sufferings.

——An APOLOGY for the People called *QUAKERS*. Containing some REASONS for their not complying with human injunctions and institutions in matters relative to the Worship of GOD.
Published by the Meeting for Sufferings of the said People at Philadelphia, *in Pursuance of the Directions of their Yearly Meeting, held at* Burlington *for* Pennsylvania *and* New Jersey, *the 24th day of the Ninth Month,* 1756.

FRIENDS. Philadelphia Meeting for Sufferings, *continued.*
Signed on behalf and by appointment of our said Meeting for Sufferings, held at *Philadelphia*, the 29th of the 6th Month, 1757, by JAMES PEMBERTON, *Clerk.*
  8vo. No Printer's name, place, or *(printed)* date. ½

——MEMORIALS concerning DECEASED FRIENDS. Published by Direction of the Yearly Meeting of Friends, held in Philadelphia, in the Fifth Month, 1841.
  Philadelphia : Printed by S. B. Chapman & Co., 1841. . . . . 12mo. [1841.] 2

——MEMORIALS, &c., *in the Fifth Month, 1848.* Published in the Fifth Month, 1848.
  Philadelphia : Printed by John Richards, No. 299, Market Street, 1848. . 12mo. [1848.] ⅓

——An Epistle from the Monthly Meeting of Friends of Philadelphia, held at Green Street, to its Members, 8th Month 23rd, 1838.
  Philadelphia : I. Richards, Printer, No. 130, North Third Street, 1838. . 12mo. [1838.] ⅓
Signed, Samuel Townsend, Lydia Longstreth.

——(No title). An Address to the Members of the Yearly Meeting on the Laws relative to Education and Military fines.
Signed on behalf of the M. for S., John J. White, Clerk (9th Month 14th, 1849.) . . . 12mo. [1849.] ⅙

——A Letter to William Bennett, of London, Great Britain, upon the subject of The Religious Controversies among the Members of the Society of Friends in America. By Pacificus. 1854.

——A TESTIMONY FOR THE TRUTH, as always held and promulgated by the Religious Society of Friends; and against the Departures from the Principles of the Society, which have appeared of latter time.
  Philadelphia : Sherman & Co., Printers.
         8vo. 1865. 3½

  NOTE.—This document was prepared by a Member and produced to a "General Meeting of Men and Women Friends of Ohio," and adopted by the Meeting and signed on its behalf by Joshua Maule, Clerk.—It was also approved of and adopted by a "General Meeting of Men and Women Friends," for Pennsylvania, New Jersey, &c., and signed on its behalf by Solomon Lukens, Clerk.

——An Epistle of Encouragement to Scattered and Solitary Individuals concerned for the Maintenance of the

FRIENDS, *continued.*

    Ancient Principles of Friends in this day of declension, from the GENERAL MEETING OF FRIENDS for Pennsylvania, New Jersey, Delaware, etc. 9th mo. 7th, 1869.
        Philadelphia : Mirrihew & Son, Printers, No. 243, Arch Street. . . 12mo. [1869.] ⅖

    Signed, Jos. E. Maule, *Clerk.* 1869.

——BIOGRAPHICAL SKETCHES AND ANECDOTES of Members of the Religious Society of Friends.
        Philadelphia : Published by the Tract Association of Friends. No. 304, Arch Street. 8vo. [1870.] 26½

        CONTENTS.—David Ferris, William Hunt, Samuel Emlen, John Churchman, Rebecca Jones, Daniel Offley, William Savery, George Dillwyn, Arthur Howell, William Jackson, Peter Yarnall, Anthony Benezet, Jacob Lindley, Eli Yarnall, Sarah Harrison, John Parker, Nicholas Walu, and Moses Brown.

    Meetings in New York Yearly Meeting.

——An Account of the Times and Places of holding the Quarterly, Monthly, and Preparative Meetings, and Meetings for Worship, constituting the New York Yearly Meeting of Friends.
        New York : Egbert, Hovey & King, Printers, 374, Pearl Street (Successors to Mahlon Day's Press).

    (With *A Map.*) . . . . 18mo. 1845.

——DISCIPLINE of the YEARLY MEETING OF FRIENDS, held in New York, for the State of New York, and parts adjacent, *As Revised and Adopted in the Sixth Month,* 1810.
        New York : Mahlon Day, Printer, No. 374, Pearl Street. 8vo. 1836. 6¾

——Discipline of New York Y.M. . . . 1872.

——SIXTH ANNUAL CATALOGUE of SWARTHMORE COLLEGE, Swarthmore, Pa. 1874-75. With Minutes of the ELEVENTH ANNUAL MEETING of the STOCKHOLDERS (two views).
        Philadelphia : Friends' Book Association, 706, Arch Street. 8vo. 1874. 3½

——Fifty-seventh Annual Report on the State of THE ASYLUM for the Relief of Persons deprived of the Use of their Reason. Published by direction of the contributors, 3rd Month, 1874.

FRIENDS, *continued.*

*Philadelphia : Printed by William K. Bellows,
S. W. Corner Fourth and Apple Tree Streets.*
                                       8vo.   1874.   2½

NOTE.—This Report is signed on behalf of the Board of Managers, John E. Carter, Clerk, with a frontispiece of the Asylum. The Superintendent's Report is signed by Joshua H. Worthington, M.D., the physician to the Asylum.

Baltimore Y. M. (both branches).

——Discipline, 1806, 1844, 1860, 1881.

——DISCIPLINE of the YEARLY MEETING OF FRIENDS, held in Baltimore, for the Western Shore of Maryland, and the adjacent parts of Pennsylvania and Virginia, as revised and adopted, 1821.
Baltimore : Printed by Thomas Maund, 1821.
                                         8vo.   1821.   6

NOTE.—In the year 1828 a second APPENDIX was added to this edition, viz., " *The following alterations have been made in our discipline since its adoption and publication in the year 1821.*
                                       8vo.   [1828.]   ⅛

The Rules of the above two Y. M.'s are against the marriage of a deceased Wife's Sister or a deceased Husband's Brother.

——EXTRACTS from the Minutes of our Yearly Meeting, held *in Baltimore, for the Western Shore of Maryland, and the adjacent parts of Pennsylvania and Virginia,* by adjournments, *from the 27th of the 10th Month to the 31st of the same, inclusive,* 1828. Signed, Philip E. Thomas, Clerk.
William Wooddy, Printer, Calvert Street, Baltimore. . . . . . 12mo.   [1828.]   ⅔
Another edition, with some slight alterations   12mo.   ⅔

——EXTRACTS from the MINUTES OF OUR YEARLY MEETING, held *In Baltimore, for the Western Shore of Maryland, and the adjacent parts of Pennsylvania and Virginia,* by adjournments, *from the 26th of the 10th Month to the 29th of the same, inclusive,* 1829.
                                    12mo.   [1829.]   ¾

——EXTRACTS from the Minutes of our Yearly Meeting, held *in Baltimore, for the Western Shore of Maryland, and the adjacent parts of Pennsylvania and Virginia,* by adjournments, *from the 31st of the 10th Month to the 3rd of the 11th Month, inclusive,* 1831.

FRIENDS, Baltimore Yearly Meeting, *continued.*
>*Wm. Wooddy, Printer, No. 6, S. Calvert Street.*
>Philip E. Thomas, Clerk. . . 12mo. [1831.] $\frac{1}{3}$

——EXTRACTS from the *Minutes of our Yearly Meeting,* Held in Baltimore, by adjournments, *from the 31st of the 10th Month to the 3rd of the 11th, inclusive,* 1842. Thomas P. Stabler, Clerk.
>*Wm. Wooddy, Printer, Baltimore* 12mo. [1842.] $1\frac{1}{6}$

——Extracts from the Minutes of the Proceedings of Baltimore Yearly Meeting of Men and Women Friends, held in their Meeting House, on Lombard Street, in the City of Baltimore, 1882.
>Baltimore: *John W. Woods, Printer, over No. 12, South Street.* . . . . 12mo. 1882.

——Extracts from the minutes of the Proceedings of Baltimore Yearly Meeting of Men and Women Friends, held in their Meeting House, on Lombard Street, in the City of Baltimore, 1884.
>*Baltimore : John W. Kennedy & Co., Printers, No. 63, Second Street.* . 12mo. 1884. 140pp.

——Minutes, &c., 1885, 1886.

——Minutes of the Proceedings of Baltimore Yearly Meeting of Friends held in the Meeting House, on Lombard Street, in the City of Baltimore, 1887.
>*Press of Isaac Friedenwald, 32, S. Paca Street.*
>12mo. 1887.

——Minutes of the Proceedings of Baltimore Yearly Meeting of Friends, Held at Eastern District Meeting House, in the City of Baltimore, 1888.
>Baltimore: *Press of John W. Kennedy & Co.*

——Minutes, &c., ——— Held in Park Avenue Meeting House, ——— 1889.
>Baltimore : *Press of John W. Kennedy & Co.*
>12mo. 1889.

——Minutes, &c. ——— 1890.
>Baltimore : *Press of John W. Kennedy & Co.*
>8vo. 1890. 155pp.

——Minutes, &c. ——— 1891.
>Baltimore : *Press of John W. Kennedy & Co.*
>8vo. 1891. 132pp.

——A Defence, 1839.
>Appendix, 1840.

FRIENDS, Baltimore Association, *continued*.
    Baltimore Association of Friends.
——1867. SECOND ANNUAL REPORT of the BALTIMORE ASSOCIATION of FRIENDS, to advise and assist FRIENDS of the SOUTHERN STATES.
    Baltimore : Printed by William K. Boyle, Corner of Baltimore and St. Paul Streets. 8vo. 1868. 1⅛
        NOTE.—There is a Frontispiece to this Report, a sketch of the " RESIDENCE OF THE LATE NATHAN HUNT." *Lith. by A. Hoen and Co., Baltimore.*

——Commemorative Exercises of the Two-Hundredth Anniversary of the Friends' Meeting House, at Third Haven. Including an Account of the Settlement of Friends in Talbot County, Maryland, from the year 1657 to the present time. Easton, Md., 8—28—1884. . . . . 8vo. 54 pp.

——PROCEEDINGS of Friends' Union for Philanthropic Labour at its Third Conference held at Mount Pleasant, Ohio, *by Adjournments from 8th Month 29th, to 9th Month 2nd,* 1884.
    Richmond, Ind., Palladium Book and Job Printing House. . . . 12mo. 1884. 63 pp.

——PROCEEDINGS of the FOURTEENTH SESSION of the FIRST-DAY SCHOOL General Conference, held at MT. PLEASANT, OHIO, Eighth Month, 1884.
    New York : John B. Jackson, 4 and 6, New Chambers Street. . . 8vo. 1884. 33 pp.

    Indiana Yearly Meeting.
——The DISCIPLINE of the SOCIETY of FRIENDS of INDIANA YEARLY MEETING, revised by the Meeting held at White Water, in the Year 1838, and printed by direction of the same.
    Cincinnati : A. Pugh, Printer, Corner Fifth and Main Streets. 12mo. 1839. 4 1/12

——The Minutes of Indiana Yearly Meeting, held at Miami, Ohio. David Evans, *Clerk.*
    (Orthodox.) . . . . 12mo. [1828.] ⅓

    New England Yearly Meeting.
——RULES of DISCIPLINE of the YEARLY MEETING, held ON RHODE ISLAND, for NEW ENGLAND. Printed by direction of the Meeting.
    New Bedford: Abraham Shearman, Jun., Printer, 1809.

FRIENDS, Yearly Meetings, *continued*.
 Re-printed by direction of the Meeting, 1826.
  B. Lindsey & Co., Printers.
 Also re-printed by direction of the Meeting, 1840.
             8vo. 10¾
 Friends in Sydney. See also Alfred Allen, Wm. Tuting, Walter Barton, &c.
—— To all Lovers of the Truth in Sydney who are interested in the controversy raised by the people called 𝕮𝖍𝖗𝖎𝖘𝖙𝖎𝖆𝖓 𝕯𝖎𝖘𝖈𝖎𝖕𝖑𝖊𝖘, 𝖆𝖌𝖆𝖎𝖓𝖘𝖙 𝖙𝖍𝖊 𝕱𝖗𝖎𝖊𝖓𝖉𝖘.
  E. Mason, Printer, 62, York Street, opposite Wesleyan Church.   8vo. [1869.] ¼
 Illinois Yearly Meeting ("Hicksite").
—— Rules of Discipline, 1878.

   Miscellaneous Books and Papers.
—— 𝕭𝖊𝖉𝖋𝖔𝖗𝖉 𝕴𝖓𝖘𝖙𝖎𝖙𝖚𝖙𝖊, 𝕱𝖎𝖗𝖘𝖙-𝕯𝖆𝖞 𝕾𝖈𝖍𝖔𝖔𝖑 𝖆𝖓𝖉 𝕳𝖔𝖒𝖊 𝕸𝖎𝖘𝖘𝖎𝖔𝖓 𝕬𝖘𝖘𝖔𝖈𝖎𝖆𝖙𝖎𝖔𝖓 REPORT.
  London: Printed by Barclay & Fry, 9, College Hill, Cannon Street. 8vo. 1867. 3½
—— Second Annual Report, 1868, to the 25th, 1891.
—— Bedford Institute, First-Day School and Home Mission Association. Appeal for Subscriptions. Signed, William Beck, Edmund Pace, Charles Hoyland, 28th 11th Month, 1867.   4to. [1867.] ¼
—— Schedule, showing time and place of the various Works carried on by the Association. Signed, T. Frederick Ball, *Secretary.*   4to. (No date.) ¼
—— Friends' Meetings, Schools, Mission Work, &c., at Ratcliff. (List of).   8vo. ⅛
—— A Special Devotional Meeting at the Bedford Institute, 30th of 4th Mo., 1869. (Notice of). 8vo. 1869. ⅛
—— Appeal for Subscriptions for Thomas White, District Visitor, incapacitated by illness. Signed, Edmund Pace, John Hilton, Charles Hoyland, and T. Frederick Ball, Secretary, 11th Mo. 5th, 1869. 8vo. ¼
 Spitalfields Soup Society. Instituted 1797. Robert Hanbury, Treasurer.
—— Appeal for aid on behalf of the poor and destitute. 4to. ¼
—— Appeal for donations   4to. No date. ¼
—— Appeal for subscriptions, through the newspapers. Signed, Edwd. Marsh, Hon. Sec., 29 1 mo., 1868. 4to. ¼
—— Form of acknowledgment of receipt. 8vo. ⅛

FRIENDS, Miscellaneous Books and Papers, *continued*.

—— Engraving of the interior of "Soup Kitchen, 53, Brick Lane, Spitalfields." . . . . 4to. (1868.) ¼

—— Appeal for donations, which some of the Committee thankfully acknowledge. . . . 4to. 1868. ½

—— Notice of the house being open every day. 8vo. N.D. ⅛

Friends' Educational Society.

—— On the Means of Intellectual Improvement, open to young persons in the Society of Friends, after leaving school. Presented to the Friends' Educational Society, 1856, by John Newby.
York : William Simpson, 15, Low Ousegate.
8vo. 1856. 2

Friends' Foreign Mission Association, 1868.

TREASURER—James Hack Tuke, Hitchin.
SECRETARY—Henry Stanley Newman, Leominster.

EXECUTIVE COMMITTEE—

Isaac Brown	John Morland
William Beck	Josiah Newman
C. L. Braithwaite	George Palmer
William Brewin	Thomas Pease
Robert Charleton	S. Pumphrey, Jun.
George Dymond	Alfred Ransom
Joseph S. Fry	William Ransom
J. T. Grace	Isaac Robson
Henry Hipsley	Frederic Seebohm
Thomas Harvey	John E. Wilson
Joseph Huntley	C. S. Wilson
Edwin Laundy	Robert Wilson

BENARES SUB-COMMITTEE.

Henry Hipsley	William Brewin
Thomas Harvey	Henry S. Newman

MADAGASCAR SUB-COMMITTEE.

James Hack Tuke	William Ransom
Alfred Ransom	Frederic Seebohm

—— REPORT of THE MISSIONARY MEETING, held in the Friends' Meeting House, Ackworth, Seventh Month Third, 1868.

"Hereby perceive we the love of God, because He laid down His life for us, and we ought to lay down our lives for the brethren."

Published by order of the Executive Committee.
8vo. 1868. 3

—— Fourth Annual Report of the Friends' **Foreign Mission Association**, 1871.

FRIENDS, Miscellaneous Books and Papers, *continued.*
    Published Order of the Executive Committee. May be obtained from the Tract Depôt, Broad Street, Leominster. . . . . . 8vo. [1871.] 4¼
Annual Reports to 1891.

——Twenty-first Annual Report of the Friends' Sabbath Schools for Men and Boys, at York, 1868. Signed, William Sessions, Secretary, York, 31st of 12th Month, 1868. With "Twelfth Annual Report of the Girls' Sabbath School, for the year 1868." Signed, Amy J. Thorp, 31st of 12th Month, 1868.
    4to. [1869 ?] ½

——REPORT of the Fifth Conference of Teachers and Delegates from Friends' First-Day Schools in the United States, held at Philadelphia, Pa., on the 17th, 18th, 19th, and 20th of 11th Month, 1869. Published by order of the Conference.

——The same.
    Bristol: *Re-printed by Henry Hill, 2, Baldwin Street.* 8vo. 1870. 6½

——The Society of Friends (or Quakers) in Glasgow. What are they, and what do they believe?
    Glasgow: *Printed by Hugh Baird, 67, Trongate.*
    8vo. 1870. 1
    NOTE.—Reprinted from the Glasgow *Daily Express* of 1st August, 1870.

——Leominster Orphan Home. The ANNUAL REPORT for 1870. *This Home is for Boys and Girls who have lost both Parents and are destitute.* Secretary, Henry Stanley Newman; Treasurer, Josiah Newman.
    Office:—Broad Street, Leominster.
    Leominster: Printed by John Woolley, Post Office.
    8vo. 1870. 1

——Proceedings of First General Meeting held within the limits of New York Yearly Meeting at Farmington, New York, the 18th of Eighth Month, 1871.
    London: *S. W. Partridge & Co., 9, Paternoster Row. Printed at the Wayne County Journal Printing Office Palmyra, New York. Re-printed by the Dublin Steam Printing Company.*
    16mo. [1871.] 1½

——Conference of Friends at Willow Park, Dublin, on 22nd and 23rd of 8th Month, 1871.

FRIENDS, Miscellaneous Books and Papers, *continued.*
London: F. B. Kitto, 5, Bishopsgate Street Without.
S. W. Partridge & Co., 9, Paternoster Row.
Dublin: John Gough, 3, Eustace Street.
 One Penny. . . . . 16mo. [1871.] ¾
——Fire at Chicago. (A circular signed by Stafford Allen and Joseph Beck, inviting Friends to a meeting at Devonshire House, 17th of 10th mo. (1871), to consider what steps should be taken to relieve the distress. . . . . . 8vo. [1871.] ⅛
——Friends' Chicago Fund. (Circular soliciting subscriptions signed) J. Lister Godlee, *Secretary.*
        4to. [1871.] ¼
——A Summary View of the INTERNAL SLAVE TRADE, &c., in some parts of THE UNITED STATES.
 William Phillips, Printer, George Yard, Lombard Street, London. . . . Large 4to. 1827. ½
——FRIENDS' PROVIDENT INSTITUTION. *Established in the Year* 1832. (Being an Explanation of the Plan and *Primary* Object of the Institution.
 W. Alexander & Co., Printers, Castlegate, York.
       Fol. N. D. 1
——ENDOWED CHARITIES. COPIES of the GENERAL DIGEST of ENDOWED CHARITIES for the COUNTIES and CITIES mentioned in the FOURTEENTH REPORT of the CHARITY COMMISSIONERS; and, of the CHARITIES vested in the various LONDON COMPANIES, in so far as such DIGESTS have been completed, &c. SOCIETY OF FRIENDS' CHARITIES. (*Lord Robert Montagu.*)
Ordered, by The House of Commons, *to be Printed,* 4th *June,* 1875.
[*Price* 6d.] 243-(5). *Under* 6 *ozs.* Large Folio. 1875. 13
——Record for Marriages as at first concluded and sent to the various Meetings. . Large Folio. [Abt. 1760.] 1
——The CASE of the People called QUAKERS. (On Prosecutions in the Ecclesiastical Courts.) . Fol. ½
——At DEVONSHIRE HOUSE, a BOOK is kept by SARAH SHIPMAN, the Door-keeper's Daughter, where Women Servants and Nurses that are Friends, may have their names entered, &c. . . Fol. N. P. P. or Date. ½
——At a Meeting of Friends held at York, the 20th of the 5th Month, 1807, convened for the purpose of con-

FRIENDS, Miscellaneous Books and Papers, *continued.*
sidering the most eligible mode of supporting the Election of WILLIAM WILBERFORCE, Esq.—WILLIAM and HENRY TUKE, Treasurers.
 A. Bartholoman, Printer, York.   4to. [1807].   ¼

——*Report of the Association for the relief of some cases of great Distress in the Island of Antigua, particularly among the discarded Negroes—for* 1814. (Subscriptions received by WM. Allen, Plough Court; and Thomas Christy, 35, Gracechurch Street.)
 London : Printed by W. Phillips, George Yard, Lombard Street.   Fol. [1814.]   1

——CASE of the DISTRESSED GREEKS.
 Printed by Wm. Phillips, George Yard, Lombard Street, London.   Large Fol. 1823.   1

SCHOOLS.

Ackworth.

——History of Ackworth School. See HENRY THOMPSON.

——LIST OF THE BOYS AND GIRLS admitted into ACKWORTH SCHOOL DURING THE 100 YEARS from 18th of 10th month, 1779, to the Centenary celebration on the 27th of 6th month, 1879.

Compiled from the Official Registers.
 "Peopled with bright remembrances."—*Jeremiah Holmes Wiffen.*
Published by the Centenary Committee, Ackworth School, 1879.
 Samuel Harris & Co., 5, Bishopsgate Without, London.   8vo.

——Preface, xxxix. pp., and List of Scholars, 211 pp.

——Supplement.

——Centenary.

——A Spelling Book for the use of Ackworth Schools.
 London : Printed and sold by James Phillips, George Yard, Lombard Street.   12mo. 1790.   6

——Ackworth Old Scholars' Association. Signed, J. Spence Hodgson.   4to. No date.   ¼

——ACKWORTH OLD SCHOLARS' ASSOCIATION. REPORT OF INAUGURAL MEETING. With an Account appended of the SCHOOL YEAR, 1881-2.
 Darlington : Harrison Penney, Crown Street Printing Works.
         8vo. 1882.   2

FRIENDS, Schools, *continued*.
Croydon.
——Annual Examination, 6th mo. 23, 1876.
Arrangements. (A post card.) . . . 1876.
——Report of the Boys' Juvenile Literary Society, 6th Mo., 1878. Geo. Frederick Linney, 1878. The School was removed to Saffron Walden, in 1879. Annual Reports from 1868 to 1892, including Saffron Walden.

YORK SCHOOL.
——Proposed BOARDING-SCHOOL for GIRLS at YORK. The following Friends propose to open a School at York, viz.:

ESTHER TUKE,	TABITHA MIDDLETON,
MARTHA ROUTH,	SARAH GRUBB,
MARY PROUD,	SARAH SWANWICK,
ANN NORTH,	ELIZABETH HOYLAND,
SARAH PRIESTMAN.	

To be opened the 1st of 1st Month, 1785.
4to. [About 1784.] ¼

TOTTENHAM SCHOOL.
——The Managers of the TOTTENHAM SCHOOL for BOYS on the improved Plan, respectfully acquaint the Subscribers that they have issued a Notice to the Parents of the Boys who attend it, of which the following is a Copy, &c.
    W. Phillips, Printer, George-yard, Lombard-street. . . (No date.) Folio. [1812.] ½
    NOTE.—Supposed to be an improvement on the Lancasterian Plan.

Women's Epistles 1871-2 printed in London.
——*From the* Yearly Meeting of Women Friends, *held in* Mount Pleasant, Ohio, *by adjournments, from the 5th of 9th Month to the 10th of the same, inclusive,* 1871, to the next Yearly Meeting of Women Friends to be held in London. Signed, SARAH E. JENKINS, *Clerk*.
4to. [1872.] ¼

——Ditto ; *held* in Baltimore, *by adjournments, from the 21st of 10th Month to the 26th of the same, inclusive,* 1871, to the next Y. M. of Women Friends, to be held in London. Signed JULIA VALENTINE, *Clerk*.
4to. [1872.] ¼

——*From the* Yearly Meeting of Women Friends, *held in* Dublin, *by adjournments, from the 1st of Fifth Month*

FRIENDS, *continued.*

to the 8th of the same, inclusive, 1872. To the next Y.M. of Women Friends to be held in London.
Signed MARY EDMUNDSON, *Clerk.*
4to. [1872]. ¼

—— *From the* Yearly Meeting of Women Friends, *held in* London *by adjournments, from the 22nd of Fifth to the 31st of the same, inclusive,* 1872. To the Quarterly and other Meetings of Women Friends in Great Britain and Ireland. . . 4to. [1872.] ½
Signed SARAH ELIZA DYMOND, *Clerk.*

*FRY, Edmund—Continued from Catalogue, vol. 1., p. 810.
——Peace Principles scripturally maintained.
London . . . . 12mo. 1855.
Note.—Title from cover.
[*British Museum,* 8425, *b.*]

——A Sketch of the Life and Labours of the Rev. C. H. Spurgeon—with an introductory address by A. Fletcher.
London. . . . . 12mo. [1856].
[*British Museum,* 4906, *c.*]

*FRY, Edmund M.D., The Type Founder.—Continued from Catalogue, vol. 1. p. 819.

This gentleman was one of the Society of Friends. He was originally bred to the medical profession; but was more generally known as an eminent, and perhaps the most learned, type-founder of his time. His foundery was in Type-street, Chiswell-street. The substructure of the establishment (as we learn from a circular issued by Dr. Fry, in 1828, on his making known his wish to retire from business), was laid about 1764; commencing with improved imitations of Baskerville's founts, in all sizes; but they did not meet with encouragement from the printers, whose offices were generally stored with the Caslon founts, formed after the Dutch models. Dr. Fry, therefore, commenced his imitation of the Chiswell-street Foundery, established by the celebrated Wm. Caslon; which he completed at a vast expense, and with very satisfactory encouragement. But at this period, what the Doctor calls "a rude, pernicious, and most unclassical innovating system" was commenced, by the introduction of various fanciful letters. His imitations of the Baskerville and Caslon types were, in consequence of this revolution, laid by for ever; but no instance occurred to

*FRY, Edmund, M.D., *continued.*

the attentive observation of Dr. Fry, where any founts of book letter, on the present system, have been found equal in service, or nearly so agreeable to the reader, as the true *Caslon*-shaped Elziver types ; and in this sentiment we coincide with Dr. Fry. As the life of Dr. Fry is interesting to the public only as connected with his business, we venture to copy the remainder of the advertisement above alluded to, for the benefit of some future historian of the annals of the Type Foundery :—

" When that eminent printer, the late William Bowyer, gave instruction to Joseph Jackson to cut his beautiful Pica Greek, he used to say, ' Those in common use, were no more Greek, than they were English.' Were he now living, it is likely that he would not have any reason to alter that opinion.

" The Greeks of this Foundery were many of them made in Type-street, copied from those of the celebrated Foulis of Glasgow; and there are two, a Pica and a Long Primer, on the Porsonian plan. The Codex Alexandrinus was purchased at James's sale, in 1782.

" The Hebrews were also chiefly cut by Dr. Fry, subject to the direction and approbation of the most learned Hebraists.

" The two Arabics, Great Primer and English, were cut from the original drawings of, and under the personal direction of Dr. Wilkins, Oriental Librarian to the East India Company ; and have no rival, either in beauty or correctness.

" The Syriac has been made within the last two years (1828), with all its vowel-points, reduced to an English body, from the Double Pica of the eminent Assemann's edition of Ludolph's Testament.

" The English, No. 1, and Pica Ethiopics—the Pica and Long Primer Samaritans, were purchased at James's sale. The other Orientals, viz. two Malabaries—the Amharic—Ethiopic, No. 3, and Guzerattee, were all cut at this Foundery. As was the fine collection of Blacks, or pointed Gothics, except the English, No. 1,—Pica, No. 2, Long Primer, No. 1,—and Brevier, which were collected by the late John James. There is good authority for believing that this Pica Black, No. 2, was once the property of William Caxton ; Dr. Fry having recut for a reprint of a work published by that celebrated man, all the contractions and accented letters exhibited in the specimen-book.

" The Occidentals, as termed by Moxon, Mores, and others, viz. the Saxons, Hibernians, German, and Russian, were also produced at this Foundery. As were the two Plein Chants, and the Psalm Music.

" The Great Primer Script, which, it must be acknowledged, is the *ne plus ultra* of every effort of the letter founder in imitation of writing, was made for the proprietor by

FRY, Edmund, M.D., *continued.*

the celebrated Firmin Didot at Paris; the matrices are of steel, and the impressions from the punches sunk in *inlaid silver!*"

We regret to learn that Dr. Fry retired from business with a very slender provision. He was an old member of the Company of Stationers. In 1799 he published a work (in strict connexion with his profession), "Pantographia: containing copies of all the known alphabets in the world, together with an English explanation of the peculiar form of each letter; to which are added, specimens of all well-authenticated oral languages, forming a comprehensive Digest of Phonology," 8vo. This work contains 200 alphabets, amongst which are 18 varieties of the Chaldee, and no less than 32 of the Greek. (See Gent. Mag. 1799, pp. 137, 879.)

Gent. Mag., May, 1836.

He died at Dalby Terrace, City Road, London, the 22nd of 12th month, 1835, aged about 79 years, and was buried on 27th of the same month, in Friends' Burial ground, Bunhill Fields.

Peel Monthly Meeting.

FRY, Sir Edward, of *London*, continued from Catalogue, Vol. 1, p. 811.

———A Treatise on the Specific Performance of Contracts, including those of public companies.

London 8vo. 1858

[*Brit. Museum*, 6375, C.]

———Three Essays on England, China, and Opium.

FRY, Elizabeth, continued from Catalogue, Vol. 1, p. 811.

———A MEMOIR of ELIZABETH FRY: by her Daughter, Mrs. Francis Cresswell. Abridged from the larger memoir, with alterations and additions.

London: *James Nisbet & Co.* . 8vo. 1869 22

See Mrs. FRANCIS CRESSWELL.

FRY, John, of *London*. (Anon.).

———A Letter to ———, beginning " Esteemed Friend," &c., and dated, "London, 1783," being "A Vindication of a late transaction on the Stock Exchange."

Folio 1783 1

FRY, Joseph Storrs, son of JOSEPH FRY of *Bristol.* —Continued from Catalogue, Vol. 1, p. 822.

———Memoir of the late Robert Charleton.

London, pd. . . . . 8vo. [1873.] 3½

See ROBERT CHARLETON.

FRYER, Alfred, of *Elm Hirst, Wilmslow,* near *Manchester.*
——THE GREAT LOAN LAND. By ALFRED FRYER. Fifth Edition.
> This book was written by Mr. Fryer, after his return from America, for private circulation among his friends ; but it so well and completely answers most of the questions that an English investor asks concerning the merits and security of American Land Mortgages, that we have obtained Mr. Fryer's permission to republish a larger edition for more general circulation.

> LONDON : JARVIS-CONKLIN MORTGAGE TRUST COMPANY, 95, GRESHAM STREET (Bank), E.C.

SIXPENCE. 8vo. 1887. 4

FRYER, John Firth, See FIELDEN THORP.
——The York Reader.

FULLER, Adam, Banker of Lombard Street and Exchange Alley, London. In the following sheet he says he was a Prisoner in the Fleet, 18 years, at the suit of Daniel Mildred, a Friend.
——The CASE of ADAM FULLER, a Prisoner in the Fleet. Addressed to the Worthy Body of People called Quakers, in Particular, and to the Benevolent Public, in General.
> (*Axtell, Printer, No. 2, Red Lion Court, Fleet Street.*) . . . . Folio. [1772 ?] ½

FULLER, Samuel, of *Dublin.* Continued from Catalogue, Vol. 1., p. 825.
——Practical Astronomy, in the Description and Use of both Globes, Orrery, and Telescopes, wherein the most useful elements, and most valuable and modern discoveries of the true Astronomy are exhibited, after a very easy and expeditious manner, in an exact Account of our Solar System, with ten curious copper plates, done by an excellent hand. Collected from the best Authors, as Dr. Halley, Keil, Harris, Gordon, &c. For the use of Students, by S. Fuller.

> The Works of the Lord are great, sought out of all them that have pleasure therein.—Psal. cxi., 2.

> About 1732 or 1733 ?

——Some PRINCIPLES AND PRECEPTS of the CHRISTIAN RELIGION, by way of QUESTION AND ANSWER, Recommended to Parents and Tutors for the use of children, BY SAMUEL FULLER, one of the People

FULLER, Samuel, *continued.*
    called QUAKERS. *Read and approved of by their National Meeting, held in Dublin, in the 9th Month,* 1733.
        "Train up a child in the way he should go : and when he is old he will not depart from it."—Prov. xxii., 6.
        "Hold fast the form of sound words, which thou hast heard of me."—II Tim., i., 13.
        "But sanctify the Lord God in your hearts : and be ready always to give an answer to every man that asketh you a reason of the hope that is in you, with meekness and fear."—I Pet., iii., 15.
  A NEW EDITION, REVISED.
    Dublin : *David F. Gardiner, 40, Westmorland Street.* 18mo. 1830.   1

G.

G.T., of *Tullylagan, Dungannon, Ireland,* an ex-Friend, but who still feels an interest in the Society.
—— Antidote to Robert Charleton's " Thoughts on Barclay's Apology."
    Dublin : *R. D. Webb & Son, Printers, Great Brunswick Street.* . . . 12mo. 1868.   ½
    NOTE.—The writer of this pamphlet gives a short account of the lives and doctrines of George Fox and Robert Barclay, which he thinks by telling their own story will be the best way of answering Robert Charleton's Objections.

GARDNER, Anne, of *Bessbrook, Newry, Ireland.*
—— The Sacramentarianism of the "Church of England," viewed from the Stand-Point of Quakerism. By Anne Gardner. *Extracted from* " *The British Friend.*"
    Glasgow : *Robert Smeal, Partick.* London : *F. B. Kitto, Bishopsgate Street.* To be had also from Anne Gardner, Bess'rook, Newry, Ireland. (*Glasgow* : *W. G. Blackie & Co., Printers, Villafield.*) . . . 8vo. 1868.   2

GAY, Claude,—*continued* from Catalogue, vol. I, p. 834.
—— *Swear not at all. Bless, and Curse not.*
                4to. No Printer's Name, Place, or Date.   ¼
—— SWEAR NOT AT ALL. BLESS, AND CURSE NOT.
                 4to. N. P., P., or Date.   ¼
—— Another edition. .   Large 4to. N. P., P., or Date.   ¼
—— Journal of Claude Gay, in MS.
    NOTE.—This Journal was destroyed in the Fire at Gracechurch Street Meeting House, in 1821.

GIBBONS, Abraham, of *Lampeter*, *Lancaster* County, *Pennsylvania*.
——Recollections of Abraham Gibbons. In Comly's Miscellany, Vol. 4, p. 161.

GIBBONS, William, M.D., of *Wilmington, Delaware*.
——Sketch of "Friends," (Hicksite) in a work, entitled, "An Original History of the Religious Denominations at present existing in the United States." Compiled by I. Daniel Rupp.
Philadelphia : Published by J. Y. Humphreys, Harrisburg : Clyde and Williams. 8vo. 1844.

*GIBBONS, George W., of *Philadelphia*.
——The Chimerical System Shaken, on the so generally believed principles of the supposed revolution of the earth and its course around the Sun, refuted from the authority of Scripture testimony and right reason. By Geo. W. Gibbons, who believes the earth to be immoveable, as the Scriptures of Truth do declare.
Philadelphia : 8vo. 1854.

GILBERT, Benjn., *continued* from Catalogue, Vol. 1, p. 843.
——Account of Benjamin Gilbert, p. 276, Vol. 3. Hazard, Register of Pennsylvania.
——Narrative reprinted with some additional particulars, pp. 311.

GILKES, Louisa E., Widow of GILBERT GILKES, of London.
——A Selection from the Letters of Lydia Ann Barclay. [Edited by L. E. GILKES]. 8vo. 1862.
See LYDIA A. BARCLAY.
She died at Fritchley, Derbyshire, the 25th of 12th month, 1881, aged 67 years.

GILPIN, Charles, *continued* from Catalogue, Vol. 1, p. 845.
——Water Supply of Sidcot School.
——Christians strangling Christians. [Anon.]
C. Gilpin, 5, Bishopsgate Street Without.
8vo. [1846?] ⅛
He died at 10, Bedford Square, London, on the 8th of 9th Month, 1874, aged 59 years, and the interment took place in Friends' Burial Ground, Winchmore Hill, on the 14th of the same month.

*GILPIN, Thomas, of *Philadelphia*.
——The Representation of minorities of electors to act with the majorities in elected Assemblies. By Thomas Gilpin.
Philadelphia. 1844.

*GILPIN, Thomas, *continued.*
—— Essay on the position of the organic remains as connected with a former Tropical belt of the earth. By Thomas Gilpin.
    Philadelphia :   8vo. 1844.

‖ GOMELDON, Jane, of *Newcastle-on-Tyne*, Cousin of Sydney Parkinson.
—— Letter and some Verses. See Parkinson's *Voyage, &c.*

GOTHERSON, Dorothea, was the youngest daughter of THOMAS SCOTT, Esquire, of *Egerton, Kent,* and JANE, daughter of JOHN KNATCHBULL, of *Mersham, Kent,* Esquire, was baptized Sepr. 22nd, 1611, in *Godmersham Church.* She was married to Major DANIEL GOTHERSON, of Cromwell's Army. Both she and her husband joined the Society of Friends, some time before 1660; she afterwards became a Minister. Her husband dying in Sept., 1666, she remarried JOSEPH HOGBEN, of *Kent*; and afterwards about 1680, emigrated to *America,* and settled on *Long Island, New York.* For further particulars concerning her see the following book,

—— DOROTHEA SCOTT, otherwise GOTHERSON and HOGBEN. Annotated by G. D. SCULL.
    Printed for Private Circulation *by Parker & Co., Oxford.* 4to. 1882. 3½
    NOTE.—With facsimile, autograph and genealogies.

—— DOROTHEA SCOTT, otherwise GOTHERSON AND HOGBEN, of EGERTON HOUSE, KENT, 1611-1680. A New and Enlarged Edition. By G. D. SCULL, Editor of "The Evelyns in America," Member of the Historical Society of Pennsylvania, &c., &c. [Frontispiece of Egerton House, Kent.]
    Printed for Private Circulation *by Parker & Co., Oxford.* 4to. 1883. 29

GOUGH, John, *continued* from Catalogue, vol. 1, p. 855.
—— PRACTICAL ARITHMETIC; adapted to the Commerce of Great Britain, Ireland, and America, for the use of schools, corrected according to the late assimilation of the currency, weights and measures. BY JOHN GOUGH. To which is added AN APPENDIX of Concise Methods of Calculation, and a Short Treatise on Algebra. The Questions are numbered to answer. Mr. Telfair's Key.

GOUGH, John, *continued.*
> *Dublin : Published by James Duffy, and sold at his Wholesale Warehouse, 25, Anglesea Street, Price 3s. 6d. bound.* . . 12mo. 1839. 14½

*GRAHAM, John, of *Sunderland*, continued from Catalogue, vol. 1, p. 858.

——*Simon Pure Unmask'd* : or, The ERRORS of QUAKERISM Display'd. A DIALOGUE betwixt a QUAKER SPEAKER and a LAY PROTESTANT. Wherein will be pointed out several (of the many) Errors, Sophistry, and Inconsistancies of their Champion, *R. Barclay*, in his *Apology* for their Principles ; also the AUTHOR'S REASONS for embracing, and afterwards renouncing them. *By* JOHN GRAHAM. (With a Postscript.)

And a Frontispiece.
> ACTS, chap. xix., ver. 13, 14, 15, 16.
> *" Then certain of the vagabond Jews, Exorcists, took upon them to call over them which had Evil spirits, in the Name of the* LORD JESUS, *saying, We adjure you by* JESUS *whom Paul preacheth.*
> *And there were seven Sons of one* Sceva *a Jew, and Chief of the Priests, which did so.*
> *And the Evil Spirit answered and said,* JESUS *I know, and Paul I know ; but who are ye ?*
> *And the Man in whom the Evil Spirit was leapt on them, and overcame them, and prevailed against them, so that they fled out of that house naked and wounded.*

> *Newcastle : Printed by John White, and sold by the Booksellers in Town and Country,* MDCCXLV. 8vo. 1745. 5

*GRANT, Ann, was the daughter of Geo. and Ann Miller, of *Edinburgh.*

——A Solemn Appeal to the Unconverted.
> Small 8vo. [about 1840 ?] 30 pp.

She died at *Stoke-upon-Trent,* the 31st of 7th Month, 1857, aged 59 years.

*GRAVES, George,—*continued* from Catalogue, vol. 1, p. 862.

——The *Naturalist's Pocket-book*, or TOURIST'S COMPANION, being a brief Introduction to the different Branches of 𝕹atural 𝕳istory, with approved methods for collecting and preserving *The Various Productions of Nature.*

*GRAVES, George, *continued.*
>By GEORGE GRAVES, F.L.S. Author of BRITISH ORNITHOLOGY, OVARIUM BRITANNICUM, and Editor of the New Edition of CURTIS'S FLORA LONDINENSIS.
>
>**London** : *Printed by W. and S. Graves, and sold by Sherwood, Neely, and Jones, Paternoster Row* . . . . . 8vo. [1817.] 21½
>
>NOTE.—With 8 plates, plain and coloured, and descriptive letterpress.

*GRAYSON, William Sandyfirth, of *Leeds*, afterwards of *London*.
——"What we are waiting for." Signed *G*. In "The Daily News, Jan. 1871."
Reprinted by the Peace Society.

GREEN, Joshua, of *Saffron Walden*.
——THE UNITARIAN OPINION of " A Reasonable Faith," by "THREE FRIENDS" from "THE CHRISTIAN LIFE," a Unitarian Journal, January 17th, 1885.
>H. D. & B. Headley, "Kent Examiner" Office, Ashford . . . 8vo. 5th Mo., 1885. ¼

GREEN, Joseph Joshua, his Son, of *Stansted Mountfitchet, Essex*, now of " *Ashmole House,*" *Hampstead, London, N.W.*
——**Two Hundred Years' History of a Country Business,** 1687-1887. JOSHUA GREEN & COMPANY, STANSTED MONTFITCHET, ESSEX. Edited by JOSEPH J. GREEN.
>*Ashford* : *H. D. & B. Headley, Invicta Printing Works, 44, High Street* . . 4to. 1887. 2
>
>NOTE.—The Title on the cover is "**Ye Hystorie of a Countre Busines att** STANSTEDE IN YE COUNTIE OF ESSEXE." Edited by JOSEPH J. GREEN.
>
>*Ashford: H. D. & B. Headley, Invicta Printing Works, 44, High Street* . . . . 1887.

——HISTORY of the WILMER FAMILY, together with some account of its Descendants. By CHARLES WILMER FOSTER, B.A., of St. John's College, Oxford, and JOSEPH J. GREEN.
>" *The glory of children are their fathers.*"
>" *Multos que pet annos stat fortuna domus, et avi numerantur avorum.*"
>*Privately Printed by Goodall and Suddick, Leeds.* 4to. 1888.
>
>A Notice of the *History of the Wilmer Family* in the *Archæological Journal*, Vol. 44, p. 213.
>
>NOTE.—Besides other illustrations this work contains Portraits of Grizell Gurnell and Samuel Hoare.

GREEN, Joseph Joshua, *continued*.
—— Genealogical Chart, showing the lineal descent of John Wilmer Green, son of Joseph J. Green, of " Ashmole House, Hampstead, from 88 families.
Headley Bros., Printers, Ashford, Kent. 4to. [1892.] ½
—— Quaker Records, being a Complete Index to "The Annual Monitor," or Obituary, from its commencement in 1813 to 1892.
Headley Bros., Printers, Ashford, Kent. 1892.

GREENWAY, R.,—*continued* from Catalogue, vol. 1, p. 868.
—— A Present from the Owners of the Ship LEEDS—INDUSTRY, to her SAILORS, being MEDITATIONS of R.G., when at SEA.
Broadside. (No Printer's Name, Place or Date).

GREER, Elizabeth, daughter of Thos. and Jane Lucas, was born in the year 1779.
—— A SELECTION from the MEMORANDA AND LETTERS of the late ELIZABETH GREER. For private circulation.
"The Righteous shall be in everlasting remembrance."—PSALM CXII. 6.
Dublin: Printed by Robert Chapman, Temple Lane, Dame Street. . . . 16mo. 1872. 2½
She died the 17th of 11th month, 1871, aged about 93 years—a minister nearly 44 years.

GRELLET, Stephen, *continued* from Catalogue, vol. 1, p. 869.
—— Memoir of Stephen Grellet, abridged Edition. By Robert Alsop. See ROBERT ALSOP.
—— Memoir of the Life of Stephen Grellet.
8vo. Philadelphia, No Date. 1
—— ETIENNE de GRELLET, the French Evangelist.
A Lecture. [By Edward Ash?]
London: Wertheim, Macintosh & Co., Paternoster Row. A. W. Bennett, 5, Bishopsgate, Without. 12mo. 1861. 2

GRISCOM, John,—*continued* from Catalogue, vol. 1, p. 874.
—— Monitorial Instruction. An ADDRESS, pronounced at the opening of the NEW YORK HIGH SCHOOL, with Note and Illustrations. By John Griscom. (With a Frontispiece of the School.)
New York: Printed by Mahlon Day, No. 376, Pearl Street. . . . 12mo. 1825. 9
" Wm. Allen, from his affectionate friend, J. Griscom."—on the copy from which the above title is taken.

GROVER, John,—*continued* from Catalogue, vol. 1 p. 875.
See "The Worthies of Sussex," by Mark Antony Lower.

——Letters, &c., of William Grover.
  Reprinted in *Friends' Family Library*, vol. 1.

GRUBB, Jonathan, of *Sudbury*,—continued from Catalogue, vol. 1, p. 876.

——The London Poor (Reported for the "Suffolk and Essex Free Press.") *A Public Lecture delivered at the Lecture Hall, Sudbury, on the Evening of the 27th of 8th Month,* 1867, by JONATHAN GRUBB.
  Sudbury : James Wright, Market Hill, &c.
    8vo. [1867.]   1

——A Word of affectionate Counsel to the younger portion of the Society of Friends. Reprinted from the "Friend" of 4th Month 1st., 1865. Price Two-pence.
  Sudbury : Printed and Published by James Wright, Market Hill.   12mo. 1865.   1

——"Lord, what wilt thou have me to do?" Acts IX. 6. *A Word to the Christian Church.* By Jonathan Grubb. *Price 1s. 6d. per 100 ; 12s. 6d. per 1000 ; 100 sent post paid for 20 stamps ; 500 sent post paid for 78 stamps by S. Jarrold, Norwich.* 32mo. [1870]   ⅛

——THE ADDRESSES by Jonathan Grubb and Caroline Talbot at the MEETING FOR YOUNG FRIENDS, held during the Yearly Meeting of 1876.
  London : Samuel Harris & Co., 5, Bishopsgate, Without.   Crown 8vo. 1876.

GRUBB, Sarah,—*continued* from Catalogue, vol. 1, p. 876.

——Life of Sarah Grubb, edition 1795, Trenton edition 1795.

——A SERIOUS MEDITATION : or a Christian's duty briefly set forth. [Anon.]
    4to. N.P.P. or date. [About 1790.]   ¼

——A SERIOUS MEDITATION : or *A Christian's Duty, briefly set forth.* [Anon.]
  G. Cooke, Printer, Dunstan's Hill, Tower Street.
    4to. No date.   ¼

——A *Christian's Duty* briefly set forth. [Anon.]
  Rodgers, Printer, Whitby.   4to. No date.   ¼

*GUMERSALL, Thomas B.. of *London*, Accountant.
——Gummersall's Tables of Interest, &c.
  Interest and Discount Tables, computed at 2½, 3, 3½, 4, 4½, and 5 per cent., from 1 to 365 days, and from £1 to

*GUMERSALL, Thomas B., *continued*.
 £20,000 ; that the Interest or Discount on any sum, for any number of days, at any of the above rates, may be obtained by the inspection of one page only. Each Rate occupies eighty pages ; the last five of which are devoted to the same number of pounds from 1 to 11 months, and from 1 to 10 years. They are also accompanied with Tables of Time and Brokerage, being altogether a vast improvement on Thompson and others. By T. B. Gumersall, Accountant, London.
 " This work is pre-eminently distinguished from all others on the same subject by facility of reference, distinctness of type, and accuracy of calculation." — *Banker's Circular*.
 Eleventh Edition, in 1 vol. 8vo. (pp. 500), price 10s. 6d., cloth, or strongly bound in calf, with the Rates per Cent. cut in at the foredge, price 15s. 6d.
London : Effingham Wilson, Royal Exchange.

GUMMERÉ, John, was born near *Willow Grove, Philadelphia*, in 1784. Professor.
——A Treatise on Surveying, containing the theory and practice to which is prefixed a short system of Plane Trigonometry ; the whole clearly demonstrated by a large number of appropriate examples particularly adapted to the use of Schools, by John Gummeré, A.M., Fellow of the Am. Phil. Soc., and Cor. Mem. of the Acad. of Nat. Sciences. 1st Editn. 8vo. 1814.
——Reprinted, 14th Edition.
 Philadelphia . . . . 8vo. 1838. 418 pp.
——An Elementary Treatise on Astronomy ; in two parts ; the first containing a clear and compendious view of the theory ; the second a number of practical problems, to which are added Solar, Lunar, and other Astronomical tables. By John Gummeré, A.M.
——3rd Edition, enlarged.
 Philadelphia . . . . 8vo. 1842. 560 pp.
——Memorials of the Life and Character of John Gummeré. By William J. Allinson. . . . 8vo. 6 leaves.
 He died 31st of 5th Month, 1845, aged 61 years.

*GUMMERE, Samuel R., of *Philadelphia*.
——A Treatise on Geography for the use of Schools.
 Philadelphia . . . . . , 18mo.
——The Progressive Spelling Book, in two parts, containing a great variety of useful exercises in Spelling, Pronunciation and derivation ; including extensive tables of words derived from their Greek and Latin Roots.

*GUMMERE, Samuel R., *continued*.

——A Compendium of the Principles of Elocution on the basis of Dr. Rush's Philosophy of the Human Voice, to which is added a copious selection of exercises for reading and declamation. By Samuel R. Gummeré.
    Philadelphia . . . . 12mo. 1857. 262 pp.

GURNEY, Bartlett, of *Norwich*.
——Account of, with a Portrait of him.
    See the Supplement to the "Record of the House of Gournay," p. 1059.
    He died in 1803.

——Chapman Hannah, of the Whitby family, first Wife of Bartlett Gurney. (Portrait.)
    See the same work, p. 1059.

GURNEY, Catherine and Rebecca, of *Charlbury*, in *Oxfordshire*.
——Notice of intended Girls' School at Hertford.
    8vo. N. D. ¼

GURNEY, Hannah, daughter of JOSHUA MIDDLETON.
——The Sincere QUAKER (8 lines of verse).
    Published May 28th, 1748, by Thomas Bakewell, against Birchin Lane, in Cornhill. A fine line engraving. . . Folio. 1748.

GURNEY, Hudson,—*continued* from Catalogue, vol. 1, p. 879.
——Portrait of *Hudson Gurney, Esq., J. Opie, Esq., R. A. pinxt*, 1797. . . . . Fol. or large 4to.

GURNEY, John, of *Norwich*, *continued* from Catalogue, Vol. 1, p. 880.
——THE WOOLLEN MANUFACTURER'S GLORY, Inscrib'd to the immortal Praise of JOHN GURNEY, of Norwich, Factor, *who by his celebrated extempore Speeches, February, 1719-20, before ye Honourable House of Commons, turn'd the Scale of the Contention between the* WOOLLEN and Linnen MANUFACTURERS.
    [Then follows his Portrait, and underneath 21 lines of verse] ON THE NORWICH QUAKER.
    Sold at Spittle Fields Coffee House, by I. & W. Groves, Weavers, in Angel Alley, near ye Weavers Arms, in Bishopsgate-street; and by the Print Sellers, &c. Price 3d. [*Copper plate.*] . . . . Broadside. [1720] 1

GURNEY, John, of *Keswick*, last of *Norwich*. Nephew of the above John Gurney, *continued* from Catalogue, Vol. 1, p. 880.

——Lines "To the Memory of the late John Gurney, of Keswick." In "The Gentleman's Magazine," Vol. xl., p. 280. June, 1770.

  Signed *Crito*, dated *Essex*, April 12th, 1770. By Edmund Rack, of *Thetford*.

 Reprinted in "The Record of the House of Gournay, &c." . . . . Supplement p. 1061.

"Last Sunday, the 22nd of 4th mo., 1770, died in the 55th year of his age, Mr. John Gurney, one of the people called Quakers. He was the largest dealer in Irish Worsted in the Kingdom, and by his upright conduct joined to great capacity was equally useful to the trade of this City; as he lived with the utmost credit, his death is deservedly lamented, and his memory will ever be held dear by his family, to whom he approved himself a most tender husband, a kind father, and indulgent Benefactor: in every degree he merited the affection demonstrated, through a tedious and painful illness, which he endured with true Christian fortitude, having left them the consolation that his death was, as his life, an example worthy of imitation."—*Norwich Mercury*.

GURNEY, Joseph John,—*continued* from Catalogue, vol. 1, p. 881.

——Some Account of John Stratford, &c. The 19th Thousand.

 Norwich: Printed by S. Wilkin, Upper Hay-market, to be had also of Messrs. Bacon & Kinnebrook, Matchett, Stevenson & Matchett, Parsons, Stacy, Kitton, and Jarrold.

         12mo. 1829.   2/3

——SERMONS AND PRAYERS, delivered by Joseph John Gurney, in the Friends' Meeting House, 𝕷𝖎𝖛𝖊𝖗𝖕𝖔𝖔𝖑, 1832.

   Second Edition with additions.

 Liverpool: Thomas Hodgson, South John Street, London: Whittaker, Treacher, & Co.

         12mo. 1832. $3\frac{1}{2}$

   NOTE TO THE SECOND EDITION.

"Great pains have been taken to ensure the fidelity of the following Discourses, but the publisher considers it due to their eminent and highly gifted Author to state, that as they are published without his consent, or the benefit of his revision, of course he is in no wise reponsible for any inaccuracies that may have occurred.

GURNEY, Joseph John, *continued*.

The last three prayers were delivered in places of temporary accommodation during the repair of the Friends' Meeting House.—*Liverpool, 11th mo., 1832.*

——Familiar Letter to Henry Clay of Kentucky, describing a Winter in the West Indies. By Joseph John Gurney.

New York: Press of Mahlon, Day & Co., 374, Pearl Street. James Egbert, Printer. . 8vo. 1840. 12¾

——Reminiscences of Chalmers, Simeon, Wilberforce, &c. By Joseph John Gurney.

(*Privately printed without any name, place, or date.*) . . . . . 8vo. [1834 ?] 10¼

——De L'Institution et de L'Observation, du JOUR DU REPOS, extrait principalement des Remarques de J. J. Gurney, sur L'Histoire, et L'Autorité du Jour du Repos et sur la Manière de L'Observer; Traduit de l'anglais par J. J. Pacaud, Interprète près les tribunaux.

Paris : Imprimiere de E. Duverger, Rue de Verneuil. No. 4. . . . . . 16mo. 1838. 1¼

——SERMONS AND PRAYERS, delivered in the City of Philadelphia, by JOSEPH JOHN GURNEY. Taken in Shorthand.

Philadelphia : Kay and Brother, 122, Chesnut Street. (J. Richards, Printer.) 12mo. 1838. 4

NOTE.—On the back of the title page is : " Entered according to Act of Congress, in the year 1838, by Edward Hopper, in the Clerk's Office of the District Court, for the Eastern District of Pennsylvania."

——Auszüge aus den Lehren des Christenthums nach ihrem einfluffe auf das Leben des Menschen, Bon Joseph John Gurney.

Knenznach, 1850: *Druck von Friedrich Mohlleben.*

16mo. 1850. 2½

——ESSAI sur L'Exercise Habituel de L' AMOUR DE DIEU, considéré comme Préparation pour le ciel, Traduit de L'Anglais de JOSEPH JEAN GURNEY, sur la cinquième édition, par J. J. Pacaud, Bibliothécaire a Sainte—Geneviève.

Nous l'aimons parce qu'il nous a aimés le premier.
1 JEAN, IV., 15.

Paris : Typographie de Firmin Didot Frères, Imprimeurs de l'Institut, Rue Jacob 56.

12mo. 1839 11⅓

GURNEY, Joseph John, *continued*.
>NOTE.—The dedication to Richard Philips is prefixed to this edition in French.

——A DECLARATION, by the late JOSEPH JOHN GURNEY, of his faith respecting several points of Christian Doctrine.
>*Boston: Printed by S. N. Dickinson & Co.*
>　　　　　　　　　　　　　　　　8vo. 1847. 1¾

——A Declaration of his faith, &c.
——Reprinted.
>*Manchester: W. Irwin.*
>*London: F. B. Kitto.* (Richard H. Southall's edition.)
>　　　　　　　　　　　　　　　　　　　1870.
>>NOTE.—Annexed to this edition is the Yearly Meeting's Epistle to its junior members, published in 1850. For a Review of this edition, see "The British Friend."

——Bemærkninger over Bennernes Gamfunds sœregne Anskueffer oy skikke. uf Joseph John Gurney.
>*Stavanger: Paa Bennesamifundets Forlag.*
>　　　　　　　　　　　　　　　　8vo. 1856. 29¼

——Are you prepared for heaven?
>*London: The Religious Tract Society, &c.*　4pp.

——DE L'HABITUDE ET DE LA DISCIPLINE Traduit de L'Anglais de Joseph Jean Gurney.
>*Paris: Ch. Meyrueis et Ce, Libraires—Editeurs,*
>*Rue de Rivoli, 174.*　　．．12mo. 1857. 10½

——(Life of) Joseph John Gurney.
>*London: The Religious Tract Society, 56, Paternoster Row, &c.*　．．12mo. No date. 1⅓
>>NOTE.—No. 16 of the R. T. Society's "Biographical Series."

——SERMON preached by the late JOSEPH JOHN GURNEY, at FRIENDS' MEETING HOUSE, Arch Street, Philadelphia, Seventh Month, 1840.
>*Philadelphia: Merrihew & Son, Printers, No. 243, Arch Street.*　．．．18mo. 1867.　⅔
>*Reprinted Manchester: William Irwin.*　1870.
>>NOTE.—This Sermon is believed to be the last J. J. G. preached in the United States. It was reprinted from a public Newspaper, and done up in a glazed cover with a printed title in gold letters.

ᶜGURNEY, John Henry, of *Northrepps Hall*, near *Norwich*, son of Joseph John Gurney,—*continued* from Catalogue, vol. 1, p. 895.
——Portrait of John Henry Gurney.
    He died the 20th of 4th month, 1890, aged 71 years.

‖GURNEY, John Henry, Jun. Son of the above.
— —Rambles of a Naturalist in Egypt and other Countries, with an Analysis of the Claims of certain Foreign Birds to be considered British, and other ornithological notes. By J. H. Gurney, Jun., F.L.S.
    London: Jarrold & Sons, 3, Paternoster Buildings.
        8vo. [1877.]

GURNEY, Priscilla,—*continued* from Catalogue, vol. 1, p. 896.
——HYMNS selected from various authors, for the use of young persons, by PRISCILLA GURNEY.
Second edition.
    London : *Printed for Harvey and Darton, Gracechurch Street, by S. Wilkin, Norwich; and to be had of all other Booksellers.*   16mo. 1821.   9

——HYMNS selected from various Authors, FOR THE USE OF YOUNG PERSONS, by Priscilla Gurney.
Third edition.
    LONDON : *Printed for Harvey and Darton, Gracechurch Street, by S. Wilkin, Norwich; and to be had of all other Booksellers.*   16mo. 1822. $6\frac{3}{8}$

——Hymns, &c.—6th edition.
    (Same imprint as the fifth.)   18mo. 1825.   6

Reprinted,—7th edition.

Reprinted,—8th edition, with additions.   18mo. 1834.

*GURNEY (Mrs.), wife of John Henry Gurney.
——Mrs. Gurney's Apology. In justification of Mrs. ————'s Friendship.
    Philadelphia: William Brotherhead, No. 218, South Eighth Street. . . . . 8vo. 1860. $3\frac{1}{2}$

GURNEY, Samuel, son of Samuel and Elizabeth Gurney, of *Upton*, in *Essex*, was born there in the year 1816; in 1837 he married Ellen, daughter of William Foster Reynolds, of *Carshalton*, in *Surrey*. He was returned a Member of Parliament for Penryn, in the Fourth Month, 1857. He died the 4th of 4th month, 1882, aged 66 years, and was buried in the new ground, adjoining Wanstead Meeting House.
    For further particulars see an interesting account of him in *The Annual Monitor* for 1883.

H.

H. C.—Charlotte Hanbury ?
——To Friends interested in Mission Work in England.
      8vo. (5th Mo., 1866.) ⅛

H. H.—See HANNAH HUNT.
——Songs of the Spirit. By H. H. . 1868

H. M., of *Gloucester*. A Beaconite ?
——REMARKS on the DISUSE OF ALL TYPICAL RITES, addressed to THE SOCIETY OF FRIENDS.
 "My Father, if the prophet had bid thee do some great thing, would'st thou not have done it ?" II Kings, v. 13.
 Gloucester ; Printed by J. E. Lea, Westgate Street ; and sold by Hamilton, Adams, & Co., London. Price Threepence. . . . 8vo. 1837. 1½

H. W. See WILLIAM HODGSON.

HACK, James, died the 17th of 3rd month, 1829, aged 71 years. (In Catalogue Vol. 1, p. 900, as James, Jr.)

*HACK, James, Junr. (his Son), he left Friends and joined the Church of England, and died at *Torquay*, about 1860 ?

HACK, Maria, Wife of STEPHEN HACK and Sister of JOHN and BERNARD BARTON. *Continued* from Catalogue, vol. 1. p. 900.
——Lectures at Home. Discovery and Manufacture of Glass : Lenses and Mirrors : The Structure of the Eye. By Maria Hack.
 London : Printed for Darton and Harvey, Gracechurch Street. . . . 12mo. 1834. 9⅓
——ENGLISH STORIES OF THE OLDEN TIME. By MARIA HACK.
  "If chance thy home
 Salute thee with a Father's honour'd name,
 Go, call thy sons ; instruct them what a debt
  They owe their ancestors."
        AKENSIDE.
      Vol. 1. Vol. 2.
 London : Harvey and Darton, Gracechurch Street.
      12mo. 1839. 38 sheets.
——Grecian Stories, by Maria Hack. With thirty-nine illustrations by Gilbert, engraved by Wright and Folkard.
 "I find that men as high as trees will write Dialogue wise yet no man doth them slight for writing so."—BUNYAN.

HACK, Maria, *continued.*
  London : Harvey and Darton, Gracechurch
    Street. 12mo. 1840. 15½
——Familiar ILLUSTRATIONS of the Principal Evidences
 and Design of Christianity. By Maria Hack.

> As the intellectual faculties expand, the more obvious proofs
> of Revealed Religion ought to be gradually developed.
> GISBORNE.

Second edition.
  London : *Printed for Harvey and Darton, Grace-
   church Street.* . . . 18mo. 1828. 9¾
——LECTURES AT HOME. By MARIA HACK.

> "Why should not children be instructed in those wonderful
> works of Nature and Art, which we daily use without
> ever reflecting how they are produced?"—ROLLIN.

(Seven plates). Second Edition.
  London: *Harvey and Darton, Gracechurch Street.*
           8vo. 1841. 14

HADDOCK, Theophilus, *continued* from Catalogue, Vol. 1,
 p. 902.
——BAPTISM SPIRITUAL ; or the Beauty of a Believer
 Baptized : in a Letter to WILLIAM TANNER.

> For by one Spirit are we all baptized into one body,
> whether we be Jews or Gentiles, whether we be bond or
> free ; and have been all made to drink into one Spirit."—
> I Corinthians, xii. 13.
>
> "Blotting out the hand-writing of ordinances that was
> against us, which was contrary to us, and took it out of
> the way, nailing it to His cross. Wherefore then if you
> be dead with Christ from the rudiments of the world ;
> why then, as living in the world, are ye subject to ordi-
> nances ? Touch not, taste not, handle not : which are
> all to perish with the using after the commandments
> and doctrines of men. Which things have indeed a
> show of wisdom, in will worship, and humility, and
> neglecting the body : not in any honour to the satisfy-
> ing of the flesh."—Colossians ii. 14, 20 to 23.

  LONDON : *Printed for the Author, and published
   by Darton and Harvey, No. 55, Gracechurch
   Street; and sold at No. 8, Orange Street,
   Leicester Fields, and by the Booksellers in
   Town and Country.*
[*Price Sixpence.*] 12mo. 1797. 1⅝

HALL, Hannah, of *Ohio, North America.*
——A Brief Account of the Travels and Work in the
 Ministry of HANNAH HALL, of Ohio.
  Philadelphia : *J. B. Lippincott Company.*
  See JOSHUA MAULE. 8vo. 1886.

HALLOWELL, Benjamin, of *Philadelphia?*
—Young Friends' Manual, 1867.
    Reprinted—Third edition . . . . 1884.

HAMPTON, William, Son of Abner and Rachel Hampton, of *Rahway, East Jersey.*
—Some Account of his last sickness and death.—In Comly's Miscellany, Vol. 4, p. 29.
    He died the 24th of 2nd month, 1781.

HANBURY, Cornelius, *continued* from Catalogue, Vol. 1., p. 909, and others.—The Wars of the Boors, &c.
    He died the 7th of 3rd month, 1869, aged 73 years. For further particulars see an interesting Memoir of him in "*The Annual Monitor,*" for 1870.

HANBURY, Daniel, of *Plough Court, Lombard Street, London.*
    Several Books or Tracts from the Pharmaceutical Journal, in the British Museum.

HANBURY, Daniel, Jun., F.R.S.
—Memoir ? title.
    He died 24th of 3rd month, 1875, aged 49 years.

HANSON, Elizabeth, *continued* from Catalogue, Vol. 1, p. 912.
—God's Mercy surmounting Man's Cruelty.
    To be sold by Samuel Keimer, in Philadelphia, and Hewston Goldsmith, in N.Y. 1724, Dec. 24.
    NOTE.—Mr. Rich must have taken this title [Edition 1787] orally from some Cockney, as he speaks of the captive as Elizabeth *Anson.* "The Captivity took place in 1725, and a relation of it made in 1741 to Samuel Hopwood, about which time it was probably first printed. The Third edition was printed at *Danvers* in 1780, it is therefore to be supposed that this is the Fourth.
    See "*An Essay towards an Indian Bibliography, &c.* By *Thos. W. Field, New York, printed 1873. 8vo.*

HARDING, Robert, of *Great Henny,* near *Sudbury, Suffolk.*—A Minister.
—" Do Try," for " God is Willing."
    Sudbury : J. Wright, Printer, 12, Market Hill.
        32 mo. [1868.] ½

*HARFORD, John Scandred, of *Frenchay,* and afterwards of *Blaise Castle.* Continued from Catalogue, Vol. 1, p. 914.

*HARFORD, John Scandred, *continued*.

——Some Account of the LIFE, DEATH, and PRINCIPLES of THOMAS PAINE. BY JOHN S. HARFORD, Esq.
Bristol: Printed and published, &c.
8vo. 1820. 5½

——The Life of Thomas Burgess, D.D., F.R.S., F.A.S., &c., &c., &c., late Lord Bishop of Salisbury. By John S. Harford, Esq., D.C.L., F.R.S. (With a Portrait of Thomas Burgess.)
London: Printed for Longman, Orme, Brown, Green, & Longmans, Paternoster Row.
8vo. 1840. 36
Re-printed—The second edition.

——Memoir of the Rev. Richard Chapple Whalley, B.D., late Rector of Chelwood; illustrated by Select Letters and Sermons. By John S. Harford, Esq., D.C.L.
London: James Nisbet and Co., 21, Berners Street. (J. Chilcott, Printer, Clare Street, Bristol.)
8vo. 1846. 18¾

——Recollections of William Wilberforce, Esq., M.P. for the County of York during nearly thirty years. With brief notices of some of his personal friends and contemporaries. By John S. Harford, Esq., D.C.L., F.R.S.
London: Longman, Green, Longman, Roberts, & Green. 8vo. 1864. 21⅛

HARFORD, Mary, of

——The WINTER SCENE; to amuse and instruct the rising generation. By MARY HARFORD. With copper-plates.
LONDON: *William Darton, 58, Holborn Hill; sold also by Harvey and Darton, 55, Gracechurch Street; and John Harris, St. Paul's Church-yard.* . . . . 18mo. No date. 3

*HARLAN, Josiah, of *North America*.

——A Memoir of India and Afghanistan with observations on the present exciting and critical state and future prospects of those countries. Comprising remarks on the Massacre of the British Army in Cabul, British policy in India, a detailed, descriptive characters of Dost Mahomed and his court, &c. With an appendix on the fulfilment of a text of David, our reference

*HARLAN, Josiah, *continued.*
 to the present prophetic condition of Mahomedan nations throughout the world, and the speedy dissolution of the Ottoman empire. By J. Harlan, late Counsellor of State, Aid-de-camp and General of the Staff to Dost Mahomed.
 Philadelphia. . . . . 12mo. 1842. 208pp.
—— A Personal Narrative of General Harlan's eighteen years' residence in Asia. Comprising an account of the manners and customs of the Oriental nations with whom the Author has had official and familiar intercourse, by General Josiah Harlan.
 Philadelphia. . . . . . . 1843.

*HARLAN, Richard, M.D, *North America,* Naturalist.
—— Fauna Americana; being a description of the mammiferous animals inhabiting North America. By Richard Harlan, M.D.
 Philadelphia. . . . 8vo. 1825. 318pp.
—— Refutation of certain misrepresentations against the Author of Fauna Americana, by R. Harlan, M.D.
 Philadelphia. . . . . 8vo. 1826. 42pp.

HARRIS, Isabella, of *Leighton-Buzzard.*
— - Family Memorials. (Edited by M. A. H.) Privately printed.
 London : Printed by Richard Barrett. . 8vo.

HARRIS, John Tindall, of *New Egham, near Staines,* continued from Catalogue, Vol. I, p. 916.
—— THOUGHTS on SPIRITUAL ETHNOLOGY. By Ignotus.
 London : Saml. Harris & Co., 5, Bishopsgate Without. 8vo. 1874. 1½
—— THE WRITINGS of the APOSTLE JOHN : with Notes, critical and expository. By the late John Tindall Harris.
 Vol. 1. THE GOSPEL AND EPISTLES.
 Vol. 2. THE REVELATION.
 Edited by W. R. Brown, of Cambridge (with Portrait of J. T. Harris).
 London : Hodder & Stoughton, 27, Paternoster Row. S. Harris & Co., 5, Bishopsgate Street, without 8vo. 1889. 47
 (Cambridge : Printed by C. J. Clay, M.A., & Sons, at the University Press.
 He died the 13th of 5th Month, 1887, aged 69 years.

HARRIS, Theodore, of *Leighton-Buzzard, Beds.,* Banker.

—— Reasons for supporting the 𝕭𝖆𝖓𝖐 𝕹𝖔𝖙𝖊𝖘 𝕴𝖘𝖘𝖚𝖊 𝕭𝖎𝖑𝖑, etc.

  Richard Barrett, Printer, 13, Mark Lane.
          Folio. [1865.] 1

HARRISON, George, *continued* from Catalogue, vol. 1, p. 917.

—— A Plain STATEMENT OF FACTS relative to 𝕿𝖍𝖊 𝖂𝖎𝖑𝖑 of THE LATE SAMUEL SOUTHALL, of Pennsbury, near Wandsworth, in the County of Surrey. BY GEORGE HARRISON.

  𝕷𝖔𝖓𝖉𝖔𝖓 : *Printed by T. Bensley, 4, Crane Court, Fleet Street.* 8vo. 1820. 1⅝

—— A Declaration against the above, [Signed] John Wilkinson, Wm. Dillworth Crewdson, Isaac Stephenson, William Backhouse, Robert Eaton, William Pryor, William Phillips, Thomas Edmonds, Joseph Coventry, Henry Bath, Caleb Lucas, Samuel H. Lucas, John Coleby.

  Printed by W. Phillips, George Yard, Lombard Street, London.

  Gracechurch Street, 1st of 6th mo., 1820. 8vo. ⅛

—— Report to the Monthly Meeting of Kingston, in the case of a complaint of Sarah Southall and Samuel Fossick, against George Harrison, from the Joint Committee appointed thereon ; namely, the Committee of the Monthly Meeting united, by authority of the said Meeting, with a Committee appointed on the 25th of 9th month, 1821, by the Quarterly Meeting of London and Middlesex. (Signed by) Thomas Sturge, Peter Bedford, Thos. Brewster, Thomas Christy, Joseph Foster, Samuel Gurney, John Eliot, Luke Howard, Wm. Foster Reynolds, Richard Brewster.

  William Phillips, Printer, George Yard, Lombard Street, London. . . . 4to. [1822.] ½

HARTSHORNE, Henry, M.D., of *North America,* Professor.

—— Water versus Hydropathy, or an essay on water and its true relations to medicine. By Henry Hartshorne, M.D.

  Philadelphia . . . 12mo. 1847. 132 pp.

HARTSHORNE, Henry, M.D., *continued*.

——Memoranda Medica, a note-book of medical principles, being a concise syllabus of Etiology, Semiology, general Pathology, and general Therapeutics, with a glossary for the use of students. By Henry Hartshorne, M.D., &c.
Philadelphia . . . . 12mo. 1860. 190 pp.

——A Monograph on Glycerin and its uses. By Henry Hartshorne, A.M., M.D.
Philadelphia . . . . . . 1865. 68 pp.

——Essentials of the Principles and Practice of Medicine, a handy book for students and practitioners. By Henry Hartshorne, M.D.
Philadelphia . . . . 12mo. 1867. 418 pp.

——Summer Songs, by H. H., M.D.
"And the Raven, too, shall sing, will he, will he? but we will not listen? We'll then pass on."
Philadelphia 1865

HARVEY, Sarah Grace, Wife of Thomas Harvey, of *Leeds*.
——A Plea for the Oppressed: An Address to the Christian Women of England. [Anon.]
Leeds: Printed by Edward Baines and Sons.
12mo. 1870

HARVEY, Thomas, of *Leeds, continued* from Catalogue, Vol. 1, p. 923.
——The POLYNESIAN SLAVE TRADE: Its Character and Tendencies; with Reasons adduced for its total and immediate prohibition. By T. Harvey. Fifth Thousand.
Leeds: Printed by McCorquodale & Co., Bank Street. 8vo. 1872. 1½

——Postscript to a Pamphlet entitled, the POLYNESIAN SLAVE TRADE, &c. By T. Harvey.
8vo. [Same imprint.] 1872. ¾

——and ISAAC ROBSON.—The MENNONITES OF SOUTH RUSSIA: their present situation in reference to their Christian Testimony against all War. By ISAAC ROBSON, and THOMAS HARVEY.
"*Bear ye one another's burdens, and so fulfil the law of Christ.*"
NOT PUBLISHED.
Birmingham: Printed by White & Pike, Moor Street Printing Works . . 8vo. [1872.] 1

HARVEY, Thomas, *continued.*

> NOTE.—On the back of the title page is printed, "*It is requested that no part of this pamphlet may be copied or re-printed without the sanction of the writers.*"

——and ISAAC ROBSON.—Narrative of the Visit of ISAAC ROBSON and THOMAS HARVEY to the South of Russia, &c. (Confidential.)
R. Barrett and Sons, Printers, Mark Lane.
          8vo. [1868.] 2½
See ISAAC ROBSON.

> He died the 25th of 12th month, and was interred in Friends' burial ground, Adel, near Leeds, on the 29th of the same month, 1884, aged 72 years.

*HARVEY, W. H., Professor.

——Charles and Josiah ; or Friendly Conversations between a churchman (W. H. H.), and a Quaker (Jonathan Pim ?)
Dublin 8vo. 1862

——Memoir of W. H. Harvey, M.D., F.R.S., &c., &c.
London : Bell and Daldy.
See "The Friend" for 10th Mo., 1870, page 244.

*HARVEY, William Henry, M.D., of *North America.*

——Nereis Borealis Americana, or contributions to a history of the Marine Algæ of North America, by William Henry Harvey, M.D., U.R.G.A., in three parts, published in the Smithsonian Contributions.
Washington City. . . . . 1857.

*HARWOOD, John, *continued* from Catalogue, vol. 1, p. 923.

——To all People That profess the Eternal TRUTH of the Living GOD. This is A true and real demonstration of the cause why I have denied, and do deny the Authority of *George Fox;* which is the original ground of the difference betwixt us, whatsoever may be pretended or deceitfully alledged against me, which I do in simplicity desire Friends to peruse impartially, and weigh in the ballance of Equity, that they may clearly discern and sensibly feel the depth of the ground of the matter in difference betwixt us, that so none may be blinded through false pretences or vain reports, but that every particular in *Israel* may see and perfectly know the Truth, before they judge of this matter.

This is only to go amongst Friends in all Countreys,

*HARWOOD, John, *continued.*
   Nations, and Islands where George Fox's *Papers of Enmity against the innocent hath passed.*
                         4to. Printed in the year 1663.   1
—— The life of innocency vindicated that was manifested in two famous ministers in their day, viz., J. N. & J. P., who are both deceased. And the liberty of God's people maintained in the order of their practices in yᵉ Church of God.

   Impositions reproved, and the immediate motion & order of God's Spirit in al justifyed concerning the holy order of yᵉ Spiritual Worship of God.

   In an answer to several particulers published in a Postscript signed by G. F., and in another paper signed by J. B., Intitled, A Testimony in yt wᶜʰ seperates between the precious and the vile.

> By a servant of the Lord Jesus and a lover of the life of righteousness in al, though never so much dejected, and at present a sufferer for the truth in Oxford Castle.—J. H.
>
> Blessed are they that are revyled and persecuted for truth & righteousness' sake, for theirs is yᵉ Kingdom of God, &c. The 12th month, 166⅔.

   Query; whether printed ?—In *Manuscript.* In the British Museum.

HAUGHTON, James, of 34, *Eccles St., Dublin.*
—— A Voice from Erin. In "The Liberty Bell." By Friends of Freedom (p. 59).
   Boston, Massachusetts   .   8vo. 1842

HAWEIS, T. Rev.
—— A Short ACCOUNT of the LAST DAYS of the RIGHT HONOURABLE and MOST RESPECTED LADY, Selina, Countess Dowager of Huntingdon. FROM AUTHENTIC TESTIMONIALS. By the Rev. T. HAWEIS, LL.B. HER CHAPLAIN.
      "The Memory of the Just is blessed."—PROVERBS x. 7.

   LONDON : *Printed and Sold by J. Chalmers, No. 81, Old Street. Sold also by C. Dilly, in the Poultry; of J. Matthews, in the Strand; Mrs. Trapp, Paternoster Row; and at the Vestries of her Ladyship's Chapels.*
   [PRICE SIXPENCE.] . . . 8vo. [1791.] 1

> NOTE.—Shortly before the decease of LADY HUNTINGDON, DR. LETTSOM visited her. In the pamphlet as above is inserted a Letter of his addressed to Lady ANN ERSKINE, and dated, "Basinghall Street, June 18, 1791."

HAWXHURST, Thomas, was born in the township of Oyster Bay, Queen's County, New York, in the year 1752.

——Testimony of New York Monthly Meetin, concerning Thomas Hawxhurst.
 New York: James Egbert, Printer, 374, Pearl Street (successor to M. Day's Press).
         8vo. 1852.
 He died 6th of 10th, 1843, in the 92nd year of his age, and 57th of his ministry.

HAZARD, Rowland G., of *North America*.
——Language—its connection with the present condition and future prospects of man. By a Heteroscian.
 Providence, Rhode Island. . 12mo. 1836. 153 pp.

——Essay on the characters of William Ellery Channing. By Rowland G. Hazard.

HEATH, Noble (the son of George Heath, the son of Topp Heath, owner of Landed Estates near Hexham) was born May 16th, 1796, in the village of Stella, (So. bank of R. Tyne) County of Durham, England, was educated principally in Newcastle-on-Tyne. When nearly 14 years old, being in delicate health, was sent to sea, made several voyages in the West Indies and gained a robust constitution, since which has been a remarkably healthy man.

 The war of 1812 prevented his returning to England—he being then in the State of Maine, U.S.—and he was variously employed in that State for several years. Here he became a Member of Friends' Society, and warmly attached to many worthy Friends, who were very kind to him. He has ever since remained a devoted Friend. It was in Maine that he first became a Teacher, and he afterwards taught in New York City (in the Senior department of the New York High School; in the School of the Brothers Peugnet, friends of Lafayette; in that of R. T. Huddart, &c.), where he assisted in the education of many who are now Merchant Princes of New York, Bank Presidents, Cashiers, &c., &c. After this he taught in the School of A. Bolmar, at West Chester, in Pennsylvania, and was a Professor in Girard College, Philadelphia.

 Returning to New York in 1858, he had a Private School at Hastings-upon-Hudson, where one of his pupils was the son of Capt. now Admiral Farragut.

HEATH, Noble, *continued*.

His services as a Teacher extend (at times and in various places) over an interval of half a century, and he is now affectionately remembered by many an eminent man.

As an Author, he first translated (from the French) the Arithmetic of Bezout, which he published by the Harper's in 1825.

At the request of Mr. Griscom, and his associate, Mr. Barnes, he prepared in 1827 "a treatise on Arithmetic," for the use of the High School. But his principal work was a much larger and more complete Arithmetic, which was published in 1856 in Philadelphia, Pennsylvania. This work received the highest encomiums of the Provost and Professors of the University of Pennsylvania. About a year later he published "The People's Spelling Book," containing important strictures and rules on Pronunciation, together with a universal system of English Syllabication."

But although these works were admired by all who read them, they have never become popular School books.

In the intervals of time between his engagements as Teacher, he followed a variety of occupations. Was at one time Assistant Engineer on the Erie Canal, at another time he was in the Tanning Business. At another was a Manufacturer. He is now a Farmer, living on a little place on Long Island, near New York, healthy and vigorous at 74.

He was married 30th June, 1826, to Hannah Hardy, and has now living three children (and fourteen grand-children, of whom he is very fond). He has always been known as a hard student, and independent and affectionate man.

He speaks seven languages and is certainly one of the greatest Mathematicians living, as well as a man of excellent literary taste.

Yours very Cordially,
NOBLE HEATH, Jr.

W. H. HENDERSON, Esq.
London.

Communicated in a letter to W. H. Henderson (by the Author's Son, Noble Heath, Jr.), and by him kindly lent to me to copy.

HEATON, William, of *Birkenhead*.
—— A Lecture on the Nature, Object, and Limit of Human Knowledge. By Wm. Heaton.
Birkenhead: Printed by Charles Willmer. 1869.

HENSHAW, Frances, *continued* from Catalogue, Vol. 1, p. 936.
—— A Serious Call, In tender Compassion, &c.
Dublin: Printed by I. Jackson. . 12mo. 1745.

*HEWES, Joseph, one of the Signers of the American Declaration of Independence, 1776, was a native of *New Jersey*, and graduated at Princeton College. He became a Merchant, and when about thirty years of age removed to North Carolina. In 1774 he was sent as a delegate to Congress, and continued to be a Member till his death, 1779, aged 50. His parents were Quakers, and he had always been considered as belonging to the Sect, but when the Quakers held a general convention in 1778 of the Members of their sect residing in Pennsylvania and New Jersey, and put forth a "Testimony," denouncing the Congress, and all its proceedings, he broke off all communion with them.
Rev. J. L. Blake's "General Biographical Dictionary, 8th edition revised, Boston, published 1853.

HILDEBURN, Charles R., of *Philadelphia*.
—— A Century of Printing. The ISSUES OF THE PRESS in Pennsylvania, 1685-1784. By Charles R. Hildeburn.
Vol. I. 1685–1763. Royal 8vo. 1885.
Vol. II. 1764–1784.
Philadelphia. . . . Royal 8vo. 1886.

HEYRICK, Elizabeth, was born at *Leicester* on the 4th of 12th month, 1769, and was the eldest daughter of John Coltman and Elizabeth Cartwright. She was married to John Heyrick, of Leicester, a Solicitor, but the practice of the law becoming distasteful to him, he entered the Army as Cornet in the Dragoons. After a union of eight years, Captain Heyrick expired suddenly. Shortly after which she became acquainted with some members of the Society of Friends, and adopting their principles was ultimately united with them.
—— A Village Dialogue.

HEYRICK, Elizabeth, *continued*.

——A Christmas-Box, for the advocates of BULL-BAITING, particularly addressed to the Inhabitants of Uppingham. [Anonymous.]
    London : *Printed by Darton and Harvey, No. 55, Gracechurch Street.* . . 16mo. 1809. ¾

——Cursory remarks on the evil of unrestrained Cruelty ; particularly on that practised in SMITHFIELD MARKET. [Anon.]
    London : *Printed for Harvey and Darton, Gracechurch Street.* 8vo. 1823. 1½

——An Appeal, not to the Government, but to the People of England, on the subject of West Indian Slavery.

——No British Slavery, or an Invitation to the People to put a speedy end to it.

——An Enquiry, which of the two parties is best entitled to freedom, the Slave or the Slave-holder ?

——Appeal to the Electors of Great Britain on the Choice of a New Parliament. . . . . . 1826.

——A Brief Sketch of the Life and Labours of Mrs. Elizabeth Heyrick. [Edited by   Ellis ?]
    Leicester : *Printed by Crossley and Clarke.*
                                        12mo. 1862. 1

    NOTE.—Besides the foregoing, she was the Author also of about 9 or 10 more tracts, being in number *18* altogether.

HICKS, Edward, Jun., of *Bishopsgate, London*.

——List of Books, Prints, &c.
    The Friends' Book and Tract Depôt, 14, Bishopsgate Without. . . 48mo. 1st mo., 1892. ¼

HICKS, Edward, of *New York, North America*.

——MEMOIRS of the LIFE AND RELIGIOUS LABORS of EDWARD HICKS, late of Newtown, Bucks County, Pennsylvania. Written by Himself.
    Philadelphia : Merrihew and Thompson, Printers, No. 7, Carter's Alley. . . 12mo. 1851. 15¼

——Sermon Delivered. . . . . . 1830.

HICKS, Elias, *continued* from Catalogue, Vol. 1, p. 938.

——Letters of ELIAS HICKS, including also observations on the Slavery of the Africans and their descendants, and on the use of the produce of their labor.
    Philadelphia : Published by T. Ellwood Chapman, No. 5, South Fifth Street. . 8vo. 1861. 15

HIGGINS.—The History of TIM Higgins. The Cottage Visitor. (*Wood-Cuts*). [By ABIGAIL ROBERTS, of *Mountrath, in Ireland.*]
Dublin : Printed by C. Bentham, Eustace Street.
18mo. 1823. 5

NOTE.—My copy of this little book has written inside on the cover, "The Rt. Honble. Lady Grenville."

HILL, Richard, was born at *South River*, in *Maryland, Sept. 8th, 1698*. He was the son of HENRY and MARY HILL, and the grand-son of RICHARD HILL, a Sea-Captain, who emigrated to *Maryland* in 1673. In 1721 Dr. Hill married DEBORAH, the daughter of DR. MORDECAI MOORE, of *Hill's Point*, near *Annapolis*. DR. MOORE'S wife was DEBORAH, the youngest daughter of THOMAS LLOYD, the confidential friend of WILLIAM PENN, and the first Governor of *Pennsylvania*.

——Letters of DOCTOR RICHARD HILL and his Children : or the History of a Family, as told by themselves. Collected and arranged by John Jay Smith.
Privately printed for the Descendants: Philadelphia, 1854. . . . Large 8vo. 466 pp.

This book, besides the letters, contains : " A Genealogy of the LLOYD FAMILY." [From Burke's History of the Landed Gentry of Great Britain.] Also " The Lloyds of America," and the following illustrations, viz. :—
Dr. Richard Hill's Villa, Madeira. (A coloured lithograph).
Portrait of Mary Lamar.
 „   Margaret Hill, Æt. 15.
 „   Harriet Scott and child.
The Achada, Dr. Richard Hill's Country House in Madeira. (Coloured).
Portrait of Rachel Hill Wells.
 „   Henry Hill.
 „   Margaret Morris. (Æt. 76).
 „   Margaret Morris Collins. Æt. 19.
This book also contains a reprint of the " Private Journal kept during a portion of the Revolutionary War, for the amusement of a Sister. By Margaret Morris, of Burlington, N.J." 50 copies only of which were originally printed for private circulation in 1836.

HILTON, John, *now of 76, Bow Road, London, E.*, continued from Catalogue, Vol. 1, p. 951.

——THE CRY OF THE POOR.—From the Tower Hamlets. Independent, December 7th, 1867.
A strip Folio. 1867. ½

HILTON, John, *continued.*

——Never too late to try. By John Hilton.
> *Eightpence per 100, 250 copies for 24 stamps, sent post paid by Samuel Jarrold, Norwich.*
> 8vo. No date. ¼
>> NOTE.—*No. 198 of " Norwich Tracts."*

——Sketches and Anecdotes. By JOHN HILTON. [Conveying wholesome Truths for Life's Guidance.]
> *London : John Kempster & Co., 9 & 10, St. Bride's Avenue, Fleet Street, E.C.* . 8vo. [1876] 4

——A DEFENCE OF LEGISLATION on THE LINES OF LOCAL OPTION. A LECTURE by JOHN HILTON, *delivered before the Members and Friends of the* BALLOON SOCIETY OF GREAT BRITAIN, in the ROYAL AQUARIUM, Westminster, February 20th, 1885.
> *Manchester : United Kingdom Alliance, 44, John Dalton Street. London : National Temperance Publication Depot, 337, Strand, W.C.*
> 8vo. [1885.] 1¾

——The Balloon Society of Great Britain and Prohibition. (A Lecture by John Hilton).
> *Reprinted from the " Alliance News" of February 25th, 1888.* . . . . 4to. [1888.] ¼

——ADDRESS delivered by JOHN HILTON at the ANNUAL MEETING of the BEDFORD INSTITUTE, held at Devonshire House, on 3rd day, 3rd of 12th month, 1889. . . . . 12mo. [1889.] ⅙

——Presentation of a Four Hundred Guineas' Testimonial to Mr. John Hilton. Brief Report of the Meeting.
> 8vo. [Dec. 1890.] ¼

——The Temperance Worker, Sept. 1890. Containing "Biographical Sketch of Mr. John Hilton." (With Portrait).
> 12mo. [1890.]

——The Christian, April 24th, 1891, containing Portrait and Sketch of Mr. and Mrs. John Hilton.

——Occasional Papers by Teachers in the Ratcliff Friends' First Day Schools. [With an Introduction by John Hilton.]
> *London : John Reeves, Friends' Mission Institute, Commercial Road, E. T. Humphrey's & Co., Printers, High Street, Stepney, E.* 8vo. [1892?] 2

HILTON, John, *continued*.

——TO THE GLORY OF GOD. 𝔄𝔫 𝔄𝔡𝔡𝔯𝔢𝔰𝔰 to Members of the Society of Friends. 𝔍𝔰𝔰𝔲𝔢𝔡 𝔟𝔶 𝔱𝔥𝔢 𝔉𝔯𝔦𝔢𝔫𝔡𝔰' 𝔗𝔢𝔪𝔭𝔢𝔯𝔞𝔫𝔠𝔢 𝔘𝔫𝔦𝔬𝔫.
> London : *Edward Hicks, Jun., 14, Bishopsgate Street, Without.* . . Square 16mo. 1891. ½

HILTON, Marié, Wife of JOHN HILTON.

——The SECOND YEAR of THE CRECHE : being Facts, Anecdotes, and Report. By MARIE HILTON.
> London : *Morgan & Chase, Paternoster Buildings.*
> 16mo. 1872-73. 58pp.

——The THIRD YEAR of THE CRECHE : with particulars of the Infant Infirmary, Children's Home, Servants' Home, &c. *From February, 1873, to February, 1874.* By MARIE HILTON.
> London : *Morgan and Scott (Office of "* 𝔗𝔥𝔢 𝔒𝔥𝔯𝔦𝔰𝔱𝔦𝔞𝔫*,") 12, Paternoster Buildings. And may be ordered of any Bookseller.*
> 16mo. [1874.] 102pp.

——The CRECHE ANNUAL. (Twentieth Year.) Being Facts, Anecdotes, and Report. By MARIE HILTON.
> London : *Morgan and Scott (Office of " The Christian,") 12, Paternoster Buildings.*
> 16mo. 1890-91. 8½

——EXTRACT *from the* "HOSPITAL," *March 12th*, 1887. A WORLD OF BABIES. By one of the Crowd. (Relates to the " Crèch.") . . . 16mo. ¼

——Faith's Record. No. 11., Vol. xxi.
> Imperial 8vo. Chicago, November, 1891.
> NOTE.—Contains an Article about Mrs. Hilton's Crèche, at page 166.

——OUR HOMES IN DANGER. By MARIE HILTON. A PAPER Read at a Conference convened by the BRITISH WOMEN'S TEMPERANCE ASSOCIATION, *In the Council Chamber, Oxford, Oct. 30th, 1879.*
> London : *National Temperance Publication Depôt, 337, Strand.* . . . 16mo. [1879.] ½
> Re-printed—
> „   —Third Edition . 8vo. [No date.]

——WOMAN'S RESPONSIBILITIES in relation to TEMPERANCE. By MARIE HILTON. With an introduction by the REV. CANON BASIL WILBERFORCE, M.A.

HILTON, Marié, continued.
London : National Temperance Publication Depôt,
33, Paternoster Row, E.C.
Twelfth Edition. . . . 8vo. [No date.] 1

HILTON, John Deane, Son of JOHN and MARIE HILTON.
—— A DASH OF BITTER. By DEANE HILTON. (A new Temperance Story.)
London : Swan Sonnenschein & Co., Paternoster Square. . . . . 8vo.
—— The Off Chance. By DEANE HILTON.
London : A. W. Hall, 2, Racquet Court, Fleet Street, E.C. . . . 8vo. [1892.] 180pp.
"A Story illustrating the Evils of Gambling."

HINDLE, Christopher.
—— Joy in Suffering and Heavenly Visions of Christopher Hindle, who died at the early age of 14½. (By Isaac Pickard, of Harrogate).
Leeds : Printed by Edward Baines and Sons.
18mo. 1869. ⅓

HINE, John Green, continued from Catalogue, Vol. 1, p. 952.
—— A New Year's Greeting. . . . . . 1861.
—— Strict Harmony between SCRIPTURE AND GEOLOGY. A LECTURE on the First Chapter of the Book of Genesis, to show the strict and entire Harmony that exists between the Mosaic Account of the Creation of the World, and the recent discoveries of Geology. By JOHN G. HINE, of Nottingham.
A. Goater, Nottingham. . Large 8vo. [1867.] 2¾
NOTE.—On the Cover, "Illustrated Syllabus to the Lecture on the First Chapter of the Book of Genesis. Designed by J. G. Hine. Price One Shilling.
Copyright reserved. Entered at Stationers' Hall.
He died at Tottenham the 22nd of 3rd mo., 1884, aged 66 years.

HOAG, Huldah, wife of Joseph Hoag, was the daughter of Nathan and Elizabeth Case, and was born the 5th of 8th mo. 1762, at Little Nine Partners, Dutchess County, State of New York.
—— TESTIMONY of FERRISBURG MONTHLY MEETING, concerning HULDAH HOAG.
New York : James Egbert, Printer, 374, Pearl Street, (successor to M. Day's Press.)
8vo. 1852. ⅝
She died the 8th of 4th mo., 1850, aged 87 years and 8 months.

*HOARE, Louisa, wife of SAMUEL HOARE, of *Hampstead*, *continued* from Catalogue, Vol. 1, p. 955.

——Friendly Advice to Parents, on the Management and Education of their Children. By the Author of "Hints for the improvement of early education and Nursery discipline."
>London : *Printed for the Religious Tract Society; and sold by J. Davis, 56, Paternoster Row; J. Nisbet, 21, Berners Street; and other Booksellers.* . . . 18mo. No date. 2⅓

——Hints for the Improvement of Early Education and 𝔑𝔲𝔯𝔰𝔢𝔯𝔶 𝔇𝔦𝔰𝔠𝔦𝔭𝔩𝔦𝔫𝔢.
>13th edition.
>London : *J. Hatchard & Son, Piccadilly.*
>12mo. 1836. 8½

——The WORKHOUSE BOY; containing his Letters, with a short account of him. By the Author of "Friendly Advice to Parents on the Management and Education of their Children." (With a Frontispiece).
>LONDON : *The Religious Tract Society, instituted 1799. Sold at the Depository, 56, Paternoster Row, and 65, St. Paul's Churchyard; and by the Booksellers.* . . 18mo. No date. 2

>>She died the 6th of 9th month, 1836, and was buried in *Hendon Churchyard*.

HODGKIN, John, *continued* from Catalogue, Vol 1, p. 958.

——Observations on the Proposed Establishment of a 𝔊𝔢𝔫𝔢𝔯𝔞𝔩 𝔑𝔢𝔤𝔦𝔰𝔱𝔢𝔯. By John Hodgkin, of Lincoln's Inn, Barrister at Law.
>London : *S. Sweet, Law Bookseller and Publisher, Chancery Lane* . . . 8vo. 1829. 3¾

——Case and Claims of the Emancipated Slaves.
>8vo. 1865.

>>He died at *Bournemouth*, the 3rd of 7th Month, 1875, aged 75 years. For further particulars concerning him, see *The Annual Monitor* for 1876, p. 185.

HODGKIN, Thomas, M.D., *continued* from Catalogue, Vol. 1, p. 959.

——On the INFLUENCE of PHYSICAL AGENTS ON LIFE. By W. F. Edwards, M.D., F.R.S. 𝔗𝔯𝔞𝔫𝔰𝔩𝔞𝔱𝔢𝔡 𝔣𝔯𝔬𝔪 𝔱𝔥𝔢 𝔉𝔯𝔢𝔫𝔠𝔥 by DR. HODGKIN AND DR. FISHER. To which are added in the APPENDIX, some observations on Electricity, by Dr. Edwards, M. Pouillet, and Luke Howard, F.R.S.; on Absorption, and the uses

HODGKIN, Thomas, M.D., *continued.*
  of the Spleen, by Dr. Hodgkin ; on the Microscopic Characters of the Animal Tissues and Fluids, by J. J. Lister, F.R.S., and Dr. Hodgkin ; and some Notes to the Work of Dr. Edwards.
  London : Printed for S. Highley, 32, Fleet Street, and Webb Street, Maze Pond, Borough.
  8vo. 1832. 31½
  NOTE.—This book is entered in the printed Catalogue, but not correctly.

——On Negro Emancipation and American Colonization. By Dr. Hodgkin.
  Printed by Richard Watts, Crown Court, Temple Bar . . . . . 8vo. [1832.] 1½

——On the British African Colonization Society. To which are added some particulars respecting the American Colonization Society ; and a Letter from Jeremiah Hubbard, addressed to a Friend in England, on the same subject.
  8vo. Printed for Dr. Hodgkin, 1834. 2
  (By R. Watts, Crown Court, Temple Bar.)

——On the Importance of studying and preserving the Languages spoken by uncivilized Nations, with the view of elucidating the Physical History of Man. By Dr. Hodgkin. [*From the London and Edinburgh Philosophical Magazine and Journal of Science* for July, 1835.]
  London : Printed by Richard Taylor, Red Lion Court, Fleet Street . . . 8vo. 1835 1½

——Report on the effects of Acrid Poisons. By Thomas Hodgkin, M.D. [*From the* Report of the British Association for the Advancement of Science *for* 1835.]
  London : Printed by Richard Taylor, Red Lion Court, Fleet Street. . . . 8vo. 1836 1⅛

——The History of an unusually-formed Placenta, and imperfect Fœtus, and of similar examples of Monstrous Productions. By Dr. Hodgkin. With an Account of the Structure of the Placenta and Fœtus, by Sir Astley Cooper, Bart.
  8vo. 1½

——On some points connected with the Pathology of Bone. By T. Hodgkin, M.D., Lecturer on Morbid Anatomy at Guy's Hospital. Read before the Hunterian

HODGKIN, Thomas, M.D., *continued.*
Society, in the session of 1832-33. In the " British Annals of Medicine," No. 1, Friday, January 6th, 1837.
8vo. 1837.
——A Lecture introductory to the course on the Practice of Medicine. Delivered at St. Thomas's Hospital, at the commencement of the Session, 1842-3. By Dr. Hodgkin.
London : *Richard Watts, Crown Court, Temple Bar.* . . . . . 8vo. [1843?] 1½
——On the expediency of continuing the Medical Section of the British Association for the Advancement of Science. By Dr. Hodgkin. . . 8vo. 1845? ¼
——Cases illustrative of some consequences of Local Injury. By Thomas Hodgkin, M.D. Received June 2nd.— Read June 27th, 1848. [*From Transactions of the Medico-Chirurgical Society,* Vol. xxxi.]
Richard Kinder, Printer, Green Arbour Court, Old Bailey. . . . . 8vo. [1848.] 2
——Description of a Remarkable Specimen of Urinary Calculus : to which are added, some remarks on the structure and form of Urinary Calculi. By Dr. Hodgkin. Published in the Guy's Hospital Reports, No. IV. 8vo. 1
——Fifty-four Objections to Tobacco, [By Thomas Reynolds], with prefatory remarks by the late Thomas Hodgkin, Esq., M.D. Second Thousand.
S. W. Partridge, 9, Paternoster Row, E.C.
[One Half-Penny.] . . . . . 16mo. ¼
——On the Physical, Moral, and Social effects of Tobacco. By Dr. Hodgkin.
Read at Bradford, on the occasion of the Meeting of the National Association for the promotion of Social Science, 1859.
Printed by Wm. Byles, Observer Office, Bradford.
8vo. [1859.] 1

HODGKIN, Thomas, Banker, of Newcastle-upon-Tyne, son of John Hodgkin.
——On the Jewish Calendar, or the Feasts and Fasts of Israel. By Thomas Hodgkin.
(Lithograph). . . . Folio. No date. 44 pages

HODGKIN, Thomas, *continued.*

——The DUTIES OF NEUTRALITY : A Plea for the Prohibition of the Export of Arms to Belligerents. By THOMAS HODGKIN, B.A., Lond. *Reprinted from the "Friend."*
 London : *F. B. Kitto, Bishopsgate Without.*
          8vo. 1871. 2¾

——ITALY AND HER INVADERS, 376-476. By THOMAS HODGKIN, B.A., Fellow of University College, London.
 Vol. I.
  Book I. The Visigothic Invasion.
 Vol. II.
  Book II. The Hunnish Invasion.
  Book III. The Vandal Invasion and the Herulian Mutiny.
 Oxford : At the Clarendon Press.
 (Many plates and maps). [*All rights reserved*]
          8vo. 1880.
 Vol. I. Contents xix pp.   Vol. II. Contents xxii.
  Text 522 pp.   Text 680 pp.

HODGKIN, Jonathan Backhouse, son of John Hodgkin.

——THREE PHASES OF QUAKERISM. AN ADDRESS by J. B. Hodgkin. Issued by The Bedford Institute First-Day School and Home Mission Association.
 London : The Bedford Institute, Spitalfields, E.
          8vo. 1889. ¾

HODGSON, William, *continued* from Catalogue, Vol. I, p. 961.

——Select HISTORICAL MEMOIRS of the RELIGIOUS SOCIETY OF FRIENDS, commonly called QUAKERS ; being a succinct account of their character and course during the seventeenth and eighteenth centuries. By WILLIAM HODGSON.
  " We are nothing ; Christ is all."--GEO. FOX.
 Third Edition.
 Philadelphia : J. B. Lippincott & Co. 12mo. 1881. 17¼

——THE LINES, SENTIMENTS AND SUFFERINGS of some of the REFORMERS AND MARTYRS, before, since, and independent of THE LUTHERAN REFORMATION. By WILLIAM HODGSON.
 Philadelphia : J. B. Lippincott & Co.
        12mo. 1867. 465 pp.

HODGSON, William, *continued.*
— —The Society of Friends : and Secessions and Departures therefrom. Signed W. H.
(From *Zell's Encyclopedia*).
4to. (No Printer's name, place, or date). [1870?] ¼
— —The SOCIETY OF FRIENDS in the NINETEENTH CENTURY : A HISTORICAL VIEW of the successive convulsions and schisms therein during that period. BY WILLIAM HODGSON.

"I will weep for thee with the weeping of Jazer, O vine of Sibmah! The spoiler is fallen upon thy summer fruit, and upon thy vintage."—JEREM. xlviii, 32.
"Yet the blessed Truth shall outlive it all, and emerge out of the very ruins, if it must come to that."—
JOHN BARCLAY.

Vol. 1.
Philadelphia : For sale by Smith, English & Co., 710, Arch Street; and by the Author, 103, N. Tenth Street, or 1,411, N. Eleventh Street.
8vo. 1875. 22
— —The same, Vol. II. 8vo. 1876. 27¾

HOLME, Benjamin, *continued* from Catalogue, Vol. 1, p. 964.
— —Invitation Sérieuse, faite En L'Amour de Jésus-Christ, a Tous les Hommes; Les exhortant à se tourner vers l'Espirit de Christ au dedans d'eux-mêmes; afin de pouvoir bien comprendre les choses de Dieu, et lui rendre leur service agréable, Avec quelques Observations sur les sujets suivans; 1. L'Universalité de l'amour de Dieu en envoyant son Fils, afin qu'il mourut pour tous les hommes; 2. Les Ecritures Saintes. 3. Le Culte. 4. Le Baptême. 5. La Cène. 6. La Perfection. 7. La Résurrection. 8. Le Serment. Par BENJAMIN HOLME. Traduit de L'Anglois.
Londres: Imprimé Guillaume Phillips, George Yard, Lombard Street. . . 12mo. 1813. 3⅝

HOOPER, Joseph, *continued* from Catalogue, Vol. 1, p. 973.
— —A DISCOURSE on the best means of improving the SCIENCE of MEDICINE, delivered at the Anniversary of the MEDICAL SOCIETY OF LONDON, in 1787. BY JOSEPH HOOPER.

————Ergo fungar Vice cotis; Acutum Reddere Quae ferrum Valet, exors ipsa secandi.—Hor. de Arte Poetica.
Published by order of the Society, and Printed by J. Phillips, George Yard, Lombard Street.
8vo. 1788. 3

HOPKINS, Stephen, Governor of Rhode Island, was a native of Massachusetts, and bred a Farmer. In 1742, he removed to Providence and engaged in mercantile business. He was from 1751 to 1754, Chief Justice of the Superior Court. In 1755, he was elected Governor, and remained in office, excepting four years, till 1768. In 1774 he was a Member of Congress. His signature to the Declaration of Independence indicates a trembling hand, this was owing to a nervous affection. He retired from Congress in 1779, and died 1785, aged 78. He published, at the order of the Assembly, "Rights of the Colonies examined, 1765; and an " Account of Providence," in 2 Hist. Col. ix., 166-203.
Blake's Biogl. Dicy., 8th edition. Boston, 1853.

Hopkins' History of Providence first appeared in the *Providence Gazette*, in 1762. It has since been re-published in the Collections of the Massachusetts Historical Society. The Author was Stephen Hopkins, who for several years sustained the office of Governor of the Colony of Rhode Island. It contains the History of the Town of Providence, from its settlement down to 1645. It is entitled to confidence, for its general correctness.

*HOWARD, Luke, *continued* from Catalogue, Vol. 1, p. 980.
——Some Observations on Electricity. By Dr. Edwards, M. Pouillet, and Luke Howard, F.R.S. See the Appendix to a work, "On the Influence of Physical Agents on Life, by W. F. Edwards, M.D., F.R.S. Translated from the French by Dr. Hodgkin and Dr. Fisher. . . . . 8vo. London, 1832.
——The Doctrine of Universal Redemption by Christ, &c. —Signed, L. H. . 4to. Fifth Month, 22, 1835. ½
——Remarks on an Epistle of Counsel. . Fol. 1836.
——Barometrographia.
——Papers on Meteorology, relating especially to the Climate of Britain, and to the variations of the Barometer. By Luke Howard, Esq., F.R.S. Being Part 1 of the Appendix to Barometrographia.
London : *Taylor and Francis, Red Lion Court, Fleet Street.* . . . Large 4to. 1854. 10
——Papers on Meteorology, relating especially to the Climate of Britain, and to the variations of the Barometer ; communicated to the Royal Society at various periods from 1821 to 1845. By Luke Howard, Esq., F.R.S. Being Part 2 of the Appendix to Barometrographia.
London : *Richard and John E. Taylor, Red Lion Court, Fleet Street.* . . Large 4to. 1850. 10

*HOWARD, Luke, *continued*.
——Short Memoirs of Luke and Mariabella Howard. 1864.
——On the Modifications of Clouds, &c. (Plates). Third Edition. [With Preface by W. Dillworth Howard and Eliot Howard.]
London : John Churchill, New Burlington Street.
Large 4to. 1865.

*HOWARD, Robert, of *Tottenham*, was the Son of LUKE HOWARD.
——Letter to Friends. (Being, Reflections on a Paper, entitled, " A Testimony to the Authority of Christ in His Church, &c." . . . . 4to. [1841.] ½
——An Answer to the "Challenge to Dissenters," *lately circulated in this Village* (Tottenham), showing what is "The Church," and who dissents from it.—R. H., of *Bruce Grove*. . . . . 8vo. No date. ¼

*HOWARD, John Eliot, Son of LUKE HOWARD, *continued* from Catalogue, Vol. 1, p. 978.
——"The Island of Saints:" or, Ireland in 1855. By John Eliot Howard.
Seeley, Jackson and Halliday : Fleet Street. B. Seeley : Hanover Street, London, MDCCCLV.
Small 8vo. 1855. 19
NOTE.—Contains 11 Lithotint Illustrations and 3 Woodcut Engravings (including the Frontispiece of "Cattle driven to hear Mass.")
——Illustration of the Nueva Quinologia.
——Observations on the Present State of our Knowledge of the genus Civichona. . . . . . 6pp.
——Hymns for Christians. Arranged by J. E. Howard.
London : Groombridge and Sons, Paternoster Row.
18mo. No date.
——ΠΡΟΣ ΕΒΡΑΙΟΥΣ. The EPISTLE TO THE HEBREWS. A revised translation, with notes. By JOHN ELIOT HOWARD.
London : Yapp and Hawkins, 70, Welbeck Street. S. W. Partridge & Co., 9, Paternoster Row.
12mo. 1872. 4 1/2
——**Christ Crucified** : The One Meeting-Point between God and the Sinner. By J. E. HOWARD.
London : William Yapp, 4, Old Cavendish Street, Oxford Street. . . . Small 8vo. 1858. 3
——Lectures on Puseyism.
——The Shepherd the Stone of Israel.
——Christ the Provider.
——Bethany.
——Indwelling of the Holy Ghost.

*HOWITT, William, *continued* from Catalogue, Vol. 1, p, 999.

—— GERMAN EXPERIENCES : addressed to THE ENGLISH ; both stayers at Home and Goers abroad. By WILLIAM HOWITT, author of "The Rural and Social Life of Germany," etc.
 LONDON : *Longman, Brown, Green, and Longmans, Paternoster Row.* . . Small 8vo. 1844. 23

—— The Book of the Seasons ; or, The Calendar of Nature. By William Howitt. (Illustrated.)
 Sixth edition.
 London : William Tegg & Co., 85, Queen Street, Cheapside. 8vo. 1856. 23

—— Reminiscences of Ackworth School. . 1831.

—— Life in Germany.
 Routledge, ... 1849.

—— WOODBURN GRANGE. A Story of English Country Life. By William Howitt. In three volumes.
 London : Charles W. Wood, 13, Tavistock Street, Strand. 8vo. 1867. 60
  At Vol. 1. Chap. IX, p. 263, "The Friends' Party."
  Vol. 3. Chap. VII, p. 242, "A Quaker Wedding, and another wedding."

—— THE ENGLISH IN INDIA ; Reprinted from "Colonization and Christianity." A Popular History of the Treatment of the Natives by the Europeans in all their Colonies. By William Howitt.
  " Most of the countries in India have been filled with tyrants who prefer piracy to commerce ;—who acknowledge no right but that of power ; and think that whatever is practicable is just."—*The Abbe Raynal.*

 Second Edition. With an Appendix.
 London : Longman, Orme, Browne, Green, and Longmans. Printed by Manning and Mason, Ivy Lane. 16mo. 1839. 3½
 Price 8d., or £3 per 100.

·· —— Life in Dalecarlia : the Parsonage of Mora. By Fredrika Bremer. Translated by William Howitt.
 London : Chapman and Hall, 186, Strand.
        16mo. 1845. 11

—— The Northern Heights of London ; or Historical Associations of Hampstead, Highgate, Muswell Hill, Hornsey, and Islington. By William Howitt.
 London : Longmans, Green, and Co., Paternoster Row. . . . square crown 8vo. 1869.

*HOWITT, William, *continued.*

———The Mad War Planet, and other Poems, by William Howitt.
    London : Longmans, Green, and Co.
                                      12mo. 1871. 190pp.

———Some account of the "The Late William Howitt," in "The Freeman," March 14th, 1879.
    William Howitt died at Rome 3rd of 3rd mo., 1879, and his remains were interred on the 5th of the same month in the Protestant cemetery of that city. He had completed the 84th year of his age.

*HOWITT, Mary, *Continued* from Catalogue, Vol. 1, p. 1003.

———Hope on ! Hope ever ! or, The Boyhood of Felix Law. A Tale for Youth. By Mary Howitt, author of "Strive and Thrive," etc., etc. (Frontispiece.)
    The third edition.
    London : *Published by Thomas Tegg, 73, Cheapside.*
                                    18mo. 1844.   6

———An Easter Offering. By Fredrika Bremer. Translated from the unpublished Swedish manuscript, by Mary Howitt.
    London : *Henry Colburn, Publisher, Great Marlborough Street.*   small 8vo. 1850. 14½

———THE ANGEL UNAWARES. By Mary Howitt. And other stories. Containing The Angel unawares, by Mary Howitt. The Christmas Rose. By H. J. Wood. Margie's Remembrances. By F. M. Peard. Illustrated.
    London : *Groombridge and Sons, 5, Paternoster Row.*   12mo. [1860.]   6
    NOTE.—The Angel unawares forms No. 23 of "The Magnet Stories, for Summer days and Winter nights."
    One of the illustrations is a plate of "a Man Friend, Samuel Tregethin, sitting in the parlour of a gentleman, and laying his hand on a little girl's head."

———OUR COUSINS IN OHIO. By MARY HOWITT. With four illustrations on steel, from original designs by Anna Mary Howitt.
    London : *Darton & Co., Holborn Hill.* [*Printed by John Wertheimer & Co., Circus Place, Finsbury Circus.*]   Small 8vo. 1849. 19
    NOTE.—Contains an interesting account of Thomas Bales, "an old Quaker preacher," also of "a curious, antiquated and very primitive Quaker, of Pennsylvania," &c., &c.

*HOWITT, Mary, *continued.*
——No Sense like Common Sense; or, Some passages in the Life of Charles Middleton, Esq. By Mary Howitt; author of " Strive and Thrive," " Hope on, hope ever," " Sowing and Reaping," &c., &c.
London: *William Tegg* . . 18mo. 1862. 5
——" Memoir of Elihu Burritt." By Mary Howitt. With a portrait of E.B. In "The People's Journal," No. 44, Oct. 31, 1846, pages 239-246.
——Mary Howitt's Illustrated Library for the Young.
London: *W. Kent & Co., 51 & 52, Paternoster Row* - . . . . . 4to. 1856.
——Mary Howitt; an Autobiography. Edited by her daughter, Margaret Howitt. 2 vols.
London: *William Isbister, 15 & 16, Tavistock Street, Covent Garden* . . . 8vo. 1889
For a Review of this book, see "The Friend" for 12th Month 2nd, 1889.
In 1870, W. and M. Howitt left England for Italy, and settled in Rome.
Mary Howitt died in Rome, of bronchitis, on the 30th of 1st mo., 1888, aged nearly 89 years.

HOYLAND, John, *continued* from Catalogue, Vol. 1, p 1008.
——An Epitome of the History of the World, from the Creation to the Advent of the Messiah, exhibiting the 𝔉𝔲𝔩𝔣𝔦𝔩𝔪𝔢𝔫𝔱 𝔬𝔣 𝔖𝔠𝔯𝔦𝔭𝔱𝔲𝔯𝔢 𝔓𝔯𝔬𝔭𝔥𝔢𝔠𝔦𝔢𝔰, particularly in relation to the Jews; evincing the connexion of divine dispensations through a period of four thousand years. By John Hoyland.
I may assert Eternal Providence,
And justify the ways of God to men.
Milton.
In Two Volumes. Vol. I, Vol. II.
Third Edition, with additions.
𝔏𝔬𝔫𝔡𝔬𝔫: *J. Robins & Co., Albion Press, Ivy Lane, Paternoster Row.* . . . 8vo. 1821. 47¾

HOYLAND, Margaret, of *Waterford.* A Minister.
——*The following Account was related,* &c., to E. B. and other friends. (On Scriptural Examination at Ackworth School, &c.) . . . . 8vo. [1871] ⅛

HUBBERT, John, *continued* from Catalogue, Vol. 1, p. 1010.
——A Serious Check to the Y.M.'s Inquisitors. . 1817
——Apology for a Speech, &c. . . . . 1832. ¼

HUBBERTHORNE, Richard, *continued* from Catalogue, Vol. 1, p. 1010.

—— A Brief Memoir of RICHARD HUBBERTHORNE, one of the earliest Ministers in the Society of Friends; who died in Newgate, a prisoner for the Truth's sake, Anno MDCLXII.
Sunderland: Printed by Thomas James Backhouse, Fawcett Street. MDCCCXLII.
8vo. 1842. 3/4
NOTE.—The half title is, "A BRIEF MEMOIR of RICHARD HUBBERTHORNE, not Published," on the back of which is, "And my speech and my preaching were not with enticing words of man's wisdom, but in demonstration of the Spirit and of power : That your faith should not stand in the wisdom of men, but in the power of God." I Cor., ch. 2. v. 4, 5.

HUBBS, Rebecca, was the daughter of Paul and Rebecca Crispin, of *Moorestown*, *New Jersey*, and was born the 3rd of 12th mo., 1772.

—— A MEMOIR of REBECCA HUBBS, a Minister of the Gospel in the Society of Friends, late of Woodstown, N.J.
Philadelphia : To be had at Friends' Book Store, 304, Arch Street. . . . 16mo. [1884].
She died the 29th of 10th Mo., 1852, in the 80th year of her age.

HUNT, David, of *Iowa*, *North America*.

—— The Doctrine of the New Testament regarding Baptism, the Last Supper, War, Oaths, &c., being an address by David Hunt, of Iowa, North America.
Darlington : Harrison Penney.
London : F. B. Kitto, 5, Bishopsgate Street, Without. 8vo. 1867. 2

—— Essays on Religious Subjects, including the Ordinances, Deity of Our Lord and Saviour Jesus Christ, Resurrection of the Dead, &c. By David Hunt.
Published for the Author, New Vienna, Ohio. 1874.
NOTE.—The etc. is, " Musings or things that shall be."

HUNT, Hannah, of *Guildford*.
—— Songs of the Spirit. By H. H. . . . 1868.

HUNT, James, of *Kingsessing*, *Philadelphia County*.
—— Some account of James Hunt, written by his mother. in *Comly's Miscellany*, Vol. 4, p. 173.
He died of pulmonary consumption, the 28th of 5th Month, 1832, in the 53rd year of his age.

HUNT, John, *of New Jersey*.
——Notices of Benjamin Lay. By John Hunt. In *Comly's Miscellany*, Vol. 4, p. 274.
HURNARD, James, of *Colchester, Essex*, continued from Catalogue, Vol. 1, p. 1023.
——The Setting Sun : a Poem in Seven Books. [ANON.]
    London : *F. Bowyer Kitto, 5, Bishopsgate Street Without, E.C.* 8vo. 1870. 2 3
    Reprinted—2nd edition with his name.
HURNARD, Louisa Bowman (his Wife), Daughter of Chas. Smith, of *Coggeshall, Essex*.
——Ripe and Ready (in verse). L. B. H.
    London : *Morgan & Chase, 38, Ludgate Hill.*
                                        8vo. [1869 ?] ⅛
    She died the 20th of 4th Mo., 1884, aged 50 years.
HUSSEY, Asahel H., of *Mount Pleasant, Ohio*.
——Perfect in Christ. AN ADDRESS given by A. H. HUSSEY, *Mount Pleasant, Ohio*, at the International Conference, June, 1885.
    London : *J. Snow & Co., 2, Ivy Lane, E.C. Price 4d. per dozen.* . . . 12mo. [1885.] ¼
    The Christian Herald for (with Portrait of him), 1885.
HUSSEY, Gertrude Colden, was the third Daughter of ROBERT L. and ELIZABETH COLDEN MURRAY, of *New York*. She was married to GEORGE F. HUSSEY, of *New Bedford*, in the 23rd year of her age ; and at the period of her death resided at *West Farms*, in the *Westchester County, State of New York*. She died the 14th of 9th Mo., 1848 ?
——A Short Account of the Last Sickness and Death of Gertrude Colden Hussey. [Edited by MARY MURRAY ?]
    New York, Printed. . . . 12mo. 1853. ¾
    NOTE.—This account is published with Memoirs of Caroline Murray Ferris (her sister). See C. F. FERRIS.
HUTCHINSON, Anna, was born at *Richmond*, in *Yorkshire*, in the year 1787, trained up in the Church of England ; in 1817, united herself to the Wesleyan Methodists ; soon after joined Friends.
——A TESTIMONY of Darlington Monthly Meeting, concerning ANNA HUTCHINSON, of Bishop Auckland, who died the 23rd of 12th Mo., 1853, and was interred in Friends' Burial Ground, at Bishop Auckland, on the 26th of the same, aged nearly 67 ; a Minister 30 years.
    Darlington : *Printed by Harrison Penney, Prebend Row.* . . . . 24mo. 1854. ⅓

I.

IRWIN, William, *continued* from Catalogue, Vol. 1, p. 1026.

——The "TENDER MERCIES" of THE STATE CHURCH, as exhibited in A SEIZURE OF GOODS, Value upwards of Nine pounds, for a demand of One Shilling and Fourpence, for Tithe Rent-Charge, at the instance of THE RECTOR OF WILMSLOW.
Manchester: Printed and Published by W. Irwin, 53, Oldham Street. . . 8vo, [1851.] ½

——Brief Remarks on the past and present condition of the Society of Friends, with especial reference to its decadence, and the results of the Recent Changes in Discipline and Practice; with a Recommendation of its original terms of Church-Fellowship as the only Basis of Restoration. Not Published.
Manchester: Printed by William Irwin, 24, Deansgate, for private circulation among members of the Society of Friends. 8vo. [1867.] 1

———A Letter of Remonstrance to Robert Charleton, with reference to his "Thoughts on Barclay's Apology; addressed to the Society of Friends, and especially to the Members of the Meeting for Sufferings."
8vo. 1868. ¼

———A Refutation of William Tallack's Remarks on Barclay's Apology and 𝕮𝖍𝖊 𝕸𝖆𝖓𝖈𝖍𝖊𝖘𝖙𝖊𝖗 𝕾𝖈𝖍𝖎𝖘𝖒, as continued in his Book entitled "George Fox, the Friends, and the Early Baptists." By William Irwin.
Manchester: William Irwin, 24, Deansgate.
8vo. 1868. ⅝

——To William Ecroyd and William Thistlethwaite, [And for perusal by others whom it may concern.]
———William Irwin.
[PRIVATE.] 4to. Manchester, 7th Mo. 29th, 1869. ¼

——ROBERT ALSOP *versus* ROBERT BARCLAY, "THE APOLOGIST." A Letter to a Friend, on Robert Alsop's pamphlet, entitled, "What is the Gospel?" By WILLIAM IRWIN. *Reprinted from "The British Friend," of 4th Month 1st, 1873.* With an introduction by George Pitt.
Manchester: William Irwin, 24, Deansgate.
8vo. 1873 1¼

NOTE.—At the end of this pamphlet is a list of "Books. Pamphlets, &c., illustrating the Christian Principles,

IRWIN, William, *continued.*
> Practices, and Discipline of the Society of Friends; printed and sold by William Irwin, 24, Deansgate, Manchester."

—— BRIEF REMARKS on THE PAST AND PRESENT CONDITION of the Society of Friends, with some suppressed facts respecting the recent Conference on "Christian Work," and a Review of Robert Alsop's Beaconite pamphlet. *By* WILLIAM IRWIN.
> Stand fast, therefore, in the liberty wherewith Christ hath made us free, and be not entangled again with the yoke of bondage.—GAL. v. 1.
>
> *Manchester: William Irwin, 24, Deansgate.*
>
> 8vo. 1873. 3
>
> He died the 5th of 5th month, 1878, aged 63 years.

J.

JACKSON, John, a Mathematician, of *Warrington*, in *Lancashire*, died 27th of 9th Mo., 1875, aged 81 years. See "*The Annual Monitor,*" *1877, p. 69,* where may be found the following account of him.
> "John Jackson was known in the past generation as a mathematician, when Warrington had become famous for its Academy and a considerable succession of literati, commencing with Dr. Aikin and his family, especially his daughters, Lucy Aikin and Anna Letitia Barbauld. Dr. Kendrick of that town, in a small tractate, issued in 1853, accompanied with profiles of the 'Warrington Worthies,' has the following notice of our departed friend:—'John Jackson, born at *Crosedale Beck, Yorkshire,* December 4th, 1793; a much respected member of the Society of Friends: author of "Puzzles and Paradoxes relating to arithmetic, geometry, geography, &c., with their solutions," and a frequent contributor on these subjects to the "Gentlemen's and Ladies' Diary," where his solutions of many abstruse calculations have shewn him to be a clever mathematician.'
>
> "John Jackson opened a school at Warrington in 1821, which he conducted for about 30 years, when he retired to a life of quiet repose with the affectionate regard and esteem of his many pupils and friends. He used to say with an innocent pleasantry, speaking both figuratively and literally, that he had long 'sat under his own vine and his own fig tree,' specimens of both being cultivated in the garden attached to his house in Academy Place.
>
> "The *Warrington Advertiser,* in announcing the close of his long life, speaks of him as 'kindly hearted, simple minded, and guileless.' His remains were interred in the Friends' Burial Ground at Penketh."

JACKSON, John, of *Warrington, continued.*
——The JACKSON COLLECTION at the WARRINGTON LIBRARY. Reprinted from the "Warrington Examiner."
"*Examiner*" *Office, Cairo Street, Warrington.*
8vo. No date. ½

JACKSON, John,—*continued* from Catalogue, vol. 2, p. 3.
——Narrative of a Visit . . . . 1844.
——Sermon . . . . . . 1849.
——Sermons . . . . . . 1851.
——A Dissertation . . . . . . 1855.

JACOB, Anne (Isaac), of *Ireland,* afterwards ANN BLACK, of *Peckham, London.*
——To those calling themselves, &c., folio, 1841.

JACOB, Joshua, *continued* from Catalogue, Vol. 2 p. 5.
——Anyone who gives money to a lawyer denies the truth of God, and the faith of Jesus, etc.
[*Brit. Museum, 1890. b.*] Broadside folio. [1840?] 1
7

JACOB, Thomas Greer, of *Belfast,—continued* from Catalogue, Vol. 2, p. 5.
——American Colonization Society. (*From* "The Belfast Guardian" *of the 15th and 19th of April, 1833.*)
12mo. [1833.] ½

JAMES, Paul Moon,
——Poems. 2nd Edition, with additions.
Small 12mo. *Manchester.* 1853.

JANNEY, Samuel M.—*continued* from Catalogue, Vol. 2. p. 7.
——Essays on Practical Piety and Divine Grace. By S.M.J., *Philadelphia.*
——Life of William Penn, 3rd Edition. . . 1871.
Reprinted . . . . . . 1878.
——CONVERSATIONS on RELIGIOUS SUBJECTS, and FAMILIAR DIALOGUES. By S. M. JANNEY. Fourth Edition, much enlarged. Two volumes in one.
Philadelphia : *T. Ellwood Zell, 439, Market Street.*
16mo. 1860.
NOTE.—The above is a general title to the following, viz :
——CONVERSATIONS on RELIGIOUS SUBJECTS, between a Father and his two Sons. By S. M. Janney.
Philadelphia : *T. Ellwood Zell, 439, Market Street.*
16mo. 1860. 6¾

JANNEY, Samuel M., *continued.*
> CONTENTS.—On Repentance and Conversion.—On Divine Worship.—On the Original and Present State of Man.—On the Divine Being.—On Salvation by Christ.—On Baptism and the Lord's Supper.

——FAMILIAR DIALOGUES on THE CHRISTIAN MINISTRY and THE HOLY SCRIPTURES. By S. M. JANNEY.
> *Philadelphia* : *T. Ellwood Zell, 439, Market Street.*
> 16mo. 1860. 2½

——AN EXAMINATION of the causes which led to the separation of the Religious Society of FRIENDS in America, in 1827-28. By Samuel M. Janney, author of " Life of William Penn," " Life of George Fox," &c.
> *Philadelphia* : *T. Ellwood Zell, 17 & 19, South Sixth Street* . , - 12mo. 1868. 350 pp.

——PEACE PRINCIPLES exemplified in the EARLY HISTORY OF PENNSYLVANIA. By SAMUEL M. JANNEY. Author of the " Life of William Penn," " Life of George Fox," " History of Friends," &c., &c.
> Blessed are the peacemakers, for they shall be called the children of God.—MATT. v. 9.
> The work of righteousness shall be peace ; and the effect of righteousness, quietness and assurance for ever.—ISAIAH XXXII. 17.
> Portrait of Willm. Penn, with fac-simile autograph.
> *Philadelphia* : *Friends' Book Association, 706, Arch Street* . . . 12mo. 1876. 7¼, or 172 pp.

——Conversations on religious subjects.
4th Edition
> *Phila.* . . . . . . 12mo. 1860.

——The Last of the Lenape, and other poems.
> *Phila. [printed] Boston* . . . 12mo 1837.

——A Religious Discourse (delivered) at a Meeting for Worship in Richmond, Virginia.
> *Springdale* . . . . . . 8vo. [1845.]

——Memoirs of Saml. M. Janney.
2nd Edition 1881
> He died. See *Herald of Peace.*

JENNINGS, Richard, was a native of *Scarborough*, and was educated at *Ackworth School.* After leaving there he   and twice forfeited his membership in the Society of Friends.

JENNINGS, Richard, *continued.*

——A short notice of RICHARD JENNINGS, presented to the subscribers to the CAPE TOWN Friends' School.
Printed by John L. Linney, Low Ousegate, York.
8vo. [1848?] ½

He died 17th of 1st month, 1848, aged nearly 48 years, and was buried at *Cape Town, South Africa.*

JENNINGS, Samuel, *continued* from Catalogue, Vol. 2, p. 11.

——Truth Rescued from Forgery and Falsehood, being An Answer to a late Scurrilous piece, Entituled, The Case Put and Decided, &c., Which Stole into the World without any known Author's name affixed thereto, And renders it the more like its Father, Who was a Lyer and Murtherer from the Beginning. By Samuel Jenings.
Printed at Philadelphia by Reynier Jansen.
4to. 1699. 4
Reprinted in Philadelphia, (100 copies) . about 1882.

JEWELL, Joseph, *continued* from Catalogue, Vol. 2, p. 12.
——A SHORT SKETCH of a LONG LIFE, accompanied with a few useful hints, by JOSEPH JEWELL.

O Lord, I know that the way of man is not in himself: it is not in man that walketh to direct his steps.—Jeremiah x., 23.

And Moses said unto the children of Israel, See, the Lord hath called by name Bezaleel the son of Uri, the son of Hur, of the tribe of Judah : and he hath filled him with the spirit of God in wisdom, in understanding, and in knowledge, and in all manner of workmanship.—Exodus xxxv., 30, 31.

Newbury: Printed by M. W. Vardy, Northbrook Street, ... 18mo. 1840. 2¹/₁₈
NOTE.—Contains addresses "To Farmers."—"To Carters." —"To Herdsmen."

JOHNSON, Jane, of *Philadelphia.* Editor of "*Friends' Intelligencer*"?

——A Daily Scriptural Watchword and Gospel Promise.
Philadelphia.
Reprinted, 2nd edition.

——Thoughts for the Children, or Questions and Answers, designed to encourage serious and profitable Reflection in the Young Mind.
Philadelphia. . . . 32mo. 64pp.

JOHNSON, Jane, *continued.*

——" A Treasury of Facts "—a Book designed for Children, in Six Numbers, being a revision of " Early Impressions." Compiled by Jane Johnson. 6 Nos.
    Philadelphia. . . . . 32mo.

——Essays upon some of the Testimonies of Truth as held by the Society of Friends, by Jane Johnson.
    Philadelphia. . . . 18mo. 71pp.

——Talks with the Children ; or, Questions and Answers for Family Use or First-Day Schools. By Jane Johnson.
    Part First.
    Philadelphia : . . . 18mo. 71pp.

Ditto.   Part Second.
    Philadelphia : . 18mo. 108pp.

JOHNSON, Mary C., Daughter of ELIJAH COFFIN.

——The Life of Elijah Coffin, with a reminiscence by his Son, Charles F. Coffin ; edited by his daughter, Mary C. Johnson. Printed for the family only.
    E. Morgan & Sons (Cincinnati). 8vo. 1863. 307pp.

JOHNSON, Thomas, *continued* from Catalogue, Vol. 2, p. 13.

——Concerning the *Spectator*, with to James' Evening Post. . . . . . 48mo. 1716.

JONES, J., of *North America.*

——The Flower of Deception unveiled, . 1829.

JONES, Augustine, of *Lynn, Massachusetts.*

——Society of Friends. The PRINCIPLES, METHODS, AND HISTORY of the Society of Friends : an Essay by Augustine Jones, of Lynn, Mass. First delivered, as a Discourse, in the Church of the Disciples, in Boston, on First Day, 2nd Mo. 8, 1874. Being the eighth of the Series upon the " Universal Church."
    Lynn, Mass : Geo. C. Herbert, Publisher, No. 5, Central Avenue, Lynn, Mass.
    Price, 20 cents. . . . . . 8vo. 1874.
    See Thomas Kimber for a Review of the above ; and CHARLES E. PRATT, for an answer to Thomas Kimber.

*JOYCE, George, last of *Rotterdam*.
—— The Rotterdam Quaker's Excommunication, and damning of George Joyce, who was formerly known by the style of Cornet Joyce : notorious for his carrying away of King Charles the first from Holmby House to the Isle of Wight, faithfully translated out of Dutch into English. Licensed according to order by Roger Lestrange.
  London : *Joseph Moxon, Ludgate Hill.* 4to. 1691. 1

K.

K. (T., Jun.), of *Philadelphia*.
—— George Fox : an Apostle of Evangelical, Spiritual Christianity. By T. K., Jun.
 From Friends' Review."
  Philadelphia : . . . 12mo. 1874. 1½

KEESE, Catherine R., of *North America*
—— Memoir of. . . . . . . 1866.

*KEITH, George, *continued* from Catalogue, Vol. 2, p. 18.
—— A Refutation of Three Opposers of Truth, by plain Evidence of the Holy Scriptures, viz. : 1. Pardon Tillinghast, who pleadeth for Water-Baptism, its being a Gospel Precept, and opposeth Christ within, as a false Christ ; to which is added, something concerning the Supper, &c. II. Of B. Keach, in his Book called, A Tutor for Children, where he disputeth against the Sufficiency of the Light within, in order to Salvation, and called Christ in the heart, A false Christ in the secret Chamber. III. Of Cotton Mather, who in his Appendix to his Book, called Memorable Providences relating to Witchcrafts, &c., doth so weakly defend his Father, Increase Mather, from being justly chargeable with abusing the honest People called Quakers, that he doth the more lay open his Father's Nakedness ; and besides the Abuses and Injuries that his Father had cast upon that People, C. Mather, the Son, addeth New Abuses of his own. And a few words of a Letter to John Cotton, called a Minister, at Plymouth in New England. By George Keith.
  Philadelphia, Printed and sold by William Bradford, Anno 1690.
     sq. 8vo. Title, 1 leaf ; pp. 1-73

*KEITH, George, *continued.*

> This is entered in my Catalogue, but not having seen a copy I could not give the full title, which I now do from Hildeburn's "Issues of the Press of Pennsylvania."
> A Copy of the Book is in the *American Antiquarian Society, Worcester, Massachusetts.*

—— [and THOMAS BUDD.] False Judgments Reprehended: And a Just Reproof to Thos. Everndon and his Associates and Fellow-Travellers for the False and rash judgment T. E. gave against G. K. and his faithful Friends and Brethren, at the Publick Meeting at Philadelphia, the 27. of 10. Mon., 1692; and also for their bringing with them their Paquet of Letters (Saul-like to Damascus) containing the false judgment of a Faction of men, calling themselves the Yearly Meeting at Tredaven, in Maryland, the 4. of 8th Mon., '92 ; and another false judgment contained in another Letter from William Richardson, All which will return upon their own heads.

[*Philadelphia : William Bradford,* 1692].
Sq. 8vo. pp. 8.

—— An Appeal from the twenty-eight Judges to the Spirit of Truth and true Judgment in all faithful Friends, called Quakers, that meet at this Yearly Meeting at Burlington, 7th Mo., 1692.

Philadelphia : William Bradford.
Folio, 1 leaf. 1692.

Reprinted Philadelphia : William Bradford.
4to. 1692. 1
„ Same imprint. 4to. 1692. 1

—— A True Copy of George Keith's Paper, delivered to Mr. George Layfield, at POCAMOK in MARYLAND.

> NOTE.—This paper is printed and inserted in a Book, entitled : "An ANSWER to George Keith's LIBEL. Against a CATECHISM published by *Francis Makemie.*

Printed at Boston, 1694.   .   .   .   Small 8vo.

> See Joseph Smith's "Bibliotheca Anti-Quakeriana, &c,"
> p. 282.

—— The great Doctrine of **Christ Crucified**, Asserted in Three Declarations or Sermons, Preached by Mr. GEORGE KEITH. Exactly taken in **Shorthand** as they were lately delivered by him at the Meetings of the Christian People, called QUAKERS, in LONDON.

London : Printed for Nath. Crouch, at the Bell in the Poultry, near Cheapside.   .   8vo. 1694.   4

[In *Sion College Library.*]

*KEITH, George, *continued.*

——The MAGICK of QUAKERISM; or the Chief Mysteries of QUAKERISM Laid open. To which are added, a Preface and Postscript relating to the CAMISARS; in answer to *Mr. Lacy's* Preface to the *Cry from the Desart.* 𝕿𝖍𝖊 𝕾𝖊𝖈𝖔𝖓𝖉 𝕰𝖉𝖎𝖙𝖎𝖔𝖓, to which is now added Some Brief Remarks upon *Mr. Lacy's* Book of his Prophetical Warnings; showing the Invalidity of his Arguments for his pretended Inspirations. By *George Keith,* M.A., *Rector of* Edburton, *in* Sussex.

LONDON, *Printed for Brabazon Aylmer Senior and Junior, at the Three Pigeons, in Cornhill.*
          8vo. 1707. 6½

KEITHIAN CONTROVERSY,—*continued* from Catalogue, Vol. 2, p. 43.

BETHUN, D.

——The PRINCIPLES of CHRISTIANITY Illustrated and clear'd from several OBJECTIONS; as Also some OBSERVATIONS on the Papers call'd, *A Serious Call to Quakers,* Put out by *George Keith,* by *D. Bethun,* A Gentleman of the Church of ENGLAND.
       4to. Printed in the YEAR 1705. 3

KELTY, Mary Ann, (*continued* from Catalogue, Vol. 2, p. 51,) was the daughter of an Irish Surgeon resident in *Cambridge,* and born in that town in 1789. She left Cambridge in 1832, and spent the rest of her life at 5, Hanover Street, Peckham, London. She was much attracted by the lives of the early Quakers, though she never became a member of the Society.

——Peace in Poverty. A Memorial of ANN SAVAGE, with extracts from her diary. Compiled by Mary Ann Kelty.
London: Published by Harvey & Darton, Gracechurch Street. . . . 18mo. 1841. 3⅙

——Straightforwardness essential to the Christian. By Mary Ann Kelty.
𝕻𝖗𝖎𝖓𝖙𝖊𝖉 𝖋𝖔𝖗 𝕲𝖗𝖆𝖙𝖚𝖎𝖙𝖔𝖚𝖘 𝕮𝖎𝖗𝖈𝖚𝖑𝖆𝖙𝖎𝖔𝖓.
Ipswich: Rees and Gripper. . . 18mo. 1867. 1½

——Reminiscences of Thought and Feeling; by the Author of Visiting my Relations.
London: William Pickering. . . 8vo. 1852. 18½

——Alice Rivers, etc. [By M.A.K.] . 8vo. 1852.

——Life by the Fireside. [By M.A.K.] . 8vo. 1853.

KELTY, Mary Ann, *continued.*
——A Devotional Diary. . . 8vo. 1854.
——The Unity of Truth. . . . . 12mo. 1867.
——The Solace of a Solitaire ; a record of facts and feelings.
 London. Edinburgh, printed. . . 8vo. 1869.
  She died at *Peckham,* the 8th of the 1st month, 1873, aged
  about 83 years.

KENDALL, John, of *Colchester, continued* from Catalogue
 Vol. 2, p. 52.
——The Life of Thomas Story, carefully abridged, &c.
 Reprinted,—*Philadelphia : Printed by Joseph Cruk-
  shank.* 12mo. 1805. 14½
— —Abstract of Thomas à Kempis. . . 12mo. 1804.

KIMBER, Thomas, of *Philadelphia.*
——Review of an Essay by Augustine Jones, of *Lynn,
 Massa.,* upon the Principles, &c., of the Society of
 Friends, in "The Christian Worker," 1874.

KERSEY, Jesse, of *Pennsylvania, continued* from Cata-
 logue, Vol. 2, p. 56.
——A Treatise on Fundamental Doctrines of the Christian
 Religion, &c.
 Republished with additional matter, &c. by the Author.
  Printed by Joseph Painter, West Chester, Pa.
          16mo. 1842. 3¾

KEWELL, Ann, of *Southwark, London.*
——Essay on Christianity. [Anon.]
 Barnes, Printer, Stone's End, Borough.
        24mo. No date. ⅙
— —Another edition.
 *W. H. Barnes, Printer, 44, Bridge House Place,
 Newington Causeway.* 24mo. No date. ⅙
  She died at *Old Ford, London,* the 21st of 5th month,
  1869, aged 64 years, and was buried at *Barking.*

KILHAM, Hannah, *continued* from Catalogue, Vol. 2, p. 58.
——SCRIPTURE SELECTIONS on the PRINCIPLES of the
 CHRISTIAN RELIGION. 𝔄𝔡𝔞𝔭𝔱𝔢𝔡 𝔣𝔬𝔯 𝔖𝔠𝔥𝔬𝔬𝔩𝔰 and
 for private instruction. Questions correspondent with
 the selections in a separate tract. By Hannah Kilham.
 5th Edition.
  *Printed and sold by Christopher Bentham, Sheffield;
  sold also by Darton, Harvey and Darton,
  London ; Beilby and Knotts, Birmingham ;
  and by other Booksellers.* . . 18mo. 1817. 1⅓

KILHAM, Hannah, *continued*.

——AFRICAN LESSONS. WOLOF and ENGLISH. In Three Parts. Part First.—EASY LESSONS and NARRATIVES FOR SCHOOLS. Part Second.— EXAMPLES IN GRAMMAR, FAMILY ADVICES, SHORT VOCABULARY. Part Third.—SELECTIONS from the HOLY SCRIPTURES. [Anon.]
 London : *Printed for a Committee of Friends for promoting African Instruction, by William Phillips, George Yard, Lombard Street.*
         12mo. 1823. 8¼

——Specimens of African Languages, also AKU and BASSU.
 London : *P. White, New Street, Bishopsgate.* 1828.

——FAMILY MAXIMS. By Hannah Kilham.
 Birmingham : Printed by T. Groom, Islington Row ; by Richard Davies, Temple Road.
        24mo. [1841?]. ⅓

KING, Esther Richardson, Wife of HENRY KING, of *Birkenhead*.

——Brief Account of her last illness and death.
 Printed for Private Circulation, J. R. Williams & Co., Printers, Rainford Square, Liverpool.
     12mo. [1853]. ⅝ or 19 pp.
  She died the 13th of 11 Mo., 1853, aged 28 years.

KING, *Continued* from Catalogue, Vol. 2, p. 62.

——For the King and both Houses, &c., that they may see the moderation of other powers.
     Folio B. [About 1670 ?] 1

KIRKBRIDE, Thos. S., of *Philadelphia*.

——Report of the Pennsylvania Hospital for the Insane, for the year 1865. (*Frontispiece*.)
 Philadelphia. . . . 8vo. 1866. 3½

——Report for 1867.
 Philadelphia.   . 8vo. 1868. 3½

——Report for 1868.
 Philadelphia. . . 8vo. 1869.

——Report for 1869.
 Philadelphia. . . 8vo. 1870. 3¾

——Report for 1870.
 Philadelphia. . . 8vo. 1871. 3¾

KITE, Nathan, of *Philadelphia*.

———Thomas Scattergood and his times, and numerous papers relating to the History of Friends throughout the volumes of the Friend. (Philadelphia.)
Reprinted in "*The British Friend.*"

KNOTT, Thomas, *continued* from Catalogue, Vol. 2, p. 72.

———The SPEECH of THOMAS KNOTT, (*one of the Society of Friends, and not 19 years of age*), delivered at the Anniversary Meeting of the Bible Society at Newcastle, *December 5th, 1816*.

 Manchester: *Printed and sold by T. Rogerson, Market Place; sold also by Mrs. Richardson, and the other booksellers; by Wilcockson, Preston; Baily, Lancaster; Brown, Wigan; Wilcockson, Blackburn; Gardner, Bolton; Baines, Leeds; and Alexander, York.*

 Price Threepence.   8vo.   No date.   ¾

———SPEECH of Mr. Thomas Knott, (a young man belonging to the Society of Friends), *Delivered at the Annual Meeting of the Newcastle Bible Society held at the Circus, on Monday, September 27th, 1817.*— Copied from the "Tyne Mercury," of Nov. 4th, 1817.

 Printed by J. Mitchell, Newcastle.   12mo.   1817.   ⅓

KNOTT, Mary, *continued* from Catalogue, Vol. 2, p. 72.

 "MRS. MARY KNOTT.—This lady is the daughter of the late RICHARD ABELL, of Cork, and descended of an old and respectable mercantile family in that city. She was born about the year 1784, and married, several years since, MR. JOHN KNOTT, of Dublin, in which city she has continued to reside. In 1836 she published "Two Months at Kilkee," the result of a visit paid to that neighbourhood, in search of health, in the previous year. This work bears the impress of kindly feeling, and of a mind deeply devoted to the improvement and amelioration of the condition of the humbler classes. It displays careful observation, and is written in a style, clear, natural, and unaffected."

 See "*Historical and Descriptive Notices of the City of Cork and its vicinity, &c. By J. Windle. A new and enlarged edition. Cork, printed, p. 149.*

 ABRAHAM ABELL, Esq., a short notice of, in the same work.

L.

L. (J. E.) ———(Joseph E. Lyndall?) of *Dublin*.

——A TESTIMONY concerning THE SOCIETY OF FRIENDS, (so called) AT FRITCHLEY, in Derbyshire.
  5th month, 1881. . . . 16mo. [1881.]   ⅛
   NOTE.—This writer speaks thus of the above-named body of Friends, "They are an outward copy of the Early Friends, whose words they steal, and whose ways they imitate."

LAKE, George, of *Southport*.

——To the Ministers and Elders of the Lancashire and Cheshire Quarterly Meeting at Manchester.
  (A Circular). . . 10th of 4th mo., 1869.

——A Brief Statement of Facts.—Example is before Precept.
  London : Printed for the Author. 12mo. [1872.]   ½

*LAMBIER, James Henry, a Native of *Boston, Massachussets*, his Parents were *Quakers*.

——The AMERICAN J. H. Lambier, late a Captain in the French Imperial Horse Guards. One of the largest men in the World, from the United States of America.
  Ipswich : Printed by King and Garrod.
     12mo. [1833?]   ½ sht. or 12 pp.
   This extraordinary was in stature 6ft. 10¾in., in weight, nearly 21 stone.

LAMBOLL, William—*continued* from Catalogue, Vol. 2, p. 75.

——Letter, 1680. . . . . Folio. B.

LAMB, Eli M., of *187, McCulloh Street, Baltimore*.

——Questions on Books of Old Testament. . 1868.
——Questions on Books of New Testament. . 1872.
——Hints to Teachers. . . . . . 1873.

*LANCASTER, Joseph, *continued* from Catalogue, Vol. 2, p. 77.

——EDUCATION for THE POOR. Joseph Lancaster intends to deliver another Lecture, &c., At the Welsh Charity School Room, Liverpool.
  Printed by James Smith, for W. Robinson, Castle Street . . . . large B. N.D.   1

——AN ADDRESS to the Friends of the Education of the Poor, by the Society instituted for the Purpose of establishing Schools on the Lancastrian Plan of

*LANCASTER, Joseph, *continued.*

Education, for children of both sexes of the labouring class of Society, *Inhabitants of Spitalfields and the neighbouring Parishes.* Signed by William Allen, Joseph Allen, John Arch, David Barclay, Gurney Barclay, Peter Bedford, T. F. Buxton, and others.
William Phillips, Printer, George's Yard, Lombard-street . . . large 4to. [1811.]   ½

—— PUBLIC FREE SCHOOL, Borough Road, George's Fields (*Between* STONE'S END *and the* OBELISK), for the Instruction of Youth in Reading, Writing & Arithmetic (A Circular).
Ann Kemmish, Printer, 17, King Street, Borough.
Small B. N.D.   1

—— SPEAK THE TRUTH. [ANON.]
BE HONEST.
BE OBEDIENT.
BE DILIGENT, &c., &c.
Barnes and Rutter, Printers, Kent Street.
Oblong B. N.D.   1

—— (Circular) Publishing by Subscription. By J. LANCASTER. A SPELLING BOOK, &c.
G. Cooke, Printer, Dunstan's Hill, Tower Street.
8vo. N.D.   ⅛

—— Form of Recommendation to be given by a Subscriber to the Boy recommended to the Royal British Institution in Chichester.
Mason, Printer, East-street (Chichester). 8vo. 1811.   ⅛

—— Faults in Writing, Faults in Reading. [ANON.]
Kemmish, Printer, Borough. . 8vo. No date.   ⅛

—— Directions for writing with accuracy and freedom. [ANON.] . . . . . . 8vo. No date.   ⅛

—— A Collection of Cuttings, or Paragraphs, &c., by and respecting Joseph Lancaster and Lancasterian Schools, from the following newspapers, viz. :—

"The Tyne Mercury, or Northumberland, Durham and Cumberland Gazette," February 27th, 1810.
The same, March 6th, 1810.
"The Norwich Mercury and Yarmouth, Lynn and Ipswich Herald," March 24th, 1810.
"The Bury and Norwich Post," March 28th, 1810.
"The Bath Journal," 26th March, 1810.
"The Ipswich Journal," April 5th, 1810.

*LANCASTER, Joseph, *continued*.

"The Bath Chronicle," A Letter by Wm. Matthews, April 16th, 1808.
"The Bath Journal," March 7th, 1810.
"The Bath Chronicle," May 17th, 1810.
"The Coventry Herald," June 22nd, 1810.
"Felix Farley's Bristol Journal"
"Edinburg Star," October 9th, 1810.
"Hampshire Courier," September 17th, 1810.
"Clyde Commerciel Advertiser," Glasgow, October 10th, 1810.
"Glasgow Weekly Packet and Clydesdale Chronicle," October 10th, 1810.
"County Press for Northampton, Bedford, &c.," November 14th, 1810.
"National Register," January 21st, 1810.
"Boston Gazette," November 20th, 1810.
"The Leeds Mercury," December 1st, 1810, and December 8th, 1810.
"Wright's Leeds Intelligencer," December 3rd, 1810, and October 22nd, 1810, and December 11th, 1810.
"Nottingham Journal," December 1st, 1810.
"Nottingham Review," November 30th, 1810.
"The Tyne Mercury," December 4th, 1810, and December 11th, 1810.
"Plymouth and Dock Telegraph," September 1st, 1810.
"Tyne Mercury." October 9th, 1810.
"Northamptonshire County Press," November 21st, 1810, and December 12th, 1810.
"London Times," March 22nd, 1811.
"Carlisle Journal," April 27th, 1811.
"Surrey and Sussex Gazette," May 16th, 1811.
"The Morning Herald," May 18th, 1811.
"The Day," May 18th, 1811.
"The Morning Post," May 18th, 1811, and October 9th, 1811.
"The Bristol Mercury," May 20th, 1811.
"The Public Ledger," May 22nd, 1811.
"Exeter Flying Post," October 3rd, 1811.
"Times," August 10th, 1811.
"Shrewsbury Chronicle," November 1st, 1811.
&c., &c.

——Joseph Lancaster begs to represent to the respectable inhabitants of the Borough of Southwark, &c. . . soliciting Subscriptions from the Inhabitants of Southwark. . . Single-leaf Folio. No Date.

Joseph Lancaster.—His Portrait (an oil painting) is in the Bethnal Green Museum, London.

LANCASTER, Lydia, *continued* from Catalogue, Vol. 2, p. 82. She was the daughter of THOMAS and DOROTHY RAWLINSON, of *Graithwaite*, in *Lancashire*.

LAUNDY, Edwin, *continued* from Catalogue, Vol. 2, p. 85.
——A Chart of Bible History.
>He died at Edgbaston, Birmingham, the 16th of 10th Month, 1875, aged 64 years, and was interred in Friends' Burial Ground, Birmingham.

LAWSON, John, *continued* from Catalogue, Vol. 2, p. 88.
>John Lawson died the 18th day of September, 1689, in the 74th year of his age, and was buried in Friends' Ground, Moorside, Lancaster Moor.—See "*Friends' Examiner for 1879*, for inscription on his coffer-tomb.

LATCHMORE, Joseph, of
——True Story of the Settlement of New Jersey. By Joseph Latchmore.
>*In "British Friend," 2nd Mo., 1879.*
>An account of Elizabeth Estaugh, daughter of John Haddon, of *Bristol.*

LANGSTROTH, Huson, *continued* from Catalogue, Vol. 2, p. 83.
——Some Serious Reflections respecting our duty to God, our children, and ourselves. By Huson Langstroth.
>In *Comly's Miscellany, Vol. 4, p. 34.*

LAWTONITES, OR LAWTONIAN QUAKERS.

LAWTON, Abraham, of *Athens, Greene County, New York, United States of America.*
——An ANTIDOTE for THE SERPENT'S Meat, the Ground Work of the Critical Philosopher, JOHN JACKSON, late of Darby, Pennsylvania. Examined by the Light of Truth through ABRAHAM LAWTON, of Athens, Greene Co., New York. Seventh Month, 1859.
>12mo. No Printer's name or place. [1859.] ½

——A PLEA for LIBERTY OF CONSCIENCE, and against Libertinism of Conscience in the PROFESSING SOCIETY OF FRIENDS.
>*Philadelphia*: *Merrihew & Thompson, Printers, Lodge Street, north side of Penns., Bank.*
>12mo. 1861. 1

——MOSES, A FRIEND TO GOD, and THE SOCIETY OF FRIENDS: or Something held up, as on a pole, unto that professing people; particularly what is called the Select Body, and THE EXECUTIVES OF THAT SOCIETY.
>*Philadelphia*: *Merrihew & Thompson, Printers, Lodge Street, North side Pennsylvania Bank.*
>12mo. 1861. 1½

LAWTON, Abraham, *continued.*

—— A Just and Equitable Law, *To stop the mouths of gainsayers of the order of God in divine worship; and that the pure conscience may enjoy Christian liberty in the truth.*—Athens, Greene Co., N. Y., 4th mo. 26th, 1862. 12mo. No Printer's name or place. [1862.] ¼

—— An Epistle for the Encouragement of Friends, who stand by faith which justly belongs unto them, etc., etc,
Philadelphia: Merrihew & Thompson, Printers. Corner of Lodge Street and Kenton Place.
12mo. 1862. ½

—— A Testimony against perverse Friends, with their doctrines and practices, that corrupt a common hireling ministry, and, through subtlety, appeal to them for judgement to pass condemnation upon faith and doctrine. By Abraham Lawton, of Athens, Greene County, New York.
Philadelphia: Merrihew & Thompson, Printers. Corner of Lodge Street and Kenton Place.
12mo. 1862. 1

—— An Epistolary Call to Men; being An Invitation to come unto God, *The fountain of all good, by following the manifestation of His streams of Life that flow from that eternal source to make glad the inheritors of His substance, as witnesses that He is their fountain.* Given forth in Athens, Greene County, New York, in the 6th Month, 1863, by Abraham Lawton and his Friends.
12mo. No Printer's name or place. [1863.] ⅔

—— and Joseph Bancroft. Narrative. "At a meeting of some Friends, held in Philadelphia on the 11th of the 11th month, 1864."
12mo. No Printer's name or place. [1864?] ¾

> Note.—The title page to the pamphlet from which I took the above is wanting (if it had one). It begins, "By Way of Preface," by Joseph Bancroft, then follows, "Prefatory Essay," by Abraham Lawton, then "Narrative."

—— On the dignified name of Friends, in Truth's cause. Written by Abraham Lawton, of Athens, Green County, N.Y., 1st month, 1865.
12mo. No Printer's name or place. [1865.] ⅛

LAWTON, Abraham, *continued.*

——An Epistle for the encouragement of every mind sincerely seeking after God, and after his dominion only, by Truth overturning every other kingdom, power, and glory : that he may take his own power and reign ; and they be clothed with true zeal, and so be preserved from lukewarmness and indifference. Also the inexpressible value of acknowledging the great mystery of godliness, confirmed and vindicated. By Abraham Lawton, 6th month, 1865.
Philadelphia : Merrihew & Son, Printers, No. 243, Arch Street, below Third. . 12mo. 1865. ½

——*An explanation of the Saviour's scourge of small cords, which he uses for the salvation of the house of God, through prayer and fasting from the bond of iniquity made manifest in vain form, by temple merchants; who do not the truth, neither bring their deeds to the light, that they may be made manifest that they are wrought in God, the only one good, and the pure fountain of life that giveth light for the purpose of sight, that God is man's only Saviour, and gives light to fill his whole body; that there may be no cause of stumbling in God's true and faithful witnesses, by whom every word must be established out of their own mouths for a testimony, as a rod of iron against the evil doer, and against that nation that is laden heavily with iniquity ; and that must be smitten with the rod of the mouth of the just one, because the breath of his lips can only slay the wicked.* Written in Philadelphia, 9th month, 1864, by Abraham Lawton, of Athens, Greene County, New York, with

——The Use and Calling of the Generation of Light set forth, for the great gain of the children and generation of this world who are wiser in calculation than the children of light. Abraham Lawton, 2nd month, 1865.
12mo. No Printer's name or place. [1865?] 1

Note.—The pagination in the above two pieces runs on.

——Man's imperative duty to God in Divine Worship, set forth, *for the promotion of the cause of Truth, and for the encouragement and blessing of the meek learners of the true faith, which gives the victory over sin, and makes men free, by true and saving knowledge of the one good, that is God ; to whom all praise is due.*

LAWTON, Abraham, *continued.*
ABRAHAM LAWTON, *12th mo., 1865.*
with,

——The word Friend examined and put before men, that they may prove the ground of friendship, in truth that is God's mutual pillar of society, &c., &c. The words *deceiver,* and the *deceived* also brought to view, &c., &c. Written by ABRAHAM LAWTON, of Athens, Green County, New York, 8th month, 1865.

12mo. [1865]

NOTE.—The above two treatises appear to be the end of some pamphlet, the remainder of which is wanting in the vol. from which I took the titles, the pagination commencing at page 73, and ending at page 96.

——*The Confederacy of Esau's unjust nest examined, and the habitation of his rock on high uncovered: which they who are of him have set among the stars, by pretensions of duties that are in the woe of the hypocrite's hope that shall fail.* Written by ABRAHAM LAWTON, of Athens, Greene County, N.Y., *6th month, 1865.*

12mo. N.P. or place. [1865] $\frac{1}{2}$

——and JOSEPH BANCROFT. An ADDRESS TO FRIENDS; with an Answer to the Query, "CAN ALL PROFESSING TO BE FRIENDS BECOME UNITED?" (by ELI K. PRICE.)

Philadelphia: Merrihew & Son, Printers, No. 243 Arch Street, below Third . 12mo. 1865. $\frac{1}{3}$

NOTE.—There is an addition on the *last page* of the above, by EVAN T. FLINN, of *Stanton, 12th month, 1865.*

——A TESTIMONY TO THE AUTHORITY OF THE SIMPLE TRUTH. A GIVEN STANDARD OF TRUTH. AN EPISTLE to the CHURCH OF CHRIST'S FRIENDS. Written by ABRAHAM LAWTON, *Athens, New York.* Put forth by the Friends of Truth, to whom they have been committed.

Philadelphia: Thomas William Stuckey, Printer, 624, Weaver Street. . . 12mo. 1867. $1\frac{1}{12}$

——A DECLARATION Concerning the Just, True, and Real Calling, and Special Use and Peculiarity of the PEOPLE OF GOD in the world: who only are the friends of God, and of Christ, and of men; being "redeemed to God by the blood (which is the life) of the Lamb, out of every kindred, and tongue, and people and nation " (Rev. v. 9): which is only known and to be known by men who abide in the blessed

LAWTONITES, *continued.*

dominion of the Truth over all plurality of names and callings; in the One name and calling of good, which is One. Written and set forth by ABRAHAM LAWTON, Athens, N.Y., having been submitted to some friends who met in Philadelphia, on the 8th of Ninth month, 1868.
Stuckey, Printer, 403, North Sixth Street, Philadelphia . . . . 12mo. [1868.] ½

——A TRUE CAUSE of the DECLENSION of the People called Quakers, or SOCIETY OF FRIENDS. By Abraham Lawton.
Philadelphia: Thomas William Stuckey, Printer, 624, Weaver Street. . . 12mo. 1868. 1

——MINUTES of a MEETING OF SOME FRIENDS held in Philadelphia, at No. 915, Spring Garden Street, the 8th of Twelfth Month, 1868 (with an "Epistle, by ABRAHAM LAWTON.)
Stuckey, Printer, 403, North Sixth Street, Philadelphia. . . . . 12mo. [1868]. ½

——A Summary. . . 1868.

ANONYMOUS.
——Why the Friends of Truth should meet together.
Stuckey, Printer, 624, Weaver Street, Philadelphia. . . . . 12mo. No date. ⅙

BANCROFT, Joseph, of *Wilmington, Delaware.*
——AN EPISTLE to all Friends everywhere.—"At a meeting of some Friends held in Philadelphia, by adjournment, the 5th and 6th of the 5th month, 1865, for the purpose of establishing elect principles by reform, which is the only way the true seed can come," &c.
Signed on behalf of the meeting,

Joseph Bancroft, *Clerk.*

12mo. No Printer's name or place. [1865.] ½

——A REPORT from a MEETING OF SOME FRIENDS, held in Philadelphia, by adjournment, on the 1st and 2nd of Eleventh Month, 1865. To which is appended, AN APPEAL TO THE SOCIETY OF FRIENDS EVERYWHERE. By JOSEPH BANCROFT.
Philadelphia: Merrihew & Son, Printers, No. 243, Arch Street. . . . . 12mo. 1865. ⅔

LAWTONITES, *continued.*

——AN ADDRESS TO THE ELECT IN GOD THE FATHER AND IN CHRIST, the Mysterious Door into the one true Sheepfold; whom neither the World nor the Princes thereof do know.
Philadelphia: *Merrihew & Son, Printers, No. 243, Arch Street, below Third.* . 12mo. 1865. ½
NOTE.—The above "Address" is signed by Joseph Bancroft, on behalf of a Meeting held in Philadelphia, 5th Mo. 11th, 1866.

——AN EXPOSTULATORY ADDRESS to all WHO PROFESS THE NAME OF CHRIST, and more particularly to all of them WHO CLAIM THE NAME OF FRIENDS, *given forth in the Love of God to all men, by one who is known amongst them by the name of* JOSEPH BANCROFT, First Month, 1867.
Philadelphia: *Thomas William Stuckey, Printer, 624, Weaver Street.* . . 12mo. [1867] 1¼
NOTE.—Appended to the above (the pagination running on) is:

——"A MESSAGE from the SPIRIT OF TRUTH unto the HOLY SEED, who are chosen out of the World, and are lovers and followers of the Light. By James Nayler.
LONDON: *Printed in the year 1658, and Reprinted in 1715.*
Philadelphia: *Thomas William Stuckey, Printer, 624, Weaver Street.* . . 12mo. 1867. ⅚

——At a Meeting of some Men and Women Friends, held in Philadelphia on the 8th of the Second Month, 1867, as agreed upon in the Eleventh Month last. Joseph Bancroft *was named to serve the Meeting as Clerk.* . . . . N. P. or place. [1867.] ⅙

——"INNOCENCY WITH HER OPEN FACE, presented by way of APOLOGY," for the Meetings of those Friends who are convinced by the Truth of the necessity of Members to the Body of Christ, who is the Truth. (Signed on behalf of the Meeting by JOSEPH BANCROFT.
Stuckey, Printer, 624, Weaver Street, Philadelphia.
12mo. [1867.] ⅓

FLINN, Evan.
——THE TESTIMONY OF JESUS CHRIST.
Stuckey, Printer, 624, Weaver Street, Philadelphia.
12mo. [1867.] ½

LAWTONITES, *continued.*

KEESE, Samuel, of *Peru, New York.*

——The CONCILIATOR : being a serious inquiry into and a rational elucidation of THE MEANS OF SALVATION, shewing the way to reconcile man to man, and all men to God. By SAMUEL KEESE.

New York: *Wm. C. Bryant & Co., Printers, 41, Nassau Street, Corner of Liberty.*
12mo. 1866. 1$\frac{7}{12}$

——THEOLOGY SIMPLIFIED, available for all. In three parts. By Samuel Keese. **Part first**: THE BEING OF GOD, His primary elements recognized, His Son owned and Angels described.

"God is light and in Him is no darkness at all."—ST. JOHN.

New York: *Smith & Son, Steam, Book, and Job Printers, No. 15, Spruce Street.*
12mo. 1867. 2$\frac{7}{12}$

NOTE.—Contains, "THE POWER OF INFLUENCE and the FRUIT OF OBEDIENCE," An Essay, suggested by the Life and Death of Catherine R. Keese, of Peru, N. Y. "Family Government," &c.

PRICE, Eli K.

——An ADDRESS TO FRIENDS; or, Can all professing to be Friends become united ?

Philadelphia: *Merrihew & Son, Printers, No. 243, Arch Street, below Third.* 12mo. 1865. $\frac{1}{2}$

NOTE.—The above was answered by Abraham Lawton and Joseph Bancroft.

*LAY, Benjamin, *continued* from Catalogue, Vol. 2, p. 92.

——Notices of Benjamin Lay. By John Hunt, of New Jersey.

In Comly's Miscellany, Vol. 4, p. 274.

——Life of Benjamin Lay. By L. Maria Child.

Published by the American Anti-Slavery Society.
1842 or '43.

LEADBEATER, Mary, *continued* from Catalogue, Vol. 2, p. 95.

——Extracts and Original Anecdotes; for the improvement of youth by Mary Leadbeater. Second edition.

Dublin: *Printed and Published by Christopher Bentham, 19, Eustace Street, sold also by William Alexander, York.* 18mo. 1820. 5

LEADBETTER, Mary, *continued.*
—— The Pedlars.
> NOTE.—This was the last work she published, it was written for the Kildare-street Education Society, and consists of dialogues descriptive of the natural and artificial natural curiosities of various parts of Ireland, etc.

—— TALES for COTTAGERS, accommodated to the present condition of the IRISH PEASANTRY. By MARY LEADBETTER, and ELIZABETH SHAKLETON.
> DUBLIN: *Printed by James Cumming & Co., Hibernia Press Office,* for John Cumming, Lower Ormond Quay; and Gale, Curtis, & Fenner, Paternoster Row, London. 12mo. 1814. 9⅔

—— Cottage DIALOGUES among the Irish Peasantry. Part I. By Mary Leadbeater.
Fourth Edition.
> Dublin: *Printed at the Hibernia Press Office, 1, Temple Lane, for J. Cumming, 16, Lower Ormond Quay.*
> 12mo. 1813. 6 5/6

—— Part 2nd. Dublin . . . . 12mo. 1813.

—— The LANDLORD'S FRIEND, intended as a Sequel to COTTAGE DIALOGUES. By Mary Leadbeater.
> Dublin: *Printed at the Hibernia Press Offices, 1, Temple Lane, for J. Cumming, 16, Lower Ormond Quay.* . . . 12mo. 1813. 5

LEAN, William, *continued* from Catalogue, Vol. 2, p. 97.
—— A letter to Robert Charleton; occasioned by his "Thoughts on Barclay's Apology."
8vo. 1868. ½

LEAN, William Scarnell, *continued* from Catalogue, Vol. 2, p. 97.
—— Familiar Notes on Modes of Teaching English. By William Scarnel Lean, Principal of the Flounders Institute, Ackworth.
> *London: Longmans, Green, & Co.*
> *All Rights Reserved.* . . 8vo. 1874. 1¾

LEAPER, Joseph, of *London.*
—— Some Account of the PRESENT STATE of the CULTIVATION, &c., of EAST INDIA SUGAR, *by the* Labour *of* Free People. Sold, wholesale and retail, *by* JOSEPH LEAPER, No. 157, Bishopsgate Street, Without, London. . . . . . . Folio.

LEAPER, Joseph, *continued.*

——EAST INDIA SUGAR, RAW and REFINED, sold wholesale and retail, by JOSEPH LEAPER, *No. 157,* Bishopsgate Without, London.
    Single leaf. . . . . Folio. *circa.* 1794. ½
      NOTE.—On the back is the following printed endorsement. JOSEPH LEAPER, (No. 157), Bishopsgate Without, HAVING recently imported a quantity of MAPLE TREE SUGAR from CANADA, offers it to the Public for Sale, being the first introduction of this Sugar on a Commercial Plan," and on my Copy is the following invoice :
      " London, 7th Mo. 5th, '94.
    Thos. Hodgkin.
      Of Joseph Leaper.   £ s. d.
    28lb E. I. Sugar, 6¾d.   - - 0 15 9
                 Recd. J. Leaper."

LEATHAM, William Henry, M.P. for *Wakefield,* son of WM. LEATHAM, of *Heath,* near *Wakefield,* a banker, was born at *Wakefield* in the year 1815, married in 1839 Priscilla, daughter of Samuel Gurney, of *Upton, Essex,* and Lombard Street. Residence, *Hemsworth Hall, Pontefract, Yorkshire.*
Continued from Catalogue, Vol. 2, p. 97.

LEDDRA, William, *continued* from Catalogue, Vol. 2, p. 98.
——NARRATIVE of the MARTYRDOM, AT BOSTON, of William Robinson, Marmaduke Stevenson, Mary Dyer, and William Leddra, in the year 1659. *With other particulars.* Price Sixpence.
            12mo. *Manchester, printed.* 1841. 2
    See WILLIAM ROBINSON.

*LEEDS, Daniel, of *Philadelphia* (continued from Catalogue, Vol. 2, p. 99), was married at *Burlington Meeting* 2nd mo. 21st, 1681, and on that occasion is described as late of *Shrewsbury,* in *East Jersey,* and as being a " Cooper" by trade. He was in *New Jersey* in 1676, and a resident of *Burlington* in 1680. In 1682 he was Surveyor General and a member of the Assembly of *West Jersey.* Two years later he is mentioned as contributing £4 towards a Meeting-house in *Burlington.* His first quarrel with his co-religionists was about his Almanac for 1688, but he did not withdraw from the Society of Friends until the Keithian Schism. His first wife died in 1682.

——An Almanac for 1688. By Daniel Leeds.
    Philadelphia : William Bradford. .   1687.

*LEEDS, Daniel, *continued.*

——An Almanac for 1690. By Daniel Leeds.
Philadelphia: William Bradford. . 1689.

——An Almanac for 1691. By Daniel Leeds.
Philadelphia: William Bradford. . . 1690.

——An Almanac for 1692. By Daniel Leeds.
Philadelphia: William Bradford. . . 1691.

——An Almanac and Ephemerides For the Year of Christian Account 1693. By Daniel Leeds, Philomath.
Printed and Sold by William Bradford.
Small 8vo. pp. (51) 1693.

——An Almanac for 1689. By Daniel Leeds.
Philadelphia: William Bradford, 1688.

> No copy is known to be extant. Jacob Taylor, in his Almanac for 1706, says, "That unparalleled Plagiary and unreasonable Transcriber, D. Leeds, who hath now for 19 years, with a very large stock of Impudence, filched matter out of other men's works, to furnish his spurious Almanacs." This, and the existence of an Almanac for the year 1693, is the only evidence I can find of there being an unbroken series of Leeds Almanacs.

——The Temple of Wisdom for the Little World, In Two Parts. The First, Philosophically Divine, treating of the Being of all Beeings, and whence everything hath its original, as Heaven, Hell, Angels, Men, and Devils, Earth, Stars, and Elements. And particularly of all Mysteries concerning the Soul; and of Adam before and after the Fall. Also, a Treatise of the four Complexions, with the Causes of Spiritual Sadness, &c., To which is added a Postscript to all Students in Arts and Sciences. The Second Part, Morally divine, contains, First, Abuses stript and whipt, by Geo. Wither, with his discription of Fair Virtue. Secondly. A Collection of divine Poems, from Fr. Quarles. Lastly. Essays and Religious Meditations of Sir Francis Bacon Knight. Collected, Published and intended for a general Good, by D. L.

12mo. *Printed and Sold by William Bradford, in Philadelphia.* . . . *Anno.* 1688.

> Collation: Title, 1 leaf; Preface, pp. (3); To the Doctors, pp. (3); Text, pp. 1-125, (1); Second Title, and To the Reader, pp. (2); Text, pp. 3-48; Third Title, 1 leaf, pp. 50-86; Errata, 1 leaf.

*LEEDS, Daniel, *continued*.
> The postscript to the first part, which occupies the last three pages, is signed " Daniel Leeds."
>
> NOTE.—The Titles of the above Almanacs, and "The Temple of Wisdom," are from Hildeburn's " Issues of the Press of Pennsylvania, 1885."

LEEDS, Josiah W., of *Philadelphia*.

——The Theatre. An Essay upon the Non-Accordance of Stage-Plays with the Christian Profession. By Josiah W. Leeds.
> *Philadelphia : 528, Walnut Street.   Published for the Author.* . . 8vo. 1884. pp. 85.
> Reprinted.—*Newport, Mon.: Published by John E. Southall, 106, Dock Street.* . 8vo. 1890. 5½

LEEDS, Samuel, *continued* from Catalogue, Vol. 2, p. 99.
> I find this Friend was last of *Ipswich*, where he died about the year 1773.
> See Elliot's Life of Dr. Fothergill, p. XII.

LE'TALL, Benjamin, of *Woodhouse, near Sheffield*.

——An Examination of the Methods of performing Public Worship, pursued by various Christian Professors, and the Ordination of their Ministers considered, with an enquiry into the Christian's ultimate appeal of faith and manners.
> *Manchester : Printed and Sold by William Irwin, 24, Deansgate.* . . 8vo. 1871.

LE'TALL, William J.

——Short Answers to Enquirers about the Views of Friends, by many Known as "Quakers."
> *York : Printed,* . . . 8vo. 1892.

LETCHWORTH, Robert, of *Chesterton, Cambridgeshire*.

——(and Edward Sammon, and others). A DISCOVERY of the EDUCATION of the Schollars of Cambridge, *etc*.
4to. 1659. 2
> See Catalogue, Vol. 2, p. 653.

LETCHWORTH, Thomas, *continued* from Catalogue, Vol. 2, p. 100.

——*Multum in Parvo* contra *Parvum in Multo*. Or a Six Days CANDID REVIEW of a six years' uncandid Controversy.—See ANONYMOUS in Catalogue, Vol. 1, p. 68. . . . . . 8vo. 1773. 6

LETCHWORTH, Thomas, *continued*.

—— Proposals for Publishing by Subscription, An Abridgement of the Works of John Woolman.

4to. [1774 ?] ¼

—— A Morning and Evening's Meditation, or, a Descant on the Times. A Poem. By T.L.

London, Printed. Philadelphia, Re-Printed and Sold by B. Franklin, and D. Hall.

8vo. 1766. 58pp.

Note.—This edition consisted of 500 copies.

—— Twelve Discourses, delivered chiefly at the Meeting House of the People called Quakers, in the Park, Southwark.

Reprinted.—*Salem.* . . . 8vo. 1794.

LETTSOM, John Coakley,—*continued* from Catalogue, Vol. 2, p. 101.

—— Le VOYAGEUR NATURALISTE, ou INSTRUCTIONS Sur les moyens de ramasser les objets d'Histoire Naturelle, & de les bien conserver. Avec des observations propres à étendre les recherches relatives aux connoissances humaines en général. Par M. JOHN COAKLEY LETTSOM, Docteur-Médecin, Membre de la Société Royale de Londres, & de celle des arts.

> Traduit de l'Anglois sur la seconde édition corrigée & augmentée, auquel on a joint *l'Art de calmer les flots de la Mer*. Ouvrage aussi traduit de l'Anglois, qui renferme la preuve d'un phénomene qui mérite d'être placé parmi les découvertes curieuses & utiles de la Physique moderne.

A AMSTERDAM; *Et se trouve* A PARIS, *Chez* LACOMBE, *Libraire, rue Christine.*

MDCCLXXV. 12mo. 1775. 12

—— Letter to Lady ANN ERSKINE, dated from "Basinghall Street, June, 18, 1791," on the decease of LADY HUNTINGDON, inserted in "A Short Account of the last days of LADY HUNTINGDON, &c., by the Rev. T. HAWEIS."

8vo. [1791.]

—— See WILLIAM FALCONER. (In my "Bibliotheca Quakeristica, &c.") "A Dissertation on the Influence of the Passions, &c." 12mo., 1796, contains an explanation of the origin of the FOTHERGILLIAN MEDAL, with an address by Dr. Lettsom.

LETTSOM, John Coakley, *continued.*

——HINTS designed to promote BENEFICENCE, TEMPERANCE, and MEDICAL SCIENCE; Vol. 1.
    London : *Printed by H. Fry, for C. Dilly, 1797,*
                                                      8vo.

CONTENTS.   *Page.*
I. HINTS designed to promote the establishment of a DISPENSARY, for extending MEDICAL RELIEF to the POOR at their own habitations. . . . 1
II. HINTS for the establishment of a MEDICAL SOCIETY in London. 31
III. HINTS respecting FEMALE CHARACTER. . . 58
IV. HINTS for establishing a SOCIETY for promoting USEFUL LITERATURE. 67
V. HINTS respecting the IMMEDIATE EFFECTS of POVERTY. 89
VI. HINTS respecting the DISTRESSES of the POOR. . 102
VII. HINTS respecting a SUBSTITUTE for WHEAT BREAD 173
VIII. HINTS respecting the EFFECTS of a LITTLE DROP 180
IX. HINTS respecting the EFFECTS of TAVERN FEASTS 199
X. HINTS respecting WILLS and TESTAMENTS . . 223
XI. HINTS respecting CRIMES and PUNISHMENTS . 230
XII. HINTS for establishing an INFIRMARY for SEA-BATHING the POOR of LONDON. . . . 243
XIII. HINTS for promoting a BEE SOCIETY . . . 256

Plates.
Plate I.   A morning walk in the Metropolis . . 93
Plate II. Tavern Feast 199
Plate III. Sea-Bathing Infirmary at Margate . . 243
Plate IV. Plan of a Colony of Bees 259

——A short account of Mr. Hewson, by Dr. Lettsom, compiled from Mrs. Hewson's papers. In the "Transactions of the Medical Society of London," Vol. 1, Art. 2. . . . . . . 8vo. London, 1810.

——Recollections of Dr. Rush. By Dr. Lettsom.
    London : *Printed by J. Nichols, Son, and Bentley, Red Lion Passage.* . . . 8vo. 1815. 1 *sheet.*

——An EULOGY on JOHN COAKLEY LETTSOM, M.D., &c. By T. J. PETTIGREW 8vo. 1816. 4½
                See J. T. PETTIGREW.

———*Part Second.* A CATALOGUE of the Medical and remaining part of the LIBRARY of the late John Coakley Lettsom, M. and LL.D., *Member of several Academies and Literary Societies.* Among which are :
    A most extraordinary Collection of Tracts, on all subjects of Literature, in 520 vols. ; to which is a copious Manu-

LETTSOM, John Coakley, *continued*.

    script Index, made by the late Dr. Lettsom; the Bills of Mortality from the commencement; Merian Topographia generalis, in 19 vol., *red morocco*, A VERY FINE SET; Grainger's Biography, illustrated with many rare and scarce English Portraits, bound in 12 vols. *in atlas folio, in blue morocco*; many transactions of Literary and Medical Societies: Solvyn's Collections of Etchings, descriptive of the Manners, &c., of the Hindoos, PRINTED AT CALCUTTA; and likewise many Books printed in America, chiefly presented to the late Doctor.
    Which will be Sold by Auction,
    BY LEIGH AND SOTHEBY,
Booksellers, at their House, No. 145, Strand, opposite Catherine Street,
On Wednesday, April 3, 1816, and Two following days, at Twelve o'Clock.
To be viewed to the Time of Sale, and Catalogues to be had at the Place of Sale.

Wright and Murphy, Printers, 31, Little Queen Street, Holborn, London.
[*Brit. Museum, 130 K, 7.*] . 8vo. [1816.] 2.

The following Sales are announced at the end of Leigh and Sotheby's Catalogue of the Library of the late Rev. Samuel Henley, D.D., F.S.A., April 11, 1816, and four following days.

" Messrs. LEIGH and SOTHEBY will have the honour to submit the following Libraries for Public Sale, during the present season.

The entire Collection of Coins and Medals of the late DR. LETTSOM, consisting of Greek, Roman, Saxon and English, in Copper, Silver and Gold. Likewise two very fine carved Medal Cases."

——MUSEUM LETTSOMIANUM. The entire Museum of the late DR. LETTSOM, consisting of an extensive Collection of fine Minerals, Shells, Bronzes, Carvings in Ivory, Models in Wax, Inlaid Marbles, Curiosities from the South Seas, and a most valuable Human Skeleton, prepared by himself, &c., &c." ("Fine Cork Models of Ancient Buildings in Rome ").

LEVICK, James J.—M.D. of *Philadelphia*.
——The Early History of Merion. And An Old Welsh Pedigree. By James J. Levick, M.D.
    Extracted from The Pennsylvania Magazine of History and Biography, Vol. IV., 1880.
    Collins' Printing House, 705, Jayne Street. Philadelphia. . . 8vo. No date. 2¾

LEVIS, Elizabeth, of *North America*.

——Some Friendly Advice and Cautions, recommended to the serious consideration of the professors of Holy Truth. By Elizabeth Levis. In *Comly's Miscellany*, Vol. 4, p. 182.

LEWIS, Enoch, *continued* from Catalogue, Vol. 2, p. 107.

——A DISSERTATION ON OATHS. By Enoch Lewis.
 Uriah Hunt: 101, Market Street. Nathan Kite: Appletree Alley, Near Fourth Street.
         12mo. 1838. 4⅙

LEWIS, Evan, *continued* from Catalogue, Vol. 2, p. 108.

——The Friend, or Advocate of Truth. New Series, was edited by him.

*LIGHTFOOT, Hannah, The Pretty Quaker.

——Biographical Notice of Hannah Lightfoot. By Joseph Smith. (In MS.)

LILBURNE, John, *continued* from Catalogue, Vol. 2, p. 110.

——To the Parliament of the Commonwealth of England: The Humble Petition of John Lilburn, Gentleman, prisoner in Newgate. . Tuesday, 12 July, 1653.
 NOTE.—A copy of this petition is inserted in his Trial at the Old Bailey. 4to. 1653. p. 27.

——Several Informations and Examinations taken concerning Lieu.-Col. John Lilburne, concerning his Apostasie to the Party of Charles Stuart, and his intentions in coming over into England out of Flanders.
 NOTE.—This book is stated to be "a most base, wicked, false, lying, villanous, perjured book," and was answered in the following, viz: see his Trial at the Old Bailey, p. 33.

——Malice detected, to the said most false, perjured, and calumnious Book against Mr. Lilburne; and some few short observations upon 4 of the Witnesses.
 NOTE.—Printed at the latter end of "A Conference with the Soldiers, &c."

——John Lilburn, Revived.
 Writ at *Bridges* in *Flanders*. Printed, March, 1653.

——A Declaration against him in *Spanish*, by Don Manuel Suarez.—See His trial in the Old Baily, p. 35.

——An Act for the execution of a Judgement given in Parliament against Lieut.-Col. John Lilburne. Friday, 30th Jany., 1651.—See p. 40 of the Trial at the Old Baily.

LILBURNE, John, *continued.*

—— The TRIALL of Mr. JOHN LILBURNE, Prisoner in Newgate, at the Sessions of Peace, Held for the City of LONDON, at Justice-Hall, in the Old Baily; sitting upon Wednesday, Thursday, Friday, and Saturday, the 13, 14, 15, and 16 of *July,* 1653.
     4to. London, printed in the yeer, 1653. 5½

—— The EXCEPTIONS of *John Lilburne,* Gent., PRISONER, at the BARRE, to a Bill of Indictment preferred against him, grounded upon a pretended Act, intituled, *An Act for the execution of a Judgement given in Parliament against Lieutenant Collonel* John Lilburn: which Judgement is by the said Act supposed to be given the 15 day of January, 1651.
  London: Printed for Richard Moon, at the Seven stars, in Pauls Church-yard, near the great North-door. . . . 4to. 1653. 1

—— Memoir of John Lilburne, in French. See:—"Portraits Politiques des Hommes des différents Partis—Parlementaires,—Cavaliers, Republicains Niveleurs Par M. Guizot. Quatrième édition.
  Paris, Didier et Co., Libraires,—Editeurs, 35, Quai des Augustins. . . . 8vo. 1858.

—— The Life of John Lilburne, in Vol. 6, p. 44 of "British Biography," &c. . . . 8vo. London, 1770.
  See R. BARCLAY, for the whole title of "British Biography."

—— LIEUT. COLONEL J. LILBURNE TRYED and CAST: or, *His Case and Craft Discovered.* Wherein is shewed the Grounds and Reasons of the Parliaments proceeding, in passing the Act of Banishment against him, and wherefore since his coming over hee hath been committed to the Tower by the PARLIAMENT. Here likewise is laid open the partiall, corrupt and illegall verdicts of his JURIES, both the former and later. Being to satisfie all those in the Nation that are truly godly, and wel affected to the Peace of the Common-wealth: And to stop the Mouths of others; proving what is done in order to his present Imprisonment, is according to the rules of Justice and Equity contained in the morall Law of God and nature, or sound naturall Reason. *Published by* AUTHORITY.
  LONDON: *Printed by M. Simmons, in Aldersgate Street.* 4to. 1653. 23½

LILBURNE, John, *continued.*

"Colonel *John Lilburn*, a great stickler against monarchical government in the civil wars, who, under the name of Colonel *Titus*, frightened *Oliver Cromwel* in the height of his power, by writing the famous pamphlet entitled, *Killing no Murder.*"

See " *The Geography and History of England.*"
—*London : Printed for J. Dodsley, in Pall Mall, 1765*—p. 53, Durham, " *Remarkable Persons.*"

It is very curious whilst going to press with this "Supplement" to JOHN LILBURNE, that a copy of " *The Weekly Times and Echo, April 24, 1892,* should come into my hands, containing the following article, "THE ANNALS OF TOIL," by J. Morrison Davidson, NO. XXI.—" FREE-BORN JOHN," THE LEVELLER.

> The most turbulent, but the most upright and courageous of mankind.—HUME'S HISTORY OF ENGLAND.

> I thank you for your friend Lilburne, and desire you to send me as many of his books as you can. I learn much by them ; and in earnest I find a great benefit by reading his books, for though they want judgment and logic to prove what they promise, yet they bring good materials to prove somewhat else they do not think of.—CLARENDON PAPERS, VOL. 2., p. 363.

Such was the opinion of Royalist Chancellor Hyde regarding " Free-born John," the Leader of the Ultra-Republicans, or Social Democrats of England in the 17th century, etc., etc.

L.R., *i.e.*, Robert Linklater, a native of the *Shetland Isles*, and who attended Ratcliff Meeting for some years. He has issued and had printed the following small papers :—

> " Especially to the Younger Members of the Society of Friends."

> " Giving Credit to the statements of the Early Members of the Society of Friends. They seemed to feel themselves raised up as a people to bear testimony in favour of a more Spiritual Christianity than most arrive at," &c.

Robert Linklater's small paper on Shetland Goods.
6, Bishopsgate Street Without, and Paynton Street, Poplar.
" Letter to Joseph Smith, London," 4th mo. 16, *1866*, MS.
He died at *Newton*, near *Kimmuck*, the 27th of 5th month, 1869, aged 32 years.

LISTER, Joseph Jackson, *continued* from Catalogue, Vol. 2, p. 125.

—— " On the Microscopic characters of the Animal Tissues

LISTER, Joseph Jackson, *continued.*

and Fluids, by J. J. Lister, F.R.S., and Dr. Hodgkin." See the Appendix, page 424, of "On the Influence of Physical Agents on Life, by W. F. Edwards, M.D., F.R.S. 𝕿𝖗𝖆𝖓𝖘𝖑𝖆𝖙𝖊𝖉 𝖋𝖗𝖔𝖒 𝖙𝖍𝖊 𝕱𝖗𝖊𝖓𝖈𝖍, by Dr. Hodgkin and Dr. Fisher. . . . . . 8vo. 1832.

He died the 24th of the 10th Mo., 1869, aged 83 years, and was buried in Friends' Burial Ground, Stoke Newington.

LISTER, Joseph, of Glasgow, Professor, son of J. J. Lister, of *London.*

——Testimonials in favour of Joseph Lister, Esq., F.R.C.S. Eng., and Edin. Candidate for the office of Assistant-Surgeon to the Royal Infirmary of Edinburgh.

Ballantyne & Company, Printers, Paul's Work.
8vo. [1852 ?]   1

"Sir Joseph Lister, Bart., M.D., F.R.S., Surgeon Extraordinary to the Queen, was 64 years of age yesterday."
—*Echo,* Monday, April 6, 1891.

LISTER, Thomas, *continued* from Catalogue, Vol. 2, p. 126.

——Moral advancement the Hope of England. A Poem.

——Speech at the Festival of the East London Auxiliary Temperance Society.

. See *The New British and Foreign Temperance Intelligencer,* Vol. 2, No. 83 and 84, p. 193, June 16, 1838.

For further particulars, see an account of him in the "Naturalists' Journal," 4th Mo., 1888, Edited by Scholars in Friends' Schools.
He died in the 3rd Month, 1888.

LITTLEBOY, Sarah, of *Great Berkhampstead.*

——MEMORANDA relating to the late SARAH LITTLEBOY, of Boxwells, Great Berkhampstead. With selections from her poetry and manuscripts.

"So must, so let it be ;—we say, Amen ;
If Jesus is our refuge, all is well."
The Berkhampstead Graveyard.

FOR PRIVATE CIRCULATION ONLY.

[*London : R. Barrett and Sons, Printers, Mark Lane.* . . . . 4to. 1873. 24½ sheets.

(Photographic Portrait of Sarah Littleboy, with fac-simile autograph, "Thy very affectionate mother, S. Littleboy").

——Account of the last illness of William Littleboy, *who died the 28th of First Month, 1837.* (Commencing

LITTLEBOY, Sarah, *continued.*

at page 187 of the above vol.) [Preface by her son, the late John Eeles Littleboy, of Hunton Bridge, the compiler.]

——Visit to the Grave of William Penn, at Jordans, in Buckinghamshire. See ANON. *Catalogue, Vol. 1, p.* 115. . . . . 1853.

LIVINGSTONE, Patrick, was born near *Montrose*, in 1634, *continued* from Catalogue, Vol. 2, p. 126.

——Good Advice to the People to whom this may come. (Written in "Aberdeen Prison.")

John Harrison, Printer, Manchester.
8vo. No date. ¼

——Good Will to the People in and about Aberdeen. (Written in Aberdeen Prison.)

[*John Harrison, Printer, Manchester.*]
8vo. No date. ¼

He died (see Catalogue, Vol. 2, p. 127) the 15th of 4th Month, 1694, aged about 60 years, and was buried in Bunhill Fields.

LOGAN, George, M.D., was a native of Pennsylvania. He was an active member of the Board of Agriculture, and of the Philosophical Society. He published experiments on Gypsum, and on the rotation of Crops, 1797. He died in the year 1821, aged 66 years. For further particulars concerning him, see *Blake's Biographical Dictionary, 8th Edition, Boston, 1853.*

LOGAN, James, *continued* from Catalogue, Vol. 2, p. 129.

——The Charge Delivered from the Bench to the Grand Jury, At the Court of Quarter Sessions, held for the County of Philadelphia, the Second Day of September, 1723. Published at the Desire of the said Grand Jury. Together with their Address.

Philadelphia: Printed and Sold by Andrew Bradford, at the Sign of the Bible, in the Second Street, 1723. . . Sq. 8vo. pp. 16.

——A Dialogue, showing What's therein to be found. A Motto being Modish, for want of good Latin, are put English Quotations.

Philadelphia: Printed by S. Keimer, in the Year MDCCXXV. . . Small 8vo. 1725. pp. 40.
Errata 1 leaf.

LOGAN, James, *continued.*

——A Memorial from James Logan, in behalf of the Proprietor's Family and of himself, Servant to the said Family.
> *Philadelphia*: [*Printed by Andrew Bradford, 1725.*]

——The Antidote In some Remarks on a Paper of David Lloyd's, called A Vindication of the Legislative Power, Submitted to the Representatives of all the Freemen of Pennsylvania, by J. Logan. 25th Sept., 1725.
> [*Philadelphia: Andrew Bradford, 1725.*]   Folio. 2
> Reprinted, 2nd Edition.
> *Philadelphia : Andrew Bradford.*

——A more Just Vindication of the Honourable Sir Wm. Keith, Bart., Against the unparalled Abuses put upon him in a Scandalous Libel, call'd, A just and plain Vindication of Sir William Keith, &c.
> [*Philadelphia: Printed by Andrew Bradford, 1726.*] . . . . . . Folio. pp. 4

——By the Honourable James Logan, Esq., President of the Council of the Province of Pennsylvania. A Proclamation.
> . *Philadelphia: B. Franklin, 1737.* . . Folio. 1 leaf.

——(Letter) to Robert Jordan and others, the Friends of the Yearly Meeting for Business, now convened in Philadelphia. Stenton, 22nd Sept., 1741.
> *Philadelphia: B. Franklin.* . Folio. 1 sheet.
> NOTE.—Only 30 copies privately printed.
> Reprinted in the "Pennsylvania Magazine of History and Biography", Vol. VI.

——The Latter Part of The Charge Delivered from the Bench to the Grand Inquest, at a Court of Oyer and Terminer and Gaol Delivery, held for the City and County of Philadelphia, At Philadelphia the 24th Day of September, 1733. Published at the Request of the said Inquest. With their Address.
> [*Philadelphia: B. Franklin, 1733.*] . Folio. pp. 3.

———Cato's Moral Distichs Englished in Couplets. [Translated by JAMES LOGAN.]
> *Philadelphia: Printed and Sold by B. Franklin, 1735.* . . . . 4to.

LOGAN, James, *continued.*

——The Charge Delivered from the Bench to the Grand Inquest, at a Court of Oyer and Terminer and Gaol-Delivery, held for the City and County of Philadelphia, April 13, 1736.
> *Philadelphia: Printed and Sold by B. Franklin, M,DCC,XXXVI.* . . Small 4to. pp. 24.
>> For some particulars concerning him, See *Blake's Biographical Dictionary*, 8th edition, Boston, 1853.

LONGSHORE, Thomas Ellwood, of *North America.*

——George Fox interpreted. . . . . . 1881.

LOWER, Thomas, M.D., of *Marsh Grainge, County of Lancaster*, (was the Brother of Richard Lower, Physician to Chas. 2nd). He married Mary, daughter of Judge Fell, Swarthmore Hall, the 26th of 6th Month, 1668.
> He died at *Hammersmith*, 5th of 3rd Mo., 1720, aged 88 years.

LLOYD, Charles, *continued* from Catalogue, Vol. 2, p. 132.

——"To a Brother, who had been afflicted with a long sickness."

——"To the Sabbath."
> NOTE.—The above are inserted in a privately printed vol., entitled: "British Melodies," &c. See Anon.
>> *Norwich: Printed. No date.*

LLOYD, David, of *Philadelphia.*

——A Vindication of the Legislative Power, Submitted to the Representatives of all the Free-men of the Province of Pennsylvania, now sitting in Assembly.
> *Philadelphia:* [*Andrew Bradford, 1725.*]
>> Folio. pp. 4.
>> Signed by David Lloyd and dated the 19th of the month called March, 1724-5.

——A Defence of the Legislative Constitution of the Province of Pennsylvania. As it now stands Confirmed and Established by Law and Charter. With some Observations on the Proceedings published by Sixteen Members of Assembly, in a Paper, entitled, The Votes and Proceedings of the House of Representatives: Recommended to the consideration of all the Free-men of the Province.
> [*Philadelphia: Printed by Andrew Bradford, 1728.*] . . . . . . Folio. pp. 11.

*LLOYD, Llewellyn,
—— Field Sports of the North of Europe. Comprised in a Personal Narrative of a Residence in Sweden and Norway in the Years 1827-28. By L. Lloyd, Esq. 2 Vols.
  Reprinted, 2nd edition, with additions.
  London : Henry Colburn and Richard Bentley, New Burlington Street. . . 8vo. 1831. 54⅓

LUCAS, Francis, of *Hitchin*.
—— Sketches of Rural Life and other poems.
  London : Printed, . . 8vo. 1889.

LUCAS, Samuel, of Hitchin. His brother. Account of him in a Hitchin Newspaper.

LUCAS, William, of *Hitchin*. Brother of Samuel.
—— 𝕿𝖍𝖊 𝕺𝖑𝖉 𝕭𝖎𝖙𝖈𝖍𝖎𝖓 𝕮𝖔𝖆𝖈𝖍. A Local Sketch. The following was written by our late lamented townsman, Mr. William Lucas, in the year 1849, at which time the Great Northern Railway opened, and the Coach ceased to run. Mr. John Kershaw, the respected Proprietor, died at Biggleswade, October, 1863. Copied from *The Hertford Mercury, 1849.*
          Broadside. [1849.] 1

LUKENS, Susan, of *Chester Co., Pennsylvania.*
—— Gleanings at Seventy-five, by Susan Lukens, of Ercildown, Chester County, Pa.
  Philadelphia : Porter and Coates. . . 1873.
    NOTE.—This book includes some very readable incidents of Early and other Friends, with poetry by the Gleaner ; the principal poem is the Painter of Seville. The remainder being mostly reminiscences of her friends and of precious seasons with Friends. Daniel Hough's Letter.

LUNDY, Benjamin, *continued* from Catalgue, Vol. 2, p. 136.
—— The Genius of Universal Emancipation. . . 1821.
—— The Life, Travels and Opinions of BENJAMIN LUNDY, including his Journeys to Texas and Mexico ; with a sketch of contemporary events ; and a notice of the Revolution in Hayti. Compiled under the direction and on behalf of his children. (With a *Portrait*).
  Philadelphia : Published by William D. Parrish, No. 4, North Fifth Street. . 12mo. 1847. 13

LUNN, Mary, one of the People called Quakers. She has left £50 to the Quaker's Workhouse, Clerkenwell; £50 to the Quaker's Meeting, nr. Gracechurch Street; and £10 to the Poor of Wandsworth Meeting.
> *Gents' Magazine, August, 1775.*

LURTING, Thomas, *continued* from Catalogue, Vol. 2, p. 137.

——The Fighting Sailor turn'd Peaceable Christian, etc.
> *London: Printed, and Re-printed by Samuel Keimer, [Philadelphia.] 1725.* Small 8vo. pp. 47.

LURY, John Elton, *continued* from Catalogue, Vol. 2, p. 138.

——"Principle Out and Out." To the Editor of the *Hampshire Advertiser.*
> *Reprinted from "The National Temperance Chronicle," June 1st, 1850.* . . . 8vo. ¼

LURY, Samuel H., of *Bristol.*

——How we are Saved by Christ. Testimony of the Scripture thereon.
> *Bristol, printed,* 12mo. No date. 1

M.

M. W.

——A Brief Declaration to all the World.
> 4to. [No name or date.] 16—. ½

*MACDERMID, John, of *Edinburgh.*

——A COMPENDIUM of THE PRINCIPLES of ARITHMETICAL SCIENCE: designed to facilitate the business of the Tutor, as well as the task of the Pupil; and to enable learners to go through their arithmetical studies in about half the usual time appropriated to that branch of education; insuring to them also a power over numbers, or a degree of facility in mental calculations hitherto known only in singular or extraordinary instances, and unattainable by the usual methods of teaching. BY JOHN MACDERMID.
> EDINBURGH: *John Anderson, Jun., 55, North Bridge Street; Simpkin, Marshall & Co., London; W. Curry, Jun., & Co., Dublin.*
> 8vo. 1836. 11½

MACKELLOW, John, was born at *Wadhurst*, in *Sussex*, in 1772.

—— Autobiography of John Mackellow, (with a Photopraphic Portrait in his 90th year). [Edited by Jane Barron Smith.]
 London: Printed by Richard Barrett, 13, Mark Lane. 8vo. 1863. 5

MACY, Obed, of *Nantucket, North America.*

—— The HISTORY OF NANTUCKET; being a compendious account of the first settlement of the Island by the English, together with the Rise and Progress of the WHALE FISHERY; and other historical facts relative to said Island and its Inhabitants. In Two Parts. BY OBED MACY. (With a Frontispiece of the Island of Nantucket. Drawn by Wm. Coffin).
 " We know that all things work together for good, to them that love God.—ROMANS VIII. 28.
 Gather up the fragments that remain, that nothing be lost.—JOHN VI. 12.
 BOSTON: *Hilliard, Gray & Co. (J. D. Freeman, Printer, No. 110, Washington St.)*
           8vo. 1835. 20

 NOTE.—At the end of this book is added a list of "Hilliard, Gray & Company's School Books."
 In the work itself is inserted: "A letter from Zaccheus Macy, forwarding to the Historical Society an account of the former Indian divisions of the Island, &c." 1792, also an "Account of the names of the old Sachems and some of the most respectable Indians, and their habitations, taken from the best authors that could be had yᵉ 15 yᵉ 3 Mo., 1763. At that time there were living near about 370 of the natives on the Island of Nantucket—per me the subscriber." Nantucket, yᵉ 2d 10th Month, 1792. By Zaccheus Macy.
 And many other interesting pieces, see Peter Folger, Peleg Folger, Rachel Wilson.

MACY, Silvanus J., of Nantucket.

—— Genealogy of the Macy family. . . 1868.

MACY, Zaccheus. See OBED MACY.

MAJOLIER, Christiné. See CHRISTINE ALSOP.

MAPS OF FRIENDS' MEETINGS, &c.

—— A Map of Friends' Meetings in Ireland. . . 1794.

—— A Map of the MEETINGS of FRIENDS in ENGLAND AND WALES, *exhibiting the boundaries* of the respective QUARTERLY MEETINGS.

MAPS OF FRIENDS' MEETINGS, &c., *continued.*
  *Dean & Son, Lith., 12, Clements Lane, Lombard
     St. . . . . . .* [No date.]
  ——A Travelling Map of *Great Britain and Ireland,*
     distinguishing the places where Meetings are held.
     By Joseph Pease, Jun., of Darlington.
     *London : Published by William Phillips, George
        Yard, Lombard Street.* 4to size (when folded).

MARRIAGE, Francis, *continued* from Catalogue, Vol. 2,
  p. 141.
     He died the 12th day of the 2nd Mo., 1878, aged 68 years.
     DEATH OF MR. FRANCIS MARRIAGE.—This week we have to
     record the death of a venerable, though somewhat
     eccentric philanthropist—formerly well-known as what
     may be called "a character" in Chelmsford, and after-
     wards in the metropolis—which took place at Blackmore
     on Tuesday last. The deceased was Mr. Francis
     Marriage, a member of a family of the Society of
     Friends which for two or more generations has occupied,
     and still retains, a good and honourable position in this
     neighbourhood. He was the second son of Mr. Joseph
     Marriage, of Bishops Hall Mill ; and for some time he
     carried on the business of a miller and merchant in this
     town and at Springfield Wharf. But it is less in a com-
     mercial than in an intellectual and philanthropic view
     that his memory is entitled to notice. With a large and
     liberal mind he united the qualities of the ripe scholar
     and linguist, and his knowledge of languages often
     brought him into contact with foreigners, whom he was
     ever ready to counsel and assist. In the cause of educa-
     tion he always took a deep interest, and was the means
     of erecting several Schools in the county ; and he may
     be said to have been the father of the Temperance
     Societies in this district, having expended considerable
     time and money on the advancement of those principles.
     His principal eccentricity was the adoption of the garb
     of his sect in the 17th century ; but from familiarity
     with his pleasant and portly form, this did not attract
     peculiar notice in Chelmsford, though in the Metropolis,
     to which he removed to take a place of trust, it made
     him conspicuous in the Law Courts and occasionally in
     the House of Commons, to which his interest in public
     matters often led him. About twelve months ago, be-
     coming somewhat feeble from age, he returned to Essex,
     and had resided at Blackmore, where he died at the age
     of 68. A short time before this sad event he was walk-
     ing from Ongar to his home, when he was assailed by
     three roughs, who threw him down and robbed him of
     his watch. This, possibly, in his feeble state, might
     have accelerated his death—if so, it was a sad end for
     a man of his cultivated mind and gentle spirit.

MARRIAGE, Francis, *continued.*

> FUNERAL OF MR. FRANCIS MARRIAGE.—The remains of Mr. Francis Marriage, whose death at Blackmore, at the age of 68, we noticed in our last, were on Saturday afternoon consigned to their last resting-place in the Friends' Cemetery, Broomfield Road, Chelmsford, in the presence of a large concourse of mourners from various parts, who had assembled to pay this last tribute of respect to the memory of a man of whom it may truly be said that to know him was to respect and love him. The sad procession reached the Cemetery at about three o'clock, the chief mourner being deceased's only surviving brother—Mr. Joseph Marriage, of Holloway, in the carriage with whom were Mr. Manning, of Cornhill, an old friend of deceased, and the Rev. Mr. Warley, of Blackmore; while in another conveyance were three female neighbours of deceased who had been most kind to him in his last illness. At Roxwell the procession had been joined by Mr. Wm. Bott's carriage, in which were Mr. and Mrs. Wm. Bott; Mr. and Mrs. E. Marriage, of Colchester; Mr. Chas. Marriage, of Reigate; and Mr. Thos. Marriage, of Chelmsford, all cousins of deceased. At the gate of the Cemetery the procession was met by a deputation of the elder members of the Chelmsford Temperance Society, which was founded at a meeting held at deceased's house at Chelmsford in 1837; while among the relatives of the deceased present near the graveside were Mr. Henry Marriage, Mr. Lawrance Marriage, Mr. Joseph Smith, of Saling; Mr. Chas. Hicks, of Stansted; Mr. Burgess, of Leicester; Mr. Jno. Marriage, of Moulsham Lodge; Mr. F. Marriage, of Barnes Farm, Springfield; Mrs. Henry Marriage, of Coval Hall; Miss Caroline Marriage, &c. The service at the grave was conducted in the usual simple manner of the Society of Friends, Mr. H. S. Corder, of Writtle, offering prayer, after which Mr. Chas. Hicks delivered an address. In addition to the relatives and friends, a goodly number of residents in the neighbourhood—by whom deceased was formerly known—were present in the graveyard to show their respect for the memory of an old and honoured friend, who, with not a few harmless eccentricities, was one of the kindest, most upright, and most loveable of men. *Essex Paper.*

MARRIAGE, Joseph, *continued* from Catalogue, Vol. 2, p. 142.

—— A Letter, &c., on the Case of Joseph Marriage. Chelmsford, 8th Mo., 1844. . . 4to. [1844.] ¼

MARRIAGE, Mary A., of *Moulsham Lodge, Chelmsford, and Grassmere, Mitcham.*

MARRIAGE, Mary, A., *continued*.

—— 𝔒ur 𝔏ittle 𝔑agged 𝔉riends, and their late Teacher.
London: F. Bowyer Kitto, 5, Bishopsgate Without. 16mo. 1868. 2

MARSH, John Finch, of *Croydon*, was the Son of THOMAS and CATHARINE MARSH, and was born in the year 1789, at *Chatham*, in *Kent*.

—— A MEMOIR of JOHN FINCH MARSH, of Croydon, who died in the Autumn of 1873. By his daughter, [Priscilla Pitt.]
[*Manchester*: *Printed by William Irwin, 35, Fennell Street.*] *Obtainable of Hannah Marsh, 32, Park Lane, Croydon, S.; or G. & P. Pitt, Mitcham, Surrey.* 8vo. [1873.] 7

*MARSH, Josiah, of *Woodside*, nr. *Epping, Essex*.

—— A Popular Life of George Fox, the first of the Quakers, compiled from his Journal and other authentic sources; and interspersed with remarks upon the imperfect reformation of the Anglican Church, and consequent spread of dissent. By Josiah Marsh.
London: *Charles Gilpin, 5, Bishopsgate Without.*
8vo. 1847. 27

He died the 2nd of 5th Mo., 1873, aged 83 years; and his wife the 5th of 3rd Mo., 1877, aged 77 years.

MARSH, Thomas W., of *Dorking*, in *Surrey*.

—— 𝔖cripture 𝔗ime 𝔒ard. A Comparison of the Modern reckoning of time, with the HOURS OF THE DAY AND WATCHES OF THE NIGHT. *Price 1d.*
London: *W. Macintosh, 24, Paternoster Row.*
16mo. [1876.] 1/16

—— The same on coloured paper . . 12mo. [1876.] 1/12

—— Some Records of THE EARLY FRIENDS in SURREY AND SUSSEX, from the original Minute-Books and other sources.
Compiled and edited by Thos. W. Marsh.
Concluding chapter by Anne W. Marsh.
𝔚ith nine 𝔓lates.
London: *S. Harris & Co., 5, Bishopsgate Without.*
4to. 1886. 21

List of Plates.
I.—Fac-simile of Page from the earliest Horsham Minute Book (as frontispiece).
II.—Capel Meeting-house.
III.—Reigate Old Meeting-house.

MARSH, Thomas W., *continued.*
>   IV.—Ifield Meeting-house.
>   V.—Thakeham Meeting-house.
>   VI.—Interior of Thakeham Meeting-house.
>   VII.—Dorking Old Market-house.
>   VIII.—" Ye House of Thomas Wright in Capill" (supposed).
>   IX.—Bregsell's Farm-house.

*MARSHALL, Christopher, of *Philadelphia.*

—— Passages from "The Remembrancer" of Christopher Marshall, member of the Committee of observation and inspection of the Provincial Conference and of the committee of safety (1774-1776, during the American Revolution). Edited by William Duane, Jr., Member of the Pennsylvania Historical Society, Philadelphia. . . . . 12mo. 1839. 140 pp.

MARSHALL, Charles, a Druggist, *continued* from Catalogue, Vol. 2, p. 142.

—— A Plain and Candid RELATION of The Nature, Use, and Dose of several *Approved Medicines.* Published, to the intent that the afflicted with Sickness may have the benefit of them. By *Charles Marshall.* They are to be sold at his House, near the *Castlegate,* within the City of BRISTOL.
>   London, *Printed in the year* 1670. . . . 2
>>   NOTE.—At the end of this pamphlet, "*These Medicines are also to be sold at* John Furlies, *the younger, at* Colchester."

MARSHALL, Humphry, a Botanist and industrious Horticulturist, died about 1805. He published Arburtum Americanum, the American grove, or alphabetical catalogue of forest trees and shrubs.
>   *Philadelphia.* . . . 8vo. 1785 and 1786.

MARSHALL, Samuel, of Kendal. *Meteorologist.*

MARTEN, T., of *Lewes.*

—— T. MARTEN'S PROPOSALS for publishing by subscription, A New Edition of his Book, call'd Quakerism no Delusion, with considerable Additions.
>   4to. N.D. ¼

*MARTIN, Henry, of *Manchester, continued* from Catalogue, Vol. 2, p. 148.

—— ELECTORS of WORCESTER. (Signed "Lion.")
>   *T. Hayes, Britannia Printing Office,* 56, *Broad Street, Worcester.* . . . B. [1830.] 1

MARTIN, Isaac, of *Bridgetown, Rahway,* in *East New Jersey, North America,* was born in *New York,* in 1758.

—— A Journal of the Life, Travels, Labours and Religious Exercises of Isaac Martin, late of Rahway, in East Jersey, deceased.
Philadelphia : Printed by William P. Gibbons, Sixth and Cherry Streets. . 12mo. 1834. 6⅔

He died the 9th of the 8th Month, 1828, in the 71st year of his age, having been an approved Minister about 38 years.

MARTIN, Josiah, (Correction).

On perusing the following Sermon, I find that a "MR. MIDDLETON, of *Bristol,* was the Author of the pamphlet, attributed to JOSIAH MARTIN by MORRIS BIRKBECK, entitled : "An Enquiry into the Inward Call to the Holy Ministry, &c." See my Catalogue, Vol. 2, page 152.
The Nature and Reasonableness of the Inward Call and Outward Mission to the Holy Ministry consider'd.
A SERMON Preach'd before the Right Reverend Father in GOD, THOMAS, LORD BISHOP OF OXFORD, at the Ordination, held at *Christ Church,* on *Sunday, Dec. 22nd, 1745.* And before the UNIVERSITY of *Oxford,* at *St. Mary's,* on *Sunday, March 2nd,* 1745-6. By WILLIAM PARKER, B.D., Rector of *Little Ilford,* in *Essex,* Minister of *St. Catharine Cree, London,* and F.R.S. THE SECOND EDITION.
OXFORD : *Printed at the* THEATRE *for* JAMES FLETCHER, *in the Turl, and Sold by* R. BALDWIN, *in Paternoster Row, London. MDCCLIV.*

MASON, B., of *North America.*

—— The Doctrine of particular. . . . . 1830.

MASON, Susanna, of *North America.*

—— A Selection from the Letters. . . . . 1836.

MATHER, Joseph Benson, of Australia. A Minister.

—— Hymns.
Hobart Town, printed.

*MATHER, Ralph, *continued* from Catalogue, Vol. 2, p. 158.

—— Representation of the Case of the Cotton Spinners in Lancashire.
London. . . . . . 8vo. 1780.

*MATHER, Ralph, *continued.*

—— Rational Reflections on Tale-bearing and detraction. By Ralph Mather.

> *Reprinted (Anonymous.)*
> 12mo. Printed in the year 1797. ½
> NOTE.—I find that Ralph Mather was a Methodist after a Quaker, then a Swedenborgian. See White's Swedenborg, 2nd edition, p. 689.

*MATHER, William, of *Bedford,* *continued* from Catalogue, Vol. 2, p. 159.

—— A VERY USEFUL MANUAL, or the Young Man's Companion, CONTAINING Plain and easy directions for Spelling, Reading and Uniting English, with easy Rules, for their attaining to Writing and Arithmetick, and the Englishing of the Latin Bible without a Tutor; Likewise the Plotting and Measuring of Land, Globes, Steeples, Walls, Barrels, Timber, Stone, Boards, Glass, &c. The Exchange of Mony, Weights and Measures, Purchase of Annuities. Leases, &c., Together with some secrets of Navigation, Astronomy, Astrology, Dialling, Geometry, Law, Religion, Physick, Philosopher's Stone, ordering of Bees, Husbandry, &c. And several other considerable and necessary matters; Intended for the good of all, and for promoting love to one another. As by the Table annexed particularly appears. Collected by *William Mather.*

> London, *Printed by T. Snowden, and sold at the Bell in Exchange Alley, in Cornhil,* 1681.
> Small 12mo. 1861. 18 sheets.

MAULE, Joshua, of *Colerain, Ohio, North America.*

—— TRANSACTIONS AND CHANGES in the SOCIETY OF FRIENDS, and incidents in the Life and Experience of JOSHUA MAULE. With a sketch of the original Doctrine and Discipline of FRIENDS. Also a Brief Account of the TRAVELS AND WORK IN THE MINISTRY of HANNAH HALL, of Ohio.

> *Philadelphia: J. B. Lippincott Company.*
> 8vo. 1886. 24 or 384 pp.

*MATTHEWS, William, *continued* from Catalogue, Vol. 2, p. 164.

> *Extracted from Bath Chronicle, May 17th, 1810.*
> ADVERTISEMENT, beginning: "As Persons who have taken a warm interest in the establishment of

*MATTHEWS, William, *continued*.
the *Bath and Bath Forum Lancastrian Free-School*,
we use the liberty of noting the efforts of one of
its adversaries," &c.
Signed Wm. Matthews.
        Wm. Davis.
Bath, May 14th, 1810.
*Richard Cruttwell, Printer, St. James's Street,
Bath.* . . . . Single leaf 8vo. ⅛

McGIRR, W., of *North America*.
——Letters upon divers subjects. . . . . 1854.

MESSER, Joseph, of *Upper Holloway*, now of Ware. 1872.
——and others. Circular, soliciting subscriptions for a
new School-room at Westminster Meeting House for
a First-day School. . . . 8vo. [1862.] ⅛

MICKLE, Isaac, of *North America*.
——Reminiscences of Old Gloucester ; or incidents in the
History of the counties of Gloucester and Camden,
New Jersey, by Isaac Mickle.
Philadelphia. . . . . . 1845.

MILLER, Daniel, of Croydon.
——To the Owners and Drivers of Horses and other
Animals. [ANON.]
Clouter, Printer, Croydon. . 8vo. [1868.] ¼

MILLER, Ellen Clare, *of Edinburgh*.
——Eastern Sketches : Notes of Scenery, Schools, and
Tent Life in Syria and Palestine. By Ellen Clare
Miller.
Edinburgh : William Oliphant and Company.
                                         8vo. 1871. 1 3⁄8

*MILLER, William Allen, Professor of Chemistry at King's
College. Son of William Miller and Francis Bowyer
Miller (Vaux), once of London, but who afterwards
lived and died in Birmingham.
——The Importance of Chemistry to Science. An Intro-
ductory Address to the Medical Classes of King's
College. Delivered October 1st, 1845.
——Inaugural Lecture at King's College. Given October
6th, 1845.
——Practical Hints to the Medical Student. An Intro-
ductory Lecture at the Opening of the Medical
Session at King's College, London, October 1st, 1867.

*MILLER, William Allen, *continued.*

——The Bible and Science. An Address delivered at the Church Congress in Wolverhampton, 3rd October, 1867.

——Work on Chemistry.

MILLER, Frances Bowyer, formerly VAUX.

——Tales of Travel. . . . . . 12mo.

——The Twelfth Cake.

——Pleasures of Farm life.

 See also under VAUX.

MILNE, George A., of *Goldsmith Street, Dublin.*

——A Chronological Summary of Facts connected with 𝕿𝖍𝖊 𝕿𝖜𝖔 𝕰𝖕𝖎𝖘𝖙𝖑𝖊𝖘 *forwarded to Dublin Yearly Meeting of 1878 by the two Bodies, claiming to be* WESTERN YEARLY MEETING. With Minute of Dublin Y.M., 1883. . . . . 8vo. [1883.] 1

*MILLS, Thomas, kept a bookshop in Bristol. He was not originally a Quaker, but professing to be convinced of the truth of Quaker principles, he was admitted into membership in 1778. Eleven years later, he was publicly disowned. But he continued to use the garb and speech of a Quaker, and even to attend the Quaker Meetings to the last. His daughter, Selina, married Zachary Macaulay; and was the mother of the Essayist and Historian. These facts are matters of history, whatever inference may be drawn from them by the curious.—*Inquirer.*
 From "Friends' Review," Vol. IX., p. 743.

MITCHILL, Samuel L., of *New York.*

——An Elementary Introduction to the Knowledge of MINERALOGY, &c. By William Phillips, Member of the Geological Society. *With Notes and Additions on American Articles,* BY SAMUEL L. MITCHILL, Professor of Mineralogy, Botany and Zoology, in the University of New York; President of the Lyceum of Natural History, &c.

 𝕹𝖊𝖜 𝖄𝖔𝖗𝖐: *Printed and Published by Collins and Co., No. 189, Pearl Street.* 12mo. 1818. 12½

MOORE, Ann, of *Bucks County, Pennsylvania.*

——Journal. Being a Narrative of some parts of her Life, Travels and Religious Labours.
 In *Comly's Miscellany,* Vol. 4, p. 289.

MOORE, Charles, M.D., of *Philadelphia*.

——A Claim for the "Flitch of Bacon." In the Letter of Dr. Richd. Hill, p. 315. . . . 8vo. 1854.
> He died the 19th of 8th Month, 1801, in his 77th year, at his dwelling in Montgomery County, and his remains were interred at North Wales.

MOORE, Milcah Martha, was the daughter of Richard Hill, M.D., and was married to Charles Moore, M.D., 1767, as above. She died 8th Month, 24th, 1829. (See ANON. 1787, &c.)

——Miscellanies, moral and instructive, &c.
> Vol. I. 3rd edition.
> *Philadelphia* . . . 1829.

MORGAN, William, formerly a Clergyman.

——His Thesis on taking his degree as Doctor of Physic in Holland.
> See SARAH BOCKETT.

MORRALL, Michael Thomas, of *Newcastle*.

——History and Description of NEEDLE MAKING: Fifth Edition. By Michael T. Morrall, F.S.A., Newcastle; 7, High Street, Manchester; and Balmoral House, Matlock. (With a Portrait of Michael Thomas Morrall, F.S.A., Newcastle).
> *Manchester : Printed by H. Briddon, 55, Faulkner Street.* . . (1st pd. 1852). 16mo. 1866. 1¾
> Errata, 1 leaf.
> He died 30th of 10th Month, 1891, aged 73 years, and was interred in St. Giles Church (The Parish Church) Yard, Matlock Town.

MORRIS, Margaret, of *Burlington, New Jersey*.

——Private Journal kept during a portion of the Revolutionary War, for the amusement of a sister. By Margaret Morris, of Burlington, N.J.
> Only 50 copies Printed for private circulation (in Philadelphia) . . . . . 1836.

Reprinted in the "Letters of Doctor Richard Hill, &c." Edited by John Jay Smith. 8vo. Philadelphia, 1834.

——Portrait of Margaret Morris. In the "Letters of Dr. Richard Hill."

——The Private Diary of Margaret Morris, daughter of Doctor Richard Hill. In the "Letters of Dr. Richard Hill."

*MORTON, Samuel George, M.D., Ethnologist.

—— Crania Americana; or, a Comparative View of the Skulls of various Aboriginal Nations of North and South America; with an Essay on the Varieties of the Human Species. By Dr. S. G. Morton. With 78 beautiful Plates and Coloured Map.
Philadelphia :
Imperial Folio. 1849.

An edition. . . . . . . 1839 (?).

—— An Illustrated System of Human Anatomy, special, general, and microscopic. By Samuel G. Morton, M.D., with 391 engravings on wood.
Philadelphia :
8vo. 1849.

—— Crania Egyptiaca or Observations on Egyptian Ethnography, derived from Anatomy, History, and the Monuments. By Samuel G. Morton, M.D.
Philadelphia. . . . . . . 1844.

—— Types of Mankind; or Ethnological Researches, based upon the Ancient Monuments, Paintings, Sculptures, and Crania of Races, and upon their Natural, Geographical, Philological, and Biblical History. Illustrated by Specimens from the Inedited Papers of S. G. Morton, M.D., and by additional Contributions from Professor Agassiz, Dr. Usher, and Professor Patterson. By J. C. Nott and George R. Gliddon.
Reprinted, 2nd edition.
Philadelphia :
Royal 8vo. 1854. 738 pp.

—— Catalogue of the Skulls of man and the inferior animals in the collection of Samuel George Morton, M.D.
Reprinted, 3rd edition.
Philadelphia : 1849.

MOTT, James, and *continued* from Catalogue, Vol. 2, p. 188.
MOTT, Lucretia.

—— Three Months in Great Britain. By James Mott.
Philadelphia: J. Miller M'Kim, No. 31, North Fifth Street (Merrihew & Thompson, Printers, No. 7, Carter's Alley). . . 12mo. 1841. 3½

°₀° Contains an account of his visit (accompanied by his wife, Lucretia Mott) to Manchester Meeting; their visit to the "Evangelical Friends;" Isaac Crewdson in the

MOTT, James and Lucretia, *continued.*
    Gallery; the Causes which led to the Separation of the Beaconites; their attending the Anti-Slavery Convention; Two Friends [Josiah Forster and Jacob Post] waiting in a back room to see them; their taking tea at the "Crown and Anchor"; Josiah Forster's disclaiming fellowship with them received with a general burst of disapprobation, manifested by cries of "down, down; order, order: shame, shame," &c., &c.

——Life and Letters of James and Lucretia Mott. Edited by their Granddaughter, Anna Davis Hallowell. With Portraits.
    Boston : Houghton, Mifflin and Company, &c.
                          8vo. 1884.

MOTT, Robert.
——Account of his last sickness and death.
    In *Comly's Miscellany*, Vol. IV., p. 49.

MOTT, Abigail, daughter of Uriah and Mary Field, was born in the year 1766. Wife of Richard Mott.
——MEMOIR of PURCHASE MONTHLY MEETING concerning ABIGAIL MOTT.
    New York : James Egbert, Printer, 374, Pearl Street (Successor to M. Day's Press.)
                          8vo. 1852. 1¼
    She died the 8th of 8mo., 1851.

MOTT, Valentine, Dr., Surgeon, Author.

†MUCKLOW, William, *continued* from Catalogue, Vol. 2, p. 190.
——Liberty of Conscience Asserted against Imposition: Proposed in Several Sober Queries to those of the People called QUAKERS; who have assumed such an Authority, contrary to their Former *Testimonies*: As also unto those that have *Submitted* unto it before they found *Convictions* in themselves; for them to *weigh* and *consider* in the Ballance of True Judgment.—*William Mucklowe.*
      Broadside.—*London*, printed in the year 1673¾. 1

——A Bemoaning LETTER of an Ingenious *Quaker*, To a Friend of his. Wherein the GOVERNMENT of the QUAKERS Among Themselves, (As hath been Exercised by *George Fox*, and others of their Ring-Leaders) *is* brought to Light. Wherein their Tyrannical and Persecuting Practices are Detected and Redargued. Also a *Preface to the Reader*, giving an

†MUCKLOW, William, *continued.*
 account how the said Letter came to the hand of the Publisher. By G.I.
  LONDON, Printed for *A. Baldwin* in *Warwick Lane*, 1700 (Price Sticht 6d.)   8vo. 45 pages.

MULFORD, Isaac, Dr., Historian.

MURRAY, Lindley, *continued* from Catalogue, Vol. 2, p. 192.

——The Power of Religion on the Mind, in Retirement, Sickness, and at Death ; exemplified in the Testimonies and Experience of Men distinguished by their Greatness, Learning, or Virtue. [ANONYMOUS.]
 York : Printed by Lucas Lund, in Low Ousegate.
          12mo. 1787. 9

——An English Spelling-Book.
 41st Edition . . . . 18mo., *York*, 1832.

——KEY TO THE EXERCISES adapted to MURRAY'S English Grammar, calculated to enable private learners to become their own Instructors in Grammar and Composition. By the Author of the Exercises.
 Ninth Edition, improved.
 Dublin : Printed at the Hibernia Press Office, Temple-Lane, for John Cumming, and William Pickering & Son, Lower Ormond-Quay.
          12mo. 1820. 7

——INTRODUCTION TO THE ENGLISH READER : or, A Selection of pieces in Prose and Poetry ; calculated to improve the younger classes of Learners in reading ; and to imbue their minds with the love of Virtue. To which are added, Rules and Observations for assisting children to read with propriety. By LINDLEY MURRAY, Author of an English Grammar, etc.
 Derby : Printed by and for Henry Mozley & Sons.
          12mo. 1836. 8
 (Including a list of books of 4 pages at the end.)

——Abridgment of Murray's English Grammar. A new edition, with copious Parsing Questions.
 London : T. Fox, No. 1, Bear Street, Leicester Square, (J. Howitt, Printer, Clumber Street, Nottingham.) . . . 18mo., 1840. 3

——Key to the Exercises, &c.
 The 27th Edition.

MURRAY, Lindley, *continued.*
London : Printed for Longman, Brown, Green, & Longmans, Paternoster Row ; and Harvey & Darton, Gracechurch Street. . 12mo. 1847. 9½
—— ENGLISH GRAMMAR, adapted to the Different Classes of Learners ; with An Appendix, containing Rules and Observations, for assisting the more advanced Students to write with perspecuity and accuracy. By Lindley Murray. With corrections and additions.
London : William Tegg & Co., 85, Queen Street, Cheapside. 12mo. 1857. 13⅔

N.

NAISH, Francis C., Son of ARTHUR JOHN NAISH, of *Birmingham.*
——The TRIUMPH OF IRON. A Poem ; by Francis C. Naish.
London : Simpkin, Marshall, & Co.,
Birmingham : R. Davies.
Middlesborough : Burnett & Hood.
Glasgow : Porteous Brothers.
Price One Shilling. . . . 12mo. 1873. 1½

NAMELESS AND PSEUDONYMOUS.
——A Letter *to a Person of* Quality, in *Relation to the* Affirmation *of the* QUAKERS. (Signed N.N., Not a Friend).
Folio. *No Printer's Name or Place.* [*Circa* 17—]. ½
——Some brief Observations on Reason and Revelation, and their Use in Matters of Religion. In a Letter to a Friend ; Signed, " RATIONALIS."
Folio. No Printer's Name, Place, or Date. 1
——A PARALLEL between the EARLY CHURCH and the SALVATION ARMY. By a Member of the Society of Friends 8vo. 1886. 1

NAPPER, Robert Peter, of *Newport*, in *Monmouthshire.*
——Views in Wales. By R. P. Napper. (13 Views with letterpress descriptions).
Photographed by the British and Foreign Portrait Company. (By R. P. Napper.) Large 4to. (No Date).
He died the 31st of 10th Mo., 1867, aged 48 years.

NEIGHBOUR, Alfred, *continued* from Catalogue, Vol. 2, p. 235.
——The Apiary ; or Bees, Bee-Hives, and Bee-Culture, &c.
    3rd edition, enlarged, 8vo. 1878.
  He died at West Hampstead the 19th of 12th month, 1890, aged 65 years, and was buried in Friends' Burial Ground, Isleworth.

NEWBY, John, of *Ackworth*.
——On the Means of Intellectual Improvement open to young persons in the Society of Friends, after leaving School. Presented to the Friends' Educational Society, 1856, by John Newby.
  York : William Simpson, 15, Low Ousegate.
          8vo. 1856.   2
——Priscilla Quertier, of *Guernsey*, Aged 13½ years. (A Memoir). From the *French*.
  Bradford, printed.   12mo. 1872. 2½
  He was the Editor of The Annual Monitor, from 1868 to 1877 inclusive.
  He died the 16th of 6th month, 1877, aged 72 years. See an interesting account of him in *The Annual Monitor for 1878*.

†NEWMAN, Edward, of *Peckham*.
——Circular to raise funds for the assistance of Henry Doubleday, of Epping. . . 8vo.   ¼

NEWMAN, Henry Stanley, of *Leominster*.
——ORPHAN HOME, Leominster, *for destitute children, lawfully begotten, who have lost both parents by death*.
          4to. [1869.]   ¼
——God with us. By Henry Stanley Newman, Leominster.
  London : F. Bowyer Kitto, 5, Bishopsgate, E.C. ; Tract Depôt, Broad Street, Leominster.
  Reprinted. . . . . Small 8vo. [1872.]   3
——Days of Grace in India ; a Record of Visits to Indian Missions. By H. S. Newman. With Language, Map, and Illustrations.
  London : S. W. Partridge & Co., 9, Paternoster Row, E.C. ; Leominster: The Orphans' Printing Press, 10 and 12, Broad Street.
         8vo. [1882.] 21 Sheets.
——The Young Man of God.—Memories of Stanley Pumphrey. By Henry Stanley Newman. (With Portrait).

NEWMAN, Henry Stanley, *continued*.
    Reprinted—[Second Edition.] . 8vo. [1882.] 1 9
    London : S. W. Partridge & Co., 9, Paternoster
    Row; Leominster: Orphans' Printing Press.
                                  Crown 8vo. 1883. 17
—— Journal of the East India Association.—A Paper read by Henry S. Newman. 8vo. 1886
—— The AUTOBIOGRAPHY of GEORGE FOX, from his Journal. Edited by HENRY STANLEY NEWMAN.
    London : S. W. Partridge & Co., 9, Paternoster
    Row, E.C.; Leominster: The Orphans' Print-
    ing Press, 10 and 12, Broad Street. 4to. [1886.]
    Preface and Contents. xxxii. Text, 422 pp.
—— Palestine Lessons to my Class, through the Land of Promise in the Pathway of our Lord. 8vo. [1888.]
—— Christian Solidarity. . . . . 8vo. [1888.] 9½
—— What I saw in India. With Coloured Map of India, and 113 Illustrations of Native Manners, Customs and Scenery. . . . Foolscap 4to. 180 pages
—— The Story of the Orphan Homes.
    Red Line Edition. . . . Foolscap 4to. 172 pp.
—— The Story of the Orphan Homes, Leominster. By H. S. Newman. (Illustrated.)
    Leominster: The Orphans' Printing Press, 10
    and 12, Broad Street. . Demy 16mo. 124 pp.
—— THE FRIENDS.
    " I have called you Friends." JOHN xv. 13, 14. 15.
    Leominster: The Orphans' Printing Press.
                                16mo. No date. ½
—— A Narrative of the Ancient Monastery of Leominster.
—— Herefordshire Friends of the Olden Times. 2d.
NICHOLITES.
—— Some account of the Religious People called "Nicholites."
    In Comly's Miscellany, Vol. 4, p. 241.
NODAL, John H., of near *Manchester*.
—— The Bibliography of Ackworth School.
    Manchester: Printed. . . 8vo. 1889.
NORRIS, Isaac, of *Pennsylvania*.
—— Friendly Advice to the Inhabitants of Pennsylvania.
    Philadelphia : Jacob Taylor. . . 1710 ?
    Reprinted,—*Philadelphia : Andrew Bradford.*
                                  Folio. 1728.

NORRIS, Isaac, *continued.*
——A Modest Reply to the Speech of Isaac Norris, Esq., etc.
  Philadelphia : Andrew Bradford.
          Folio. 1727. pp. 4.
——A Confutation of the Reply to the Speech, &c.
  Philadelphia : Andrew Bradford.
          Folio. 1727. pp. 4.
——The Speech Delivered from the Bench in the Court of Common Pleas held for the City and County of Philadelphia, the 11th day of September, 1727.
  Philadelphia : Andrew Bradford.
          Folio. 1727. pp. 3(1)
  He died in 1735, being at that time Chief Justice of Pennsylvania. Bowden's History of Friends in America, Vol. 2, p. 273.

O.

OCKANICKON, A North American Indian King, who died in *Burlington, New Jersey*, and was buried in Friends' Burial Ground.
——A True ACCOUNT of the Dying Words of Ockanickon, an 𝔍𝔫𝔡𝔦𝔞𝔫 𝔎𝔦𝔫𝔤, &c.—(See John Cripps).
      London, printed, 4to. 1682. 1
OGDEN, J. Melchoir.
——In Memoriam.
OLIVER, Daniel, of *Newcastle-upon-Tyne.*
——A Little Memoir written by himself. Mentioned in Geo. Richardson's life, p. 318.
OPIE, Amelia.—*Continued* from Catalogue, Vol. 2, p. 243.
——The Negro Boy's Tale. By Mrs. Opie.
  Printed by Richard Peart, 38, Bull Street, Birmingham. . . . Large 4to. No date. ¼
———The Father and Daughter, 𝔄 𝔗𝔞𝔩𝔢 𝔦𝔫 𝔓𝔯𝔬𝔰𝔢. By Mrs. Opie. With a Frontispiece.
  "Thy sweet reviving smiles might cheer despair,
  On the pale lips detain the parting breath,
  And bid hope blossom in the shades of death."
          Mrs. BARBAULD.
  Fourth Edition.
  London : Printed for T. N. Longman and O. Rees, Paternoster Row, by R. Taylor & Co., Black Horse Court. . . . 8vo. 1804. 15

OPIE, Amelia, *continued.*
——EXTRACTS from 𝔐emoranda on 𝔙arious 𝔒ccasions, taken from the Memoir of the late CHARLES SIMEON, M.A., *Minister of Trinity Church, Cambridge.*
   Printed by Josiah Fletcher, Haymarket, Norwich.
                           (4 pages). 12mo. No date. $\frac{1}{6}$

——The Poor Man's Dog. By Mrs. Opie. In "Affection's Offering," &c., page 105.
   London : Charles Tilt, 86, Fleet Street.
                                    18mo. 1831.

——"The Poor Hindoo," and "An Evening Walk at Cromer, 1795."
    NOTE.—The above are inserted in a volume privately printed at Norwich, entitled " British Melodies," &c.

OPIE, John, the Painter, and husband of Amelia Opie. (Not a Friend).
——OPIE AND HIS WORKS : being a *Catalogue of 760 Pictures,* by JOHN OPIE, R.A. Preceded by *A Biographical Sketch.* By JOHN JOPE ROGERS, M.A., *Sometime Hon. Sec. and Treas. of the Arundel Society.*
    Si quid novisti rectius istis,
    Candidus imperti ; si non, his utere mecum.
                                  Horace.
   London : Paul and Dominic Colnaghi, & Co., 13 and 14, Pall Mall, East.
   Truro : Netherton & Worth. . . 8vo. 1878.
    He was born at St. Agnes, near Truro, in Cornwall, in the Month of May, 1761 ; and died in London on the 9th of April, 1807, at the age of 46 ; and his funeral took place at St. Paul's Cathedral.

OSBORN, Charles, *Continued* from Catalogue, Vol. 2, p. 248.
——A Testimony, concerning the Separation which occurred in Indiana Yearly Meeting of Friends, in the Winter of 1842 and 1843 ; together with sundry remarks and observations.
   Centreville : R. Vaile, Printer. . 12mo. 1849. $2\frac{1}{4}$

OTIS, Job, of *Sherwoods, New York.*
——Journal of Job Otis.
——" Israel to Dwell alone," from above, p. 150-153.
   J. E. Southall, Dock Street, Newport, Mon.
                                  8vo. No date. $\frac{1}{8}$

OVEREND, John, M.D., late of *Doncaster*, *continued* from Catalogue, Vol. 2, p. 249.
  Derby.—July 21, 1832. Death.
> "At Bolsover Hill, aged 30 John Overend, M.D., eldest son of the late Hall Overend, Esq., of Sheffield, Surgeon, and nephew to the late John Overend, Esq., of Lombard-street."
>
> *Gent's Mag.*, *1832*. *Vol. 102*. *Part 2*. *Page 187*.

P.

P., R.
——An Essay concerning the Resurrection of the Same Body, &c. 8vo. 1735. 1½

PANCOAST, Joseph, of *North America*.
——Operative Surgery; comprising a Description of the Various Processes of the Art, including all the New Operations; exhibiting the State of Surgical Science in its present advanced condition. With 80 plates, containing 486 separate illustrations. By Joseph Pancoast, M.D.
  Reprinted, 2nd Edition.
    „   3rd Edition, revised and enlarged.
  Philadelphia . . . . 4to. 1852.

PARKER, Alexander, *continued* from Catalogue, Vol. 2, p. 257.
——" To all that say we (whom the world do in scorn call Quakers) do deny Ministers and Magistrates, &c." (at the end of Edward Burrough's " Declaration to all the World of our Faith, &c." See Edward Burrough and George Whitehead. . . . . 4to. 1659.
——and Geo. Whitehead. A Few Seasonable Wordes, &c.
                                    B. 1665. 1

PARKINSON, Sydney, *continued* from Catalogue, Vol. 2, p. 260.
——A JOURNAL of a VOYAGE to the SOUTH SEAS, in his Majesty's Ship, The Endeavour. Faithfully transcribed from the Papers of the late SYDNEY PARKINSON, Draughtsman to JOSEPH BANKS, Esq., on his late Expedition, with DR. SOLANDER, round the World. Embellished with Views and Designs, delineated by the Author, and engraved by Capital

PARKINSON, Sydney, *continued*.
>Artists. (With Portrait of Sydney Parkinson and 27 plates.)
>>LONDON: *Printed for* STANFIELD PARKINSON, *the Editor: And Sold by* MESSRS. RICHARDSON & URQUHART, *at the Royal Exchange;* EVANS, *in Paternoster Row;* HOOPER, *on Ludgate Hill;* MURRAY, *in Fleet Street;* LEACROFT, *at Charing Cross; and* RILEY, *in Curzon Street, May-Fair.*
>>>Large 4to. 1773. 29¾

PARLIAMENT.
>—— REPORT from Select Committee on Quakers' Affirmation. *Ordered, by* The House of Commons, *to be Printed, 11th February,* 1833. . Folio. 1833. 4
>>NOTE.—Contains the Case of John Archdale's, with his Letter, dated, London, the 3rd of the month called January, 1698-9. Begins, "Sir, Upon the Call of the House, &c."

>—— 3 WILL. IV.—Sess. 1833.—A BILL [as amended by the Committee] To allow Quakers and Moravians to make Affirmation in all Cases where an Oath is at present required.—*Ordered, by* The House of Commons, *to be Printed,* 22nd May, 1833. 312.
>>Folio. 1833. 1

PARRISH, Edward, of *Philadelphia, Pennsylvania.*
>—— Practical Pharmacy, an Introduction to ; designed as a Text-book for the Student, as a guide to the Physician and Pharmaceutist, with many Formulas and Prescriptions. By Edward Parrish. With 243 Illustrations.
>>*Philadelphia:* 8vo. 1856.

PARRISH, Isaac, of *Philadelphia, Pennsylvania.*
>—— Memoir of Thomas Shipley and Edwin T. Atlee.
>>*Philadelphia: Printed* 1837.

*PARRISH, Joseph, of *Philadelphia, Pennsylvania.*
>—— A Letter from a Young Woman to a Member of the Religious Society of Friends. With his Reply. [ANON.]
>>*Philadelphia:* 1828.
>>*Philadelphia:* 24mo. 1840. ½
>>Reprinted (with his name). 5th Edition. *Philadelphia: T. E. Chapman, No. 5, South Fifth Street.* . . . . . 24mo. 1862. ½

PARRISH, Samuel, of *Philadelphia, Pennsylvania.*
——Sketches of Friends. Historical, Biographical, and Anecdotal.
    In the " Friends' Intelligencer," commencing 12th month, 18th, 1869, No. 42, Vol. xxvi., and ending

PARSONS, Samuel B., of *New York.*
——The Rose; its History, Poetry, Culture, and Classification. By S. B. Parsons. With 2 large coloured plates and other engravings.
    New York: Royal 8vo.

PASCHALL, Ann S., of *Philadelphia.* (" Hicksite ").
——The Home Circle.
    Philadelphia : Friends' Book Association, 706, Arch Street. . . . . . 1876 ?
    Suitable for First-day Schools and Libraries.

PASKELL, Thomas, of *Pennsylvania, North America.*
——An Abstract of a LETTER from Thomas Paskell, of PENNSILVANIA, To his Friend, J. J., of Chippenham.
    London : Printed at the sign of the Book in Gracechurch Street. . Folio Broadside. 1683.   1

PASTORIUS, Francis Daniel, of *Germantown*, had been previously engaged by Friends to keep their School in the City (Phila.) and to do the writing of the Society. [Reiner Jansen, being Printer].
——New Primmer, with Dedication, &c., to W. Penn.
    NOTE.—The minutes of the Philadelphia Monthly Meeting show the purchase of a large number for use in the Friends' Schools.

PAXSON, Jacob, of *Abington, Montgomery* County, Pennsylvania.
——Testimony concerning him. In Comly's Miscellany, Vol. 4.
    He died the 13th of the 7th month, 1832, aged nearly 87 years.

PEACOCK, Thomas Bevill, M.D., of *London.*
——On the Influenza, or Epidemic Catarrhal Fever of 1847-8. By Thomas Bevill Peacock, M.D., Licentiate of the Royal College of Physicians, Physician to the Royal Free Hospital, and to the City of London Hospital for Diseases of the Chest.
    London : John Churchill, Princes Street, Soho. (Richard Barrett, Printer, 18, Mark Lane).
                                         8vo.   1848.   12

PEACOCK, Thomas Bevill, *continued*.
——On the Weight and Dimensions of the Heart, in health and disease. By Thomas B. Peacock, M.D., F.R.C.P., Physician to St. Thomas's Hospital, and to the Hospital for Diseases of the Chest, Victoria Park.
    Reprinted from the Monthly Journal of Medical Science. [*Richard Barrett, Printer, Mark Lane, London.*] . . . . 8vo. 1854.
        He died the 30th of 5th Mo., 1882, aged 69 years.

PEARSON, Agatha, of *Birmingham*.
——Scriptural Association with the Women's Queries. [ANON.] . . . . 48mo. 1850. 16 pages.
        She died the 14th of 5th month, 1838, aged 47 years.

PEASE family, or Backhouse?
——Select Family Memoirs. Compiled by *James Backhouse*.
    Printed at York, 1831.

PEASE, Gurney, of *Darlington*.
——Pedigree of Pease, of Darlington.
    Privately printed for the late Gurney Pease, of Darlington.

PEASE, Joseph, of *Darlington, continued* from Catalogue, Vol. 2, p. 278.
——A 𝕮𝖗𝖆𝖛𝖊𝖑𝖑𝖎𝖓𝖌 𝕸𝖆𝖕 OF GREAT BRITAIN and IRELAND. *Containing all the direct and principal cross Roads, Mail Coach Routes and Stages where Post horses may be procured, with their distances accurately marked.* By *Joseph Pease, Jun., of Darlington.*
    The Publisher of this Map trusts that it will be found particularly serviceable to the Society of Friends, as he has taken great care to distinguish all the places where they have meetings.
    Published by William Phillips, George Yard, Lombard Street, London. . Large size. 1824.
        NOTE.—The imprint is on the case.

——And John Hodgkin and others.— Circular or letter on the right distribution of a pamphlet, on "*The Christian Ministry, &c.*" . . . 8vo. [1867.] ⅛

PEASE, Louisa, daughter of FREDERICK ASHBY, of *Staines*, and Wife of —— PEASE.
——SELECTIONS from Private MEMORANDA AND LETTERS of LOUISA PEASE, who died August 12, 1861. (Aged 28 years.)
    London: Printed by Richard Barrett, 13, Mark Lane. 8vo. 1862. 4¾

PEASE, Martha Lucy, daughter of Henry and Mary Aggs, was born at Upton House, Essex, 15/5 mo., 1824.

——A Memoir of Martha Lucy Pease. [Wife of Thos. Pease, Bristol.]
"Those that seek me early, shall find me." Proverbs viii. 17.
Printed for Private Circulation, 4to.   .   1859. 8¼

She died the 8th of 11th month, 1853, aged 29 years.

PEASE, S. E.

——Hints on Nursing the Sick and other Domestic Subjects. Compiled by S. E. Pease. Intended for the Use of Girls' Schools.
London : S. W. Partridge & Co., 9, Paternoster Row. Price Fourpence. [*John Bellows, Steam Press, Gloucester.*] . . . 8vo. [1871.] 3

3rd Edition, revised.   .   12mo. 1875. 2

[PENN, Wm.] *continued* from Catalogue, Vol. 2, p. 282.

——The Excellent Priviledge of Liberty & Property Being the Birth-Right of the Free-born Subjects of England. Containing I. Magna-Charta, with a learned Comment upon it. II. The Confirmation of the Charters of the Liberties of England and of the Forrest, made in the 35th year of Edward the First. III. A Statute made the 34 Edw. I., Commonly called De Tallagoe non Concedendo ; wherein all Fundamental Laws, Liberties and Customs are confirmed. With a Comment upon it. IV. An Abstract of the Pattent granted by the King to William Penn and his Heirs and Assigns for the Province of Pennsilvania. V., And Lastly. The Charter of Liberties granted by the said William Penn to the Free-men and Inhabitants of the Province of Pennsilvania and Territories thereunto annexed in America. Major Hereditas venit unicunq; nostrum a Jure & Legibus, quam a Parentibus.

[*Philadelphia : William Bradford. 1687.*]
16mo. (8) 63pp.

——By the Proprietary of the Province of Pensilvania, and Counties annexed With the Advice of the Council : A Proclamation.

Philadelphia : *Printed by Reiner Jansen. 1699.*
Folio. 1 leaf.
This is a Proclamation against Pirates.

PENN, Wm., *continued.*
——The Case of W. P., Esq.
        s. sh. folio. [*London*, 1680.]
———The Case of W. P.
        s. sh. folio. [*London*, 1720.]
——Trial of Penn and Mead.
        8vo. *Sheffield*, 1794.
——Sandy Foundation. . . . . . 1825.
     Philadelphia Edition, 1855.
——No Cross, No Crown, &c.
 9th Edition, *Dublin*.   8vo. 1749.
 American Editions.   . 1796.
    ,,   . 1797.
    ,,   . 1879.
 German, *London*. . 12mo. 1847.
——A Letter from William Penn.
        folio. 1683.
 Reprinted, fac-simile, by *Coleman*.
——Mr. Penn's Advice in the Choice of Parliament Men.
    s. sh. folio. [*London*.] 1688.
——Some Fruits of Solitude, &c.
    8th Edition, *London*. 1785.
    and 16mo. 1790.
——Fruits of Solitude.
 London. [Birmingham printed.] . 4to. 1863.
——Tender Counsel and Advice, &c.
 The Fifth Edition.
  PHILADELPHIA : Printed by ENOCH STORY, in
   Strawberry Alley. . . . 12mo. 1783.
 The Fifth Edition.
  *Dublin : Printed by Robert Jackson, No. 20, Meath
   Street.* 8vo. 1791. 1½
——Life of Wm. Penn.—See HEPWORTH DIXON.
—— ,, ,, —See SAMUEL M. JANNEY.
—— ,, ,, —See JOHN STOUGHTON.

PENINGTON, Isaac, *continued* from Catalogue, Vol. 2,
 p. 335.
——A Brief Account concerning the People called QUAKERS,
 in reference to Principle, Doctrine, and Practice ; as
 held and maintained by them unitedly at their
 origin. *Written about the year 1676, by* ISAAC
 PENINGTON, *a Minister amongst them.*
  𝔑𝔬𝔱𝔱𝔦𝔫𝔤𝔥𝔞𝔪 : *Printed by G. Butters, Chapel Bar.*
        8vo. 1854. ¾
  NOTE.—On the last page of the cover are some " Remarks."

PENINGTON, Isaac, *continued.*

—— On the Pure, Constant, eternal, unchangeable Nature of God's Truth. . . 4to. Nottingham. 1854.

*PENNYMAN, John, *continued* from Catalogue, Vol. 2, p. 365.

—— A Collection of the Several Books and Writings of Geo. Fox, the Younger [Edited by J. P[ennyman ?] See GEO. FOX THE YOUNGER.

—— Begins,—" Oh People ! my Bowels yearn, my Bowels yearn towards you, whose desires in any measure are after the Lord, &c."

> *These words were formerly conveyed through* G.F. *the younger, only the words, viz.,* I SAY, *with the words adjoyning (in Capital letters, within several Parentheses) I have added who am required thus to publish them, this 22nd day of the Month called July, in the year accounted* 1670. JOHN PENNYMAN.

4to. No Printer's name or place. [1670.]

This extract I give here, as it is evidently connected with John Pennyman.

MR. J. W. PENNYMAN.

James White Pennyman, Esq., of Ormesby Hall, in the County of York, J.P., died, at his seat in Cleveland, on the 1st instant. He was born Nov. 5, 1792, the eldest son of Colonel James Worsley, by Lydia, his Wife, sister of Sir Thomas Wollaston White, Bart., and grandson of the Rev. James Worsley, of Stonegrave, by Dorothy, his Wife, daughter of Sir James Pennyman, Bart., of Ormesby. At the death of his Cousin, Sir William Henry Pennyman, Bart., in 1852, he succeeded to the Ormesby estates, and assumed the surname and arms of Pennyman. He married, March 24th, 1828, Frances, daughter of the Rev. James Stovin, D.D., and leaves a Son, James Stovin Pennyman, Esq., now of Ormesby Hall, and a daughter, Frances Maria, married to Captain Forbes Mac Bean. The Pennymans are an Ancient Yorkshire family, of Saxon extraction, and were raised to the degree of Baronet shortly after the Restoration. Through the marriage of his great grandfather, Thomas Worsley, Esq., of Hovingham, with Mary Frankland, of Thirkelby, Mr. Pennyman was sixth in direct descent from the Lord Protector Cromwell.

From, " *The Illustrated London News*, Feb. 12th, 1870."

John Pennyman was buried in the Dissenters' burial ground, Bunhill Fields, and the following inscription is on his Grave-stone :—

*PENNYMAN, John, *continued*.

" Here
Lyeth the Body of
JOHN PENNYMAN, who
was required (by *Abraham's* God)
to offer up (as *Abraham* did)
An unusual Sacrifice at the *Royal
Exchange* in *London*, upon the 28th
Day of *July*, 1670. (An Account
of which he then caused to be
Printed, and hath ordered it to
be Reprinted in the Book of his
Life). And for a perpetual Memorial of which, he order'd
this Inscription to be set in
this Place. He departed this
Life the 2nd Day of *July*, 1706,
in the 78th Year of his Age."

NOTE.—This Inscription is printed in a scarce pamphlet, entitled, " Inscriptions upon the Tombs," and is in the Dissenters' Burial-place, near Bunhill Fields. *London:* E. *Curll.* 1717.

PERIODICAL PUBLICATIONS, *continued* from Catalogue, Vol. 2, p. 372.

——The St. James's EVENING POST. Numb. 185. From Thursday, August 2, to Saturday, August 4, 1716.

Contains An Advertisement, Sign'd Thomas Johnson, John Whiting, and John Halsey. Occasioned by the Spectator, No. 5, July 11th, 1716.

——The BEREAN. A Religious Publication.

" *These were more noble than those of Thessalonica, in that they received the* WORD *with all readiness of mind, and searched the Scriptures daily, whether those things were so.*" " *Prove all things; hold fast that which is good.*"— ACTS xvii. 11 ; I. THES. v. 21.

February, 1824, to April, 1825.
VOL. I.
WILMINGTON, DEL.

Printed by Mendenhall & Walters, No. 81, Market Street. . . . . . 8vo. 1825. 408 pp.

NOTE.—This periodical was published every other Tuesday, and this volume contains No. 1 to 26. It was suspended for about a month, for "On the night of the 30th May (1824) our whole (says the editors) printing establishment was destroyed by fire, the origin of which remains unknown to us. Every article was consumed, even to our books, and subscription list, together with the over copies of ' The Berean.'"

PERIODICAL PUBLICATIONS, *continued.*

    List of some of the Contents of Vol. I.
Biographical Sketch of Calvin and Servetus.
Letter of Queen Caroline to her daughter, Princess Charlotte, about that interesting People vulgarly called Quakers.
Biog. of Cotton Mather.
,,   Benjm. Franklin.
,,   George Keith.
,,   Charles Leslie.
,,   James Naylor.
,,   Wm. Penn.
Letter of John Locke.
Sermons of E. Hicks.
Cruelty to Slaves, &c., &c.

——THE BEREAN, *continued,* April, 1825, to June, 1826. (26 Nos.)
Vol. II.
WILMINGTON, DEL.
Printed by S. E. Merrihew, No. 103, Shipley Street.
8vo.   1826.   408 pages.

    Contents.
Bates's Doctrines.
Review of W. C. Brownlee.
On "Creeds."
Memoir of Wm. Dell.
Epis. of Geo. Fox.
Elizth. Fry.
Account of George Mason.
Quakerism in England.
Notes of Saml. Spavold's testimony.
    By Anthony Benezet, &c., &c.

THE BEREAN, July, 1826, to July, 1827. (26 Nos.)
Vol. III.
1827.
Luther Rice, famous "Baptist Beggar."
Quakerism and Episcopacy amalgamating in England.
Biog. of Martin Luther.
Inconsistency of Martin Luther.
And numerous interesting articles relating to Friends and others, &c., &c.

——THE HANGMAN. (Published every Wednesday morning, for Thirteen weeks.)
    CHARLES SPEAR, Corresponding Editor.
    BELA MARSH, Agent, 25, Cornhill.
    REDDING & Co., General Agents, State Street.
    Terms.—25 cents for the whole Thirteen Numbers. Single Numbers, 2 cents.

    Vol. 1.   BOSTON, WEDNESDAY, JANUARY 22, 1845. . . . . Number 4.

PERIODICAL PUBLICATIONS, *continued*.

NOTE.—Contents. (Some are). Active Benevolence.
                                              Elizabeth Fry.
  Poetry. The Human Sacrifice.
              By John G. Whittier. &c., &c.
                         Large folio. 1845. ½
  This is the only number I have met with.—J.S.

——THE WESTERN FRIEND, devoted to Religion, Morality,
  Literature, General News, and the Markets.
  Number 1.—Cincinatti, Eleventh Month 11, 1847.
  Vol. 1. . . . . . . 26 Nos.
  Vol. 2. . . 26 Nos., ending 12 mo. 7, 1848.

——𝕋𝕙𝕖 ℙ𝕒𝕣𝕥𝕙𝕖𝕟𝕠𝕟. A Monthly Magazine.
  Price 6d. , . No. 12. 9 Mo. (September) 1848.
  Edited by R. Dymond, Jun., G. Scholefield, and
  F. W. Dymond.
  Exeter : Printed by W. Roberts, 197, High Street.
                                 8vo. 1848.
  London : B. Farrand, 68, St. John Street, Smith-
  field. . No. 13. 10 Mo. (October), 1848.

——The Annual Monitor for 1868, (New Series, No. 26)
  or Obituary of the Members of the Society of Friends
  in 𝔊𝔯𝔢𝔞𝔱 𝔅𝔯𝔦𝔱𝔞𝔦𝔫 𝔞𝔫𝔡 𝔍𝔯𝔢𝔩𝔞𝔫𝔡 for the year 1867.
  [Edited by John Newby, of Ackworth.]
  London : Sold by F. B. Kitto and E. Marsh :
    William Sessions and George Hope, York :
    John Gough, Eustace Street, Dublin.
                                18mo. 1867. 7
                  Contents.
  Preface, 1 page.
  Obituary, 1 to 247.
  Table showing the Deaths during the years 1864-65, 1865-66,
    and 1866-67.

——The Annual Monitor for 1869 to 1892. New Series.

Pennsylvania Hospital.
——Report of the Board of Managers of the Pennsylvania
  Hospital to the Contributors at their Annual Meeting,
  held Fifth Month 6th, 1867. Together with the
  Accounts of the Treasurer and Stewards. (Frontis-
  piece.)
  Philadelphia : Collins, Printer.   8vo. 1867. 3

——Report, &c. . .   8vo. 1868.
——Report, &c. . . . . .   8vo. 1869.

PERIODICAL PUBLICATIONS, *continued.*
——Report, &c. Held Fifth Month 2nd, 1870. (Frontispiece.)
  Philadelphia: Collins, Printer, &c. . 8vo. 1870. 2¼
——Ditto, to 1892.
——An Account of the Times and Places for holding the Meetings for Worship and Discipline of the Society of Friends in Great Britain and Ireland, for the year 1868. Published by direction of the Yearly Meeting.
  London: Edward Marsh, 12, Bishopsgate Street Without. 18mo. 1868. 3⅓
——Ditto, 1869 to 1892.
——𝔗𝔥𝔢 𝔐𝔬𝔫𝔱𝔥𝔩𝔶 𝔑𝔢𝔠𝔬𝔯𝔡. A Journal of Home and Foreign Missions, First-Day Schools, Temperance and other Christian Work in the Society of Friends. No. 1. Vol. 1.
  Birmingham printed. . . . . 1869.
——The Manchester Friend, Vols. 1 and 2. 1872, 1873.
——The FRIENDS' ALMANACK for 1874, The 37th Year of the Reign of Queen Victoria; containing information useful to Members of the 𝔖𝔬𝔠𝔦𝔢𝔱𝔶 𝔬𝔣 𝔉𝔯𝔦𝔢𝔫𝔡𝔰, and others connected with it, also A Text for every Day in the Year.
  𝔏𝔬𝔫𝔡𝔬𝔫: *Published by G. H. Farrington, 11, Knight Rider Street, Doctors' Commons, E.C. And to be had of all Booksellers.*
    32mo. [1874.] 2
——Natural History Journal.
  James Edmund Clark, B.A., B.Sc., 20, Bootham, York.
  Price 3s. yearly, (9 issues yearly).
——Herald of Peace. A Semi-Monthly, devoted to the Cause of Peace and general religious improvement.
  Edited by W. E. Hathaway and Willet Dorland, Chicago, Illinois, printed.

PERRY, Stephen, of *Needham-Market, Suffolk.*
——A Dialogue on the Corn Laws between a Gentleman and a Farmer, on board of the Orwell Steamer.
  Printed by Stephen Piper. . . . . 8vo.
   NOTE.—Afterwards adopted and largely circulated by the Anti-Corn Law Leagues.
   See also "ANONYMOUS."
   He died at Needham Market the 3rd of 4th Month, 1871, aged 75 years.

PETTITT, Wyatt J., of *Dover*. See Bibliography of Bees.

PHILLIPS, James, of *London*, Bookseller and Printer.

——Letter, dated London, 1st of 3rd Month, 1785, " On the slowness of the sale of Friends' Books," &c.
Folio. [1785.] ½

[PHILLIPS, John], of *Philadelphia*.

——A Paraphrastical Exposition on a Letter from a Gentleman in Philadelphia to his friend in Boston, concerning a certain Person who compared himself to Mordecai.
[Philadelphia : William Bradford.]
Small 4to. [1693.] 8 pp.

PHILLIPS, John, of *Cockermouth*.

——A Hand of Love stretched forth for the help of those who have mournfully fallen into the Pit of darkness, where the saving Light by Man is not enjoyed. Or a Dissuader from Drunkenness. (In verse.)
Cockermouth : Printed at the office of W. H. Moss, Bookseller. . . . . 8vo. No date. ¼

PHILLIPS, Richard, continued from Catalogue, Vol. 2, p. 409.

——An Experimental Examination of the Last edition of the 𝔓𝔥𝔞𝔯𝔪𝔞𝔠𝔬𝔭𝔬𝔢𝔦𝔞 𝔏𝔬𝔫𝔡𝔦𝔫𝔢𝔫𝔰𝔦𝔰; with remarks on Dr. Powell's Translation and Annotations. By Richard Phillips.
LONDON: *Sold by William Phillips, George-yard, and T. Underwood, 40, West Smithfield.*
8vo. 1811. 10½

PHILLIPS, William, continued from Catalogue, Vol. 2, p. 409.

——An Elementary Introduction to the Knowledge of MINERALOGY;—*With Notes and Additions on American Articles*, BY SAMUEL L. MITCHILL, Professor of Mineralogy, Botany, and Zoology in the University of New York; President of the Lyceum of Natural History, &c.
𝔑𝔢𝔴 𝔜𝔬𝔯𝔨 : *Printed and Published by Collins & Co., No. 189, Pearl-street.* . 12mo. 1818. 12½

——Outline of Geology.
New York : 12mo. 1818 ?

PICKARD, Isaac, of *Harrogate*, in *Yorkshire*.

——Joy in Suffering, and Heavenly Visions of Christopher Hindle, who died at the early age of 14½ years.
Leeds : Printed by Edward Baines & Sons.
18mo. 1869. ⅓

PILKINGTON, George, *continued* from Catalogue, Vol. 2, p. 423.
——An Address to the ENGLISH RESIDENTS in the Brazilian Empire by George Pilkington.
"Who slew all these?"
Rio De Janeiro. Printed by Laemmert, Ouvires Street, corner of Cano. . . 8vo. 1841. 1½

PIM, Jonathan, *continued* from Catalogue, Vol. 2, p. 423.
——Charles and Josiah; or, Friendly Conversations between a Churchman and a Quaker.
See W. H. Harvey, M.D., Dublin. . . 1862.
——IRELAND and the IMPERIAL PARLIAMENT. By JONATHAN PIM, M.P.
Dublin: Hodges, Foster, & Co., 104, Grafton Street; London: W. Ridgway, 169, Piccadilly.
Price Sixpence. 8vo. 1871. 1½
——Transactions of the Central Relief Committee of the Society of Friends during the Famine in Ireland in 1846 and 1847. (With an Appendix).
Dublin: Hodges and Smith, Grafton Street; London: W. & F. G. Cash. . 8vo. 1852. 30

PITT, Andrew, of *Hampstead.*
——"*Answer of a Quaker to Frederick, Prince of Wales, on his declining to interfere in Behalf of the Quakers on the Subject of Tythes.*" In "The Cabinet Magazine; or, Literary Olio." No. 6, for April, 1797, page 347. . . . . . 12mo. 1797.
——Biography of him, in "Park's History of Hampstead."

PITT, George, of *Berkeley Cottage, Mitcham, Surrey.*
——The BRUISING OF THE SERPENT'S HEAD and of THE CHURCH'S HEEL; or AN ESSAY on the Causes of Decline of the Society of Friends. 1858.
8vo. No Printer's name or place. [1872.] 3
NOTE.—This pamphlet was written in 1858 and intended only as a private memorandum and was laid aside unused, but a relative of the Author's, turning it up, prints it for private circulation. See the Preface.
——ROBERT ALSOP *versus* ROBERT BARCLAY, "THE APOLOGIST." A Letter to a Friend on Robert Alsop's Pamphlet, entitled: "What is the Gospel?" By WILLIAM IRWIN With an Introduction by George Pitt.
Manchester: William Irwin, 24, Deansgate.
See WILLIAM IRWIN. 8vo. 1873. 1¼

PITT, George, *continued.*
——IMMEDIATE REVELATION *True*, and GEORGE FOX *Not* Mistaken. A Testimony *for* George Fox, and *against* his Detractors and Traducers, especially against one who has lately published a pamphlet, signed, "E. A." "A Member of the Society of Friends," entitled, George Fox, his Character, Doctrine, and Work. By George Pitt.
    Manchester: Printed by William Irwin, 35, Fennell Street. . . . 8vo. [1873.]   2
——Can a TRUE CHRISTIAN MINISTER Exact TITHES? or Reasons for not paying Tithes. By George Pitt.
    Manchester: William Irwin, Cathedral Chambers, Half Street. 8vo. 1874.   1½
——GREATEST OF ALL TRUTHS or Salvation by Christ INWARDLY REVEALED, being A DISCOURSE upon the *Universal Love and Goodness of God to Mankind in and through Jesus Christ.* With a Preface by George Pitt, (31st of 12th Month, 1875.)
    Croydon: Printed by Jesse W. Ward, "Advertiser" Offices, Katharine Street. . 8vo. 1876.   1
——There Being No GOSPEL for TITHES, How did they become LAW? or, An Examination of the TITLE DEEDS of the English Church as by LAW established, by A PLAIN MAN. Introduced by George Pitt.
    Croydon: Printed by Jesse W. Ward, "Advertiser" Offices, Katharine Street. 8vo. 1876.   7
      NOTE.—This book is a reprint of Cobbett's "Legacy to Parsons," with an introduction by George Pitt.
——WHY AM I A LIBERAL and NOT A TORY? or, An Appeal to the Electors of Mid Surrey. By George Pitt.
Reprinted, Second Edition.
    Croydon: Printed by Jesse W. Ward, "Advertiser" Offices," Katharine Street. 8vo. 1880.   1¼
——MID SURREY ELECTION. TO THE LIBERAL ELECTORS OF MITCHAM. Manor House, Mitcham, *8th 4th Mo.,* 1880.
    Jesse W. Ward, Printer, Katharine Street, Croydon. . . Large Broadside. [1880.]   1
——"Polly put the Kettle on, and We'll all have TEA." (Being an Invitation to Tea, to Manor House, for "The Destitute of Mitcham.") 2nd 2nd Mo., 1880. GEORGE PITT.

PITT, George, *continued.*
    W. *Field, Printer, Whitford Lane, Mitcham.*
                      Large Broadside. [1880.]   1

—— The Town Crier and Surrey Cartoons. A Humorous and Satirical Paper. Jan. 10, 1880. Vol. 1, No. 4. Our Cartoon.
        No. 4. Mr. George Pitt.
        Mr. Pitt's Dinner Party.

—— The Croydon Review and Railway Time Table. No. 4. February, 1880.
    "The Mitcham Dinners, by Mr. George Pitt," p. 8.

—— —— The Croydon Review, &c. No. 5. March, 1880.
        Free Teas by George Pitt.
    " Polly put the kettle on, and we'll all have Tea," p. 8.

—— —— The Croydon Advertiser and Surrey County Report. Saturday, Jan. 3, 1880.
        Hungry Souls at Mitcham, p. 5.

—— —— Ditto. Saturday, Jan. 10, 1880.
        George Pitt's Dinners, p. 7.

—— —— Ditto. Saturday, Jan. 17, 1880.
        Mitcham Free Dinner Parties—
    the other side of the Question, p. 3.

—— —— Ditto. Saturday, Feb. 7, 1880.
    George Pitt " Puts the Kettle on," p. 5.

—— —— BE MEN ! A few Words to the New Voters. By George Pitt. 14/7mo. 1885. B.   1885.   1

—— —— ROUND THE WORLD. A Sketch of a Visit to INDIA, CHINA, and JAPAN, and Home across the Pacific Ocean, United States, and the Atlantic. By GEORGE PITT.
    Reprinted from " 𝔗𝔥𝔢 𝔅𝔯𝔦𝔱𝔦𝔰𝔥 𝔉𝔯𝔦𝔢𝔫𝔡."
    Glasgow : *Robert Smeal, Crosshill.*   8vo. 1885.

—— —— AUTOBIOGRAPHY of a MITCHAM WORKING MAN. —London House, Mitcham, 12th Mo. 25th, 1886.
                              B.   1

—— —— BERKELEY MUTUAL IMPROVEMENT SOCIETY, MITCHAM. ESSAY BY MR. G. PITT on "Emigration."
    Reprinted from the "Sutton and Epsom Advertiser," March 2nd, 1889.   . . .   B. 1889.   1

—— Berkeley Mutual Improvement. MR. GEORGE PITT ON "EDUCATION."
    Reprinted from the "SUTTON AND EPSOM ADVERTISER," November 15th, 1890.   . B. 1890.   1

PITT, George, *continued.*
——Remarkable Travels Round and Over the World. By George Pitt (Prospectus of).
      17th of 9th Mo., 1886. Folio.

PITT, Priscilla (his Wife.)
——The Berkeley Mutual Improvement Society. For the Breaking-up (verse) . . . 17/4, 1889. 8vo. ¼

POLE, Thomas, *continued* from Catalogue, Vol. 2, p. 425.
——The ANATOMICAL INSTRUCTOR; or, an ILLUSTRATRATION of the modern and most approved methods of preparing and preserving the different parts of the HUMAN BODY, and of QUADRUPEDS, by Injection, Corrosion, Maceration, Distention, Articulation, Modelling, &c., with a variety of Copper Plates. By THOMAS POLE, Member of the Corporation of Surgeons in London.
  LONDON: *Printed by Couchman and Fry; and sold by the Author, No. 11, Talbot Court, Gracechurch Street; and by W. Darton & Co., No. 55, Gracechurch Street.* . 8vo. 1790. 26

——A SYLLABUS of a course of Lectures on the Theory and Practice of Midwifery, including the Diseases of Women and Children: Read by THOMAS POLE, at his Theatre, *in* Thomas's Street, between Thomas's and Guy's Hospitals, in the Borough of Southwark, London. With a Prefatory Address to his Pupils.
  London: *Printed by Stephen Couchman, Throgmorton Street.* 8vo. 1797. 7½

POLLARD, William, *continued* from Catalogue, Vol. 2, p. 427.
——Considerations addressed to the Society of Friends on THE PEACE QUESTION. By William Pollard. (*Reprinted, with additions, from the* FRIENDS' EXAMINER.)
  London: Printed by R. Barrett and Sons, 13, Mark Lane. . . . . . 8vo. 1871. ½

——New Game of Proverbs. In Quartetts.

*POTTER, Alonzo, Bishop of Episcopal Church, Philadelphia.
——Political Economy; its Objects, Uses, and Principles considered. With a Summary for the Use of Students. By A. Potter, D.D., Bishop of Pennsylvania.
  New York:
           18mo. 1841.

*POTTER, Alonzo, *continued.*
———The Principles of Science, applied to the Domestic and Mechanic Arts, and to Manufactures and Agriculture; with Reflections on the Progress of the Arts, and their Influence on Natural Welfare. By Alonzo Potter, D.D.
New York :
12mo. 1850.
———and G. B. Emerson. The School and the Schoolmaster; a Manual for the use of Teachers, Employers, Trustees, Inspectors, &c., of Common Schools, in Parts. Part 1, by Dr. Potter; Part 2, by G. B. Emerson, A.M.
New York. . . . 12mo. 1842.
By Horatio Potter. ?
———LECTURES ON THE EVIDENCES OF CHRISTIANITY; delivered in Philadelphia by Clergymen of the Protestant Episcopal Church, in the Fall and Winter of 1853-4; With an Introduction, by ALONZO POTTER, D.D., Bishop of Pennsylvania. 8vo.
Philadelphia : *E. H. Butler & Co.* 8vo. 1855. pp. 408

> The lectures in this volume were delivered during the past winter in Philadelphia, at the instance of some of the leading members of the Episcopal Convention of Pennsylvania. The subjects of which they treat were selected with special reference to the present exigencies of public opinion, and to the wants of young men of cultivated and thoughtful habits. Among the names of the lecturers, we noticed several of the most distinguished preachers in the Church.—*New York Daily Tribune, Tuesday, December 26, 1854.*

PRATT, Charles E., of *Boston, Massachusetts.*
———A Reviewer Reviewed. The QUAKER DOCTRINE of the Inward Light vindicated; with some criticism of Thomas Kimber's Review of an Essay by Augustine Jones, upon the Principles, Methods, and History of the Society of Friends. By CHARLES E. PRATT, Boston, Mass.
Geo. C. Herbert, Publisher, No. 5, Central Avenue, Lynn, Mass. . . 8vo. 1874. 2¾ or 44pp.
Price 20 cents.

*PRICE, Eli K., of *Philadelphia*, Law Writer, &c.
———DISCOURSE on THE TRIAL BY JURY. Read before the American Philosophical Society, May 1, 1863.
Philadelphia : *Caxton Press of C. Sherman, Son, and Co.* . . 12mo. 1863. 24 pages.

*PRICE, Eli K., *continued*.
——Discourse on THE FAMILY as an element of Government. Read before the American Philosophical Society, January, 1864. [ANONYMOUS.]
    Philadelphia : *Caxton Press of C. Sherman, Son, and Co.*
                            12mo. 1864. 50 pages.
——Centennial Meeting of the Descendants of PHILIP AND RACHEL PRICE.
    Philadelphia : *Caxton Press of C. Sherman, Son, and Co.* . . . 12mo. 1864. 86 pages.

Eli K. Price, in his "Centennial Meeting of the Descendants of Philip and Rachel Price," printed 1864, says:
    "He wrote and published a professional work, and prepared Acts of Assembly at other times. He wrote, and with the aid of his brother Philip, printed and circulated the 'Memoir of Philip and Rachel Price,' which was printed at Glasgow in 'The British Friend,' and wrote and printed for our relatives the Memorial of 'Rebecca,' his daughter, and of her mother, and now presents them this contribution towards their family history. He ceased to be a member with Friends by the best act of his life, that which gave him one of the best of women to be one of the best of wives. This was at the period of the separation, &c.

Rebecca Embree Withers, Wife of HANSON L. WITHERS, Daughter of ELI K. and ANNA E. PRICE, was born in *Philadelphia*, Third Month, 10th, 1829, and died First Month, 17th, 1861.
——Memorial of our Daughter, for her Child. [Edited by ELI K. PRICE.]
    Printed for Eli K. Price. . . 8vo. 1862. 14

PRICE, Rebecca Embree, see REBECCA EMBREE WITHERS.

PRICE, Anna E., Wife of Eli K. Price, Daughter of James and Rebecca Embree, of *West Bradford, Chester County, Pennsylvania*, born 5th Mo. 22nd, 1799.
——Memorial of her, at the end of the above vol.

PRICE, Eli K.
——Memorial of our Daughter, for her Child.
    See R. E. WITHERS.   8vo. 1862.

PRICHARD, James Cowles, *continued* from Catalogue, Vol. 2, p. 432.
——On the different Forms of Insanity, in relation to Jurisprudence, designed for the use of persons concerned in legal questions regarding unsoundness of mind.

PRICHARD, James Cowles, *continued*.
> By James Cowles Prichard, M.D., F.R.S., M.R.I.A., Corresponding Member of the Academy of Moral and Political Sciences in the National Institute, &c., &c.
>> Reprinted, 2nd Edition.—Hippolyte Bailliere, Publisher, 219, Regent Street. . 12mo. 1847. 11

PRIDEAUX, Frances.
——Claudia. By Mrs. Frederick Prideaux.
> " It is old and plain."
>> Twelfth Night.
> *London : Smith, Elder and Co., 65, Cornhill.*
>> 8vo. 1865. 14¼

PRIDEAUX, John, of *Plymouth*.
——Relics of WILLIAM COOKWORTHY, Discoverer of the CORNISH CHINA-CLAY AND STONE, about A.D. 1755; Founder of the BRITISH PORCELAIN MANUFACTURE, about 1760; and an eminent Minister of the Society of Friends. Collected by JOHN PRIDEAUX, Member of the Plymouth Institution and Natural History Society, and of the Royal Institution, Polytechnic, and Geological Societies of Cornwall.
> *London : Messrs. Whittaker and Co., Ave Maria Lane. Plymouth and Devonport : Roger Lidstone. Bristol : T. Kerslake. Newcastle-under-Line : Crewe. Stafford : R. & W. Wright. Truro : Heard & Son. St. Austell : Andrews.* 8vo. 1853. 2½
>> NOTE.—With a Portrait (a Profile) and a Shadow on the Cover.

PUSEY, Caleb, *continued* from Catalogue, Vol. 2, p. 440.
——Some brief Observations Made on Daniel Leeds his Book, Entituled The Second Part of the Mystery of Fox-Craft. Published for the clearing the Truth against the false Aspersions, Calumnies, and Perversions of that often-refuted Author. By Caleb Pusey. With a Postscript by Thos. Chalkly, wherein D.L. is justly rebuked for falsely citeing him.
> *Printed at Philadelphia by Joseph Reyners.*
>> Small 4to. 1706 4½
>> NOTE.—Chalkley's Appendix is entitled : " A Small Broom, &c." See THOS. CHALKLEY.
>> In the Library of the Meeting for Sufferings, Philadelphia.

Q.

QUERTIER, Priscilla. See JOHN NEWBY.

QUINBY, M., of *New York*. See BIBLIOGRAPHY OF BEES.

R.

R.M. See MATILDA RICKMAN.

RATHBONE, Hannah Mary, Widow of RICHARD RATHBONE and daughter of the late JOSEPH REYNOLDS, of *Bristol*. See *Evening Standard, Thursday, March 28th, 1878*.

——The Diary of Lady Willoughby.

——Letters of Richard Reynolds, with a Memoir of his Life. By his Grand-daughter, Hannah Mary Rathbone. (With a Portrait of Richard Reynolds.) *London : C. Gilpin.* . . Large 12mo. 1852. 13½

——The Strawberry Girl, with other Thoughts and Fancies in Verse. By H. M. Rathbone, *Authoress of " The Diary of Lady Willoughby."* (Frontispiece.) *London : Longman, Brown, Green, Longmans and Roberts.* 8vo. 1858. 7

She died at Ivy Lodge, Aigburth, near Liverpool, the 26th of 3rd month, 1878, in the 80th year of her age.

RATHMELL, Mary, of *Leeds*, was born in 1761. She was of the Methodist persuasion. About the 24th year of her age she married W. Rathmell, soon after she quitted the Methodists and joined Friends.

——SPIRITUAL PROGRESS of MARY RATHMELL. A MOTHER'S LEGACY to her daughters. *Philadelphia : For Sale at Friends' Book-store, 304, Arch Street.* . . . 8vo. [1883 ?] 1¾

She died the 4th of 11th Mo., 1796, aged 35 years, and was interred in Friends' Burial Ground at *Leeds*. A few years after her death, her husband and two daughters joined Friends.

*RAUNCE, John, *continued* from Catalogue, Vol. 2, p. 472.

——A Brief DECLARATION against *Judicial Astrologie* or, The Diabolical *Art* of *Astrologie* opened, arraigned, and condemned. Wherein is handled these following particulars, viz. :—

1. *The deluded* Astrologer.
2. *The delusion of the* Astrologer.
3. *Diabolical* Divination.
4. *Horary* Questions.

*RAUNCE, John, *continued.*
    5. *The Events of* Astrology.
    6. *The* 12 Houses.
    7. *The* 7 Planets.
    8. *The* 7 *Planitary* Angels.
    9. *Calculation by Man's* Nativity.
    10. *Predictions by Stars to the alteration of a Kingdom to War or Peace. Or to the good or ill success of any particular Man.*
    By John Raunce, *sometime a* Practitioner *of the said Art.*
    Isa. 47. 13. 14.—*Let now the* Astrologers, *the* Star-gazers, *the monethly* Prognosticators, *stand up, and save thee from these things that shall come upon thee. Behold, they shall be as Stubble; the fire shall burn them, they shall not deliver themselves from the power of the flame,* &c.
    Astrologia accusata pariter & Condemnata. Or the DIABOLICAL ART of JUDICIAL ASTROLOGIE, Receiving the DEFINITIVE SENTENCE OF FINAL CONDEMNATION: Being Delivered in this following Discourse, where the said Art is briefly and manifestly opened, justly arrainged, diligently examined, and experimentally condemned by him, who was a *Student* in the same.
    Omnis planta quam non plantavit Pater ille meus cœlestis, eradicabitur.—Matth. 15. 13.
    By John Raunce, *sometime a practitioner of* Astrologie, *and* Student *in the Magick Art.*
    Preface dated, "*From my Study,*" November 8, 1650.
    County of Buckingham: John Raunce, of the Burrough of Chipping Wickham.
    LONDON: *Printed by J. Clowes, for W. Learner, at the Blackmore in Bishopsgate-street,* 1650.
                                        4to. 5¼ Sheets.
    LONDON: *Printed for W. L. at the Blackmore in Bishops-gate Street.* . . 4to. 1650. 1 Sheet.
    NOTE.—Subscribed at the end—"Farewell."
    John Raunce, of the Burrough of Chipping Wickham, in the County of Buckinggham.
July the last, 1650.

REBANKS, Thomas, of *Kendal,* in *Westmoreland.*
——ADVERTISEMENT (of his School).
                                          8vo. No Date. ⅛
——Another Edition.
    Kendal: Printed by Thomas Ashburner.
                                          8vo. No Date. ⅛

REES, Charlotte, was born in the year 1783, of respectable parents (*continued* from Catalogue, Vol. 2, p. 476).
——Louisa, a moral tale (a Manuscript of about 150 pages in folio, written about the age of 9 years, and "in-

REES, Charlotte, *continued.*
    tended to show that though Vice might flourish for awhile, Virtue in the end would prevail").

——A Poem on the death of the King of France. (Written at about 10 years of age.)
        Two or three other Poems, Query, the Titles, &c. ? written before 1793.
        About 60 poetical productions since.

——SERMONS, from the FOLLOWING TEXTS, viz. : 2 COR., iv., 8, 9, 10 ; ISAIAH lxv., 13, 14 ; EXODUS xiii., 21, 22 ; PSALM xxxvi., 7, 8 ; MICAH vi., 8.
    By CHARLOTTE REES, written before she was TWELVE YEARS of Age. And published for her Benefit. [Edited, with Preface, by SHURMER BATH, of *Bristol.*]
    BRISTOL : *Printed by W. Pine & Son, 1796.*
                                              8vo. 1796. $5\frac{3}{4}$
        NOTE.—At the end of these Sermons is added one of her poetical productions, viz., "THOUGHTS in a BURIAL GROUND, Written at the Age of Twelve Years," 3 pages, and a long list of "Subscribers." 16 pages. Amongst the Subscribers are 9 names of the GURNEY FAMILY, of *Norwich.*

REYNOLDS, Richard, of *Bristol, continued* from Catalogue, Vol. 2, p. 478.

——A Sketch of THE LIFE of the late RICHARD REYNOLDS, of Bristol, the great Philanthropist, *who died at Cheltenham, the 10th day of September,* 1816. To which is added, the Requisition to the Mayor of Bristol, for Founding a Commemoration Society ; and the Speeches delivered on the occasion, to honour the Memory of this Great Man, who annually distributed £10,000 in alleviating the Distresses of his Fellow-creatures ! ! ! Together with INTERESTING ANECDOTES, from his most intimate friends.
    Bristol : *Printed and Published by Mary Bryan, 51, Corn-street ; and sold by all the Booksellers.* 8vo. 1816.   2

——The Loss of Righteous and Merciful Men lamented and improved. A SERMON—occasioned by the death of RICHARD REYNOLDS. By Samuel Lowell.
                                              8vo. 1816. $2\frac{1}{8}$
        See SAMUEL LOWELL, in Miscellaneous Catalogue.

RICHARDSON, Charles, Son of John and Sarah Richardson, was born at Newcastle, the 27th of the 12th month, 1826, and died there the 24th of 3rd month, 1846, aged about 19 years.

RICHARDSON, Charles, *continued.*
—— The ADVANTAGES OF EARLY PIETY, displayed, in A SHORT MEMOIR of the late CHARLES RICHARDSON.
  Newcastle: Printed for private circulation.
  (W. Irwin, Printer, Manchester.)
           18mo. 1848. 1½

RICHARDSON, Hannah W., of *Philadelphia.* See "Nameless" in my Catalogue.

RICHARDSON, John G., of *Moyallon House, Co. Down, Ireland.*
—— Bessbrook and its Founder: J. G. Richardson, Esq. (With a Portrait, *engraved by* R. and E. Taylor,) in "Home Words," vol. 1, p. 178, also "View of the Town of Bessbrook," at p. 181.

RICHARDSON, Jane M., his wife.
—— A CALL to PRAYER; or, What we need as a Church. By Jane M. Richardson.
  Glasgow: Robert Smeal. . . 16mo. 1874. ½

RICHARDSON, Joshua, of *Newcastle-upon-Tyne,* civil engineer.
—— An Account of the Public Meetings holden in the several Towns in Scotland through or near which The Railway from Newcastle to Edinburgh & Glasgow is proposed to go, with the Resolutions passed at the Meetings, together with the General Report on the Line, by Joshua Richardson, Esq., M.I.C.E.L., with a coloured map of the Railway, engraved by Collard.
  Newcastle-upon-Tyne: *Printed by John Hernaman, 69, Pilgrim Street.* . Large 8vo. 1837.
—— Second General Report of the Newcastle-upon-Tyne, Edinburgh, and Glasgow Railway. Addressed to the Provisional Committees. By Joshua Richardson.
  Newcastle-upon-Tyne. . . . 8vo. 1837.

RICHARDSON, R., of *North America.*
—— Memoir of Josiah White, 1873.

RICHARDSON, Thomas, of *Holly Lodge, Shotley Bridge.*
—— Fragments of Family History, compiled by him.
  He died the day of month,

RICHARDSON, William Henry, of *Jarrow-on-Tyne.*
—— Work of the Future for the Society of Friends. [ANON.]
  London: W. Isbister & Co. . . 8vo. 1874. 3⅛
  Reprinted,—Second edition
  London: Daldy, Isbister & Co. . 8vo. 1874. 3⅛

RICKETSON, Shadrack, M.D., of *New York.*
——Means of preserving health and preventing disease, by Shadrack Ricketson.
  New York. . . . . . . 12mo. 1806.
——A Brief History of the Influenza which prevailed in New York in 1807, by Shadrack Ricketson.

RICKMAN, Joseph, of *Newbury, Berkshire.*
——" From the Metropolis." . . . . 4to. 1810.

RICKMAN, Matilda, of *Wellingham, near Lewes,* afterwards of *Fritchley, near Derby.*
——The Happy Choice. [ANON.]
  " There is a path which no fowl knoweth, and which the Vulture's eye hath not seen:
  " The Lion's whelps have not trodden it, nor the fierce lion passed by it."
  " And unto man he said, Behold, the fear of the Lord, that is wisdom; and to depart from evil is understanding.—
       JOB xxviii., 7, 8, 28.
  Gloucester: John Bellows, Steam Press.
      Small 8vo. [1872.]   1
——An Affectionate Address to the Inhabitants of Fritchley. (Signed M. R.)
  John Bellows, Steam Press, Gloucester.
      Small 8vo. [1872.]   1

*RICKMAN, Thomas Clio, *continued* from Catalogue, Vol. 2, p. 489.
——ELEGY, written at the Bank. *After the manner of Gray.* By Thomas Clio Rickman.
  Printed and sold by Clio Rickman, Upper Mary-le-bone Street.
  Price TWO-PENCE. . . . 4to. No date.   ½
———The LIFE of THOMAS PAINE, Author of Common Sense, Rights of Man, Age of Reason, Letter to the Addressers, &c., &c. By THOMAS CLIO RICKMAN. (With Portrait of Thomas Paine.)
    To counteract foul SLANDER's lies,
    And vindicate the good and wise,
     Has been my only aim ;
    If skillness I've perform'd my part,
    The error lies not with my HEART,
     My HEAD's alone to blame.
  London : *Printed and Published by Thomas Clio Rickman, Upper Mary-le-bone Street; and to be had of all Booksellers.* . 8vo. 1819. 18½

*RICKMAN, Thomas Clio, *continued*.

EXTRACTS FROM RECORDS OF LEWES MONTHLY MEETING.
(CONCERNING THOMAS CLIO RICKMAN.)

1779.
11 mo. 14. Thomas Rickman, Senior, presented to us a certificate on behalf of Thomas Rickman, Doctor, being removed from the Monthly Meeting of Reading in Barkshire, to reside within the compass of this Monthly Meeting to the following import:

To Friends of Lewes Monthly Meeting in Sussex.

Thomas Rickman being, by mutual consent, discharged from his apprenticeship and removed to Lewes.

We certifie that during his residence within the compass of this meeting he was in general of a sober, morral conduct, constant attender of meetings, both on the First-day and week-day, and we would hope under no engagement relative to marriage. Desiering he may happily experience a growth and establishment in the blessed Truth, we commend him to your Christian care and tender regard, and conclude with the salutation of unfeigned love.

Your Friends and Brethren.
(Signed by Friends of Reading Monthly Meeting.)

(A " Thomas Rickman, *Junior*," appears both before and after this date to have been present at the Monthly Meeting for Lewes, also after the *disownment*, so that he must have been another of the same name.)

1780.
12 mo. 10. From the various reports spread remote respecting the conduct of Thomas Rickman, late apprentice in Barkshire, and recommended to us by certificate, we appoint the following Friends . . . to querie with him on the subject of missconduct, and make their report, that if clear of the charge, his conduct may be vindicated.

1781.
1 mo. 14. (The Minute was continued, the Friends not having reported.)

1781.
2 mo. 11. The Friends appointed to visit Thomas Rickman, late of Barkshire, report they had visited him, and that he received their advice corderly [cordially ?] and with some degree of tenderness, and this Meeting desiers their watchful care in future over him for good.

1781.
5 mo. 13. (The report of the Friends not being satisfactory) " the case is continued with desiers he may be brought to a true sence of making to free with the reputation of others."

1781.
9 mo. 9. (From report made the meeting) " concludes to close the minute With a fervent wish he may be very careful

*RICKMAN, Thomas Clio, *continued.*

of the like attempt respecting the reputation of others, But look well to his own future conduct."

1783.
4 mo. 13. This meeting having reason to apprehend that Thos. Rickman, late of Barkshire, has an intention of marriage with a person not of our Society, we appoint John Ticehurst and William Tupper to advise him against any proceeding of this nature by the request of this meeting the first convenient time that should offer.

1783.
5 mo. 11. Wm. Tupper reports that John Ticehurst nor himself hath not had any opportunity to visit Thos. Rickman, late of Barkshire, and since that time they were appointed he appears to be married by the Priest to a person not of our profession, we now appoint the following Friends to visit him on that subject and other misseonduct [names follow, John Ticehurst desiring to be excused from the appointment].

1783.
6 mo. 18. (By adjournment.) Wm. Tupper and Thos. Cruttenden report they had fixed a time to visit Thos. Rickman, late of Barkshire, but was refused by a letter from him to them signifying he was not prepared to receive their visit, their further care respecting the affaire is requested of them.

1783.
8 mo. 10. (Report was made that he declined giving the Friends any opportunity to visit him as " yett.")

1783.
9 mo. 14. (The meeting received a report from the Friends that visited him and " there appearing from him no satisfaction to them nor to this meeting ") some Friends were appointed " to draw up a Testimony against the next meeting."

1783.
10 mo. 12. (One of the Friends presented the document) " on which after reading we desier it may be produced at our next sitting with some little alteration."

1783.
11 mo. 9. *Thos. Martin* presented a Testimony of Denial against Thos. Rickman, late of Barkshire, which he is desiered to deliver to him and make report thereof.

The Proceedings and Testimony of Lewes Monthly Meeting held the 9th of 11th mo., 1783, against Thos. Rickman, late of Barkshire, a member of Reading Monthly Meeting. Removed to reside within the compass of this by certificate of Recommendation. Having been visited by request of this meeting for some misconduct Inconsistent to our principles. Since that is married contrary to the Rules of our Discipline and the frequent absenting from our religious meetings for worship, also

*RICKMAN, Thomas Clio, *continued*.

other missbehaviour Inconsistant to our Religious profession, for which he hath been Revisited by order of this meeting, but has given us no satisfaction for his disorderly conduct. We do therefore declare our disapprobation of the said Thomas Rickman and signify we cannot account a person who acts so inconsistant with the principles of our religious society to be any longer a member thereof. Notwithstanding we affectionately wish that by becoming truly seneiable of his errors may be rendered fit for reception into unity with us again.

1783.
12 mo. 7. Thomas Martin informs us of Delivering the Testimony of Denial to Thomas Rickman, late of Barkshire, and was cordially received, and Thomas Rickman, Senr., is Desired to send a coppy of this meeting's proceedings to the Monthly Meeting of Reading, of which he was a Member.

1784.
2 mo. 8. Thomas Rickman reports that he hath sent a copy of his nephew's, Thomas Rickman's, disownment to the Monthly Meeting of Reading, in Barkshire.

RICKMAN, William, of *Rochester*, *Kent*.

——Memoir of William Rickman. In "*The British Friend*," Vols. 7 and 8, 1849 and 1850.

——[No. 1.] Thoughts on EDUCATION including the draft of a CONSTITUTION for a contemplated Society, to be called THE UNITED STATES Education-Improvement Society. By William Rickman, *An Instructor of Youth, in the States of Ohio, Pennsylvania, and Maryland, from 1818 to 1826*.

Baltimore: *Published by William Rickman, Pratt Street (above Howard), and sold by John J. Harrod and Henry Vicary. Price 12½ cents. William Wooddy, Printer.*
12mo. 1830. ½

He died on the 29th of 7th Month, 1839, in the 94th year of his age, and his remains were interred at Rochester.

‖RIPLEY, Dorothy (*continued* from Catalogue, Vol. 2, p. 496), was the daughter of WILLIAM RIPLEY, who was one of John Wesley's first Preachers in Whitby. She was born on the 24th of 4th month, 1767.

For further particulars see Smales's "Whitby Authors," 8vo., 1867.

——LETTERS addressed to DOROTHY RIPLEY, *from several Africans and Indians*, on subjects of Christian experience, &c.

‖RIPLEY, Dorothy, *continued.*
>   Ask of me and I shall give thee the heathen for thine inheritance, and the uttermost parts of the earth for thy possession.

Second edition.
Bristol: Printed by Philip Rose, 20, Broadmead.
[Brit. Museum,]   12mo. [No date, 1810?]   1⅔
4405. *bbb.*
―――
1

――The BANK of FAITH and WORKS UNITED. By DOROTHY RIPLEY, Citizen of this World, but going above to the NEW JERUSALEM.
>   "Faith is the substance of things hoped for, the evidence of things not seen."—HEB. XI.
>   "Through faith we understand that the worlds were framed by the Word of God, so that things which are seen were not made of things which do appear."—XI. 3.

Philadelphia - Printed for the Authoress by J. H. Cunningham, No. 70, South Third Street.
[Brit. Museum,]   12mo. 1819.   8½
4986. *b.*

――An ADDRESS to all in Difficulties. God is Love.—A Hymn from my Nativity.
Rose, Printer, Broadmead, Bristol.
[Brit. Museum,]   12mo. [1821?]   ⅝
4405. *bbb.*
―――
2
>   NOTE.—Written from Mythe, nr. Tewkesbury, 20th 11th month, 1821.

――Memoirs of WILLIAM RIPLEY, Minister of the Gospel, Whitby, England. [Edited by Dorothy Ripley.]
Philadelphia: J. H. Cunningham, Printer.
     12mo. 1827.   3⅔
>   She died on 6th day the 23rd of 12th month, 1831, at *Mecklenburgh, Virginia,* in great peace, after an illness of 5 days, aged 64 years.—*Whitby Repository, of May, 1832.*

‖RITSON, Isaac, Son of Isaac Ritson, of *Eamont Bridge, Cumberland,* was born in 1761. Though decrepid and lame,—of all the departed geniuses in this County, there are few more worthy of commemoration. After having been for some time under the tuition of Mr. Blain, a respectable teacher in the neighbourhood, he was removed to *a Quaker's School* at *Kendal,* his Parents being of that persuasion. His progress in learning was very great; at

RITSON, Isaac, *continued.*

nine years of age he had made no ordinary proficiency in the Greek language. From *Kendal* he was sent to study Mathematics under Mr. John Slee, of How-Hill, in Mungrisdale, an excellent Mathematician. This hitherto unnoticed *Village Sage*, with his pupil and many others in these neglected spots, like some wild flower, might be said to ———————" bloom unseen, "And waste their fragrance on the desert air." So clear and acute were Ritson's ideas, that he understood the propositions of the first six books of Euclid almost as soon as he read them. At the early age of sixteen he commenced teacher in *Carlisle*, but two years afterwards he resigned his School, and made a tour through the Highlands of Scotland with only a few shillings in his pocket; but such was the kindness he experienced in Caledonia, that on his return, in about twelve months, he made a pretty respectable appearance, being well clothed, and no longer the humble pedestrian, but mounted on a pony. He now opened a School at Penrith, which his restless disposition would not permit him long to retain. He went back to Scotland, and studied medicine at *Edinburgh* for two years, supporting himself, in the meanwhile, by writing *theses* for the students. At Edinburgh, Ritson formed an intimacy with the celebrated Dr. Brown; a remarkable semblance in character was perhaps the foundation of this friendship. He next proceeded to London, where he subsisted upon the products of his literary labour. He here published a translation of Homer's Hymns to Venus, and for some time wrote the medical articles in *the Monthly Review.* His Preface to Clark's Survey of the Lakes exhibits much learning and genius. Isaac Ritson died in an obscure lodging at Islington, aged only 27. Unfortunately, the numerous MSS. he left behind could never be found."

Jollie's Cumberland Guide and Directory. Carlisle printed, 1811.

RITTER, Jacob, was the son of Jacob and Elizabeth Ritter, who emigrated from *Germany* to *Pennsylvania.* He was born in *Bucks County* in the year 1757, and belonged to the Lutheran Church; he joined Friends afterwards.

RITTER, Jacob, *continued.*

——Memoirs of Jacob Ritter, a Faithful Minister in the Society of Friends. By Joseph Foulke.
"Gather up the fragments that remain, that nothing be lost."—John vi., 12.
Philadelphia : *T. E. Chapman, 74, North Fourth Street ; Wearer, 5, North Front Street ; Baker & Crane, New York.*
16mo. 1844. 3½
He died the 15th of 12th month, 1841, in the 85th year of his age. He was a Minister about 50 years. Interred in Friends' Burial Ground, Plymouth, America.

ROBERTS, Abigail. [But *Anonymous.*]
——The History of Tim Higgins, The Cottage Visitor. (*Wood cuts.*)
Dublin : *Printed by C. Bentham, Eustace Street.*
18mo. 1823. 5

——The Entertaining Medley ; being a Collection of 𝔗𝔯𝔲𝔢 𝔥𝔦𝔰𝔱𝔬𝔯𝔦𝔢𝔰 𝔞𝔫𝔡 𝔄𝔫𝔢𝔠𝔡𝔬𝔱𝔢𝔰, calculated for the Cottager's Fireside. (*Wood cuts.*) [Anon.]
Dublin : *Printed by Christopher Bentham, 19, Eustace Street.* 18mo. 1822. 5

ROBERTS, John, *continued* from Catalogue, Vol. 2, p. 498.
——Some account of the Persecutions and Sufferings of the People called Quakers, in the seventeenth century, exemplified in The Memoirs of the Life of John Roberts, 1665. By Daniel Roberts.
Philadelphia: Kimber & Sharpless, No. 50, North Fourth Street. [*J. Richards, Printer, No. 130, North Third Street.*] . 18mo. 1840. 2

——𝔖𝔬𝔪𝔢 𝔐𝔢𝔪𝔬𝔦𝔯𝔰 of the Life of John Roberts, written by his son, Daniel Roberts. A New Edition.
𝔏𝔬𝔫𝔡𝔬𝔫 : *Printed and Published by G. H. Farrington, 11, Knightrider Street, Doctors' Commons, E.C.* . . . 18mo. 1873. 2
Another Edition by Wm. Irwin.

*ROBERTS, Oade, of *Painswick, Gloucestershire.* Continued from Catalogue, Vol. 2, p. 501.
——Select Education. Oade Roberts *respectfully announces his intention of receiving, at Midsummer, the limited number of seven pupils, &c. Fifth Month, 1813.*
Walker, Printer, Gloucester. 4to. 1813. ¼

*ROBERTS, Mary, *continued* from Catalogue, Vol. 2, p. 500.
——The CONCHOLOGIST'S COMPANION. By MARY ROBERTS.
Author of "Wonders of the Vegetable Kingdom;"
"Select Female Biography;" "Annals of my Village;"
"A Calendar of Nature," Etc.
    THE NAUTILUS.
 "Light as a flake of foam upon the wind."—*Montgomery.*
 London : *Whittaker & Co., Ave-Maria Lane.*
          8vo. 1834. 14.

——The SEA-SIDE COMPANION; or, MARINE NATURAL
HISTORY. By MARY ROBERTS, Author of "Domesticated Animals;" "Conchologist's Companion;" "Select
Female Biography;" &c., &c. *With illustrative Wood-Cuts, by Baxter.*
 London : *Printed for Whittaker & Co.* [*Printed
 by Manning and Smithson, 12, Ivy Lane.*]
          8vo. 1835. 15½

——WILD ANIMALS, their NATURE, HABITS, AND Instincts;
with incidental Notices of the Regions they inhabit.
By MARY ROBERTS, Author of Domesticated Animals
considered with reference to Civilization and the Arts.
Published under the Direction of the Committee of
General Literature and Education, appointed by the
Society for promoting Christian Knowledge.
 London : *John W. Parker, West Strand.*
          8vo. 1836. 19

——The History of an Umbrella. By Mary Roberts,
Author of " Domesticated Animals," etc.
 London : *Printed by Truscott, Son, and Simmons,
 Suffolk Lane, City.* . . 12mo. No date.
 NOTE.—This book was never published, but left in an unfinished state only 36 pages having been printed off.

——*On seeing a beautiful Hyacinth, which had belonged to
a deceased Friend.* Signed, " COTSWOLDIA."
 Neave, *Gillingham (John Thompson, Printer), but
 not stated so.* . . . . 8vo. [1818?]. ⅛

——WILD ANIMALS, their Nature, Habits, and Instincts, with
incidental notices of the Regions they inhabit. By
MARY ROBERTS, Author of Domesticated Animals
considered with reference to Civilization and the Arts.
Published under the direction of the Committee of
General Literature and Education appointed by the
Society for Promoting Christian Knowledge.
The Fifth Edition.
 London : *Parker, Son, and Bourn, West Strand.*
          8vo. 1861. 19

*ROBINS, Benjamin, *continued* from Catalogue, Vol. 2, p. 502.
—REMARKS on MR. EULER'S Treatise of *Motion*, DR. SMITH'S compleat System of *Opticks*, and DR. JURIN'S Essay upon Distinct and Indistinct *Vision*. By BENJAMIN ROBINS, F.R.S.

> *Hæc eo animo accipi velim, quo ego accipiam, quoties acciderit, ut aliquis mihi errores meos indicet.—Boni autem viri munus esse puto, non aliorum peccata dissimulare; sed potius omnes homines, si fieri posset, ab inscitiæ tenebris in lucem veritatis asserere.*
>
> Petr. Nonius de Errat. Orontii Finæi. In præfat.

LONDON: *Printed for J. Nourse, at the Lamb, without Temple-Bar.* 1739. 7½

A REPLY to Mr. *Robins's* Remarks on the Essay upon *Distinct and Indistinct Vision*, Published at the End of *Dr. Smith's* Compleat System of Opticks. By JAMES JURIN, M.D., Fellow of the College of Physicians, and of the Royal Society.

> *Communi sensu plane caret, inquimus. Eheu! Quam temere in nosmet legem sancimus iniquam!*

LONDON: *Printed for W. Innys and R. Manby, at the West-End of St. Paul's.* . 8vo. 1739. 4

——A FULL CONFUTATION of DR. JURIN'S REPLY to the REMARKS on his ESSAY upon Distinct and Indistinct VISION. By BENJAMIN ROBINS, F.R.S.

> *Quid faciet in geometria, qui non didiceret?—aut, taceat, aportebit, aut ne sanus quidem judicetur.*

LONDON: *Printed for J. Nourse, at the Lamb, without Temple-Bar.* . . 8vo. 1740. 4½

——MATHEMATICAL TRACTS of the late Benjamin Robins, Esq., Fellow of the Royal Society, and Engineer General to the Honourable the East India Company. In Two Volumes. Vol. I. Containing his NEW PRINCIPLES OF GUNNERY, with several subsequent DISCOURSES on the same subject, the greatest Part never before printed. Published by JAMES WILSON, M.D.

> *Patere honoris scirent ut cunctis viam, Nec generi tribui, sed virtuti, gloriam.*—Phæd.

LONDON: *Printed for J. NOURSE, over against Katherine Street, in the Strand. MDCCLXI.*
8vo. 1761. 24¼

——Mathematical Tracts. Vol. II.
——New PRINCIPLES of GUNNERY: containing the Determination of THE FORCE OF GUNPOWDER, and *An Investigation of the Difference* in the RESISTING

*ROBINS, Benjamin, *continued.*
>POWER OF THE AIR to Swift and Slow Motions. With several other Tracts on the improvement of practical Gunnery. By BENJAMIN ROBINS, Esq., F.R.S. *And Engineer General to the Honourable the East India Company.* With an account of his Life and Writings, BY JAMES WILSON, M.D.
>>A NEW EDITION, corrected, and enlarged with the addition of several notes, BY CHARLES HUTTON, LL.D., F.R.S. *And Professor of Mathematics in the Royal Academy at Woolwich.*
>>>LONDON : *Printed for F. Wingrave in the Strand.*
>>>8vo. 1805. 24½

ROBINSON, James, he was born at *Colchester*, 31st of 12th Month, 1801, his Father was a Non-Commissioned Officer in the Army.
——Memoir of James Robinson. (With a Portrait). (With his " Reasons for quitting the Army.")
>*Birmingham* : *White and Pike, Commercial Buildings.* 18mo. 1868.   1
>>He died on the 20th of 9th Mo., 1867, in his 67th year, and his remains were interred in Friends' Burial Ground, at *Stoke-on-Trent.*

ROBINSON, Samuel, of *Clara Mills.*
——To the Inhabitants of Great Britain and Ireland. (Being the 4th Address.) . . 8vo. No date.   ¼
——A Friendly Address, dated, "Clara Mills, 10th of 1st Month, 1851. . . . . . 8vo. [1851.]   ⅛

ROBINSON, Sarah, of Manor House, Crawley, Sussex.
——Letter (soliciting aid for the salary of a Missionary and his Wife.)
>Large 4to. 9mo. 1868.   ¼

ROBINSON, William, Merchant, of *London, continued* from Catalogue, Vol. 2, p. 504.
——NARRATIVE of the MARTYRDOM, AT BOSTON, of William Robinson, Marmaduke Stevenson, Mary Dyer, and William Leddra, in the year 1659. With some particulars of the Judgments which befel their persecutors, and the State of New England. Taken from Besse's Account of the Sufferings of Friends ; and other authentic sources. [Edited by JOHN HARRISON ?]
>*Manchester* : *Printed and published by John Harrison, Market Street.* . 12mo. 1841.   2

ROBINSON, William, of *Scarborough*, Editor of "*The Annual Monitor.*"

—— FRIENDS of a HALF CENTURY ; Fifty 𝔐𝔢𝔪𝔬𝔯𝔦𝔞𝔩𝔰, 𝔴𝔦𝔱𝔥 𝔓𝔬𝔯𝔱𝔯𝔞𝔦𝔱𝔰 of MEMBERS OF THE SOCIETY OF FRIENDS, 1840-1890. *Edited by William Robinson.* First Edition.
  London : Edward Hicks, Junr., 14, Bishopsgate Without, E.C.
  𝔄𝔰𝔥𝔣𝔬𝔯𝔡, 𝔎𝔢𝔫𝔱 : *H. D. & B. Headley, 44, High Street, Joint Publishers.* . . 8vo. 1891. 21⅛

ROBSON, Isaac, of *Huddersfield, continued* from Catalogue, Vol. 2, p. 506.

—— and THOMAS HARVEY.— Narrative of the Visit of ISAAC ROBSON and THOMAS HARVEY to the South of Russia, &c. (*Confidential.*)
  R. Barrett and Sons, Printers. Mark Lane.
            8vo. [1868.] 2½
  NOTE.—Only a limited number of copies printed and not to be circulated.

—— and THOMAS HARVEY.—The MENNONITES OF SOUTH RUSSIA : their present situation in reference to their Christian Testimony against all War. By ISAAC ROBSON and THOMAS HARVEY. NOT PUBLISHED.
  "*Bear ye one another's burdens, and so fulfil the law of Christ.*"
  Birmingham : Printed by White & Pike, Moor Street Printing Works. . 8vo. [1872.] 1

See THOMAS HARVEY.

ROFE, George, *continued* from Catalogue, Vol. 2, p. 507.
 Geo. Whitehead in his "Christian Progress," (see p. 97-98.) says
  "*George Rofe* became a great Traveller in the Work of the Lord beyond the Seas, as not only in *Holland* and *Germany*, but also in the *American* Parts, as *New-England, Virginia, Bermudas, Barbadoes,* and other remote Parts. A particular Account of his Travels in those Parts and Islands, I have not ; but we have often had general Accounts, yet have desired a more particular and full Relation thereof.
  "After divers Difficulties and Dangers the said *George Rofe* passed through by Sea, and great Travels and Service in those Foreign Parts in *America*, he, with some other *Friends*, lost their Lives in a Storm at Sea, near the Coasts of *Virginia*, as has been related to us."

*ROGERS, John, Junr., of *Lisburn*, in *Ireland*.
——Letter to a Friend (on his Marriage being contrary to the Rules, &c.) dated, *Lisburn*, 12th mo., 1800. At the end of John Hancock's "Friendly Expostulation," &c.
    Belfast, printed.   .   8vo. 1802.

*ROSE, Aquila, of *London*.
——A Poem to his memory. See Elias Bockett.
    He died in Philadelphia, August 22nd, 1723, Aged 28 years.

ROWNTREE, Joshua, of *Scarborough*. Editor of *The Friend*.
——Letter to Friends, beginning, "Dear Friend, "Thou wilt have observed by a Notice in the last number of *The Friend* that I have succeeded to the Editorship of the Paper, on the retirement of John Frank from the office," &c., &c. Dated "Scarborough, 1st Month 9th, 1871."
——Notice to "The Subscribers of *The Friend*, of an advertisement respecting" D.M.P. being inaccurate, &c.
     8vo. Second Month, 1874.

RUDD, Thomas, *continued* from Catalogue, Vol. 2, p. 515.
——"We the undernamed do Certifie that We are credibly informed by Certificate from our Friends, and others, of the honest and quiet behaviour of our Friend the abovesaid *Thomas Rudd*, whose dwelling in his *Wharfe*, near *Settle*, in *Yorkshire*, and that the before recited, is the substance of his Testimony. Given forth (to prevent Mistakes and false Reports) the day above said, by us,
    James Whitehill,   *Robert Bradshaw*,
    Antho. Sharpe,   *Roger Roberts*,
    Samuel Clarridge,   *John Hutchinson*,
    Thomas Ashton,
(27/2mo., 1693)   8vo. [1693.]
    Query part of some other paper.

RULE, Joseph, a waterman—See JOHN FREE, in my "Adverse Catalogue."—Note.
——History of Joseph Rule, in "*The Friend, for 7th month, 1, 1872, p. 160.*"
    He died, and was buried at *Jordans*.

||RUSH, Benjamin, by religious profession a Presbyterian, an American Physician, was born in the State of Pennsylvania, of Parents who were Quakers, in 1745. He studied in the College of Princeton, but took his

‖RUSH, Benjamin, *continued*.
Doctor's degree at Edinburgh in 1768. On his return to Philadelphia, an attempt was made to form a medical school in that University, and Dr. Rush became Professor of Chemistry. In 1776 he was chosen a Member of Congress, and appointed surgeon-general of the Military Hospital, which office he exchanged for that of Physician-General, but soon resigned that situation also. Soon afterwards, when the Medical Colleges of Philadelphia became united, under the name of the University of Pennsylvania, Dr. Rush was appointed Professor of the Institutes of Medicine and clinical practice. He died in 1813. His works are numerous, and highly esteemed by his countrymen. The principal tracts were collected into an octavo volume, entitled, "Essays, literary, moral, and philosophical," 1798. Dr. Rush also wrote "A History of the Yellow Fever," which was translated into the Spanish and French Languages.
American Medical Register.
——Sermons to Gentlemen upon Temperance and Exercise.
Philadelphia: Printed by John Dunlap, in Market Street, MDCCLXXII. . . 8vo. 1772. pp. 44
——An Address to the Inhabitants of the British Settlements, on the Slavery of the Negroes in America. The Second Edition. To which is added, A Vindication of the Address, in Answer to a Pamphlet, entitled, "Slavery not forbidden in Scripture; or, a Defence of the West India Planters." By a Pennsylvanian.
Philadelphia: Printed and Sold by John Dunlap, MDCCLXXIII.
One leaf, pp. 28, 1 leaf. . . . 8vo. 1773. Title.
——An ENQUIRY into the EFFECTS of SPIRITUOUS LIQUORS upon the Human Body, and their Influence upon the Happiness of Society. By BENJAMIN RUSH, M.D., Professor of Chemistry in the University of Philadelphia.
PHILADELPHIA: *Printed by Thomas Bradford, in Front Street, four Doors from the Coffee House.* . . . . 12mo. [1784?] ½
——CONSIDERATIONS upon the present TEST-LAW of PENNSYLVANIA: Addressed to the Legislature and Freemen of the State. [ANON.]
Philadelphia: Printed by HALL and SELLERS.
Small 8vo. 1784. 1½
——MEDICAL INQUIRIES and OBSERVATIONS. To which is added AN APPENDIX, containing OBSERVATIONS

‖RUSH, Benjamin, *continued*.
— on the DUTIES of a PHYSICIAN, and the Methods of improving MEDICINE. By BENJAMIN RUSH, M.D., Professor of Chemistry in the University of Pennsylvania. THE SECOND EDITION.
PHILADELPHIA, *Printed*. LONDON: *Reprinted for C. Dilly, in the Poultry, MDCCLXXXIX*.
8vo. 1789. 16½
NOTE.—Dedicated "To John Redman, M.D.," President of the College of Physicians, of Philadelphia.

—— Considerations on the Injustice and Impolicy of Punishing Murder by death. Extracted from the American Museum. With additions. By Benjamin Rush, M.D., Professor of the Institutes, and of Clinical Medicine, in the University of Pennsylvania. *Philadelphia : From the Press of Mathew Carey, May 4*. 8vo. 1792. 1¼

—— Extract of a Letter from Dr. Benjamin Rush, of Philadelphia, to Granville Sharp.
London : Printed by James Phillips, George Yard, Lombard Street. . . Small 8vo. 1792. ½

—— On the PUNISHMENT of MURDER by DEATH. By B. Rush, M.D.
Philadelphia printed : London reprinted : and sold by J. Johnson, St. Paul's Church Yard ; and J. Phillips, George Yard, Lombard Street.
8vo. 1793. 1½

—— Recollections of Dr. Rush. (Being a Biographical Sketch, by Dr. Lettsom). See p. 52 of "An Eulogy, &c., on John C. Lettsom, "Note."

—— A Sketch of the Life of Benjamin Rush, M.D., with a Portrait of him from an oil painting in the possession of the Pennsylvanian Hospital, Philadelphia. Inserted in D. H. Tuke's "Insane in the United States and Canada." 8vo. 1885.

RUTTER, John, *continued* from Catalogue, Vol 2, p. 519.
—— The DEFENCE of JOHN RUTTER, delivered "On Monday the 14th of August, 1826," with additional observations. . . . . . 8vo. [1826.] 1

RUTTER, Richard Ball, of 8, *Elgin Park, Bristol*.
—— To the Younger Members of Bristol and Frenchay Monthly Meeting.
4to. 9th of 10th Month, 1886. ½
This was accompanied with "a letter from Arthur J. Naish and Cephas Butler, dated Birmingham, November 30th, 1886," there being "so much loving counsel contained in it."

S.

S., S. A.   See Sarah Ann Storrs.

SANDS, Nathaniel, Son of David and Clementine Sands.
—— Memorials of Nathaniel Sands and Sarah Hawxhurst.
New York: Published by S.S. & W. Wood, 389, Broadway. . . . . 8vo. 1857. ⅝

SANSOM, Joseph, of *North America.*
—— Letters from Europe during a tour through Switzerland and Italy in the years 1801 and 1802, written by a Native of Pennsylvania (Joseph Sansom). In 2 Vols.
Philadelphia: . . . . . 8vo. 1805.
—— A Tour to Quebec, by Joseph Sansom.
Philadelphia:

SARGENT, John Grant, of *Fritchley, Derbyshire.*
—— A TENDER PLEADING with those Friends who see and feel the present backslidden state of the Society, and are still hoping for better things therein.
Folio. [1872.]   1
—— FURTHER EVIDENCES confirmatory of the Great Defection and Departure from the Living Truth, and Truth's Principles; and the letting fall of the Testimonies which were held by the SOCIETY OF FRIENDS formerly, but are now despised as of no account, and unnecessary any longer to be borne by it.
Gloucester: Printed by John Bellows, Steam Press.
8vo. [1873.]   1
—— Selections from the Diary and Correspondence of John G. Sargent.
Newport, Mon.—Printed. . . 8vo. 1885. 21
He died the 27th of 12th Month, 1883, aged 70 years.

SAVERY, William, *continued* from Catalogue, Vol. 2, p. 538.
—— Seven Sermons.   1808.

SAY, Thomas, of *Philadelphia.*
—— A Short COMPILATION of the extraordinary LIFE AND WRITINGS of THOMAS SAY; in which is faithfully copied, from the original Manuscript, the UNCOMMON VISION, which he had when a young man. By his Son. [DR. BENJAMIN SAY.]
Philadelphia: Printed and sold by Budd and Bartram, No. 58, North Second Street.
[*Brit. Museum, 4986.*]   12mo. 1796 7¾

SAY, Thomas, Son of Dr. Benjamin Say.
——American Conchology. 1 Vol.
  Philadelphia : . . . . . 8vo.
——American Entomology. 3 Vols.
  Philadelphia : . . . . . 8vo.
  Many papers in the Journal of the Academy of Natural Sciences, and in the Transactions of the Am. Phil. Soc.

SAYCE, William J., of *Hereford*.
——What the Society of Friends Believes, and Why. By William J. Sayce.
  Leominster : *The Orphans' Printing Press.*
          8vo. [1892.] 2
 Reprinted—2nd edition. . . . 8vo. [1892.] 2

SAYERS, Joseph, of *Dorking, Surrey*.
——FAMILY QUERIES. *Written by our dear friend,* J. SAYERS, late of DORKING.
  W. Eade, Printer, Lindfield. . 8vo. No date. ⅛
——Why do you go to the Play ?
——Anecdote of the late Joseph Sayers.
  See *British Friend*, Vol. 2, p. 2, 3.

SCATTERGOOD, Thomas, *continued* from Catalogue, Vol. 2, p. 542.
——Journal of the Life and Religious Labours of Thomas Scattergood.
  Stereotype Edition. 8vo. *Philadelphia* : No date.
——BIOGRAPHICAL SKETCHES and ANECDOTES of Members of the RELIGIOUS SOCIETY OF FRIENDS (American).
  Philadelphia : Published by the Tract Association of Friends, No. 304, Arch Street.
          8vo. 1870. 26¾
 NOTE.—This book is chiefly compiled from "Thomas Scattergood and his times," with some additions. It contains :—

David Ferris,	William Jackson,
William Hunt,	Peter Yarnall,
Samuel Emlen,	Anthony Benezet,
John Churchman,	Jacob Lindley,
Rebecca Jones,	Eli Yarnall,
Daniel Offley,	Sarah Harrison,
William Savery,	John Parker,
George Dillwyn,	Nicholas Waln,
Arthur Howell,	Moses Brown.

 At page 250 is an account of Peter Price, with the Vision seen by him.

*SCHIMMELPENNINCK, Mary Ann, *continued* from Catalogue, Vol. 2, p. 542.

——Narrative of a Tour in the year 1667, to 𝔏𝔞 𝔊𝔯𝔞𝔫𝔡𝔢 ℭ𝔥𝔞𝔯𝔱𝔯𝔢𝔲𝔰𝔢 𝔞𝔫𝔡 𝔄𝔩𝔢𝔱, by Dom Claude Lancelot, Author of the Port Royal Grammars; including some account of Dom Armand Jean Le Bouthillier de Rancé, Reverend Father Abbé, and Reformer of the Monastery of Notre Dame De La Trappe; with Notes; and an Appendix, containing some particulars respecting M. Du Verger De Hauranne, Abbé De St. Cyran; Cornelius Jansenius, Bishop of Ypres; and also a Brief Sketch of the celebrated Institution of Port Royal.
    London : Printed for J. and A. Arch, Cornhill.
                                                  8vo. 1813. 18

——𝔐𝔞𝔫𝔲𝔞𝔩 of La Mère Agnès, or 𝔄 𝔊𝔦𝔣𝔱 𝔣𝔯𝔬𝔪 𝔞𝔫 𝔄𝔟𝔟𝔢𝔰𝔰 𝔱𝔬 𝔥𝔢𝔯 𝔑𝔲𝔫𝔰, a Specimen of "La Religieuse Parfaite et Imparfaite," of La Mère Agnès de St. Paul Arnauld, Abbess of Port Royal. By M. A. Schimmelpenninck.
    Bristol : Printed by Wright and Bagnall, Bridge Street. 8vo. 1829. 3

——Biblical Fragments. By Mary Anne Schimmelpenninck, Author of "A Tour to Alet," "Demolition of Port Royal," "Theory of the Classification of Beauty and Deformity," &c., &c. Vol. II.
    London : Printed for Ogle, Duncan, and Co., 37, Paternoster Row, and 295, Holborn.
    (*Printed by J. Moyes, Greville Street.*) 8vo. 1822. 21
      What God keeps is well kept.—Translated by M.A.S.
      Sketch from Nature.

SCOTT, Job, *continued* from Catalogue, Vol. 2, p. 546.

——Extracts of Letters, from Job Scott to James Bringhurst. In Comly's Miscellany, Vol. 4, p. 66.

SCOTT, John, of *Amwell, Herts. Continued* from Catalogue, Vol. 2, p. 550.

——ODE TO FANCY, written in Winter, 1760.
                (Not in his works.)

——Ode to a Friend, 1761. (Now first published.)

——Ode to Hospitality, 1761. (Now first published.)

——Ode to Leisure, 1762. (Now first published.) By John Scott, Esq., of Amwell.
    All the above Odes are in "The European Magazine," Vol.

SCOTT, John, *continued*.
>36, from July to December, 1799, pp. 46, 256, 330, and 400.

——The Poetical Works of John Scott. By Thomas Park.
>18mo. 1808.

SCULL, G. D., of *Rugby Lodge, Norham Road, Oxford*, formerly of *Philadelphia*, afterwards of *2, Langland Gardens, Frognal, Hampstead, N.W.* Member of the Historical Society of Pennsylvania; the Academy of Natural Sciences of Philadelphia; the Harleian Society of London; Corresponding Member of the New York Historical Society; the New England Historic-Genealogical Society of Boston; the Maine Historical Society; and the State Historical Society of Wisconsin.

——DOROTHEA SCOTT, otherwise GOTHERSON AND HOGBEN, of EGERTON HOUSE, KENT, 1611-1680.
>4to. 1882.
>Reprinted. 4to. 1883.
>See DOROTHEA GOTHERSON.

——The Evelyns in America.

SEEBOHM, Benjamin, *continued* from Catalogue, Vol. 2, pp. 553 and 554.

——On the Sufferings of Christ for our sake. [By Esther, his wife.]
>*W. Byles, Printer, Chapel Court, Kirkgate, Bradford.* . . . 16mo. No date. ½

——Private Memoirs of B. and E. Seebohm. Edited by their Sons. 8vo. 1873. 28

SEEBOHM, Frederic, *continued* from Catalogue, Vol. 2, p. 554.

——The Oxford Reformers of 1498, &c.
>Reprinted, 2nd Edition, revised. . 8vo. 1869.

——How can Compulsory Education be made to work in England? By Frederic Seebohm. Reprinted, with alterations, from "The Fortnightly Review": with a Postscript on Education in the Plaiting Districts.
>*London: Longmans, Green, & Co.*
>8vo. 1870. 2

——On INTERNATIONAL REFORM. By Frederic Seebohm.
>*London: Longmans, Green, & Co.*
>8vo. 1871. 9¾

——The Era of the Protestant Reformation. New Edition.
>8vo. 1877.

SESSIONS, Eliza, of 6, *Bath Villas, Gloucester*.

——Proposed HOME OF HOPE FOR THE FALLEN, GLOUCESTER.—A Letter to a Friend. . 8vo. 6mo. 1, 1872. ¼

SESSIONS, Frederick (son of the above).

——A Letter to Working Men on National Armaments. By Frederick Sessions, Gloucester.
Printed by R. Barrett & Sons, Mark Lane, London.
12mo. No date. ⅙
NOTE.—No. 68 Tract of Peace Society's 12mo. Series.

——Gospel Temperance Stories. With illustrations.
Leominster:

SEWEL, William, *continued* from Catalogue, Vol. 2, *p.* 560.

——KORT-BEGRYP van de HISTORIE der REFORMATIE van de KERK van ENGELAND : *Beginnende* Met de Regeeringe van Koning Hendrik den Achtsten, en eyndigende met het begin der Regeeringe van Koninginne Elizabeth. *In't Engelsch beschreeven door* GILBERT BURNET, Nu Bisschop van Salisbury. *En daar uyt in't Nederdaytsch gebragt door* WM. SEWEL. *Met Kópere Plaaten vercierd.*
T'AMSTERDAM, *by de Weduwe van* STEVEN SWART, *Boekverkoopster bezyde de Beurs, 1690.*
Met privilegie voor vyftien jaaren.
NOTE.—With an *engraved title page* also, and portraits of Henry VIII., Cardinal Wolsey, Archbishop Cranmer, Queen Catherine Howard, Anna Boleyn, Thomas Cromwel, Earl of Essex, and Thomas More, Chancellor.

——NEDERDUYTSCHE SPRAAKKONST, Waarin de Gronden der HOLLANDSCHE TAALE Naauwkeuriglyk opgedólven, en zelfs voor geringe Verstanden, zo ten aanzien der Spellinge als Bewoordinge duidelyk aangeweezen zyn. *De derde Druk.* Doorgaans veel vermeerderd, en met eene LYST VAN DE GESLACHTEN DER NAAMWOORDEN, die onder geene vaste Regelen betrekkelyk zyn ; Nevenseene *Verhandeling* van de REDENKONSTIGE Figuuren en andere Taalcieraaden, verrykt, Door Wm. Séwel.
TE AMSTERDAM, *By de Erven van* J. RATELBAND, *en Comp. op de hoek van de Kalverstraat, aan den Dam.* 1733. . . . 8vo. 1733. 30¼
NOTE.—This book contains a fine portrait of "Willem Séwel, Amsterdammer, oud LI. Jaaren 1705."
G. Rademaker, del. J. C. Philips sculp. 1733.

SEWEL, William, *continued.*

——A Compendious GUIDE to the *Low-Dutch Language*; containing the most necessary and essential *Grammar Rules*, whereby one may speedily, and without much difficulty, attain to the knowledge of the aforesaid Language, and the right use of the Dutch Particles *de* and *het*, so much wanted hitherto.

Korte WEGWYZER der Nederduytsche Taal; Behelzende de noodigste en weezendlykste *Letterkonstige Regelen*, om spoedig en zonder veel moeite tot kennisse dier Taale te geraaken. By WILLEM SEWEL. (In 3 parts.) The second edition, with some additions.

TE AMSTERDAM, *By* JACOB TER BEEK, *bezyden de Beurs in de Gekroonde Bybel.* 12mo. 1740. 21

——A COMPENDIOUS GUIDE to the LOW DUTCH LANGUAGE; containing the most necessary and essential *Grammar Rules*, whereby one may speedily, and without much difficulty, attain to the knowledge of the aforesaid Language, and the right use of the Dutch Particles *de* and *het*, so much wanted hitherto.

——KORTE WEGWYZER DER NEDERDUYTSCHE TAAL; Behelzende de noodigste en weezendlykste *Letterkonstige Regelen*, om spoedig en zonder veel moeite tot kennisse dier Taale te geraaken. By WILLEM SEWEL. *The Third Edition, Corrected and Enlarged.*

Te AMSTERDAM, By KORNELIS de VEER, Boekverkooper in de Beursstraat, by den Dam, 1760. *Met Privilegie.* . . 12mo. 1760. 21$\frac{1}{6}$

NOTE.—This book is in three parts. The 1st and 2nd parts have each a separate pagination. The third part, has no pagination and contains a small VOCABULARY.

——KORTE WEGWYZER DER ENGELSCHE TAALE; Behelzende de noodigste en weezendlykste *Letterkonstige* Regelen, om spoedig zonder veel moeite tot kennisse dier Taale te geraaken.

——A COMPENDIOUS GUIDE to the ENGLISH LANGUAGE; containing the most necessary and essential *Grammar Rules*, whereby one may speedily, and without much difficulty, attain to the knowledge of the aforesaid Language. Door WILLEM SEWEL.

Te AMSTERDAM, by JACOB Ter BEEK, bezyden de Beurs, in de Gekroonde Bybel, 1740.
12mo. 1740. 20$\frac{1}{2}$

NOTE.—In three parts. The 1st and 2nd have a separate pagination. The third part has no pagination.

SEWEL, William, *continued*.

SEWEL'S HISTORY (the following is from an ancient MS.)

"William Sewel's History: the Intent of its Publication I supose is to Describe the Difference between the Power and forme the Spirit and the Letter, the Living and the Dead, a voluntary humility, and a Necessitated one, the Flesh and the Spirit, or Grace and Nature, Light and Darkness in the knowledge of the Creature, the Temple of Merchandize, and the New Temple which is a praying one made by Divine Athourity Raised and Beautifyed with Precious things of Revelation, the Death of sin, the Birth of Innocence, the Power of Eternal Life, the Love of the Father, the Image of a Heavenly Body, a Baptism of Holiness, the visions of Paradize, or Bliss of Immortality, the Fight of Afflictions attending on the Excellency and Power of Godliness unto the full Discovvery of the freeness of Eternal Love in Christ Jesus.

The Points of Bearings considered in the Reading of this History, by Wm. Long."

SHARP, Thomas, emigrated from Ireland in 1681, and settled at Newton, Gloucester County, New Jersey; one of the founders of the Friends' Meeting at that place. [He was nephew of Anthony Sharp, a Friend of Dublin, Ireland). He held various responsible positions under the government of the Colony, and left several MSS. books now in the office of the Surveyor General of West New Jersey (some of which is written in verse) deprecating the want of zeal among the members of the Society of Friends.

SHEWELL, John Talwin, of *Ipswich*.

——MEMOIR of the late JOHN TALWIN SHEWELL, to which is appended Notes of his Italian Journey, and fugitive Poems.

Ipswich: Printed for Private Circulation only by William Hunt, Steam Press, Tavern-street.
4to. 1870. $58\frac{3}{4}$

NOTE—One leaf of "Errata" at the end.

SHIELDSTREAM, Charles, of *Philadelphia*.

——THOUGHTS and VIEWS on the ETERNAL GOSPEL and FALLING BABYLON: which is the dying Religion. By CHARLES SHIELDSTREAM.
8vo. *Philadelphia.* 1884. $6\frac{3}{4}$

SHOLL, Samuel.

——Historical Account of the Silk Manufactures in England.
London :　　　　　　　　　　　　　　8vo.　1811.

SIMPSON, James, Son of John and Hannah Simpson, was born in Bucks County the 19th of the 3rd Month, 1743.

——Memoirs of James Simpson. In Comly's Miscellany, Vol. 4, p. 193.

> He died the 9th of the 4th Month, 1811, aged about 68 years.

*SIMPSON, William, of *21, Darlington Street, Cheetham Hill, Manchester*.

——A Letter of Farewell addressed, "My dear Schoolfellows and Friends" (on his Resignation).—
　　　　　　　　　　8vo.　28th of 9th Mo., 1871.

SLAVERY IN AMERICA.

——The FIRST PRINTED PROTEST against SLAVERY IN AMERICA.
Reprinted from " The Pennsylvania Magazine of History and Biography."
　　　　　　　　　8vo.　*Philadelphia* :　1889.

> NOTE.—This has an introduction by GEORGE H. MOORE, of the "Lenox Library, May 19, 1889," who says, "Among the numerous revelations for which we are indebted to the zeal and ability of Mr. Charles R. Hildeburn, in prosecution of his admirable bibliographical researches, his discovery of George Keith's early testimony against slavery among the Bradford imprints is peculiarly interesting." It is among the earliest of Bradford's New York imprints. The original is entitled, "An Exhortation & Caution to Friends concerning Buying or Keeping of Negroes." Given forth by our Monthly Meeting in Philadelphia, the 13th day of the 8th Month, 1693."
>
> Copied from the original in library at Devonshire Meeting House, London, by Mr. Joseph Smith."

SLEIGH, Joseph, of *Dublin—continued* from Catalogue, Vol. 2, p. 580.

——GOOD ADVICE and COUNSEL, Given forth by JOSEPH SLEIGH, of the CITY of DUBLIN, in the time of his Sickness, to his CHILDREN. And since his Death, it being thought fit for the service of others also;

SLEIGH, Joseph, *continued*.
 therefore it was ordered into Print, that other Children, &c., may have the Benefit thereof.
      Small 8vo. Printed in the year 1683.   1¼
  NOTE.—This is the *original* edition, and is evidently printed in Dublin. At the end is a Testimony concerning him, by A.S., *i.e.*, Abel or Amos Strettle. A copy of this edition is in the Library of John Sleigh, of the Inner Temple and North Grove, Highgate.
  Joseph Sleigh was aged about 40 years when he died.

SMEAL, Robert, of *Glasgow*, *continued* from Catalogue, Vol. 2, p. 580.
——The Editor of the "British Friend" to his Readers and to Friends everywhere. . . 8vo. [1872.]   ¼
  He died the 12th of 6th mo., 1886, aged 81 years.

SMEDLEY, Esther K., of *West Chester*, *Chester County, Pennsylvania*.
——The Children's Friend. A Monthly Journal. See PERIODICAL PUBLICATIONS.

*SMILEY, Sarah F., of *Baltimore, United States*.
——WHO IS HE? An Appeal to those who regard with any doubt the Name of JESUS.
  Dost thou believe on the Son of God? Who is He, Lord, that I might believe on Him?—John ix. 35, 36. By S. F. SMILEY.
 Philadelphia: J. B. Lippincott & Co.   8vo. 1868.   6½
 Reprinted—*London*: F. Bowyer Kitto, 5, Bishopsgate Without. . . 8vo. 1869.   6½
  " again, *London*.
——CHRISTIAN WORK and CHRISTIAN SERVICE: An Address delivered by Sarah Smiley, of Baltimore, U.S., at Devonshire House, during the General Meeting of Friends, 1869.
 𝕷𝖔𝖓𝖉𝖔𝖓: F. B. Kitto, 5, *Bishopsgate Street Without*. . . . 16mo. 1871.   1/16
  NOTE.—In "*The Friend for 8th Month 1st, 1872*," Vol. XII., New Series, p. 176, will be found a brief notice of retirement of Sarah F. Smiley from membership with Friends, and of her subsequent public Baptism with water, by Dr. Pentecost, of New York.

SMITH, Ashby, of *10, Bloomsbury Square, London*.
——MISCELLANEOUS WORKS of the late ROBERT WILLAN, M.D., F.R.S., F.A.S.—Edited by ASHBY SMITH, M.D.
 London: Printed for T. Cadell, in the Strand.
  See ROBERT WILLAN.   8vo. 1821.   32½

SMITH, Charles, *continued* from Catalogue, Vol. 2, p. 581.

——On War. A Copy of a Letter sent to Sovereigns, Rulers and Governments; to which is added A Few Words for the consideration of the People.

London : Published by F. B. Kitto, 5, Bishopsgate Street Without, E.C. (Wertheimer, Lea & Co., Printers, Finsbury Circus). 8vo. [1870.] ½

Translated into French, entitled :—

——Sur la Guerre. Copie D'une Lettre adressée aux Souverains, Gouverneurs et Gouvernements, a laquelle sont ajoutés quelques mots pour la considération des Peuples.

Londres : *F. B. Kitto, Editeur, 5, Bishopsgate St. Without, E.C. (Imprimerie de Wertheimer, Lea et Cie, Finsbury Circus, Londres.*
8vo. [1870.] ½

Translated into German, entitled :—

——Ueber den Krieg. Copie eines Briefes, gerichtet an Souveraine, Monarchen und Regierungen, und einige Worte zur Ueberlegung fur das Boek.

London : *Berlag von F. B. Kitto, 5, Bishopsgate Street Without, E.C. (Gedruckt bei Wertheimer, Lea & Co., Circus Place, Finsbury, London).* . . . . 8vo. [1870.] ½

SMITH, Charlotte Fell, of *Great Saling, Essex.*

——STEVEN CRISP and his Correspondents, 1657-1692, Being a Synopsis of the Letters in the "Colchester Collection." Edited, with Notes and an Introduction. By C. Fell Smith.

London : E. Hicks, Jun., 14, Bishopsgate Without, and 2, Amen Corner, Paternoster Row. [Printed by Headley Bros., Ashford, Kent.]
8vo. 1892. 9⅛

Note.—Illustrated with a view of "Colchester Castle"; "Stebbing Meeting House, built 1675"; "Facsimile of Crisp's Answers to the Deputy-Lieutenants of Durham, 18th Feb., 1661"; "Door of the prison in Colchester Castle, where the Essex Friends were confined, 1655-70"; Portrait of "George Fox," *("from a photo-type of the painting by Sir Peter Lely")*; Portrait of "Elizabeth, Princess Palatine"; Portrait of "James Nayler," *("from the painting engraved by Francis Place")* "An Amsterdam Quaker, about 1689, in a winter dress"; "Cottage at Saling, Essex, formerly part of Meeting House, 1675."

SMITH, Frederick, *continued* from Catalogue, Vol. 2, p. 582.
——A Recommendation to INWARD RETIREMENT. With The Lord's Prayer and The Ten Commandments. [ANON.]
Printed and sold by W. Robson & Co., St. Dunstan's Hill, Tower Street.
16mo. (No date.) 1/16

SMITH, Hannah Logan, of *Philadelphia*.
——A Volume [Lettered on the back, "FROM H.L.S."] apparently never having had a title page, and "not intended for sale or general circulation." With a "Preface," addressed by Hannah Logan Smith to her Children, dated *Philadelphia*, 4th Month, 1839, and beginning, "Dear Children : I present to you a volume containing a short memoir of your father, and some account of several persons in some way or other connected with our family. There are also many extracts from books of a religious tendency, &c., &c."
The Contents of the Volume are :
1st.—A Testimony from Shropshire Monthly Meeting, for DEBORAH DARBY, p. 13.
2nd.—A Testimony respecting REBECCA BYRD, of *Marnhull*. [Sent by WILLIAM FORSTER, a respectable Minister from England, to H. L. Smith.]
3rd.—A Testimony respecting WILLIAM BYRD, of *Marnhull.*
4th.—A Testimony of Kingston Monthly Meeting, concerning ANN BREWSTER, of *Clapham.*
5th.—Account of MARY PRIOR, wife of JOHN PRIOR, of *Hertford. (From the Annual Monitor.)* p. 47
6th.—A Memorial concerning my beloved Wife, SARAH FISHER. By JOSHUA FISHER, of *Philadelphia.*
7th.—Some Account of SARAH STEPHENSON.
8th.—An Epistle to THOMAS FISHER, my late beloved Father.
9th.—Account of JAMES LOGAN FISHER. [*From Poulson's American Daily Advertiser.*]
10th.—An Address to the Inhabitants of Pennsylvania, by those Freemen of the City of Philadelphia who are now confined in the Mason's Lodge, &c.
11th.—(Lines to the) Memories of THOMAS GILPIN and JOHN HUNT, who died exiles in Virginia, 1778. Signed "*Fidelia.*"
12th.—(Lines addressed by) MARY SHACKLETON to SARAH G. DILLWYN, wife of GEORGE DILLWYN.
13th.—Testimony from the Monthly Meeting of Philadelphia, concerning HANNAH FISHER.

SMITH, Hannah Logan, *continued.*

    14th.—Obituary of BENJAMIN RIDGWAY SMITH, 2nd Month 28th, 1809.

    15th.—Biography of NICHOLAS WALN.

    16th.—(Lines) to the Memory of my dear relative and friend, MARY DICKINSON, who deceased at Wilmington the 23rd day of the 7th Month, 1803. By Hannah Griffitts.

    17th.—(Account of) Lydia Dean, from the *Salem Gazette, March 12th, 1822.*

    18th.—HANNAH POWELL. [This Obituary was written by Elizabeth Arnold, and is so true and appropriate that Anna wished it printed thus.—*From a letter sheet received from Joseph Rotch.*]

    19th.—PETER YARNALL. *To the Memory of the late pious* PETER YARNAL, *an eminent preacher of the religious Society called Quakers.*

    20th.—WIFE OF ROBERT BARCLAY (of Thrale's Brewhouse, Southwark). [Sent to Miers Fisher from one of the family. Printed from *The Times* of 4th January, 1794.]

    21st.—ELIZABETH ESTAUGH's Testimony to the Memory of her beloved Husband, John Estaugh, deceased.

    22nd.—(Lines) To the Memory of Sarah F. Corlies, deceased.

    23rd.—A Memorial concerning my beloved Wife, Hannah Smith. By John Smith.

    24th.—Some account of JOHN SMITH, towards the close of his life, by his daughter, H. Smith, who afterwards became the wife of JOHN COX, of *Burlington.*

    25th.—(Letter from) JAMES LOGAN to his son WILLIAM, on his voyage to Bristol. Sent to him at Chester. Philadelphia, 4th of 5th Month. 1730.

    26th.—To the Memory of the late JOSEPH BROWN, of *Lothersdale.* (By James Montgomery).

    27th.—PARSON PETERS to ANTHONY BENEZET (on Barclay's Apology).

    28th.—The Substance of a few expressions delivered by SAMUEL FOTHERGILL.

    29th.—On Faithfulness in Little Things.

    30th.—Thoughts on the Importance of Religion.

    31st.—On Passing Meeting. 1st Mo. 30th, 1838.

    32nd.—Extracts from an Essay on Love to God. By Joseph John Gurney.

    33rd.—Memoir of the Fisher family.

    34th.—(An account of) Visits of European Friends to America.

    35th.—(An account of) Visits of American Friends to Europe.

    36th.—Testimony from New Garden Monthly Meeting, concerning HANNAH LINDLEY.

SMITH, Hannah Logan, *continued.*
 37th.—Testimony concerning JACOB LINDLEY.
 38th.—Last illness of BENJAMIN RIDGWAY SMITH.
 39th.—Memoir of James Smith.
 40th.—An Eulogium on the Character of Benjamin Ridgway Smith, by Roberts Vaux.
 41st.—Account of Deborah Logan.
 42nd.—Postscript (containing some Memorandums supplied by E. Littell). One leaf.

SMITH, Henry Ecroyd (an Old Ackworth Scholar), *continued* from Catalogue, Vol. 2, p. 585.

——ANNALS of SMITH OF CANTLEY, BALBY, AND DONCASTER, COUNTY YORK; embracing elaborate Pedigrees of the connected Families, and biographical notices of their more eminent members. Compiled by HENRY ECROYD SMITH.
 No man of well-regulated mind, can feel indifference respecting the genealogy of his family.—RICHARD COBDEN.
 Printed for Subscribers only. (*By Hills & Co., 188, High Street West, Sunderland.*)
 (Not Published.) . . . . . 4to. 1878.
 NOTE.—This title is taken from a proof; the words in a parenthesis I believe are struck out in the copies sent out. 277 pages; Appendix, 24 do.; Works by the Compiler, 3 do., at the end.
 He died at *Middleham, Yorkshire,* 1st mo. 25, 1889, aged 66 years.

SMITH, Henry Frederick, of *Darlington.*

——Circular addressed to Friends on the Removal of his Academy from Darlington to Wood House, near Little Ilford, Essex.
      4to. No date. ¼

SMITH, John Jay, of *North America.*

———A Summer's Jaunt across the water, including visits to England, Ireland, Scotland, France, Switzerland, Germany Belgium, &c. By J. Jay Smith, Librarian of the Philadelphia and Loganian Libraries, 2 vols.
 Philadelphia . . . . 12mo. 1846.

——American Historical and Literary Curiosities; consisting of Original Documents relative to the Events of the Revolution; with a variety of Reliques, Antiquities, and Modern Autographs. Collected and Edited by J. Jay Smith and John F. Watson.
 New York . . . . Royal 4to. 1850.
 Reprinted, the 5th edition,
 Philadelphia . . Imperial 4to. 1861.

SMITH, John Jay, *continued*.

——Letter to Horace Binney, Esq., respecting (John Smith) the founder of the Philadelphia Contributionship, by John Jay Smith.
Philadelphia . . . . . 8vo. 1853.
No. 12,884, Philadelphia Library.

——Letters of Doctor Richard Hill and his Children ; or, the History of a Family as told by themselves. Collected and arranged by John Jay Smith.
Privately printed for the descendants.
Philadelphia, 1854. . . Large 8vo. 466 pp.
See RICHARD HILL.

——The Penn Family. By John Jay Smith.
[*Philadelphia printed. No date?*] . Large 8vo. 1¾

†SMITH, Joseph (an Old Ackworth Scholar), *continued* from Catalogue. Vol. 2, p. 595.

——Bibliotheca Anti-Quakeriana ; or, A Catalogue of Books adverse to the Society of Friends, alphabetically arranged ; with Biographical Notices of the Authors, together with the Answers which have been given to some of them by Friends and others. By Joseph Smith.
London : Joseph Smith, 6, Oxford Street, White-chapel, E. 8vo. 1873. 30

——BIBLIOTHECA QUAKERISTICA : A Bibliography of Miscellaneous Literature relating to the Friends (Quakers), *chiefly written by Persons not Members of their Society*; also of PUBLICATIONS BY AUTHORS in some way connected ; and Biographical Notices. By Joseph Smith, Hon. Member of the Friends' Hist. Association of Philadelphia ; Author of "A Catalogue of Friends' Books," and " Bibliotheca Anti-Quakeriana," etc.
London : Joseph Smith, 6, Oxford Street, White-chapel, E. Printed by Geo. H. Farrington, 11, Knight Rider Street, Doctors' Commons, E.C.
(Only *2 sheets* printed off.) . . . 8vo. 1883.

——Bibliography of Sugar. In "The Sugar Cane," a periodical edited by Henry Thorp, of Manchester.

——George Fox, his Journal. . Single leaf. Folio. 1882.

——Portraits of George Fox, 2 circulars. . 4to.

——Books (List of) by Ackworth Scholars and relating to the School. . . . . . . 8vo. ¼

SMITH, Joseph, *continued.*

——A Biographical Catalogue of Friends whose portraits are chiefly in the Gallery of "Friends' Institute." (*Part his*). . . . . . . 8vo. 1888.

——Short BIOGRAPHICAL NOTICES of William Bradford, Reiner Jansen, Andrew Bradford, and Samuel Keimer, Early Printers in Pennsylvania. By Joseph Smith.

London : Edward Hicks, Jun., 14, Bishopsgate Without, E.C. 8vo. 1891. 1¾

SMITH, M. D.

——A Daughter's Memorial to her Mother.

*SMITH, R. Pearsall, of *Philadelphia.*

——The Secret of Victory.

London : Morgan & Chase, 38, Ludgate Hill.

——Thy Maker is thy Husband.

(Same imprint.)

——The Way of Righteousness. A Narrative of Christian Experience.

(Same imprint.)

——Holiness through Faith. By R. PEARSALL SMITH, Author of

"The Secret of Victory," "Thy Maker is thy Husband," "The Way of Righteousness," &c., &c.

"Purifying their hearts by faith."—*Acts xv., 9.*

London : Morgan & Chase, 38, Ludgate Hill ; and may be ordered of any Bookseller.

8vo. No date. 8

——Hymns selected from Faber, by R. Pearsall Smith.

W. Isbister & Co. . . . . . 1874.

——Is Romans vii. To be the continued Experience of the Christian ?

London : Morgan & Chase, 38, Ludgate Hill.

He also wrote a number of small books (envelope series), published by Morgan & Chase.

*SMITH, H. W. (his Wife).

——The Early Friends : their Message and the Secret of their Power. [Anon.]

King & Baird, Printers, 607, Sansom Street, Philadelphia ; Smith, English, & Co.'s Bookstore, 23, North Sixth Street. 8vo. No date. 1

SMITH, Samuel, of *Burlington, New Jersey.* Continued from Catalogue, Vol. 2, p. 598.

——History of the religious progress of the People called Quakers in Pennsylvania, by Samuel Smith, from materials furnished by the Yearly Meeting.

> This History was not published at the time when it was written, but remained in the possession of James Pemberton and his heirs, and was published in Hazard's Register of Pennsylvania about the year 1833, and then more fully in the 18th, 19th, and 20th volumes of "The Friend."

SMITH, Samuel J. The Poet of Burlington, grandson of the above.

——The Miscellaneous Writings of the late Samuel J. Smith, of Burlington, N.J., collected and arranged by one of the family, with a notice illustrative of his life and character.

Philadelphia: 8vo. 1836. 222pp.

SMITH, Seth,—See JOHN H. WILLETS.

——And John H. Willets.—An Elementary Treatise on Natural Philosophy, designed for the use of Students, by John H. Willets and Seth Smith.

Philadelphia: 8vo. 1830. 470pp.

SNASHALL, John, *continued* from Catalogue, Vol. 2, p. 613.

——(*Copy of a Letter*) FROM JOHN SNASHALL, AGED EIGHTY-ONE YEARS, TO THE LATE WILLIAM GROVER, WHEN A LAD, 11th month 28th, 1768.

> "For admonition—I could recommend to thy serious view nothing like the pathetic advice and cautions as are contained in that excellent performance, "No Cross, no Crown," by William Penn, with whom I was well acquainted, dined with him divers times at his house at Worminghurst, and other Friends' houses; yet never beheld so respectable a personage everyway for presence as also so soft, courteously affable, and engaging, withal a solid cheerful demeanor and countenance, *never* to be forgotten by me."
>
> NOTE.—The above is inserted in a small paper printed at Manchester by John Harrison, in [1844?], entitled "Extracts from ' No Cross, No Crown,' and John Woolman's Works."

SNOWDON, Richard, of *Woodbury, Gloucester County, New Jersey,* of English parentage.

——A History of the Revolutionary War.

313

SOUTHALL, John Edward, of *Newport, Monmouthshire*.

——A Faithful Warning to those calling themselves Friends; more particularly in Western Quarterly Meeting, England.
Printed by John Bellows, Gloucester. 8vo. 1881. ¼

SOUTHALL, John Tertius, of *Leominster*.

——The 𝕮𝖎𝖒𝖊𝖘 𝖔𝖋 𝖙𝖍𝖊 𝕮𝖔𝖒𝖒𝖔𝖓𝖜𝖊𝖆𝖑𝖙𝖍, a Lecture delivered at the Corn Exchange, Leominster, February 28, 1865. By John Tertius Southall.
Leominster: Published by S. Partridge, the Public Library. London: A. W. Bennett, 5, Bishopsgate St. Within. . . . 8vo. 1865. 2¼

SPALDING, John, *continued* from Catalogue, Vol. 2, p. 616.

——A Few Reasons for leaving, &c. Translated into GERMAN, entitled — Johann Spalding's Grunde seiner Abtretung von der allgemeinen Artder Gottesverehrung. Ein Sendschreiben an die Mitglieder seiner vorigen Gemeinschaft. Aus dem Englischen.
Friedensthal, ber Ludwig Seebohm. 16mo. 1803. 2⅝

SPEAKMAN, Thomas H., of *Philadelphia*, Attorney-at-Law. (Of the branch called " Hicksite.")

——Divisions in the Society of Friends. By Thomas H. Speakman.
Philadelphia: J. B. Lippincott & Co. 8vo. 1869. 4

——RITUALISM and DOGMATIC THEOLOGY. 𝔄 𝔖𝔢𝔯𝔦𝔢𝔰 𝔬𝔣 𝔈𝔰𝔰𝔞𝔶𝔰 Published in 1872-3 in Friends' Intelligencer and Manchester Friend, on the Causes of the Declension in the Society of Friends. Now Republished as bearing also on the subjects of Creeds and Confessions of Faith and Rational Religion. By Thomas H. Speakman.
Philadelphia: For sale by Friends' Book Association, S.W. Cor. Fifteenth and Race Streets.
8vo. 1891. 3

SQUIRE, Thomas, of *Epping*, in *Essex*.

——A Popular Grammar of the Elements of Astronomy, adapted to the use of Students and Public Schools. By Thomas Squire. Illustrated with thirty-seven engravings. 𝔄 𝔑𝔢𝔴 𝔈𝔡𝔦𝔱𝔦𝔬𝔫.
London: Printed for Geo. B. Whittaker, Ave Maria Lane. . . . 12mo. 1825. 12⅔

STABLER, Edward, son of Edward and Mary Stabler, of
Alexandria, in the district of *Columbia*, was born
at *Petersburg* in *Virginia*, on the 28th day of the
9th Month, 1769. He died on the 18th of the 1st
Month, 1831, in the 62nd year of his age. Edward
Stabler, his father, was born near York, in England.

——A MEMOIR of the LIFE OF EDWARD STABLER,—with a
Collection of his Letters. By his Son, William
Stabler.

    *Philadelphia : Printed by John Richards, 299,
Market Street. And to be had of John Comly,
Byberry, Philadelphia County ; T. Ellwood
Chapman, No. 74, North Fourth Street, Phila-
delphia ; Baker, Crane and Day, 158, Pearl
Street, New York ; and Richard Plummer,
Baltimore.* 12mo. 1846. 13

STARK, Thomas, of *Mevagissey, Cornwall*.

——A Biographical Notice of THOMAS STARK, THE
MEVAGISSEY QUAKER, WITH NOTES ; comprehend-
ing his domestic manners, Politics, Morals, Religion ;
how he got Riches and disposed of them ; his death ;
and the respect paid to his remains on the day of his
burial. By CANTABAR [Josiah Harris, of Bath.]
    " I speak as unto wise men, judge ye of what I say."
*Published by Wood Brothers, Bath.
To be had of all Booksellers.* PRICE FOURPENCE.
                                                                8vo. [1857.] 1
    He died the 8th of 7th Month, 1857, aged 76 years.

STEPHEN, Caroline Emelia, of *Malvern, Worcestershire*,
and *Chelsea*.

——The SERVICE OF THE POOR ; being an Inquiry into the
Reasons for and against the establishment of Religious
Sisterhoods for Charitable Purposes. By Caroline
Emelia Stephen.
    London & New York : Macmillan & Co.
                                                                          8vo. 1871. 22

——Quaker Strongholds.
                                                                    8vo. 1890.
    Reprinted, 2nd edition.
        „   3rd edition.
                                                                     . 8vo. 1891.

STEVENS, John Austin.

——THE ENGLISH IN NEW YORK, 1664-1689.
    This forms Chapter X. of *Justin Winsor's History of
America, 1886.*

STEPHENSON, Marmaduke, *continued* from Catalogue, Vol. 2, p. 624.
——A Call from Death to Life, &c.
Reprinted. *Providence.* 1845.
Only 100 copies printed.
——NARRATIVE of the MARTYRDOM, AT BOSTON, of William Robinson, Marmaduke Stevenson, Mary Dyer, and William Leddra, in the year 1659. *With other particulars.* Price Sixpence.
12mo. *Manchester*, 1841. 2
See WILLIAM ROBINSON.

STERRY, Alfred, of *22, Cannon Street.*
——DECIMAL COINAGE easily accomplished; with some remarks on FOREIGN CURRENCIES. Written for perusal at a Private Essay Club.
Croydon: Printed by Gray and Warren, High Street. . . . . 8vo. 1856. ½

STEWARDSON, William, of
——Letter to Commissioners of Customs.
London . . . . . . 8vo. 1763.
——Spiritual Courtship; or, The Rival Quakeresses.
London . . . . . . 8vo. 1764.

STEWART, Louisa, now of *Enfield, Middlesex.*
——The Missing Law; or, Woman's Birthright. By Mrs. J. Stewart.
London: W. Tweedie, 337, Strand . 8vo. 1869. 3⅜

STICKNEY, Stickney Sarah, *continued* from Catalogue, Vol. 2, p. 626. (Afterwards wife of William Ellis, the Missionary).
——Negro Slave, a Tale addressed to the Women of Great Britain. . . . . . . 12mo. 1830.
She died 16th of 6th mo., 1872, and was buried in Friends' Burial Ground at *Hoddesdon,* the 21st of the same Month, aged 73 years.

STONE, Frederick D., Librarian of the Historical Society of Pennsylvania, Philadelphia, U.S. America.
——THE FOUNDING OF PENNSYLVANIA. By FREDERICK D. STONE, *Librarian of the Historical Society of Pennsylvania.*
NOTE.—This forms Chapter XII. of Vol. III. of *Justin Winsor's History of America,* and contains a Portrait of George Fox (after Honthorst), and one of William Penn (in Armour), and fac-similes of the titles of two of William Penn's tracts. The account is most interesting and valuable.

STORRS, Sarah Ann, of *70, Clissold Road, Stoke Newington.*

—— More about the FIGHT in Dame Europa's School, with John's Reasons for not joining in the Quarrel. Reprinted. SECOND EDITION. Price Threepence.
Sold by F. B. Kitto, 5, Bishopsgate Street Without; and at 70, Clissold Road, Stoke Newington. . . . . . 16mo. [1870.] ¼

STORY, Thomas, was born at *Justice Town*, Parish of *Kirklinton*, about the year 1670. He received a good education, and was intended for the Church by his Father, who was in good circumstances; but, changing his mind, he joined himself to the Quakers, and travelled much both at home and in America, preaching in Pennsylvania and other Provinces, where he was appointed to the highest offices in the State. In 1715 he returned to his paternal estate at Justice Town, and imported several species of foreign trees, such as the tulip tree, locust tree, cedar of America, scarlet oak, &c. He died in 1742. His works on various subjects were published by his Executors in a large folio volume.
Jollie's Cumberland Guide and Directory.
Carlisle: Printed. 8vo. 1811.

Continued from Catalogue, Vol. 2, p. 636.

—— Life of Thomas Story, carefully abridged, &c., by John Kendall.
Reprinted,—*Philadelphia : Printed by Joseph Crukshank.* 12mo. 1805. 14½

—— The DOCTRINES of the SOCIETY OF FRIENDS, as set forth in THE LIFE AND WRITINGS of THOMAS STORY. [Or, "Brief Memoir of Thomas Story."]
Philadelphia: Published by the Association of Friends for the Diffusion of Religious and Useful Knowledge, No. 109, North Tenth Street. [Stereotyped by L. Johnson & Co., Philadelphia. 12mo. 1859. 8⅙

—— Salvation by Christ, and its universality. Silent Waiting, Silent Teaching, and Silent Worship. By Thomas Story, a Minister of the Society of Friends. First edition, printed 1738.
London : F. Bowyer Kitto, 5, Bishopsgate Street. Carlisle : Hudson, Scott, and Sons.
16mo. 1868. 2½

STOUGHTON, John, D.D., of *Ealing, Middlesex* (Not a Member).

——WILLIAM PENN, the Founder of Pennsylvania. By John Stoughton, D.D. (With a "Portrait of William Penn" in Armour.)
London : Hodder and Stoughton, 27, Paternoster Row. 8vo. 1882. 23¼

*STROUD, George M., of *North America*.

——A Sketch of the Laws relating to Slavery, in the several states of the United States of America, by George M. Stroud.
Philadelphia : 8vo. 1827. 180pp.

Reprinted.—The 2nd edition with some alterations and considerable additions.
Philadelphia : 12mo. 1856. 305pp.

STUBBE, Henry,

was the Son of a minister (Church of England), and born at *Partney*, near *Spilsbye*, in *Lincolnshire*, on the 28th of February, 1631, and at ten years of age sent to *Westminster* School under the care of Dr. *Richard Busby*, where by the interest of Sir *Henry Vane*, junr., he became one of the King's Scholars, and in 1649 was elected student of *Christ Church* in *Oxford*. In July, 1653, he took the degree of Bachelor of Arts, and then went to *Scotland*, where he served in the Army till 1655; and in December, 1656, took the degree of Master of Arts. In the beginning of the year following he was appointed second library-keeper of the *Bodleian* library under Dr. *Thos. Barlow*, which post he held till the year 1659, when he was removed from it, as well as from his place of student of *Christ Church*, having the same year published a *Vindication* of his patron Sir *Henry Vane, An Essay on the good old Cause*, and a piece entitled, *Light shining out of Darkness*, with *an Apology for the Quakers*, in which he reflected upon the Clergy and the Universities. He retired then to *Stratford* upon *Avon* in order to practise physic there, and after the Restoration joined himself to the Church of *England, not only,* says he in the dedication to bishop *Morley* of his translation of *Casa's Arts of Grandeur and Submission, upon account of its being publicly imposed, (which in things indifferent is no small consideration, as I learned from the Scottish Transactions at Perth,) but because*

STUBBE, Henry, *continued.*
it is the least defining, and consequently the most comprehensive and fitting to be national. In 1661 he went to *Jamaica*, being honoured with the title of his Majesty's physician for that island; but that climate not agreeing with his constitution, he returned to *England*, and at last settled in *Warwick*, where he gained very considerable practice, as likewise at the *Bath*, which he frequented in the summer-season; but was unfortunately drowned in a river about two miles from that city in a journey to *Bristol* on the 12th of July, 1676, and was interred in the great church at *Bath*, his old antagonist, Mr. *Glanvill*, preaching his funeral sermon.
Birch's Life of Robt. Boyle, 1744.

STURGE, Joseph, *continued* from Catalogue, Vol. 2, p. 643.
——Joseph Sturge, 𝕮𝖍𝖊 𝕮𝖍𝖗𝖎𝖘𝖙𝖎𝖆𝖓 𝕻𝖍𝖎𝖑𝖆𝖓𝖙𝖍𝖗𝖔𝖕𝖎𝖘𝖙.
[Gloucestershire Tracts, No. 17.]
London : Morgan & Chase, 40, Ludgate Street. Cirencester : C. H. Savory, Printer and Publisher. . . . . 8vo. No date. 1¼

†SWINTON, John, *continued* from Catalogue, Vol. 2, p. 688.
——To the Inhabitants of the Whole Earth.
B. 1665. 1

T.

T., Susan. See REBECCA THURSFIELD.

TALLACK, William, *continued* from Catalogue, Vol. 2, p. 690.
——Capital Punishment, illustrated by a few very recent facts. [Prepared in view of Mr. William Ewart's Motion for its Abolition, March 15th, 1867.]
8vo. [1867.] ¼
——George Fox, the Friends, and the Early Baptists. By William Tallack. (With a Portrait of George Fox.)
London : S. W. Partridge & Co., 9, Paternoster Row. 8vo. 1868. 13
——The Unemployed Poor, The "Roughs," and the Criminal Classes. . . . . 8vo. 1868. ¼

TALLACK, William, *continued.*

——Humanity and Humanitarianism. . . 8vo. 1871.

——The Police. Misdemeanours and Intemperance. A Letter, " To the Editor of the Globe."
    In " The Globe " Newspaper, Wednesday, July 9, 1873.

——The War System of Europe, 1877-78.
    Wertheimer, Lea & Co., Printers, Circus Place, Finsbury Circus. . . 8vo. May 4, 1877. $\frac{1}{2}$

——The Quakers' "Bunhill Fields" Burial Ground.
    In " The City Press," Saturday, March 31st, 1877.

——THE ROOT-PRINCIPLE of the PEACE QUESTION. [ANON.]
    Barrett, Sons & Co., Printers, Seething Lane, London. . . . 12mo. No date. $\frac{1}{3}$

——THE WAR SYSTEM OF EUROPE. 1882. [ANON.]
    Wertheimer, Lea & Co., Printers, Circus Place, London. . . . . 8vo. 1882. $\frac{1}{2}$

——Proved Praticability of International Arbitration, 1882. [ANON.]
    Wertheimer, Lea. & Co., Printers, Circus Place, London Wall. . . . 12mo. [1882.] $\frac{1}{3}$

——FRIENDLY WORDS TO EMPLOYERS, MASTERS, AND MISTRESSES. [ANON.]
    London : S. W. Partridge & Co., 9, Paternoster Row. . . . . . . (A Card.)

——PENOLOGICAL AND PREVENTIVE PRINCIPLES, WITH SPECIAL REFERENCE TO EUROPE AND AMERICA ; and to the Diminution of Crime, Pauperism and Intemperance ; Prisons and their Substitutes, Habitual Offenders, Sentences, Neglected Youth, Education, Police, Statistics, &c. ; by William Tallack, Secretary of the Howard Association.
    Published by Wertheimer, Lea & Co., Circus Place, London Wall, London, E.C.
                                                   8vo   1889.   (420 pp.)

——Some general observations on THE PENALTY OF DEATH. By William Tallack. 1890.
    Issued by the Howard Association, *Bishopsgate Without, London.*
    Wertheimer, Lea, & Co., Printers, Circus Place, London Wall. . . . 8vo. [1890.] $\frac{1}{4}$

TALLACK, William, *continued*.

——THE COLLEGIATE AND HOTEL PRISONS OF THE
UNITED STATES, 1891. [*Issued by the* Howard
Association *for the Promotion of the best methods of
the Treatment and Prevention of Crime and Pauperism.*] Office, 5, Bishopsgate Street Without, London,
E.C.
  *Wertheimer, Lea, & Co., Printers, Circus Place,
  London Wall.* . . . 8vo. [1891.] ¼

——" The Probation of First Offenders' Act " (1887).
[Issued by the Howard Association, London, 1892.]
  *Wertheimer, Lea, & Co., Printers, Circus Place,
  London Wall, E.C.* . . 8vo. [1892.] ⅛

——Suggestions for the Diminution of Pauperism.
[*Issued by the* Howard Association, *London.*]
            8vo. 1892. ¼

——Edward Denison, M.P., Arnold Toynbee, and Social
Problems.
[*Issued by the* Howard Association, *London*, 1892.]
  *Wertheimer, Lea, & Co., Printers, Circus Place,
  London Wall.* . . . . 8vo. 1892. ¼

——The Inward Light and Christ's Incarnation. By William Tallack (Author of " Penological and Preventive
Principles ").
  *Reprinted from the Friends' Quarterly Examiner
  for January, 1892.*
  London : *Edward Hicks, Jun., 14, Bishopsgate
  Without, E.C.* . . . 8vo. [1892.] 1

TALLCOT, Joseph, of *North America*.

——Memoirs of Joseph Tallcot. (Portrait.)
   Count that day lost whose slow sun declining
   Shines on no generous deed or useful action done.
  Auburn, N.Y. : *Miller, Orton, and Mulligan,
  Printers.* . . . . . 12mo. 1855.

TANGYE, Richard, of *Birmingham*.

——REMINISCENCES of TRAVEL in Australia, America, and
Egypt. By RICHARD TANGYE. With illustrations
by E. C. Mountfort. (Portrait.) Third edition.
  London : *Sampson, Low, Marston, Searle, and
  Rivington, Crown Buildings, 188, Fleet Street.*
  [*All Rights Reserved.*] 8vo. 1884. 268pp.

TANNER, William, *continued* from Catalogue, Vol. 2, p. 692.
——Some account of the last illness and death of William Tanner, who died the 8th of 11th Month, 1866, in his 52nd year. *For private circulation only.*
            8vo. [1866.] ¾
——An Account of his funeral in *The Bristol Daily Post.*
——MEMOIR of WILLIAM TANNER, compiled chiefly from autobiographical memoranda. Edited by John Ford. (With a Preface by his Widow, Sarah W. Tanner.) *London : F. Bowyer Kitto, Bishopsgate Street Without. York : William Sessions, Low Ouseyate.* 8vo. 1868. 17
  NOTE.—This book has a Portrait and fac-simile of the autograph of William Tanner, also a view of his residence, "Ashley Farm, near Bristol": and at the end of the Volume are some "Sermons by W. Tanner."

TAYLOR, Bayard, of *North America.*
——Book of Romance, Lyrics, and Songs.
 Boston :   .   .   .   Foolscap 8vo ?   1852.
——Poems and Ballads, with Portrait.
 New York :   .   .   .   12mo.
——Poems of Home and Travel.
 Boston :   .   .   .   12mo.   1855.
——Poems of the Orient.
 Boston :   .   .   .   .   12mo.   1854.
——Views A-foot ; or, Europe seen with Knapsack and Staff. By Bayard Taylor.
Reprinted.—New edition, thoroughly revised.
 New York :   .   .   .   Crown 8vo.   1856.
——Life and Landscapes from Egypt to the White Nile ; being a Journey to Central Africa. By Bayard Taylor, Author of "Views A-foot," and "Eldorado," Illustrated with elegant tinted Plates and Engravings on Wood, from Drawings by the Author ; with a Steel Portrait.
 New York :   .   .   .   .   12mo.   1855.
——Asia Minor, Sicily, and Spain : or the Lands of the Saracen. By Bayard Taylor. With Illustrations.
 New York :   .   .   .   Post 8vo.   1855.
  " Pleasant, readable and useful, which is saying no little for Mr. Bayard Taylor. He blends various qualities into the narrative together, which lie harmoniously upon each other like the strands of a rope. . . He writes elo-

TAYLOR, Bayard, *continued.*

quently, easily, and with a vivid feeling for the picturesque."—*Athenæum.*

"The book is full of fresh and genuine interest."—*Leader.*

"Mr. Taylor writes with facility and describes with effect ; his narrative is always lively and amusing. His landscapes are variations of purple, orange and green ; every object adds a tint to the picture."—*Press.*

——India, Japan, and China. By Bayard Taylor, Author of "The Lands of the Saracen ; or Pictures of Palestine," &c. With Engravings.

New York : . . . . Post 8vo. 1855.

"The two years and four months' travel, of which this volume forms the closing part, exhibits the same resolute energy as the Author's "Views A-foot." . . . Mr. Taylor shows the skill or knack of a practised *littérateur*, and knows what to select from the objects that pass before him, as well as how to present them in the most forcible and lively manner."—*Spectator.*

"To extract passages from Mr. Taylor's pictorial descriptions, would be to cut squares out of a panorama. . . . At once bright in style, and varied and entertaining in matter."—*Leader.*

*TAYLOR, John, of *Peckham, London.*

——Christian Activity.

Reprinted from the Examiner.

——Drunkenness, an indirect cause of Crime. . . With a Map shewing the number of Public Houses in the Metropolis.

London : . . . . . . 8vo. 1860.

[*British Museum*, 8435. C. 26.]
              ———
              12.

*TAYLOR, Joseph, of *Whitby, Yorkshire.*

——Thoughts on the Production and Formation of Animal Bodies, &c., with the Natural cause of the Recovery of Persons apparently dead by drowning ; and many other things worthy of notice. By Joseph Taylor.

Whitby : *Printed by C. Webster, for the Author.* (*March 3rd*). . . 8vo. 1787. pp. 44.

NOTE.—With a sketch of himself, on his donkey, as a frontispiece. The Quakers denounced this publication. On the printed cover of the above book two additional pamphlets were advertised to be published, Query whether ?—viz., Anecdotes of the late John Elwes, Esq., price 6d. ; also, The Absurd Notion of Fortune in Marriage Refuted, by Scripture Reasoning and Experience, by Joseph Taylor, price 6d., Dec. 1st, 1791.

TAYLOR, Joseph, of *Middlesborough.*
——Statement of the Claims of the TEES COAL COMPANY, against JONATHAN BACKHOUSE, and against EDWARD BACKHOUSE, as Co-Partner with H. Stobart, in answer to the various Mis-statements that have been circulated. Also, a Statement of the Proceedings of the MONTHLY AND QUARTERLY MEETINGS in these cases in answer to the Documents issued by them. By Joseph Taylor.
 Stockton : Printed at the Office of R. Swales, High Street, 1838. . . . . 8vo. 1838. 3½

THOMAS, Abel, *continued* from Catalogue, Vol. 2, p. 732.
——Letters.
 In Comly's Miscellany, Vol. 4, p. 276.

THOMAS, David, of *North America.*
——Travels through the Western Country in the Summer of 1816, including notices of the Natural History, Topography, Commerce, Antiquities, Agriculture and Manufactures, with a Map of the Wabash Country now settling by David Thomas.
 Auburn, New York. . 12mo. 1819. 320 pp.

THOMAS, John,
——A Propheticall LOVE-SONG. By one of the Sons of Zion, in the dayes of his Youth, in his Travel towards the Holy Land through the *Wilderness.* Being a certain true Testimony by an Infallible Spirit of Prophesie, of what should befall him in his safe arrival there, with the certainty of that and his portion then. In which is intermingled the miserable Estate of all the Gentiles, the wicked World, the backsliding House of *Israel*, the Jews called by the Name of *Quakers*, as it was given forth about the beginning of the 2 Month, 1661. With several other things since, and some before, as at the beginning of each is expressed. And now Published in its season. By *John Thomas.*
 LONDON: *Printed for the Author in the year 1661.*
            4to. 2½

 NOTE.—This pamphlet is wholly poetry, it contains amongst others,
  "*To a Maid making silver on gold lace,*"
  "*Of Young* George Fox,"
  "*To a Maid known by the Name* of Anne Robinson (*I think call'd a* Quaker) *pretending service for the Lord to Jamaica ; but it's a Lye ; for the Word of the Lord was brought unto her by the Author to forbid her the Journey,*" etc.

THOMAS, John J., Son of DAVID THOMAS, Pomologist.

—— Farm Implements, and the Principles of their Construction and Use. By John J. Thomas. An Elementary and familiar Treatise on Mechanics, and on Natural Philosophy generally, as applied to the ordinary Practices of Agriculture, with 200 Engravings.
New York:
Post 8vo. 1854. 267pp.

" We should like to see this work printed, bound, and hung up in every workshop, tool-room, and farmer's bookshelf in the country. It gives the reason and explains the action of mechanical powers, and the forces of nature generally, with Illustrations so directly drawn from the farmer's daily routine, that it gives a direct meaning and value to every point, rarely found in text-books."— *Downing's Rural Essays.*

—— The American Fruit Culturist. By John J. Thomas.
New York: . . . 8vo. 1867. 500pp.

*THOMAS, Joseph, M.D., Son of DAVID THOMAS, Philologist, Geographer. See also THOMAS BALDWIN.

—— A Universal Pronouncing Gazetteer, containing Topographical, Statistical, and other information of all the more important places in the known world, from the most recent and authentic sources, with a Map by Thomas Baldwin, assisted by several other gentlemen.
Philadelphia: . . . 8vo. 1845. 550pp.

NOTE.—This, although appearing as J. Baldwin's work, was chiefly written by Dr. Thomas, being the first of his series of Gazetteers."
From a note furnished to me by an American Friend.—J.S.

—— A New and Complete Gazetteer of the United States, giving a full and comprehensive review of the present condition, industry and resources of the American Confederacy: embracing also important topographical, statistical, and historical information from recent and original sources, together with the results of the census of 1850, and population and statistics in many cases, to 1853. By Thos. Baldwin and J. Thomas, M.D.
Philadelphia: . . . 8vo. 1854. 1364pp.

THOMAS, Joseph, *continued.*

—— Travels in Egypt and Palestine. By J. Thomas, M.D.

Philadelphia: . . . 12mo. 1853. 174pp.

—— A Complete Pronouncing Gazetteer, or Geographical Dictionary of the World, containing a notice and the pronunciation of the names of nearly one hundred thousand places, with the most recent and authentic information respecting the Countries, Islands, Rivers, Mountains, Cities, Towns, &c., in every portion of the Globe. Including the latest and most reliable statistics of population, commerce, &c.; also a complete etymological Vocabulary of Geographical names, and many other valuable features to be found in no other Gazetteers in the English Language. Edited by J. Thomas, M.D., and J. Baldwin, assisted by several other Gentlemen.—2 Vols. in 1.

Philadelphia: . . . . 1855. 2,182pp.

—— A Comprehensive Medical Dictionary, containing the pronunciation, etymology, and signification of the terms made use of in Medicine and the Kindred Sciences, with an Appendix, comprising a complete list of all the more important articles of the Materia Medica arranged according to their medicinal properties. Also an explanation of the Latin terms and phrases occurring in Anatomy, Pharmacy, &c., together with the necessary directions for writing Latin prescriptions, &c., &c. By J. Thomas, M.D.

Philadelphia: . . 8vo. 1864. 704pp.

THOMPSON, Charles, an Old Ackworth Scholar, of *Morland*, near *Penrith.*

THOMPSON, Henry, of *Rawden.*

—— A HISTORY of ACKWORTH SCHOOL during its first hundred years; Preceded by a brief Account of the fortunes of the house whilst occupied as a Foundling Hospital. By HENRY THOMPSON. With Twelve Illustrations by Mary Hodgson, engraved on wood by Edmund Evans.

Published by the Centenary Committee, Ackworth School, 1879. Samuel Harris & Co., 5, Bishopsgate St. Without, London.

8vo. 1879. 47½

THOMPSON, Isaac, of *Newcastle-on-Tyne*.

——ADVERTISEMENT. Whereas THOMAS STORY, late of *Justice Town*, in the County of *Cumberland*, did write a JOURNAL OF HIS OWN LIFE, &c.
         Folio. No Date. ½

*THOMPSON, Jacob, was the Eldest Son of Merrick and Mary Thompson, of *Penrith*, born in Lanton Street, Penrith, 28 4mo., 1806.

——THE LIFE AND WORKS of JACOB THOMPSON. By LLEWELLYNN JEWIT, F.S.A., &c., &c., &c.
Illustrated with Engravings on Steel and Wood. (*Portrait*).
London : *Published for the Author by J. S. Virtue & Co., Limited, 294, City Road. (All Rights reserved.)* . . . . Large 4to. 1882. 18

THOMPSON, John, *continued* from Catalogue, Vol. 2, p. 736.
> John Thompson died the 27th day of the 7th Month, 1877, aged 80 years, and his remains were interred in Friends' Burial-ground, Hitchin. For further particulars concerning him, his funeral, &c., see the "*Hertfordshire Express*," of *Saturday*, August 4th, 1877. Vol. xvii. No. 926. Printed by Wm. Carling & Co., Market Place, Hitchin.

*THOMPSON, Katharine, daughter of John and Mary Thompson, of *Hitchin*.

——Joachim *v.* Kamern ; Diary of a Poor Young Lady. By Maria Nathusius. From the German by Miss Thompson.
Leipzig, 1869.
Bernhard Tauchnitz.
London : *Sampson Low, Son, and Marston, Crown Buildings, 188, Fleet Street. Paris : C. Reinwald, 15, Rues des Saints Péres.*
        16mo. 1869. 334 pp.

———A Hand-Book to the Public Picture Galleries of Europe. By Kate Thompson.
3rd Edition, with illustrations—*Macmillan & Co.*
           1880.
> She died the 30th of 11th month, 1885, and was buried according to the rites of the Church of England in Hitchin public cemetery.

THOMPSON, Philip, of *Woodbridge*, *continued* from Catalogue, Vol. 2, p. 737.

——The REMEMBRANCER, for such as believe in the TRUTH AS IT IS IN JESUS, of every denomination. Preceded

THOMPSON, Philip, *continued*.

by Three Chapters, explanatory of Man in the Fall, and Unbelief, Of God's Free Grace, Of Regeneration, &c. 𝔇𝔢𝔰𝔦𝔤𝔫𝔢𝔡 𝔞𝔰 𝔞 𝔓𝔬𝔠𝔨𝔢𝔱 𝔒𝔬𝔪𝔭𝔞𝔫𝔦𝔬𝔫. By a Member of the Society of Friends.

Third edition, enlarged.

WOODBRIDGE : *Printed for the Author, at the Columbian Press; and sold by B.* Smith ; Harvey and Darton, Gracechurch Street ; W. Darton, Holborn ; Edm. Fry, Houndsditch ; W. Alexander, York ; and other Booksellers. 16mo. 1823. 7

THOMPSON, Silvanus, of *York*, Son of Thomas Thompson, of Liverpool.

——MEMORIALS of JOHN FORD. Edited by SILVANUS THOMPSON. (Portrait.)

London : Samuel Harris & Co., 5, Bishopsgate Street Without. York : William Sessions, 15, Low Ousegate. . . . 8vo. 1877. 16¼

He died the 3rd of 2nd Mo., 1881, aged 63 years, and was buried at *Settle*.

THOMPSON, Thomas, of *Compton*, near *Sherborne, Dorsetshire*. Son of JONAH THOMPSON.

——Advertisement of Thos. Thompson's BOARDING SCHOOL, to be continued, after Midsummer, 1809.

Cruttwell, Printer, Sherborne. 4to. [about 1808.] ¼

THOMPSON, T., of *Gillingham, Dorset*.

——On the Discovery of a Skeleton of the Hippopotamus in Post-Pliocene Drift near Motcomb, Dorset. By T. Thompson, Esq. [*Extracted from the* GEOLOGICAL MAGAZINE, Vol. VI., No. 5, May, 1869.]

Stephen Austin, Printer, Hertford. 8vo. [1869.] ¼

THORP, Fielden, of YORK, *continued* from Catalogue, Vol. 2, p. 743.

——The YORK READER ; a collection of 𝔒𝔯𝔞𝔱𝔬𝔯𝔦𝔠𝔞𝔩, 𝔓𝔬𝔢𝔱𝔦𝔠𝔞𝔩, 𝔞𝔫𝔡 𝔐𝔦𝔰𝔠𝔢𝔩𝔩𝔞𝔫𝔢𝔬𝔲𝔰 𝔓𝔞𝔰𝔰𝔞𝔤𝔢𝔰, designed for the use of Senior Classes, and forming a Supplement to the " Ackworth Reading Book." Compiled by Fielden Thorp, B.A., Fellow of University College, London ; and John Firth Fryer, B.A.

London : Alfred W. Bennett, 5, Bishopsgate Without. 8vo. 1866. 10

THORP, Fielden, *continued*.
——A Letter to a Friend. See *Anon*.
——A Review of a Lecture on "Liberty," read at the Manchester Friends' Institute, and since printed and published.
  London : F. B. Kitto, 5, Bishopsgate Street Without. York : William Sessions, 15, Low Ousegate. 8vo. 1867. 1¼
——The Rite of Baptism. Is it to be regarded as of Permanent Obligation for the Christian Church? A Scriptural Argument. By Fielden Thorp. (With a recommendatory notice, by Robert Charleton).
  York : William Sessions, 15, Low Ousegate. 1872.
——A few considerations on the non-necessity of Water Baptism. Being (with a little alteration) a Lecture delivered by Fielden Thorp. (When read please to return to Joseph Davis, Cotham Hill, Bristol).
  (*Tanner Bros., Bristol, Lithographers*).
      Folio. No date. 16 pages.

THORP, Henry, of *Manchester*. Editor of "The Sugar Cane."
——The Sugar Cane.
  He died at *Sale*, near *Manchester*, the 24th of 10th month, 1889, aged 58 years, and was buried at *Ashton-on-Mersey*.

THURSFIELD, Rebecca, daughter of JOHN and SUSANNA FINCHER, of *Evesham*, was the wife of JOHN THURSFIELD.
——A Brief Memoir of Susan T. (Thursfield) (her daughter).
  London : James Nisbet & Co., 21, Berners Street, Oxford Street. . . . 18mo. 1863. 3⅔
  She died the 30th of 4th Month, 1887, aged 72 years.

TOWNSEND, Ann A., of *Philadelphia*. (Hicksite?)
——Biblical History Familiarized by Questions.
  Philadelphia. . . . . 18mo. 324 pp.

¶TOWNSEND, Hannah, of *Philadelphia*.
——HISTORY OF ENGLAND, in Verse, from the Invasion of Julius Cæsar to the present time. With illustrative notes, Chronological Chart of the Kings of England, Tables of Contemporary Sovereigns, and A TABLE, descriptive of the present condition of Great Britain. By HANNAH TOWNSEND.
  Philadelphia : Lindsay & Blakiston. 12mo. 1852. 6⅓

TOWNSEND, John K., of *Philadelphia*, Naturalist.

———Narrative of a Journey across the Rocky Mountains to the Columbia River, and a visit to the Sandwich Islands, Chili, &c. By John K. Townsend.
Philadelphia. . . . 8vo. 1839.

TRACT AND BOOK ASSOCIATIONS, &c., (*continued* from Catalogue, Vol. 2, p. 752), arranged in the following order, viz :—

LONDON TRACT ASSOCIATION.
DUBLIN TRACT ASSOCIATION.
BRIGHTON FRIENDS' TRACT ASSOCIATION.
LEICESTER FRIENDS' TRACT ASSOCIATION.
LEOMINSTER FRIENDS' TRACT ASSOCIATION.
PHILADELPHIA FRIENDS' TRACT ASSOCIATION.
PHILADELPHIA FRIENDS' BOOK ASSOCIATION (Hicksite?)
NEW YORK FRIENDS' TRACT ASSOCIATION.

LONDON TRACT ASSOCIATION.

———Catalogue of Books, Tracts, Pamphlets, Leaflets, &c., Published and Sold by the Friends' Tract Association at their Book and Tract Depôt, 14, Bishopsgate Street Without, London (*Adjoining Devonshire House*).—Addressed to Edward Hicks, Jun.
16mo. 1890   ¾

DUBLIN TRACT ASSOCIATION.

———SECOND REPORT of the TRACT ASSOCIATION. Dublin. 1816.
Graisberry & Campbell, Printers, 10, Back Lane, Dublin. . . . . . Fol. 1816.   1

———ASSOCIATION *for printing and distributing Tracts on Moral and Religious Subjects, chiefly such as have a tendency to elucidate and support the Principles of Christianity, as held by the Society of* FRIENDS. DUBLIN.
List of Tracts already printed.
Graisberry & Campbell, Printers, Dublin.
8vo. 1815.   ⅛

No. 69.—The DUTY OF PRAYER 𝕮onsidered and 𝕰nforced ; consisting of Extracts from various Authors ; to which are added, selections from the writings of Members of the Society of Friends, and from the acknowledged Public Documents of that Religious Body, on the same subject.

TRACT ASSOCIATIONS, &c., *continued.*

DUBLIN TRACT ASSOCIATION, *continued.*

2nd Edition—
Dublin : *Printed for the Tract Association of Members of the Society of Friends, by Webb and Chapman, Great Brunswick Street.*
12mo. 1842. ⅔

No. 70.—A Few Observations on the great Truths of the Christian Religion. By J. F[orster].
D.T.A. *Webb and Chapman, Printers, Great Brunswick Street.* . . 12mo. No date. ⅓

No. 71.—SELECTIONS from a work entitled, PIETY PROMOTED ; containing Brief Memorials and dying expressions of some of the Society of Friends. Part III.
Second Edition—
Dublin : *Printed, &c., by Webb and Chapman, Great Brunswick Street.* . 12mo. 1842. ⅔

NOTE.—This selection consists of some particulars of the children of Samuel and Rebecca Tregelles, of Falmouth, viz. :—
Robert Tregelles,
John Tregelles,
Joseph Tregelles,
Catherine Tregelles,
Henry Tregelles,
Mary Tregelles.

No. 72.—MEMOIR of DAVID FERRIS, a Minister of the Society of Friends.
D.T.A. *2nd Edition*— 12mo. N.P.N., place or date. ⅔

No. 73.—A Short Account of John Spalding, late of Reading. Written by himself.
Second Edition—
Dublin : *Printed, &c., by Webb and Chapman, Great Brunswick Street.* . 12mo. 1842. ⅔

No. 74.—A Short Account of Robert Searles, with a few extracts from his Diary.
D.T.A. *2nd Edition*—
Dublin : *Printed by Webb and Chapman.*
12mo. 1843. ½

No 75.—EXTRACTS relating to THE CHRISTIAN DOCTRINE of the Religious Society of Friends, from approved documents.
Second Edition.

TRACT ASSOCIATIONS, &c., *continued.*
DUBLIN TRACT ASSOCIATION, *continued.*
    Dublin : *Printed for the Tract Association, &c.,
by Webb and Chapman, Great Brunswick
Street.* . . . . . 12mo. 1848 $\frac{1}{2}$

No 76.—A Testimony to the Authority of Christ in his Church, and to the Spirituality of the Gospel Dispensation : also against some of the corruptions of Professing Christendom.
Second Edition.
    *Dublin : Printed for the Tract Association, &c.,
by Webb and Chapman, Great Brunswick
Street.* . . . . . 12mo. 1847. $\frac{1}{3}$

No. 77.—MEMOIRS of the LIFE OF DANIEL WHEELER, a Minister of the Gospel in the Society of Friends.
Second Edition.
    *Dublin : Printed for the Tract Association, &c.,
by Webb and Chapman, Great Brunswick
Street.* . . . . . 12mo. 1852 $1\frac{2}{3}$

No. 78.—Memoirs of the Life and Religious Experience of William Lewis, late of Bristol.
    D.T.R. *Dublin : Printed by Webb and Chapman,
177, Great Brunswick Street.* 12mo. No date. $\frac{2}{3}$

No. 79.—BRIEF MEMOIRS of THE BARCLAY FAMILY.
    D.T.R. *Dublin : Printed by Webb and Chapman,
Great Brunswick Street.* . 12mo. 1845. $\frac{2}{3}$

No. 80.—The Christian's Pathway. *Extracted principally from a letter by Stephen Crisp, dated 1668.*
    D.T.R. . . 12mo. N.P.N. Place or Date. $\frac{1}{3}$

No. 81.—The LIBERTY OF GOSPEL MINISTRY EXEMPLIFIED, in a short account of THOMAS AND JANE COLLEY.
    D.T.R. . . . 12mo. N.P.N.P. or Date. $\frac{1}{3}$

No. 82.—Concerning PERFECTION. From ROBERT BARCLAY'S APOLOGY for the True Christian Divinity, as held forth by the Society of Friends. Proposition VIII.
    D.T.R. *Dublin : Printed by Webb and Chapman,
Great Brunswick Street.* . 12mo. 1846.   1

No. 83.—A Brief Account of WILLIAM BUSH ; late Carpenter on Board the "Henry Freeling"; in-

TRACT ASSOCIATIONS, &c., *continued.*

DUBLIN TRACT ASSOCIATION, *continued.*

cluding his correspondence with Daniel Wheeler, a Minister of the Society of Friends.

𝕯.𝕿.𝕽. *Second Edition—*

Printed for the Dublin Tract Association of Members of the Society of Friends, by Webb and Chapman, Great Brunswick Street.

12mo. 1848. ⅔

No. 84.—A MEMOIR of DEBORAH BACKHOUSE, who died at the age of 34 years.

𝕯.𝕿.𝕽. *Dublin: Printed by Webb and Chapman, Great Brunswick Street, for the Tract Association of Members of the Society of Friends.*

12mo. No date. ⅓

No. 85.—On the CHARACTER AND DOCTRINE of the EARLY FRIENDS.

𝕯.𝕿.𝕽. *Dublin: Printed by Webb and Chapman, Great Brunswick Street, for the Tract Association of the Society of Friends.*

12mo. No date. ½

No. 86.—The Last days of THOMAS LEE TAYLOR.

𝕯.𝕿.𝕽. *Second Edition—*

Printed by Webb and Chapman, 177, Great Brunswick Street. . . 12mo. No date. ⅓

No. 87.—The WORK OF RIGHTEOUSNESS. (From "A Salutation of Pure Love," by Thomas Colley).

𝕯.𝕿.𝕽. *Dublin: Printed by Webb and Chapman, Great Brunswick Street, for the Tract Association of the Society of Friends.* 12mo. 1848.

No. 88.—A FRIENDLY CALL, to all People, to come out of Darkness to the True Light;—Written in York Castle, by Thomas Thompson.

Dublin: Printed for the Tract Association, &c., by Webb and Chapman, Great Brunswick Street. . . . . . 12mo. 1849. ⅓

No. 89.—A Short Account of Clara Popplestone, who died at Kingsbridge, Devonshire, in the year 1841.

Dublin: Printed for the Tract Association, &c., by Webb and Chapman, Great Brunswick Street. . . . . . 12mo. 1849. ⅓

TRACT ASSOCIATIONS, &c., *continued*.

DUBLIN TRACT ASSOCIATION, *continued*.

No. 90.—The Swiss Peasant. A Sketch of the Life of JOHANN RICKLI. (Translated by John Yeardley.)
2nd Edition—
Dublin : *Printed by Webb and Chapman, 177, Great Brunswick Street, for the Tract Association of the Society of Friends.* 12mo. 1852.

No. 91.—On Indecision in Religion.
D.T.R. *2nd Edition—*
Dublin : *Printed by Webb and Chapman, Great Brunswick Street, for the Tract Association of the Society of Friends.* . 12mo. 1852. $\frac{1}{6}$

——TRACTS on MORAL AND RELIGIOUS SUBJECTS. Published by an Association of Members of the Society of Friends.
"Godliness is profitable unto all things."—I. Tim., iv. 8.

VOLUME I. INCLUDES No. 1 to 24.
VOLUME II.   „   No. 25 to 44.
VOLUME III.   „   No. 45 to 67.
VOLUME IV.   „   No. 68 to 91.

Dublin : *Printed by Webb and Chapman, Great Brunswick Street.*
12mo. 2 Vols. are dated 1851, and 2 Vols. 1852.

NOTE.—The Introduction to each Vol. is dated, "Dublin, 4th Mo., 1836."

——The GOSPEL PRINCIPLES of the Religious Society of Friends.
Dublin : *Tract Association of the Society of Friends in Ireland. Depository : 6, Eustace Street.*
New Series, B.—No. 1. *(Printed by Robert Chapman, Temple Lane, Dame Street).*
16mo. No date. $1\frac{3}{8}$

NOTE,—There is added at the end of this tract Montgomery's "Lines to the Memory of Joseph Browne, of Lothersdale," who suffered a long imprisonment in York Castle.

BRIGHTON FRIENDS' TRACT ASSOCIATION.
——A Tract for the Season.
Price 1s. 6d. per 100, or 13s. per 1,000. Post free.
C. Hilton, Printer, 30, Duke Street, Brighton.
12mo. No date. $\frac{1}{6}$

NOTE.—This Tract is against Intemperance and dissipation, particularly at the time called "Christmas."

TRACT ASSOCIATIONS, &c., *continued*.

LEICESTER TRACT ASSOCIATION. Commenced in 1857. The Depository is at the Meeting House, North Gate Lane, Highcross Street, Leicester.

——Report for 1867 of the Leicester Tract Association, read at the Annual Meeting, held at the Meeting House, 9th of 1st Month, 1868.
Printed by E. T. Lawrence, Bookseller, 78 & 80, High Street, Leicester. . . 16mo. 1868. ¼

LEOMINSTER TRACT ASSOCIATION.

TWO-PAGE TRACTS :

 83 What cannot religion do ?
 84 A friend for the friendless
 85 Dark hours
 86 Obeying the Holy Spirit
 100 Thankfulness
 108 The mouldy loaf
 109 Providential deliverance
 111 The little coat
 123 Able Mellar
 124 Threepence a line
 129 It never dries up
 166 I'm going up
 175 Burnt to death
 182 A boy saved
 *183 Temptation overcome
 188 Heathen boy
 †189 Shot dead
 194 Who is Christ ?
 †199 Prisoners in Servia
 209 The boy who was not drowned
 210 Jesus did it
 216 The blind river
 217 Rescued from a wreck
 219 Escape from a mine
 244 The cry of the humble
 245 You will want it
 248 The Cornish fisherman
 *251 The right change
 253 Just too late, and Just in time
 256 God hears
 257 This man receiveth sinners
 *265 My little freehold, and how I came by it
 72 Family worship

TRACT ASSOCIATIONS, &c., *continued.*

LEOMINSTER TRACT ASSOCIATION, *continued.*

    74 Can a working man pray daily?
    76 Why stand ye here idle?
    77 Watch
    78 Robert's secret
    80 Robbed of a Bible
    81 I now listen to Jesus
    82 Good tidings of great joy
    87 Spry, the navvy
    88 The ragged school teacher
    89 How do you spend your money?
    90 Are you tired of trusting God!
  †95 A shield in trouble
    96 Exceeding abundantly
    97 What did the angels wipe it out with?
    98 In all their afflictions, &c. (large type)
 *99 The fatal needle
*103 A doctor's story
 104 No harm
 105 Individual duty
*107 Not a drop more, Joe
 110 The swearer's club
 112 The old ship carpenter
 113 The patchwork quilt
†114 Is your faith as strong as that?
 115 The Nestorian deacon
 117 Am I mistaken?
 118 God is your pilot
 119 The Ethiopian serenader
 120 When will you come?
 121 Make it plain
*122 The tinker and his wife
*132 Smack Dolphin, of Brixham
 134 The strawplat girl
 139 Influence of a mother's prayers
 140 The neglected Bible
 141 The wanderer's return
 142 The Shetland cottager
 144 The use of the book
 146 The negro's story
 147 Old Moses
 152 The blind Bible-reader
 154 The journey's end
 156 A wicked old sinner
 157 Freedom from sin

TRACT ASSOCIATIONS, &c., *continued.*

LEOMINSTER TRACT ASSOCIATION, *continued.*

  158 Happy Willie
  159 The cradle
  164 The blind sailor
  165 We've got a Saviour
  168 Old John, the ragman
  170 The soldier sceptic
  171 Repent
  172 Old Jack Sibley
  174 Trust your guide
  176 Brands plucked from the burning
*177 The doctor recommends it
  178 Now
  180 Who shall have the best?
  181 The hidden Bible
  185 Rub it out, father
  186 Poor, yet rich
*187 The wreck of the Schiller
  192 Content with a little
  193 A passing word
  195 The dark messenger
  197 The Lord's apple tree
†198 Christians and war
  200 The library book
  201 Begging bread
  203 Kate, the young silk-weaver
  207 How Spurgeon found Christ
  208 How old Robin became what he was
  211 After many days
  214 The Dutch Testament
*220 William, the shepherd
*224 The clown's little daughter
  225 Crumbs for hop pickers
  226 Hops
  228 Love one another
†229 The Bible better than pistols
  230 The door on the latch
*232 Elizabeth's kettle
  233 Light in the valley
  234 I have no written report
  237 The ruffian softened
  241 And the door was shut
†242 God's protecting care
*243 Take care of your children
  246 Better than bread

TRACT ASSOCIATIONS, &c., *continued.*
LEOMINSTER TRACT ASSOCIATION, *continued.*
  247 I have no time
  *249 John's hindering thing
  250 Tommy, the fisherman
  260 Nothing to pay
  269 The dairywoman
GOSPEL TEMPERANCE TRACTS :
    Illustrated Title Page.
  92 The tables turned
 135 The converted soldier
 196 God's kitten
 202 Daniel's farm
 231 How my wife signed the pledge for me
 235 Step by step
 238 How temperance cottage came to be built
 252 The blacksmith's story
 254 The mason's story
 255 The waterman's story
 258 The carpenter's story
 259 The saddler's story
 261 The hammersmith's story
 262 The navvy's story
 263 The shoemaker's story
 264 The truck-shunter's story
 267 The goods-guard's story
 268 The sailor's story
EIGHT-PAGE TRACTS :
  71 Sunlight in the cottage
  91 Captain Ball's experience
  93 Domestic service
  94 Saved, as by fire
 *136 Husband and wife
 143 I wish He'd let me do that
 *145 The fatal quarrel
 153 Come
 155 Poll Peg
 *160 Woman's love and child's faith
 *162 Sam Bowen's dream
 190 A dream
 204 Old Tom's story
 *205 Little sups
 †212 Can God protect our lives ?
 221 Wonderful discovery

TRACT ASSOCIATIONS, &c., *continued.*

LEOMINSTER TRACT ASSOCIATION, *continued.*

*227 Give it up, father
240 Lost from a Bible class
 75 Old Robin Green
 79 Ivy, the fisherman
128 The old Indian women
131 The overcoat
137 The mysterious basket
138 The race and the crown
149 Kitty Tarl
169 Watt Wallace
173 The wrong address
179 The saw-miller
191 Poor girls
206 Isaac Moore
236 Marion's prayer

ON TINTED PAPER:

Eight pages, square.

125 Watchfulness
126 Janie's new hymn book
*151 Consider
163 Wilt thou be made whole?
*218 The wreckers. A poem
†222 The unbarred door
223 Hidden face
239 Legacies; a parable

OLIVE LEAF SERIES:

Four pages.

 1 Not lonely, if alone
 2 What the sparrow chirps
 3 Hymns from Hamburg
 4 Hymns for sickness
 5 Bless me and make me a blessing
 6 A dying child's request
 7 The altered motto
 8 Mother
 9 The three bidders
10 Thirsty
*11 Aunt Jemima's crusade
12 What my little boy taught me
13 He never prays

TRACT ASSOCIATIONS, &c., *continued.*

LEOMINSTER TRACT ASSOCIATION, *continued.*

 14 On the look out
 *15 The child's first prayer
 16 The heavenly railway
 17 Barbara's hymn
 18 Nurse's story
 *19 Touch not, taste not
 20 God is the rock
 21 What shall I render?
 22 Nobodies
 23 Newness of life
 24 Keeping
 *25 A strange bargain
 26 Even Christ pleased not himself
 27 I will not leave you comfortless
 28 A tired mother's victory
 30 Weary mothers
 31 The child is father to the man
 32 What is that in thine hand?

JUVENILE SERIES:

 15 Little Jane; or the blessing of Sabbath schools
 16 I'm so happy
 17 Losing the happy
 18 Of such is the kingdom
 19 Johnny
 20 Susie; a true story
 21 A child's faith
 22 A story for the little ones
 23 I can die alone
 24 Jesus loves me
 25 Nellie
 26 Nellie's trouble
 27 A child's gift
 28 A letter to children
 29 Nellie's hymn
 30 Frankie
 31 What Tommy did for Jesus
 32 The orphan boy
 33 The very happy boy
 34 Disobedient Reuben
 35 The snow storm
 36 Rose
 37 Charlie's choice
 38 Praying for a wind

TRACT ASSOCIATIONS, &c., *continued.*

LEOMINSTER TRACT ASSOCIATION, *continued.*
    †39 Second thoughts are best
    40 Little Bertie
    41 Cecil's hard lesson
    42 A forest scene in the days of Wycliffe

SCRIPTURE SERIES:
    11 Jesus came to save sinners
    12 Come to Jesus
    13 The sinner's prayer
    14 The prayer of the poor
    15 Thanksgiving and praise
    16 The Lord is my shepherd

RED LETTER:
    Asked of God.

        ○ Temperance Tracts.   † Peace Tracts.

PHILADELPHIA.
No. 74.
    75.
    76.
    77.—Reasons why Women should be permitted to exercise the Gifts of the Holy Spirit, particularly in reference to the Ministry of the Gospel.
    Philadelphia: Published by the Tract Association of Friends, and to be had at their Depository, No. 84, Mulberry Street.   .   12mo. N.D. $\frac{1}{3}$

    97.—Memoir of John Stickland.
    Philadelphia: Published by the Tract Association of Friends, and to be had at their Depository, No. 304, Arch Street.   . .   12mo. N.D. $\frac{2}{3}$

    103.—A New Child: a Biography of Lydia Ann Nixon.
    Published by the Tract Association of Friends, at their Depository, No. 304, Arch Street, Philadelphia. . . . . 12mo. N.D. $\frac{1}{3}$

Tract and Book Association of Friends, Philadelphia, *continued.* ("Hicksite.")

——ESSAYS on some of the TESTIMONIES OF TRUTH, as held by the 𝔖𝔬𝔠𝔦𝔢𝔱𝔶 𝔬𝔣 𝔉𝔯𝔦𝔢𝔫𝔡𝔰. By the Book Association of Friends of Philadelphia.
    Philadelphia: Published by T. Ellwood Zell, 439, Market Street. . . . 12 mo. 1860.   3

TRACT ASSOCIATIONS, &c., *continued.*
 PHILADELPHIA, *continued.*
 ——Devotional Poetry for the Children.
   Philadelphia. . . 32mo. 64 pp.
 NEW YORK.
 ——CONSTITUTION of the *Tract Association of Friends* in New York, 1817.
   Samuel Wood & Sons, Printers, No. 261, Pearl Street, New York. . . . Fol. 1817. 1
TREFFRY, Roger, of *Beer Barton,* near *Plymouth, Devonshire.* (1793).
 ——A DISSERTATION on SMUT BALLS amongst WHEAT and other GRAIN, by ROGER TREFFRY, of BEER BARTON, near PLYMOUTH, DEVONSHIRE.
   Haydon, Clarence Press, Plymouth.
     [8vo. 1793. 2
     He died the 24th of the 11th month, 1818, aged 72 years, and was buried in Plymouth.
     Mary, his widow, died at Plymouth, 22nd of 6th month, 1830, aged 80 years.
     See " Friends' Mag.," 1830, p. 614.
TREGELLES, Edwin Octavius, of *Neithrop, Banbury, Oxon.*
 ——EDWIN OCTAVIUS TREGELLES, Civil Engineer and Minister of the Gospel. Edited by his daughter, Sarah E. Fox. (With Portrait).
   London : Hodder and Stoughton, 27, Paternoster Row. . . . Crown 8vo. 1892.
   He died the 16th of 9th month, 1886, aged 79 years.
*TREGELLES, S. Prideaux, of *6, Portland Square, Plymouth.*
 ——The BOOK OF REVELATION, translated **from the Ancient Greek Text**, by S. P. Tregelles.
   "—Adjuvante etiam *codicum veritate,* quam sollers emendationis diligentia procuravit : veniat ita instructus ad ambigua Scripturarum discutienda atque solvenda."
     AUGUSTINE.
   London : Samuel Bagster and Sons, 15, Paternoster Row ; Warehouse for Bibles, New Testaments, Prayer Books, Lexicons, Grammars, Concordances, and Psalters, in Ancient and Modern Languages. MDCCCXLVIII. (*Jenkin Thomas, Printer, Plymouth.*)
     12mo. 1848. 3¼

*TREGELLES, S. Prideaux, *continued*.

———A Prospectus of a Critical Edition of the Greek New Testament, now in preparation, with an Historical Sketch of the Printed Text.
            12mo. [1848.] 1⅙

TREGO, Charles B., Professor, Geologist.

———Pennsylvania; its Geography, History, &c.; with an Account of its Climate, Soil, Agriculture, Resources, &c. By C. B. Trego. Map.

 Philadelphia: . .   12mo. 1843.

TRUSTED, Joseph, of *Llydiadyway*.

———CORRESPONDENCE with the Monthly Meeting of HEREFORDSHIRE and RADNORSHIRE, relative to RENT CHARGE. [1846-'47.]

 Birmingham: *Henry Newman, Printer, Bull Street, Birmingham*. . . 8vo. [1880.] ¾

TUKE, Daniel Hack, *continued* from Catalogue, Vol. 2, p. 832.

———INSANITY in ANCIENT AND MODERN LIFE, with Chapters ON ITS PREVENTION. By DANIEL HACK TUKE, M.D., Fellow of the Royal College of Physicians, London.

  "*The dispute, then, is not about any common matter, but about being mad or not mad.*"—EPICTETUS.

 London: MACMILLAN AND CO. . 8vo. 1878. 15¼

 [*The Right of Translation and Reproduction is Reserved.*]

———THE INSANE in the UNITED STATES and CANADA. By D. HACK TUKE, M.D., LL.D., Fellow of the Royal College of Physicians, London. Co-Editor of "The Journal of Mental Science."

 London: *H. K. Lewis, 136, Gower Street, W.C.*

             8vo. 1885. 17⅛

  [*All Rights Reserved.*]

  NOTE.—This book commences with a Sketch of the Life of Benjamin Rush, M.D., and his medical practice, with a Portrait of Benjamin Rush, "From an oil painting in the Possession of the Pennsylvania Hospital, Philadelphia."

TUKE, James Hack, *continued* from Catalogue, Vol. 2, p. 831.

——A VISIT TO PARIS in the Spring of 1871, on behalf of the WAR VICTIM'S FUND of the Society of Friends. Being a Lecture delivered at the Town Hall, Hitchin, April 4th, 1871. By James Hack Tuke.
   London: F. B. Kitto, Bishopsgate Street; Hitchin: C. Paternoster. , . . . 8vo. 1871.   2

——Irish Distress, and its Remedies. By James Hack Tuke.
   London: James Ridgway, Piccadilly. 8vo. 1880.
      Reprinted.—The 2nd Edition.
                            8vo.

——THE AUSTRALASIAN COLONIES: Emigration and Colonisation. Report of inquiries made by Walter Hazell and Howard Hodgkin (*Members of the Committee of Management of the Emigrants' Information Office*) during a visit to Australia, Tasmania, and New Zealand, December, 1886—April, 1887. With an Introduction by J. H. Tuke.
   London: Edward Stanford, 55, Charing Cross, S.W. Sold also at the Emigrants' Information Office, 31, Broadway, Westminster.
                            8vo. 1887.   5¾

TUKE, John, of *Lingcroft*, near *York*.

——An Alphabetical List of Places in Yorkshire to accompany his Map.
   York: Printed for J. Tuke.   Oblong. 1792.

TUKE, William, of *York*.

——(On Election Controversy) *York*, 7th of 4th month, 1784. . . . . 4to.   ½

TURFORD, Hugh, *continued* from Catalogue, Vol. 2, p. 832.

——The Grounds of a HOLY LIFE: or, The Way to become Christians indeed. To which is added, a TREATISE ON DIVINE GRACE, and its operation upon the Heart; by Hugh Turford. [First published, 1702.] (With a Postscript.) Twenty-seventh edition.
   Manchester: Printed by George Harrison, Cross Street, for " The Manchester District Friends' Tract Association." Sold by Joseph B. Smith, at the Depository, Meeting House, Manchester. London: Joseph Smith, Oxford Street, Whitechapel. Belfast: William Halliday, Dougal Place.
                        12mo. 1860.   3½

TURFORD, Hugh, *continued*.

——The Ancient Christian's PRINCIPLE or RULE of LIFE, *revived and brought to light* : with a Description of True Godliness, and the Way by which we may conform our Lives thereunto. Also, Some Extracts from the Writings of the late JUDGE HALE.

Waterford : Printed by Matthew Power.
           18mo. 1790. 1¾

TUTING, William, of *Sydney, New South Wales.*

——An Appeal to the Rising Generation of the SOCIETY OF FRIENDS throughout the world. [Issued by Friends in Sydney.]

Gloucester : John Bellows, Steam Press.
           24mo. 1869. ⅙

  NOTE.—Signed on behalf of the Meeting (Sydney) by William Tuting.

TYLOR, Charles, *continued* from Catalogue, Vol. 2, p. 836.

——The Worship of 𝕿𝖍𝖊 𝕹𝖊𝖜 𝕮𝖔𝖛𝖊𝖓𝖆𝖓𝖙. By Charles Tylor.

London : F. Bowyer Kitto, Bishopsgate Street Without. (Foster, Old Style Printer, London).
          8vo. 1869. 1

——The Faggot : gathered and made up.
          16mo. 1876. 8

——Early Church History.   8vo. 1884. 36
  See Edward Backhouse.

——Witnesses for Christ. 2 vols. 8vo. 1887. 65

——The Huguenots in the Seventeenth Century. (Illustrated). By Charles Tylor.

London : Simpkin, Marshall & Co.
        Crown 8vo. 1892. 320pp.

TYLOR, Edward Burnet, of *Wellington, Somersetshire.*

——ANAHUAC : or, MEXICO AND THE MEXICANS, ANCIENT AND MODERN. By EDWARD B. TYLOR.

London : Longman, Green, Longman, and Roberts.
          8vo. 1861. 22¼

——Primitive Culture. 2 Vols.

——Researches into the Early History of Mankind and the developement of Civilization. By Edward Burnet Tylor, Author of " Mexico and the Mexicans."

London : John Murray, Albemarle Street.
          8vo. 1865. 24

TYNDALL, Mary.

——The Diary of Mary Tyndall, one of the Early Quakers.
London : Hall and Co., 8, Amen Corner, Paternoster Row. (R. Clay, Sons, and Taylor, Printers, Bread Street Hill.) . 8vo. 1876. 11
  NOTE.—This may be said to be a *Quaker novel*; it is "Anonymous," but was written by a Friend, a daughter of Joseph Marriage, who resided at Holloway.

TYSON, Elisha, *continued* from Catalogue, Vol. 2, p. 837.

——LIFE of ELISHA TYSON, the PHILANTHROPIST. By a Citizen of Baltimore. (*With a Portrait.*)
Baltimore : Printed by B. Lundy, 24, S. Calvert Street. . . . . . 12mo. 1825. $6\frac{1}{4}$
  He died the 16th of 2nd month, 1824, aged 75 years, and was interred in the Burial-ground attached to the Friends' Meeting House, in Old Town, Baltimore.

TYSON, Job R., of *Philadelphia*, Scholar. Author, M.C.

——A Discourse before the Young Men's Colonization Society of Pennsylvania, delivered October 24th, 1834, in St. Paul's church Philadelphia. By J. R. Tyson. With a notice of the proceedings of the Society, and of their first expedition of coloured emigrants to found a colony at Bassa Cove.
Philadelphia : Printed for the Society. 8vo. 1834. 4
  or 64 pages.

TYSON, Philip T.   Geologist.   Author.

——Geology and Industrial Resources of California. By Philip T. Tyson.
                                                                    8vo.

U.

UPSHER, Thomas, of *Colchester*, in *Essex*.

——To Friends in Ireland, and elsewhere : a Mournful Word to the Merry-hearted in Zion ; with a word of Comfort to her bowed-down Mourners. By Thomas Upsher.
Printed in Philadelphia by Reinier Jansen, 1700.

URINE, Nathaniel, of *Walsingham* in *Norfolk*, a General Shopkeeper.

——An Account of his Sufferings.—See "The Lamentable Cry of Oppression,"—of the Quakers in and about Fakenham in Norfolk.
4to. Printed in the Year 1679. 5½

V.

VARNUM, Hattel, was born in the County of *Wexford*, in *Ireland*. In the year 1728 he removed with his wife and family into Pennsylvania.

VARNUM, Abigail (his Wife).

——Testimonies concerning them. In Comly's Miscellany, Vol. 4.

> He died the 27th of the 12th month, 1747, aged 77 years, and was buried in Friends' Burial-ground, Leacock.
> She died the 14th of the 3rd month, 1760.

VAUX, Frances Bowyer.—Married William Miller, Cousin of Ann Knight.

——Henry.

——Dew-Drop.

——Disappointment.

——Ann and Jane.

——Present for Young Cousins.

——Order and Disorder.

——Promised Visit.

——DOMESTIC PLEASURES; or, 𝔗𝔥𝔢 𝔥𝔞𝔭𝔭𝔶 𝔉𝔦𝔯𝔢-𝔖𝔦𝔡𝔢. Illustrated by interesting conversations. By F. B. VAUX.

> (With a Frontispiece of "Eddystone Light House.")

> 𝔏𝔬𝔫𝔡𝔬𝔫: *Printed for Darton, Harvey, and Darton, 55, Gracechurch Street.*   12mo. 1816.   11

VAUX, Roberts, *continued* from Catalogue, Vol. 2, p. 841.

——A MEMOIR on the LOCALITY OF THE GREAT TREATY between WILLIAM PENN and the INDIAN NATIVES in 1682. Read before the Historical Society of

VAUX, Roberts, *continued.*
> Pennsylvania, September 19, 1825. By ROBERTS VAUX. (With an Appendix.)
>> *Printed, Philadelphia, 1825. Reprinted, London, 1839. [Moyes and Barclay, Castle Street, Leicester Square (Printers).]* . 8vo. 1839. 1¾

VOKINS, Joan, *continued* from Catalogue, Vol. 2, p. 844.
> ———God's Mighty Power Magnified, as manifested and revealed in His faithful handmaid JOAN VOKINS, *who departed this life the 22nd of the 5th month, 1690,* **having finished her course, and kept the faith;** also, some account of her exercises, works of faith, labour of love, and great travels in the work of the ministry, for the good of souls.
> New edition.
>> *Cockermouth: Printed by D. Fidler, Main Street, and Sold by H. T. Wake, Bookseller, Cockermouth.* 12mo. 1871. 6½

W.

WAKEFIELD, Priscilla, was the daughter of Daniel and Catharine Bell: her mother was the daughter of David Barclay (of London), son of the Apologist (*continued* from Catalogue, Vol. 2, p. 848.
> ———MENTAL IMPROVEMENT or, the **Beauties and Wonders** of Nature and Art. Three volumes in one, arranged as a series of instructive Conversations. By Priscilla Wakefield, *Authoress of Leisure Hours, &c.* (With a Frontispiece.)
> A New Edition, improved by Edward Emerson.
>> *London: Published by George Bingley & Co., and sold by all Booksellers.* . 12mo. No date. 12½

> ———The TRAVELLER IN AFRICA: containing some account of the Antiquities, Natural Curiosities, and Inhabitants of such parts of that Continent and its Islands as have been most explored by Europeans. The Route traced on a Map, for the entertainment and instruction of young persons. By Priscilla Wakefield.

WAKEFIELD, Priscilla, *continued.*
> London : *Printed for Darton, Harvey, and Darton, 55, Gracechurch Street; by James Swan, 76, Fleet Street.* 12mo. 1814. 16

——An INTRODUCTION to BOTANY, in a Series of Familiar Letters. With illustrative Engravings. By PRISCILLA WAKEFIELD, *Author of Mental Improvement, Leisure Hours, &c.*

𝕮𝖍𝖊 𝕾𝖎𝖝𝖙𝖍 𝕰𝖉𝖎𝖙𝖎𝖔𝖓.
> London : *Printed for Darton, Harvey, and Co., Gracechurch Street; J. Harris, St. Paul's Churchyard; J. Walker; Longman, Hurst, Rees, Orme, and Brown; Sherwood, Neely, and Jones, Paternoster Row; and B. & R. Crosby, Stationers' Court.* . 12mo. 1812. 8

——An INTRODUCTION to ENTOMOLOGY, or THE CLASSIFICATION of INSECTS. In a series of 𝕱𝖆𝖒𝖎𝖑𝖎𝖆𝖗 𝕷𝖊𝖙𝖙𝖊𝖗𝖘, with [12] illustrative engravings. By Priscilla Wakefield.
> 𝕷𝖔𝖓𝖉𝖔𝖓 : *Printed for Darton, Harvey, and Darton, No. 55, Gracechurch Street.* . 12mo. 1815. 8½

——The JUVENILE TRAVELLERS ; containing the Remarks of a Family during A TOUR through the PRINCIPAL STATES and KINGDOMS of EUROPE : With an Account of their Inhabitants, Natural Productions, and Curiosities. *By* PRISCILLA WAKEFIELD (Map).

𝕮𝖍𝖊 𝕾𝖊𝖛𝖊𝖓𝖙𝖍 𝕰𝖉𝖎𝖙𝖎𝖔𝖓.
> London : *Printed for Darton and Harvey, No. 55, Gracechurch Street.* . . 12mo. 1809. 19

——A Family Tour through the British Empire, &c. Reprinted—The 15th Edition. *Corrected and Enlarged.* (With a Map.)
> London : *Published by Harvey and Darton, Gracechurch Street. (Printed by Fletcher, Forbes and Fletcher, Southampton.)*
> 12mo. 1840. 23

——𝕴𝖓𝖘𝖙𝖎𝖓𝖈𝖙 𝕯𝖎𝖘𝖕𝖑𝖆𝖞𝖊𝖉, &c. (With a Frontispiece.) Fourth Edition.
> 𝕷𝖔𝖓𝖉𝖔𝖓 : *Printed for Harvey and Darton, Gracechurch Street.* 12mo. 1821. 13¾

——INSTINCT DISPLAYED ; exemplifying the extraordinary sagacity of various species of THE ANIMAL CREATION. By Priscilla Wakefield.

WAKEFIELD, Priscilla, *continued*.
LONDON: *Printed for the Executrix of the late W. Welton. Sold by* C. F. COCK, 21, FLEET STREET; *and all Booksellers*.
18mo. 1831. 188 pages.
NOTE.—This small edition is illustrated with 6 plates.

WAKEFIELD, Thomas Christy, of *Moyallon*, in *Ireland*.
—— A Brief Memoir of Thomas Christy Wakefield, compiled from his own memoranda.
Torquay: *Printed by E. Cockrem, 10, Strand*.
Small 8vo. [1862?] 2
He died the 18th of 6th month, 1861, aged 88 years, and was interred (by his own desire) in Friends' Burying-ground, in Gloucester.

WALDMEIER, Theophilus, born in Switzerland, not far from Bâle, was baptized and brought up in the Roman Catholic Church. Now of "Brumana, Mount Lebanon, near Beyrout." Member of Devonshire House Meeting.
—— BRIEF SKETCH of THEOPHILUS WALDMEIER'S EARLIER LIFE AND EXPERIENCE. *Given at the Request of his Friends*.
Birmingham: *White & Pike, Moor Street Printing Works*. . . . . . 8vo. [1874.] 1

WALKER, Isaac, son of Peter and Mary Walker, of *Dean Scales*, near *Cockermouth*, in *Cumberland*.
—— A Short Account of Isaac Walker, who died 1843, aged Eighteen years.
York: *John L. Linney, Low Ousegate; Charles Gilpin, London* . . . 24mo. 1844. ½

WALKER, John, *continued* from Catalogue, Vol. 2, p. 852.
—— MANUAL of the THEOPHILANTHROPES, or ADORERS OF GOD, and FRIENDS OF MEN. Containing the Exposition of their Dogmas, of their Moral, and of their Religious Practices; with instruction respecting the organization and celebration of their worship. ARRANGED BY CERTAIN CITIZENS, and adopted by the 𝕿𝖍𝖊𝖔𝖕𝖍𝖎𝖑𝖆𝖓𝖙𝖍𝖗𝖔𝖕𝖎𝖈 𝕾𝖔𝖈𝖎𝖊𝖙𝖎𝖊𝖘 established in Paris. Second Edition, TRANSLATED BY JOHN WALKER, *Author of Elements of Geography, and Universal Gazetteer*.
LONDON: *Printed and Sold by Darton and Harvey, No. 55, Gracechurch Street*.
Price Sixpence. . . 12mo. 1797. 1⅔

WALKER, John, *continued*.

——Selections from LUCIAN, with a Latin Translation and English Notes; to which are subjoined, A Mythological Index, and a Lexicon adapted to the Work. Compiled for the use of Schools, by JOHN WALKER, formerly Fellow of Dublin College. SEVENTH EDITION.
    Dublin : Richard Moore Tims, 85, Grafton Street. Longman, Rees, Orme, Brown, Green and Longman, London. . 12mo. 1839. 16

WALTON, Joseph, of *Philadelphia*.

——Brief Biographies of some Members of the Society of Friends, shewing their early religious exercises, and experience in the work of Regeneration.
    Philadelphia : Printed,   12mo. 1876. 5⅙

WARDEN, John A., M.D., Pomologist.

——A Treatise on Hedges and Evergreens, by John A. Warden, M.D.
    New York. . . . . . 1867.

WARING, William, of *Colora, Cecil County, Md.*

——A Call to the Fountain : to turn from Shadow and Imitation, and to press after substance, &c.
    Philadelphia : Printed,   8vo. 1873. 6¾

WARNER, Yardley.

——The Maryville Monitor.

WARRINGTON, Joseph, *of Philadelphia*.

——The Obstetric Catechism, containing 2,347 Questions and Answers on Obstetrics Proper. By Jos. Warrington. 150 Illustrations.
    Philadelphia : . . . 12mo. 1853.

WATSON, John F, of *North America*.

——Annals of Philadelphia and Pennsylvania, in the olden time : being a Collection of Memoirs, Anecdotes, and Incidents of the City and its inhabitants, and of the earliest Settlements of the inland part of Pennsylvania, from the days of the Founders. Intended to preserve the Recollections of olden time, and to exhibit Society in its changes of Manners and Customs, and the City and Country in their local changes and improvements. Embellished with engravings by T. H. Mumford. By John F. Watson, Member of the Historical Societies of Pennsylvania,

WATSON, John F., *continued.*
>New York, and Massachusetts. In 2 volumes. *Philadelphia: Published by Elijah Thomas, No. 28, S. Seventh Street.* . . 8vo. 1857. 79½
>>Amongst the illustrations are—
>>Portrait of Penn.
>>The Landing of Penn at Chester.
>>"   at Blue Anchor.
>>The Treaty Tree and Fairman's Mansion.
>>Penn's Cottage in Letitia Court.
>>Slate Roof House, Penn's Residence.
>>Old Court House, and Friends' Meeting House.
>>Anthony Benezet's House.
>>Friends' Bank Meeting.
>>"   Alms House.
>>Portrait of Nicholas Waln.
>>"   of James Pemberton.
>>Penn's Treaty with the Indians, etc., etc.

WATSON, Robert Spence, of *Newcastle-upon-Tyne.*

——The Villages around Metz.
>*Newcastle-upon-Tyne: Printed,* 8vo. 1870. 2½

WEBB, Henry,

——THE GOSPEL CHURCH delineated from the New Testament, in its Constitution, Worship, Order, Ministers, and Ministrations. An Exhibition in detail of the special privileges and authorised duties of Christian Fellowship. By HENRY WEBB.
>*London: Simpkin, Marshall, & Co., Stationers' Hall Court: [G. Hill, Steam Printer, Westminster Bridge Road.]* . . 8vo. 1871. 19

——THE GLORIOUS GOSPEL UNFOLDED, exhibiting the Harmony of the Divine Perfections, with the Grace manifested in the Salvation of Man from Sin and Misery. By Henry Webb.
>*London: Simpkin, Marshall, & Co., Stationers' Hall Court.* . . . Demy 8vo. 620 pp.

WEBB, Richard D., of *Dublin.*

——" Memories of the Past." In "The Liberty Bell." By Friends of Freedom. (p. 51.)
>*Boston, Massachusetts.* . . . . 1842.

WEIGHTMAN, Mary, of *Hoddesdon,* in *Hertfordshire,* where she kept a boarding school.

——The Polite Reasoner: in Letters addressed to a Young Lady, at a boarding school in Hoddesden, Hartfordshire.

WEIGHTMAN, Mary, *continued.*
 LONDON: *Printed for* W. BENT, *Paternoster Row.*
           8vo. 1787.

—— The JUVENILE SPEAKER: or Dialogues, and miscellaneous pieces in prose and verse; for the instruction of Youth in the Art of Reading. By the Author of the POLITE REASONER.
 LONDON: *Printed for* W. BENT, *Paternoster Row.*
          12mo. 1787. 5½

—— A Short System of Polite Learning: being a concise Introduction to the Arts and Sciences, and other Branches of Useful Knowledge.

—— The Friendly Monitor; or, Dialogues for Youth against the Fear of Ghosts, and other Irrational Apprehensions. With reflections on the Power of Imagination, and the Folly of Superstition. By the author of The Polite Reasoner, and Juvenile Speaker.
 London: *Printed for W. Bent, Paternoster Row.*
          12mo. 1791. 5½

*WEST, Benjamin, *continued* from Catalogue, Vol. 2, p. 872.

—— **Christ Rejected.** CATALOGUE OF THE PICTURE representing the above subject; together with sketches of other scriptural subjects; painted by BENJAMIN WEST, Esq., *President of the Royal Academy, and Historical Painter to the King,* now exhibiting, under the special Protection of H.R.H. THE PRINCE REGENT, at the Room, formerly the Royal Academy, No. 125, PALL MALL, opposite Market Lane.
 LONDON: *Printed by J. H. Reynell, No. 21, Piccadilly, near the Haymarket.* 8vo. 1814. 1

  WEST'S PICTURE OF THE ANNUNCIATION.—SALE EXTRAORDINARY.—Yesterday the transparent picture of the Annunciation, painted by the late BENJAMIN WEST for the Rectory Church of St. Marylebone, was brought to the hammer by Mr. GRAVES, of Mortimer-street, under the orders of the present vestry. The old select vestry voted for this picture the exorbitant sum of £800. It occupied a large space in the centre of the organ of Marylebone New Church; but in the year 1826, it was removed, and has since, for fourteen years, been lying useless in a lumber room at the Marylebone Court-house until directed to be sold. The auctioneer read the following extract from the vestry minutes of St. Marylebone, in reference to the picture, dated February the 15th, 1817:—" I have always regulated my charge for historical paintings, and under these regulations I charge

*WEST, Benjamin, *continued.*

the parish £800 for the picture now in the New Church of St. Marylebone. Were I a man of Independent fortune, I would request the Vestry to honour me by accepting this picture as a gratuitous mark of my profound respect for the parish. (Signed). BENJAMIN WEST. Newman-street, February 1817."—" Whereupon it was moved and seconded that £800 be paid to Mr. WEST. An amendment thereunto having been moved and seconded, that a committee be appointed to obtain the opinion of three academicians of the value of the transparency painted by Mr. WEST, and to get any other opinion they may think necessary, there appeared to be 12 in favour of the amendment, and 36 against it. The original question was then put by the chairman, and there appearing to be 30 in favour thereof and 10 against the same, it passed in the affirmative." After reading this document, the auctioneer proceeded to expatiate on the merits of the picture and the fame of the artist by whom it was painted in glowing terms. A considerable period elapsed ere a bidding could be got at all. At length, however, the sum of 10 guineas was offered; and, notwithstanding the auctioneer promised the receipt, with the autograph of the late BENJAMIN WEST, should be given to the purchaser, not a bidding could be obtained above the first sum offered. The purchaser of the picture is Mr. JOHN WILSON, of Charles-street, Middlesex Hospital.—*Morning Chronicle*, 30th April, 1840.

WEST, William, F.R.S., of *Leeds.*

——An Account of the Patent and other Methods of preventing or consuming SMOKE; with Acts of Parliament on the subject; evidence on Indictments for smoke nuisances; and the proceedings at a Public Meeting of Patentees and others, for exhibiting and explaining models. By William West, Professional Chemist, Leeds, Member of the Institute of Civil Engineers, etc.

London : *Simpkin and Marshall : Baines and Newsome, Leeds.* . . . 8vo. 1842. 4

NOTE.—At the end are 18 plates with explanations.

WETHERILL, Samuel (one of the Founders of the now extinct Free Quakers), of *North America.*

——The Divinity of Jesus Christ proved, being a Reply to Dr. Joseph Priestley's Appeal to the Serious and Candid Professors of Christianity, and to a pamphlet published by Lewis Nichola, entitled the Divinity of Jesus Christ considered from Scripture Evidences,

WETHERILL, Samuel, *continued*.

&c., with some observations on Arianism, by Samuel Wetherill.

Philadelphia. . . . . . 12m. 1792.

WHITALL, Alice B.

——On the Rock (a Memoir of her by *Mrs. Pearsall Smith*).

WHITE, George, F., of *New York*.

——Sermon,—in Friends' Meeting House, Cherry Street, Philadelphia, 1843.

New York : Printed, 12mo. 1843.

*WHITE, Thomas, of *Stepney*, Son of Thomas White, of *Ratcliff*; he was educated at Ackworth School, but afterwards he left the Society and connected himself with the Methodists, the latter part of his life he held some situation at the Bedford Institute, Spitalfields.

——The Drunkard's Wife's Lament, with " Caution to Landsmen and Sailors. The Idol King Tobacco."

8vo. [No date.]

Price, 4d. per hundred ; 3s. per thousand ; 4s. per thousand (post free) ; by Samuel Jarrold, Norwich.

NOTE.—No. 22 of Norwich Cheap Tracts. *The Friend* of 7th month, 1870, says, "That he acted as a Town Missionary."

He died the 25th of 6th month, 1870, at No. 9, Harman Street, Kingsland Road, London.

WHITE, William, of *Birmingham*.

——FRIENDS IN WARWICKSHIRE, in the 17th and 18th Centuries. By William White.

Birmingham : Published by White and Pike.

Small 8vo. 1873. 12.

With a Map of the " Meetings of Friends in Warwickshire during the 18th Century ; and a Frontispiece of " Eatington Meeting House."

*WHITEHEAD, John, *continued* from Catalogue, Vol. 2, p. 915.

——A Discourse [on 2 Sam. iii. 38.] delivered at the *New Chapel* in the *City Road*, on the Ninth of March, 1791, at the Funeral of the late Rev. Mr. John Wesley. By John Whitehead, M.D.

The 2nd edition.

*WHITEHEAD, John, *continued.*
> London: Printed by G. Paramore, North Green, Worship Street; and sold by Messrs. Kent, No. 116, High Holborn; Warr, Red Lion Passage; Riedel, No. 13, Crown Street, Soho; Hunt, No. 23, New Broad Street; and at the New Chapel, City Road, and all other Methodist Preaching-Houses in Town and Country. 12mo. 1791. 3⅔
>> ADVERTISEMENT (after the Title page)—
>> "The following Discourse was delivered extempore, and a Copy of it taken in short hand, by a Nephew of Mr. Marsom, Bookseller, in High Holborn. This Copy I procured, and in some places have taken the liberty to add a sentence or two, where the subject would easily admit of farther illustration. As the Discourse extended to a considerable length, I have been obliged to omit the exhortation delivered at the end of it.—JOHN WHITEHEAD."

———A DISCOURSE delivered At the *New Chapel* in the *City-Road*, on the Ninth of March, 1791, at the Funeral of the late Rev. Mr. JOHN WESLEY. By JOHN WHITEHEAD, M.D.
> *And I heard a voice from heaven, saying unto me, write, blessed are the dead which die in the Lord, from henceforth, yea saith the Spirit, that they may rest from their labours, and their works do follow them.*—Rev. xiv., 13.

The Fourth Edition.
> London: Printed by G. Paramore, North Green, Worship Street; And sold by G. Whitfield, New Chapel, City Road; Messrs. Kent, No. 116, High Holborn; Warr, Red Lion Passage, Red Lion Square; Riedel, No. 13, Crown Street, Soho; Hunt, No. 23, New Broad Street; and at the Methodist Preaching Houses in Town and Country.

[Price SIXPENCE.] 12mo. 1791. 3

WHITEHEAD, William A.
———THE ENGLISH IN EAST AND WEST JERSEY, 1664-1689. By William A. Whitehead, *corresponding Secretary of New Jersey Historical Society.*
> NOTE.—This forms Chapter XI., Vol. III., of *Justin Winsor's History of America.*

WHITTEN, Wilfred, (an old Ackworth and York Scholar) of *Newcastle-upon-Tyne, now of London.*

WHITTEN, Wilfred, *continued.*
——QUAKER PICTURES. By Wilfred Whitten.
 London: *Edward Hicks, Jun., 14, Bishopsgate*
  Without, E.C. . . . 4to. 1892. 9
  NOTE.—This forms " The Friends' Quarto Series, No. 1."
——The Temperance Caterer and Coffee Tavern Refreshment News. A monthly journal established 1878, edited by W. W. for E. Hicks, Jun., the Proprietor.
——JOHN GREENLEAF WHITTIER. By WILFRED WHITTEN.
 London: *Edward Hicks, Jr.* . . 8vo. 1892 9½
  NOTE.—This forms "The Friends' Shilling Biographical Series, No. 2."
Reprinted on large paper.
——THE ESSAYIST. A Literary and Reflective Magazine, chiefly interesting to the Society of Friends.
 It is all wholesome cates; ay, and toothsome too; and withal Quakerish.
    CHARLES LAMB, to BERNARD BARTON.
Established First Month, 1893. Monthly. Edited by W. W., for Edward Hicks, Jun., Publisher.

WHITTIER, John G., *continued* from Catalogue, Vol 2, p. 925.
——Ballads and other Poems. By J. G. Whittier.
 London: *W. Tweedie, 337, Strand.* 16mo. No date. 6¾
——The Chapel of the Hermits, and other poems. By John G. Whittier.
 London: *Sampson Low, Son, and Company.*
      8vo. 1853. 7¼
——Two Letters on the Present Aspects of the Society of Friends. By John G. Whittier.
 Reprinted from the Philadelphia "Friends' Review."
 London: *F. B. Kitto, 5, Bishopsgate Without.*
 Price 2d., or 1s. 6d. per doz. . . 16mo. 1870. ½
——A Letter from J. G. Whittier.—In " The Swiss Times," April 2nd, 1873.
 Swiss Times Company (Limited) Printing Office, Geneva.
——The Complete Poetical Works of John G. Whittier. Reprinted—The 2nd Edition.
 London: *Printed.* 16mo. 1874. 15½
——The JOURNAL of JOHN WOOLMAN. With an Introduction by JOHN G. WHITTIER.
 GLASGOW: ROBERT SMEAL. . . 8vo. 1882. 20¼

WHITTIER, John G., *continued.*

——John Greenleaf Whittier. His Life, Genius, and Writings. By W. Sloane Kennedy.
8vo. *Boston.* 1882.

——Prefatory Note to Worsdell's "Gospel of Divine Help."
8vo. 1887. ⅛

——The Writings of John Greenleaf Whittier. In Seven Volumes.

    Vol. 1. Narrative and Legendary Poems.
    Vol. 2. Poems of Nature.
    Vol. 3. Anti-Slavery Poems, 1889.
    Vol. 4. Personal Poems.
    Vol. 5. Margaret Smith's Journal.
    Vol. 6. Old Portraits and Modern Sketches.
    Vol. 7. The Conflict with Slavery, &c.

London : Macmillan & Co.   8vo. 1891.

——JOHN G. WHITTIER. By WILFRED WHITTEN. (*Portrait.*)

London : Edward Hicks, Jr., 14, Bishopsgate Without; and 2, Amen Corner, Paternoster Row. 8vo. 1892   9½

This forms "Friends' Shilling Biographical Series, No. 2."

He died on the 7th of the 9th month, 1892, aged 85 years.

WHITWELL, Hannah Maria, of *Kendal.*

——Extracts from the Letters of Hannah Maria Whitwell, who died in 1866, at the age of 87. [Edited by Josiah Forster.]

𝔓𝔯𝔦𝔫𝔱𝔢𝔡 𝔣𝔬𝔯 𝔭𝔯𝔦𝔳𝔞𝔱𝔢 𝔠𝔦𝔯𝔠𝔲𝔩𝔞𝔱𝔦𝔬𝔫 𝔬𝔫𝔩𝔶.
8vo. 1869.   2

WHITWELL, John, Mayor, of *Kendal.*

——and Others.—To our fellow Christians in the United Kingdom. . . . . . 4to. No date. ½

WHITWELL, Thomas, of *Kendal.*

———A Biographical Sketch. Edited by William Thomlinson.
8vo. [1878.] 4¾

WIFFEN, Benjamin B., *continued* from Catalogue, Vol. 2, pp. 927 and 929.

——The Confession of a Sinner, translated from the Spanish of Dr. Constantino Ponce de la Fuente, a Reformer of the XVI Century. By John J. Betts. With a Biographical Sketch by Benjamin B. Wiffen.

WIFFEN, Benjamin B., *continued.*

London : *Bell and Daldy, York Street, Covent Garden.* 8vo. 1869. 8

——EPISTOLA CONSOLATORIA. By JUAN PEREZ, One of the Spanish Reformers in the Sixteenth Century. Now translated from a reprint of the edition published by DON LUIS DE USOZ Y RIO, in 1848. With notice of the Author, by the late Benjamin B. Wiffen.

> "Ye shall be hated of all men for my name's sake ; but he that shall endure unto the end, the same shall be saved."—Mark xiii.. 13.

London : *James Nisbet & Co., 21, Berners Street.*
8vo. 1871. 15

——The Brothers Wiffen : Memoirs and Miscellanies. Edited by Samuel Rowles Pattison. (*Portraits of the Brothers.*) 8vo. 1880. 24

WIGHAM, Eliza, of *Edinburgh.*

——The Anti-Slavery Cause in America and its Martyrs. By Eliza Wigham.

London : *A. W. Bennett, 5, Bishopsgate Street Without.* [*Edinburgh : Printed by H. Armour.*] 8vo. 1863. 11

*WILLAN, Robert, a physician and medical writer of eminence, born near *Sedburgh*, in *Yorkshire*, in 1757. He was the son of a physician, who belonged to the religious sect of the Quakers ; and he studied at Edinburgh, where he took his degree as M.D. in 1780. Soon after he settled in practice at *Darlington* in *Durham*, whence he removed to *London*, and was appointed physician to a dispensary in Carey Street. In 1791 he became a fellow of the Antiquarian Society ; and his death took place in 1812, at *Madeira*, whither he had gone for the recovery of his health. Dr. Willan, who had left the Society of the Quakers, was the author of " The History of the Ministry of Jesus Christ," 1782, 8vo ; and among various medical works, he published a valuable treatise on cutaneous diseases, 4to., illustrated with engravings.—*Gent. Mag.*

See also an account of him in Watkin's Biographical Dictionary, taken from his " *Life by Bateman.*"

Continued from Catalogue, Vol. 2, p. 938.

——MISCELLANEOUS WORKS of the late ROBERT WILLAN, M.D., F.R.S., F.A.S. Comprising An Inquiry into

*WILLAN, Robert, *continued.*
the Antiquity of the Small Pox, Measles, and Scarlet Fever, Now first published :
Reports on the Diseases in London, 𝕬 𝕹𝖊𝖜 𝕰𝖉𝖎𝖙𝖎𝖔𝖓.
and
Detached Papers on Medical Subjects, collected from various Periodical Publications.
Edited by
ASHBY SMITH, M.D., Licentiate of the Royal College of Physicians in London ; Member of the Medical and Chirurgical Society of London, and of the Royal Medical Society of Edinburgh.
London : Printed for T. Cadell, in the Strand.
          8vo. 1821. 32½
WILLETS, John H., of *Philadelphia?*
——and Seth Smith.—An Elementary Treatise on Natural Philosophy, designed for the use of Students, by John H. Willets and Seth Smith.
Philadelphia :   8vo. 1830. 470pp.
WILSON, Charles, of *Sunderland.*
——Eternal Life the Gift of God through Jesus Christ.
Sunderland : Printed. . . . 16mo. 1880. ½
*WILSON, James, Chancellor of Exchequer for India.
 Biographical notice of him in the Biographical Catalogue of Friends' Institute.
WILSON, Rachel, *continued* from Catalogue, Vol. 2, p. 945.
——A Farewell to,—By John Drinker. In Comly's Miscellany, Vol. 4.
——Farewell to Rachael Wilson, of England, 1769. [Author unknown.] Inserted in Macy's "History of Nantucket," 1835, p. 298.
WILSON, Thomas B., of *North America.* Naturalist Author.
——American Ornithology. By Wilson. To which is added a Synopsis of American Birds, including those described by Bonaparte, Audubon, and Richardson. Illustrated with 26 pages or Steel Plates of nearly 400 Birds.
Boston :   1840.
New York :
      Crown 8vo. 1852. 746pp.

WILSON, Thomas B., *continued*.
    The same Work, with the Plates finely Coloured from Nature.
    Philadelphia :
——American Ornithology. By Wilson. With Notes, by Jardine. To which is added a Synopsis of American Birds, including those described by Bonaparte, Audubon, Nuttall, and Richardson. By T. M. Brewer.
    New York :   8vo. 1852.
——The Library of American Biography. Edited by Jared Sparks, LL.D.
    Vol. 2. Wilson, the Ornithologist.

WINSOR, Justin, Librarian of Harvard University, Corresponding Secretary Massachusetts Historical Society
——NARRATIVE AND CRITICAL HISTORY OF AMERICA Edited by JUSTIN WINSOR, Librarian of Harvard University, Corresponding Secretary Massachusetts Historical Society. 8 vols.
    London : *Sampson Low, Marston, Searle & Rivington.*   8vo. 1886.
    [*All rights reserved.*]
        NOTE.—This Vol. III. contains at—
        Chapter IX. New England. By Charles Deane, LL.D.
        Chapter X. The English in New York. By John Austin Stevens.
        Chapter XI. The English in East and West Jersey, 1664-1689. By William A. Whitehead.
        Chapter XII. The Founding of Pennsylvania. By Frederick D. Stone.

*WISTAR, Caspar, of *Pennsylvania*, M.D., Professor.
——A System of Anatomy for the use of Students of Medicine, by Caspar Wistar, M.D., Professor of Anatomy in the University of Pennsylvania.
    2 vols.
    Philadelphia :   8vo. 1811 & 1814.

WOOD, George, and ISAAC H. WILLIAMSON.
——The SOCIETY OF FRIENDS VINDICATED : being the Arguments of the Counsel of JOSEPH HENDRICKSON in a cause DECIDED IN THE COURT OF CHANCERY of the STATE OF NEW JERSEY, between THOMAS L. SHOTWELL, COMPLAINANT, and Joseph Hendrickson and Stacy Decow, Defendants.
    BY GEORGE WOOD AND ISAAC H. WILLIAMSON, *Counsellors at Law.*

WOOD, George, and Isaac H. Williamson, *continued*.
To which is appended
THE DECISION OF THE COURT.
TRENTON, N.J.—*Printed and published by P. J. Gray*. 8vo. 1832. 16¾

WOOD, George Bacon, M.D., of *Philadelphia*, Professor, Author.

——and Franklin Bache.—The Dispensatory of the United States of America. By George B. Wood, M.D., Professor of Materia Medica and Pharmacy in the Philadelphia College of Pharmacy, Member of the American Philosophical Society, &c., &c.; and Franklin Bache, M.D., Professor of Chemistry in the Philadelphia College of Pharmacy. one of the Secretaries of the American Philosophical Society, &c., &c.
Philadelphia : Published by Grigg & Elliot, No. 9, North Fourth Street. . . 8vo. 1833. 68
NOTE.—This work is dedicated to Joseph Parrish, M.D., and Thomas T. Hewson, M.D.

——The same, 12th edition.
Philadelphia . . . . . . 1868.

——A Memoir of the Life and Character of the late Joseph Parrish, M.D., read before the Medical Society of Philadelphia, by G. B. Wood, M.D.
Philadelphia : . . . . . . 1840.
NOTE.—This work is illustrated with 2 plates, viz., "The Pennsylvania Hospital," and "The Pennsylvania Hospital for the Insane."

——A Treatise on the Practice of Medicine. By George B. Wood, M.D., Professor of the Theory and Practice of Medicine in the University of Pennsylvania, President of the College of Physicians of Philadelphia, &c., &c. 2 vols.
Philadelphia : 8vo. 1847.
Reprinted, The 2nd edition.
 „ , The 3rd „
 „ , The 4th „
Philadelphia : . . . 8vo. 1855. 1712pp.
Reprinted, The 5th edition.
 „ , The 6th „ 1868.

——An Address on the occasion of the Centennial Celebration of the 𝔉𝔬𝔲𝔫𝔡𝔦𝔫𝔤 𝔬𝔣 𝔱𝔥𝔢 𝔓𝔢𝔫𝔫𝔰𝔶𝔩𝔳𝔞𝔫𝔦𝔞 𝔥𝔬𝔰𝔭𝔦𝔱𝔞𝔩,

WOOD, George Bacon, M.D., *continued*.
    delivered June 10th, 1851, by George B. Wood, M.D. Published by the Board of Managers.
        Philadelphia : T. K. and P. G. Collins, Printers.
            8vo. 1851.   9
——A Biographical Memoir of Dr. Samuel George Morton, by George B. Wood, M.D.
        Philadelphia :   .   .   .   .   -   .   1853.
——Introducing Lectures and Addresses on Medical Subjects delivered chiefly before the Medical Classes of the University of Pennsylvania by George B. Wood, M.D., LL.D.
        Philadelphia :   .   .   .   8vo. 1859. 460pp.
——A Treatise on Therapeutics and Pharmacology, by G. B. Wood, M.D.
    Reprinted. Third edition. Two Vols.   .   8vo. 1868.
WOOD, Horatio C., Doctor, Professor, Naturalist.
WOODARD, Luke, of *Indiana, North America*.
——A DISCOURSE on the DOCTRINES OF THE GOSPEL as held by FRIENDS, delivered by Luke Woodard, of Indiana, at Batavia, New York, 2nd Mo. 23rd, 1875. (*Reprinted from the Philadelphia Friends' Review.*)
        LONDON : *Printed by E. Newman, Devonshire Street, Bishopsgate.*   .   .   .   8vo. 1875.   1
WOOD, William Martin, who resided some time in *India*, now of *West Kensington, London, S.W.*
——The Times of India. Edited by him.
WOODS, Joseph, *continued* from Catalogue, Vol. 2, p. 955.
——Notes on some of the Schools for the Labouring Classes in Ireland. J. Woods.
        Lewes : Baxter & Son, 37, High Street ; Simpkin, Marshall, & Co. London ; John Cumming, Dublin.   .   .   .   12mo. 1841.   2¾
WOOLMAN, John, *continued* from Catalogue, Vol. 2, p. 959.
——John Woolman, by Dora Greenwell.
——   Do.   by David Duncan.
——The JOURNAL of JOHN WOOLMAN. 𝔚𝔦𝔱𝔥 𝔞𝔫 𝔍𝔫𝔱𝔯𝔬𝔡𝔲𝔠𝔱𝔦𝔬𝔫 by JOHN G. WHITTIER.
        " *The work of righteousness shall be peace ; and the effect of righteousness quietness and assurance for ever.*"—ISAIAH.
    GLASGOW : ROBERT SMEAL, CROSSHILL.
            8vo. 1882.   20¼

WORSDELL, Edward, of *Lancaster*.
—The GOSPEL OF DIVINE HELP. Thoughts on some First Principles of Christianity. *Addressed chiefly to the Members of the Society of Friends.* By EDWARD WORSDELL, B.A. . . . . 8vo. 1886.
Reprinted—The Second Edition. 𝔚𝔦𝔱𝔥 𝔓𝔯𝔢𝔣𝔞𝔱𝔬𝔯𝔶 𝔫𝔬𝔱𝔢 𝔟𝔶 𝔍. 𝔊. 𝔚𝔥𝔦𝔱𝔱𝔦𝔢𝔯.
London : *Samuel Harris & Co., 5, Bishopsgate Without, E.C.* 8vo. 1888. 12½
WORTHINGTON, John H., Physician and Superintendent of "The Asylum for the Relief of Persons deprived of the Use of their Reason, *Frankford*, near *Philadelphia*."
—Annual Reports.
WYLD, Joseph William.
—Brief Sketches of Religious Communities.
1850.

X.

X.Y.Z.—GRAVE STONES.—In the " Rough Notes, during a tour in North America ("*Friend*," *p. 135*) is a graphic Description of New Garden Meeting House and Burial Ground, &c.
In " *The Friend*," *Vol. IV., p. 150.* . 4to. 1846.

Y.

*YEWDALL, Zechariah, was born the 8th of 9th Month (Nov.), 1751, near *Eccleshall*, in the parish of *Bradford*. *West Riding of Yorkshire*. His parents belonged to the Society of Friends, and their children, eleven in all, attended meetings till grown up to maturity. But one of the chief speakers dying, the meetings from that were generally *silent*, and they being *giddy*, thoughtless creatures, were disgusted, and one after another forsook the Quakers' Meeting, which was a great affliction to his father. When about six years old the Spirit of the Lord mercifully strove with him, and at last he joined the *Methodists*.

―――The Experience of Mr. Zechariah Yewdall.   8vo.   1795.
>In The Arminian Magazine for March, 1795. Vol. XVIII., March, 1795. Commencing at p. 109, and concluding at p. 480.

YOAKLEY, Michael, *continued* from Catalogue, Vol. 2, p. 972.

―――Some Account of the Charity founded by Michael Yoakley. By James Bowden. (*Lithographed*).

    Croydon : . . . . Large 4to. 1869.

YORK Retreat, *continued* from Catalogue, Vol. 2, p. 973.

―――REGULATIONS for the Government of THE FRIENDS' RETREAT, near York. *Instituted 1792.*

    York: *William Sessions, Printers, Low Ousegate.*
                                                                                       8vo. 1878. 1¼

―――Annual Reports, from 1868 to 1892.

Z.

ZELL, Thomas Ellwood, of *Philadelphia.*

―――Zell's Popular Encyclopedia, a Universal Dictionary of English Language, Science . . . and Art.
2 Vols.
    4to. *Philadelphia,* . . . 1870, '71.

ZINSPENNING, Judith, *continued from Catalogue, Vol. 2, p. 979.*

―――Het Licht Christi de Leydsman ter Zaligheyd.― Elisabeth Hendriks en Judith Zinspenning.

    Amsterdam—Printed.   . . . 12mo. 1684.

www.ingramcontent.com/pod-product-compliance
Lightning Source LLC
Chambersburg PA
CBHW020221240426
43672CB00006B/373